Dr. Daniel Amen, board-certified in child, adoles[illegible] psychiatry and licensed in nuclear brain imaging, has discovered that there are six types of attention deficit disorder, each with its own distinctive brain dysfunctions and treatments:

Type 1—*Classic ADD*—Inattentive, distractible, disorganized, hyperactive, restless, and impulsive.

Type 2—*Inattentive ADD*—Easily distracted with a low attention span, but not hyperactive. Instead, often appears sluggish or apathetic.

Type 3—*Overfocused ADD*—Excessive worrying, argumentative and compulsive; often gets locked in a spiral of negative thoughts.

Type 4—*Temporal Lobe ADD*—Quick temper and rage, periods of panic and fear, mildly paranoid.

Type 5—*Limbic ADD*—Moodiness, low energy. Socially isolated, chronic low-grade depression. Frequent feelings of hopelessness.

Type 6—*"Ring of Fire" ADD*—Angry, aggressive, sensitive to noise, light, clothes and touch; often inflexible, experiencing periods of mean, unpredictable behavior, and grandiose thinking.

"I highly recommend *Healing ADD* for parents of children with ADD, adults with ADD, therapists, and physicians. The subtypes Dr. Amen has firmly established will help clinicians everywhere tailor ADD treatments to each and every individual. One size does not fit all."

—George Delgado, M.D., FAAFP,
associate clinical professor, University of California, Davis

"Daniel Amen's work in SPECT brain imaging, the first major breakthrough in psychiatry and psychology in the last fifty years, brings these fields out of the dark ages and into partnership with other medical disciplines. He takes complex matters of brain function, and helps layperson and professional work together as a healing team."

—Earl A. Henslin, Psy.D., BCETS,
American Academy of Experts in Traumatic Stress

"Thanks to the cutting-edge work of Dr. Amen, I have at long last been properly diagnosed with adult ADD. I am on the appropriate medication, am working with an ADD coach, and seeing each day of my life come more and more into focus. What an unexpected joy! I recommend this book to anyone who has concerns with ADD or even the slightest interest in human behavior."

—Joan Baez

continued . . .

"For patients, parents, and doctors alike, Dr. Amen's new book provides a wealth of material on ADD, backed up by illuminating and helpful brain imaging. Clear and readable, and a must for understanding this disorder."

—William R. Collie, M.D.,
Safe Harbor Clinic for Behavioral Medicine

"Dr. Amen's *Healing ADD* contains a wealth of startling new insights about ADD. A must-read for every professional in the juvenile justice system. A breakthrough work on diagnosing and treating ADD, it is certain to be a classic."

—Thomas C. Edwards,
judge, Superior Court, State of California

"*Healing ADD* should be required reading for all clinicians and educators. Dr. Amen's work should abolish the notion that ADD is merely a myth. His elegant SPECT brain studies make ADD understandable to a three-year-old and have brought psychiatry from 'witchcraft' to neuroscience."

—Claire Friend, M.D.,
child and adult psychiatrist

"Nearly a third of my practice is filled with adult ADD. Dr. Amen is a courageous pioneer, a conscientious scientist, and a caring physician—a spectacular combination."

—Frank L. Annis, M.D.,
diplomat, American Board of Psychiatry and Neurology

"*Healing ADD* provides details on multiple treatment options, including pharmacological, educational, behavioral, and herbal. It is essential reading for those who treat ADD and those who are directly or indirectly affected by ADD."

—J. Kirk Clopton, M.D., Ph.D.,
director, Golden Hills Psychiatry

"Dr. Amen's groundbreaking discoveries make the complexities of ADD easy to understand. His pioneering use of SPECT imaging confirms what other expert clinicians could only suspect. ADD is not a weakness of the human spirit. Readers of his book will understand how to help themselves, family members, or fellow human beings."

—Dennis Alters, M.D.,
child, adolescent, and adult psychiatrist
and author of *Wizard's Way*

"With the tremendous research done by Dr. Amen, we can now measure the physiology that has gone wrong and enable patients to take charge of their lives."

—René Espy, D.C., N.D.,
Zone Health Associates

"Once again challenging older concepts about attention deficit disorder, Dr. Amen writes with a clarity, simplicity, and passion I have come to admire. *Healing ADD* is a worthy extension of *Change Your Brain, Change Your Life*."

—Terence F. McGuire, M.D.,
psychiatrist

"Dr. Amen has taken a unique and useful approach in *Healing ADD*. Providing good direction for designing an effective treatment program, this will be a tremendous aid in understanding and managing the complex needs of those with ADD. An excellent book for clinicians, patients, and their families."

—Richard Gilbert, M.D.,
psychiatrist

Other Books by Daniel G. Amen, M.D.

Change Your Brain, Change Your Life

New Skills for Frazzled Parents

Would You Give Two Minutes a Day to a Lifetime of Love?

Coaching Yourself to Success

Firestorms in the Brain: An Inside Look at Violence

Secrets of Successful Students

ADD and Intimate Relationships

A Teenager's Guide to ADD

A Child's Guide to ADD

A Sibling's Guide to ADD

A Teacher's Guide to ADD

Healing ADD

The Breakthrough Program That Allows You to See and Heal the Six Types of Attention Deficit Disorder

Daniel G. Amen, M.D.

Berkley Books, New York

A Berkley Book
Published by The Berkley Publishing Group
A division of Penguin Putnam Inc.
375 Hudson Street
New York, New York 10014

Every effort has been made to ensure that the information contained in this book is complete and accurate. However, neither the publisher nor the author is engaged in rendering professional advice or services to the individual reader. The ideas, procedures, and suggestions contained in this book are not intended as a substitute for consulting with your physician. All matters regarding your health require medical supervision. Neither the author nor the publisher shall be liable or responsible for any loss, injury or damage allegedly arising from any information or suggestion in this book. The opinions expressed in this book represent the personal views of the author and not of the publisher.

Book design by Tanya Maiboroda

PRINTING HISTORY
G. P. Putnam's Sons hardcover edition / February 2001
Berkley trade paperback edition / June 2002

Berkley trade paperback ISBN: 0-425-18327-0

The Library of Congress has catalogued
the G. P. Putnam's Sons hardcover edition as follows:

Amen, Daniel G.
Healing ADD : the breakthrough program that allows you to see and heal the 6 types of attention deficit disorder / Daniel G. Amen.
p. cm.
Includes bibliographical references and index.
ISBN 0-399-14644-X
1. Attention-deficit hyperactivity disorder—Treatment. 2. Attention-deficit disorder in adults—Treatment. I. Title.
RC394.A85 A445 2000 00-62677
616.85'8906—dc21

PRINTED IN THE UNITED STATES OF AMERICA

10 9

To Antony, Breanne, and Kaitlyn

My source of eternal inspiration

Acknowledgments

This book is the product of many years, many friendships and collaborations, and many battles. I am grateful to the best teachers a physician could have—my patients. I wish to acknowledge and thank the staff at the Amen Clinic, especially through all of the growing pains over the past twelve years. In particular, I wish to thank Lisa Routh, the medical director of our Newport Beach Clinic; Shelley Bernhard, the clinic's chief operating officer; Randy Streeter, the Newport Beach Clinic's manager; my personal assistant Brenda Doty; and the professional staff, including Linda Pepper, Jennifer Lendl, Jonathan Halverstadt, Michael McGrath, Robert Dobrin, Stan Yantis, Ed Oklan, Ann Oklan, Brian Goldman, Jeri Owens, Lewis Van Osdel III, Robert Gessler, Ronnette Leonard, Blake Carmichael, and Matthew Stubblefield. In addition, I wish to thank Jane Massengill and Emmett Miller, who have made significant contributions to this book. I am also thankful to the many professionals who have helped me develop and spread this work, including Earl Henslin, Thomas Jaeger, Ed DeRosis, Dennis Alters, Cory Clark, Rick Lavine, Sheila Krystal, Jack Juni, Jack Paldi, Gregory Hipskind, Hugh Ridlehuber, Terry McGuire, Dan Pavel, Rob Kohn, Georgia Davis, Joseph Wu,

Kitty Petty, Karen Lansing, Rick Gilbert, Leon and Linda Webber, Marty Stein, Will Hawkins, Tom Brod, and Bill Klindt.

My literary agent Faith Hamlin is an amazing woman who continually pushes me to be the best writer I can be and is a constant source of wisdom and support. My editor at G. P. Putnam's Sons, Jeremy Katz, believed in this book and saw it could help millions of people who struggle with ADD. He is every writer's dream editor—smart, funny, tenacious, and a joy to work with (but he'll probably correct this sentence, if my agent doesn't correct it first). I am also appreciative to my publicist Tammy Richards, who has believed in and supported me through publicizing *Change Your Brain, Change Your Life* and this book, along with Lori Akiyama at Putnam, whose diligence, creativity, and professionalism will help get this book into the hands and minds of many people.

I also wish to thank my children, Antony, Breanne, and Kaitlyn, who not only give me great stories, but have given me love and affection, and are a continual source of pride.

Contents

For more information, the latest breakthroughs, and interactive learning, go to: www.brainplace.com.

For a full description of www.brainplace.com, please see page 410.

Introduction

An estimated 17 million people in the United States have attention deficit disorder (ADD). It is the single most common learning and behavioral problem in children. But the issue doesn't end there: It is also one of the most common problems in adults, leading to job failures, relationship breakups, loneliness, drug abuse, and a tremendous sense of underachievement. Despite its prevalence, many myths and misconceptions about ADD abound in our society. Here are just a few of them:

MYTHS

- ADD is a flavor-of-the-month illness, a fad diagnosis. It's just an excuse for bad behavior.
- ADD is overdiagnosed. Every child that acts up a bit gets placed on Ritalin.
- ADD is only a disorder of hyperactive boys.
- ADD is only a minor problem. People make too much of a fuss over it.
- ADD is an American invention, made up by a society seeking simple solutions to complex social problems.

- Bad parents or bad teachers cause ADD. If only our society had old-fashioned values, there wouldn't be these problems.
- People with ADD should just try harder. Everybody gives them excuses and coddles them.
- Everyone outgrows ADD by the age of 12 or 13.
- Stimulant medication is dangerous and highly addictive. It's just like speed.
- Medication alone is the best treatment for ADD.

FACTS

- ADD has been described in the medical literature for about one hundred years. In 1902, pediatrician George Still described a group of children who were hyperactive, impulsive, and inattentive. Unfortunately, he didn't understand that ADD is a medical disorder and labeled these children as "morally defective."
- ADD affects approximately 6 percent of the population, while less than 2 percent receive treatment. A recent article in the *Journal of the American Medical Association* concluded that there was no evidence that ADD is overdiagnosed in our society, and child psychiatrist Peter Jensen from the National Institutes of Health found that less than one in eight children who met the diagnostic criteria for ADD were taking medication.
- Many people with ADD are never hyperactive. The non-hyperactive ADD group is often ignored because they do not bring enough negative attention to themselves: They're not a big enough problem. Many of these children, teenagers, or adults earn the unjust labels "willful," "lazy," "unmotivated," or "not that smart." Moreover, females have ADD in almost the same number as males, yet are diagnosed four to five times less often.
- ADD is a serious societal problem:

  35 percent never finish high school (25 percent repeat at least one grade).

  52 percent of untreated teens and adults abuse drugs or alcohol.

19 percent smoke cigarettes (compared to 10 percent of the general population).

43 percent of untreated hyperactive boys will be arrested for a felony by age 16.

50 percent of inmates in a number of studies have been found to have ADD (75 percent in one study).

75 percent have interpersonal problems; untreated ADD sufferers have a higher percentage of motor vehicle accidents, speeding tickets, citations for driving without a license, and suspended or revoked licenses.

They also have many more medical visits and emergency-room visits.

Parents of ADD children divorce three times more often than the general population.

ADD is found in every country where it has been studied and in about the same proportions.

Poor parents or teachers can certainly make ADD symptoms worse, but ADD is largely a genetic disorder. ADD behaviors often make even skilled parents and teachers appear stressed and inept.

- The harder many people with ADD try, the worst things get for them. Brain-imaging studies show that when people with ADD try to concentrate, the part of their brains involved with concentration, focus, and follow-through actually shuts down—just when they need it to turn on.
- Many people never outgrow ADD and have symptoms that interfere with their whole lives. Half of those children diagnosed with ADD will have disabling symptoms into adulthood.
- Stimulant medications, such as Adderall, Ritalin, or Dexedrine are among the safest and most effective medications in psychiatry. Ritalin has been approved in the U.S. for approximately fifty years. In doses prescribed for ADD, these medications have little, if any, potential for abuse. In fact, work done by psychiatrist Joseph Biederman at Harvard demonstrated that children

treated for ADD have a much lower risk for drug abuse than untreated children. Untreated ADD has many more side effects than these medications.

- Stimulants are very effective medications when prescribed properly. But in order to effectively treat ADD, a comprehensive treatment approach is essential, including education, support, exercise, nutrition, and, yes, medication. Unfortunately, medications are the only treatments given to the vast majority of people diagnosed with ADD in America.

Why are there so many myths and negative reactions about ADD when physicians know so much about it? The answer is simple. ***Until now, you couldn't see ADD.*** Children, teens, and adults with ADD look like everyone else. Sure, they may be more distractible, more impulsive, and more restless. And after all, it's a lot easier just to chalk up someone's problem as bad behavior or a child as a "bad egg" than to try to help. But unless you knew the story of an ADD person's life, you couldn't see that he or she has ADD. ***Until now!***

THE GOOD NEWS

This book, I hope, will put to rest the debate over whether or not ADD is real by showing the areas of dysfunction in the brain. New brain-imaging research, conducted at my clinic, has uncovered the ADD brain. Based on our research with thousands of ADD patients using brain SPECT imaging (one of the most sophisticated functional brain-imaging studies in the world), we have been able to see where ADD resides in the brain and why it has such a negative impact on behavior. Right or wrong, humans have an innate distrust of the intangible, but seeing the ADD brain can cause the destructive myths and prejudices to fade away.

As you'll see in the pages that follow, ADD affects many areas of the brain, primarily the *prefrontal cortex* (the brain's controller of concentration, attention span, judgment, organization, planning, and impulse control), the *anterior cingulate gyrus* (the brain's gear shifter), the *temporal lobes* (where the brain houses memory and experience), the *basal ganglia* (which produce the neurotransmitter dopamine that drives the prefrontal cortex), and the *deep limbic system* (the brain's mood control center). Before-and-after imaging shows that, with effective treatment, brain function can dramatically improve and give sufferers more access to their own abilities. I want to stress something: Treatment does not make ADD sufferers different people: It removes the barriers hindering them from being the people they already are.

The first of its kind, this book will give you a completely new perspective on ADD. You'll see actual ADD brain images (many before and after treatment) and identify the six types of ADD that we have recently described (based on a combination of our work with many others in the field). You can also take a comprehensive questionnaire that will allow you to identify ADD (and which type) within yourself or others. Most important, this book offers promising new solutions.

That's right, *six* types of ADD—not the two currently believed. Understanding the nuanced complexities of ADD allows us to treat everyone more effectively while helping people who would otherwise be ignored.

Type 1: Classic ADD—sufferers are inattentive, distractible, disorganized, hyperactive, restless, and impulsive.

Type 2: Inattentive ADD—sufferers are inattentive, sluggish, slow-moving, have low motivation, and are often described as space cadets, daydreamers, or couch potatoes.

Type 3: Overfocused ADD—sufferers have trouble shifting attention; frequently get stuck in loops of negative thoughts or behaviors; are obsessive; worry excessively; are inflexible; frequently behave oppositionally and argumentatively.

Type 4: Temporal Lobe ADD—sufferers are inattentive, irritable; aggressive; have dark thoughts, mood instability, and are severely impulsive.

Type 5: Limbic ADD—sufferers are inattentive, experience chronic low-grade depression, are negative (e.g., "glass half empty syndrome"), have low energy, and have frequent feelings of hopelessness and worthlessness.

Type 6: "Ring of Fire" ADD—sufferers are inattentive, extremely distractible, angry, irritable, overly sensitive to the environment, hyperverbal, extremely oppositional, and experience cyclic moodiness.

Knowing which ADD type you or your child has is critical to establishing an effective treatment program. Treating some types of ADD with standard remedies will make things much worse. You'll learn that specifically tailored interventions, on the other hand, often lead to quick and dramatic improvement.

A STEP-BY-STEP PROGRAM FOR HEALING EACH TYPE OF ADD

After helping you properly identify if ADD is an issue for you (or someone else you know) and which type, this book will offer advice on how to treat it. You'll learn the same clear step-by-step brain enhancement program for optimizing brain function and overcoming ADD barriers that I use at The Amen Clinic. I have found this program effective, powerful, and easy to understand; while much of the program can be done outside of the doctor's office, for the medication and psychotherapeutic components you'll need to consult a doctor. A list of knowledgeable physicians and therapists, along with strategies to find competent clinicians, begins on page 380.

The Amen Clinic ADD Brain Enhancement Program is an individualized combination of strategies geared toward enhancing the brain function of each ADD type. For each type, we will recommend:

- education
- emotional and social support

- medication, vitamins, herbs, diet, exercise, targeted brainwave biofeedback strategies
- school and work strategies
- social skill strategies
- thinking skills
- coaching
- self-regulation exercises.

This book will give you a first-ever look into truly understanding ADD and the six ADD types. In addition it will give you an effective program for enhancing brain function and overcoming the ADD traits that sabotage chances for success in all aspects of living—in relationships, at work or school, and internally. ADD affects whole families, not just individuals. Therefore, the following pages will also have extensive material on the dynamics of living in an ADD household (for parents, spouses, and siblings), along with many practical suggestions for effective cohabitation.

A note for teachers, vice principals, social workers, policeman, parole officers, marital therapists, psychologists, physicians, attorneys, and even IRS agents: Many people with ADD have societal problems and this program can teach you how to work with them. Here are some common examples of the societal challenges people with ADD face:

- difficulties in school and spending excessive time in vice-principals' offices
- frequent speeding tickets and accidents
- getting in trouble with the law (Many teens with ADD tend to find trouble. For example, an ADD kid is with a group of teenagers and a police officer walks up to them. The teen with ADD is the one who will likely say something disrespectful and get himself hauled to jail.)
- problems with parole officers (The incidence of ADD in prison is very high and parole officers frequently bust their clients with ADD for not following through on their programs.)

- relationship problems (Marital therapists often unknowingly spend excessive time with ADD clients because of their difficulties in relationships. When this dynamic is ignored, the ADD person or couple may stay in therapy unnecessarily for many years.)
- legal difficulties (People with ADD are overrepresented as clients in attorneys' offices. Lawyers frequently see ADD clients in domestic disputes, divorces, civil suits, and criminal cases.)
- tax problems (IRS agents frequently encounter people with ADD. Procrastination is a common problem in ADD and many put off filing or paying their taxes until the last possible minute and beyond.)

A PERSONAL NOTE

I have not only studied ADD from a clinical perspective, I have lived it at home. Several of my own children have been diagnosed with ADD. For years I lived with the guilt that is often associated with having a family member who has this disorder. I thought that I was a terrible husband and a terrible father. These feelings were compounded by the fact that I was a psychiatrist and that I "should" have a perfect marriage and I "should" have well-behaved children. Things "should" have been better than they were. My son used to joke that our family was like the cartoon Simpson family poster that read, "OK, everybody, let's pretend that we're a nice, normal family" as they were getting ready to take a family picture. It was not until my children were diagnosed and treated properly that the clouds of guilt began to give way to understanding.

I know this disorder from the inside out. I know what it is like:

- to have trouble holding a small child because she is in nonstop motion
- to chase a child through the store
- to look on in horror as a 4-year-old child darts across a busy parking lot

- to watch a child take four hours to do twenty minutes of homework
- to watch a child stare at a writing assignment for hours, unable to get thoughts from his brain to the paper
- to go to teachers' conferences where my child has been described as bright, spacey, and underachieving
- to have to repeat myself thirty-two times to get a child up in the morning
- to be asked for help at 11:00 P.M. the night before a term paper was due when the child knew about it for four weeks
- to be angry every school morning for years because a child is continually ten minutes late
- to be amazed that a child's room can become so messy in such a short period of time
- to be always on alert in a store or at a friend's house so that my child won't touch or break something
- to be frustrated by trying to teach a child something, only to have him or her continually be distracted by something irrelevant
- to feel guilty about the negative feelings I have toward a child after I've told him or her not to do something for the umpteenth time
- to be embarrassed to the point of madness in a restaurant (and wonder why I'm spending money to suffer)
- to be interrupted without mercy while I'm on the telephone
- to live through angry outbursts that have little or no provocation.

I have used the principles in this book to guide the treatment of my patients and to help my own family. I know the information will help you.

PART 1

ADD Uncovered

CHAPTER 1

ADD in the Real World

Stories Through the Life Cycle

ADD may not make someone look different, but you can see it plainly if you know what to look for. The following case histories demonstrate what ADD "looks like" throughout the life cycle. These stories are real. The names and details have been altered, as they have been throughout this book, to protect the confidentiality of my patients.

CHILDREN

Billy

Billy, age 9, had trouble in school since starting kindergarten. The teachers seemed to call his parents at least once a month to complain about Billy's behavior. He frequently interrupted others, they said, and he had problems with distractibility, a short attention span, and hyperactivity, and he couldn't stay in his seat. Again and again Billy was told that he was impulsive and did things without thinking. The teachers reported that he got into many fights with the other children, because he "seemed to take things the wrong way." Additionally, Billy's work was sloppy, he often forgot or lost assignments, and his desk was an absolute disorganized mess!

His parents knew most of these problems firsthand. Billy was a difficult child to parent. He said things without thinking, often argued when told to do something, and became angry with little provocation. Homework was always a struggle with Billy. Work that typically took their other kids thirty minutes to finish took Billy three or four hours. While doing his homework, he was up every five minutes looking for food or bothering his older sister. In the first three years of school, Billy was labeled a willful, defiant child. He was often sad and frustrated, and he had a tendency to blame others for his problems.

His parents didn't know what to do. They had known of the problems for some time, and they alternated between blaming Billy, blaming the "lousy" school, and blaming themselves. When Billy was 5 years old, his mother took him to the pediatrician because of his high activity level and difficult nature. While she was talking to the doctor, however, Billy sat perfectly still and he was very polite and attentive to the doctor. The doctor told Billy's mother that there was nothing the matter with the boy and that she should take parenting classes. The mother left the pediatrician's office in tears because he confirmed her worst fear: She was a defective parent who caused Billy's problems. Despite the parenting classes, the problems continued.

When he was in third grade, Billy came to my office for an evaluation. It was clear from watching him that he had difficulty concentrating and was distractible, active, and impulsive. Billy had Classic ADD: He was inattentive, distractible, disorganized, hyperactive, and impulsive. I placed him on medication, talked with the school on effective classroom management techniques, and had his parents attend a parenting group designed for dealing with difficult children. I also taught Billy some specialized biofeedback techniques. Six months after ADD treatment, Billy was a different child. He was less impulsive, his attention span had increased, and he appeared calmer. Even his grades had improved. Four years later he likes himself, is effective at school, and has healthy relationships at home and with friends.

Shortly after I placed Billy on medication, I asked him about the time in the pediatrician's office when he had been 5 years old. I asked him why he had been able to sit so still during the interview. He told me that he thought the doctor was going to do brain surgery on him. You would sit still, too, if you thought someone was going to open up your skull!

Melissa

Melissa, age 5, had been affectionately labeled the "pink tornado." Ever since she could walk, she ran. Everywhere. Her parents were always on edge, wondering what she was going to do next. She climbed. She swung on cupboard doors. She ran into the street as soon as her mother's back was turned. She was her own "little wrecking crew" when she went shopping with her mom or dad. Her parents brought her to see me after she was nearly run down in a parking lot after she opened the car door and ran into a store.

Her parents also reported that Melissa was moody, irritable, oppositional, extremely talkative, and able to throw monumental tantrums. Her mother complained that she could not take Melissa anywhere without a commotion. In restaurants she wiggled, yelled out, and screamed if she didn't get her way. Other adults would stare at Melissa's parents with a look that said, "Why don't you beat that bratty child into submission!" Lord knows they spanked this child more than they thought any child should be spanked. That didn't seem to be the answer. In fact, the more they spanked Melissa, the more she would act up—almost as if she was driven for more punishment. Melissa had a very short attention span, never playing with anything for longer than a few minutes. She could tear her room apart in a moment. Her parents actually put a lock on the outside of her room to keep her out when her parents were not supervising her.

Melissa tore up my office too. She climbed up my bookcases, messed up the papers on my desk, and screamed at her parents when they asked her to settle down. It seemed that she invited her parents to spank her in front of me. Melissa had never been abused and no obvious emotional trauma was evident in her life. The parents, who cared for each other very much, wondered how long they could last as a family.

Melissa had a severe case of "Ring of Fire" ADD. It probably had genetic roots. Her mother's father was an alcoholic and her uncle on her father's side was in jail for assault. Melissa also had an aunt with bipolar disorder (manic depression). She became more active and aggressive on Ritalin. Dexedrine did the same thing to her. With the atypical response to medication, I ordered a brain SPECT study, which showed multiple overactive areas across the cortical surface of her brain. With this information, I placed her on Depakote—an antiseizure medication often helpful for cases like this—and a higher protein diet. Within several weeks she became more settled, more cooperative, more playful, more attentive, and much more relaxed. Her mother was amazed at how little she was yelling at Melissa now. The parents also took a parenting class, which helped them gain the skills necessary to deal with a very challenging child.

TEENAGERS

Louanne

Louanne's mother came to one of my lectures. When I described ADD, she started to cry, knowing that the symptoms I had listed fit her daughter's life. Shortly thereafter, she brought Louanne to see me. Louanne had a short attention span, was easily distracted, and often did not finish her assignments. She had low self-esteem and she talked incessantly without saying very much of substance. Louanne complained of low energy and no motivation. She had always wanted to be a music teacher, but she began to believe that she couldn't do the work to succeed in college. She thought that she was slow and different from her friends. She sat in my office, already demoralized at age 16.

Louanne had Inattentive ADD, a common but rarely diagnosed condition in females. I started her on Dexedrine, had her increase her exercise and protein intake, and worked with her on self-esteem and school strategies. Within a month of starting treatment,

Louanne dramatically improved. I remember her coming into my office so tickled that she could finally get her work done. In the semester after she started treatment, her grade point average went from a 2.1 to a 3.0. She was especially pleased that she could compete with her friends at school and no longer thought of herself as "dumber than them." The demoralized girl I had first met was developing into a hopeful and forward-looking woman. Her mother commented that she was more thoughtful when she spoke and voiced the secret feelings of many parents: "Just knowing that this is a medical disorder, with signs, symptoms, and treatment, has given us immense hope for Louanne."

Gregg

When Gregg first came to see me at the age of 14, he was a wreck. He had just been expelled from his third school for fighting and breaking the rules. He told off teachers for fun and picked fights with other kids on the school grounds. He also never did his homework and he talked about dropping out of school, saying he didn't need an education to take care of himself. At home he was defiant, restless, messy, and disobedient. He teased his younger brother and sister without mercy. Anytime his parents would speak to him, he'd get defensive and challenging. His parents were at their wits' end, and their next step was a residential treatment center.

When I first saw him he was a "turned off" teenager with averted eyes and nothing much to say. He told me that he didn't want to be sent away but that he wasn't able to get along with his family. He found school very hard and thought he was stupid. When I did a test of verbal intelligence on him, however, his demeanor started to change. He liked the test and seemed challenged by it. His verbal IQ score was 142, in the superior range and far from stupid. Looking back in Gregg's history, it was clear he had had symptoms of ADD his whole life. He was a fidgety kid with awful handwriting and a messy desk. His desk at school was always a mess. He had trouble waiting his turn in school, and endured being called stupid because he had trouble learning.

Due to the severity of his problems, and the potential departure of Gregg from the family, I ordered a brain SPECT study to evaluate the functioning of his brain. The study showed that he had two problems. When Gregg tried to concentrate, the front part of his brain, which should increase in activity, actually decreased. This is the part of the brain that controls attention span, judgment, impulse control, and critical thinking. His brain study also showed decreased activity in his left temporal lobe, which, when abnormal, often causes problems with violent or aggressive behavior. I diagnosed Gregg with Temporal Lobe ADD.

As I explained these findings to Gregg, he became visibly relieved. "You mean," he said, "the harder I try to concentrate, the worse it gets for me." He responded very nicely to a combination of medication (Ritalin and Carbatrol) to correct the problems in his frontal and temporal lobes. In addition, I placed him on vitamin E and ginkgo to enhance overall blood flow to his brain and did biofeedback over his left temporal lobe. He was able to remain at home, finish high school, and start college—a far cry from the stupid troublemaker he and everyone else thought he was.

ADULTS

Brett

Brett, 27, had just been fired from his fourth job in a year. He blamed his bosses for expecting too much of him, but it was the same old story. Brett had trouble with details, he was often late to work, he seemed disorganized, and he would miss important deadlines. The end came when he impulsively told off a difficult customer who complained about his attitude.

All his life Brett had similar problems, and his mother was tired of bailing him out. He dropped out of school in the eleventh grade, despite having been found to have a high IQ. He was restless, fidgety, impulsive, and had a fleeting attention span. When he was in school, small amounts of homework would take him several hours to complete, even with much nagging and yelling from his mother. Brett had mastered the art of getting people angry at him, and it seemed to others that he intentionally stirred things up.

Brett had had lifelong symptoms of Classic ADD that had gone unnoticed, even though Brett had been tested on three separate occasions. With appropriate treatment at last, his life made a dramatic turnaround. He returned to school, finished a technical degree in fire-inspection technology, and got a job. He has kept that job for eight years now and feels that he is happier, more focused, and more positive than ever before.

Larry

Larry, 62, came into therapy because his wife threatened to start divorce proceedings against him if he didn't get help. She complained that he never talked to her, he was unreliable, he never finished projects that he started, and he was very negative. He tended to be moody, tired, and disinterested in sex. As a child, he had mediocre to poor grades in school, and as an adult he went from job to job, complaining of boredom.

Larry was referred to me by his marital therapist, and rightly so: Larry had Limbic ADD, with problems that looked like a combination of ADD and depression.

Larry's SPECT study showed decreased prefrontal cortex activity and increased activity in the deep limbic system of his brain. Seeing his scan convinced him of the need for treatment. He started on an intense aerobic exercise program, took nutritional supplements, and changed his diet. Within a month his mood was better and he felt more focused. As Larry improved, the couple learned quickly in marital therapy and have been happier than when they were first married.

Lindy

Lindy, 37, was ready to leave her husband when she first came to see me. "We fight all the time," she said. "Not over big things . . . but it sure gets old." Lindy also complained of being moody, often irritable, and short with her children. Furthermore, she had trouble getting to sleep and couldn't get out of bed in the morning.

In school she was easily distracted, and keeping up with taking notes was almost impossible for her.

Lindy's husband had the same complaints of her. She was irritable, she seemed to provoke fights with him or the children, and she had to have things a certain way or she'd become very upset. "Everyone takes off their shoes and socks before they come into the house. And if she sees a strand of hair on the floor, she becomes very upset! She's the only person I've ever met who vacuums the house at 11 P.M. on Friday night." He said that there were sexual problems. When they were making love, she'd often become distracted and lose interest. She'd then tell her husband to "just get it over with." The husband often felt that she was having an affair.

Lindy's grandfather, father, and brother had problems with alcohol. She also had a niece and a nephew who were diagnosed with ADD. As I listened to her story, along with the comments from her husband, it was clear that Lindy had Overfocused ADD, where she had trouble shifting her attention. This caused her to have to have things a certain way at home and made it hard for her to take notes in school. She responded nicely to a combination of Ritalin and Prozac, exercise, and increased complex carbohydrates in her diet. After several months she was more relaxed at home, school was much easier for her, she was better with the children, and her relationship with her husband was more positive.

CHAPTER 2

The ADD Story

Despite what it may seem from the breathless media reports, ADD is not new. As early as the seventeenth century, the philosopher John Locke described a perplexing group of young students who, "try as they might, they cannot keep their minds from straying." History is full of references to people fitting the symptom pattern of inattention, restlessness, hyperactivity, and impulsivity. Abraham Lincoln's third son, Tad, fit the picture. He was described as hyperactive, impulsive (bursting into the Oval Office while chasing his brother), and inattentive. He had learning problems. His mother hired tutor after tutor to come into the White House to help Tad, but they all quit, saying that he was not teachable. One wonders if Mary Todd Lincoln didn't have ADD herself. She too struggled with impulsivity. On a number of occasions she overspent the White House budget, causing political embarrassment and ridicule for the president. One time when President Lincoln was reviewing the troops, a young Captain's wife caught his eye. Mrs. Lincoln noticed her husband looking at the young woman and started screaming at her husband in front of the whole crowd.

ADD is not even new in the medical literature. George Still, a pediatrician at the turn of the last century, described children who were hyperactive, inattentive, and impulsive. Unfortunately, he labeled them "morally defective." During the great flu epidemic of 1918, many children also contracted viral encephalitis and meningitis. Of those who survived the brain infection, many were described with symptoms now considered classic for ADD. By the 1930s the label "minimal brain damage" was coined to describe these children. The label was changed in the 1960s to "minimal brain dysfunction" because no anatomical abnormality could be found in the children. Whatever its name, ADD has been part of the psychiatric terminology since the inception of the *Diagnostic and Statistical Manual* (*DSM*) in 1952 (The *DSM* is the diagnostic bible listing clinical criteria for various psychiatric disorders). Every version of the DSM has described the core symptoms of ADD, albeit by a different name every time.

ADD CORE SYMPTOMS

There is a group of core symptoms common to those who have ADD. These include short attention span for routine tasks, distractibility, organizational problems (space and time), difficulty with follow-through, and poor internal supervision. These symptoms exist over a prolonged period of time and are present from an early age, although they may not be evident until a child is pushed to concentrate or to organize his or her life.

Diagnostic and Statistical Manual of the American Psychiatric Association (DSM)

DSM Version	Name for ADD
1	Hyperactivity of Childhood
2	Hyperkinetic Reaction of Childhood
3	Attention Deficit Disorder with or without hyperactivity
3R	Attention Deficit Hyperactivity Disorder
4	Attention Deficit/Hyperactivity Disorder

Short Attention Span for Regular, Routine Tasks

A short attention span is the hallmark symptom of this disorder. People with ADD have trouble sustaining attention and effort over prolonged periods of time. Their minds tend to wander and they frequently get distracted, thinking about or doing other things than the task at hand. Yet, one of the things that often fools inexperienced clinicians assessing this disorder is that people with ADD do not have a short attention span for everything. Often, people with ADD can pay attention perfectly well to things that are new, novel, highly stimulating, interesting, or frightening. These things provide enough of their own intrinsic stimulation (adrenaline), which activates the brain functions that help people with ADD focus and concentrate. When asked about attention span, most people with ADD say that they can pay attention "just fine." But they often spontaneously add the phrase ". . . if I'm interested." That is the most important part of the answer: People with ADD need adrenaline in order to focus.

In one study, researchers found a deficiency of adrenaline (the hormone frequently associated with stress or excitement) in the urine samples of ADD children. I often think of ADD as "adrenaline deficit disorder," because people with ADD can focus with excitement and interest, but not without it. My son who has ADD without hyperactivity (Type 2), for example, used to take four hours to do a half hour's worth of homework, frequently getting off task. Yet, if you gave him a car stereo magazine, he would quickly read it from cover to cover and remember every little detail in it.

People with ADD have problems paying attention to regular, routine, everyday matters such as homework, schoolwork, chores, or paperwork—problems that have plagued them their whole lives. The mundane is terrible for them and *not* by choice. As we will see later on, they need excitement or interest to stimulate an underactive brain.

Attention patterns are crucial to a diagnosis of ADD. A person's tendency to deny that they have attentional problems (because they can concentrate with intense interest) is often a roadblock to accepting the diagnosis or getting proper treatment. I make sure that I ask about attention span for regular, routine, everyday tasks. I also ask about attention span from those who know the person. Other people may be better observers than the person being evaluated. Parents, siblings, spouses, and friends are often to quick to complain about attention and focusing abilities, even when the person has completely denied any trouble concentrating.

In addition to clinical history (from family and friends as well as the subject him- or herself), our office also uses the Conner's Continuous Performance Task (CPT) to measure attention span and aid in making the diagnosis of ADD. The Conner's CPT is a computer-based fifteen-minute test of attention, vigilance, response time, and impulse control. On the screen, letters flash at one-second, two-second, and four-second intervals. Every time you see a letter, you hit the space bar, except when you see the letter X. Whenever you see the letter X you just let it go and do not hit the space bar. People with ADD often have erratic response times (good when the letters come fast at one second intervals, but slower when the letters come at two- or four-second intervals) and more impulsive responses, hitting an excessive number of X's. This test frustrates many people with ADD.

Distractibility

Distractibility differs from a short attention span. The issue here is not an inability to sustain attention, but rather a hypersensitivity to the environment. Most of us can block out unnecessary environmental stimuli: traffic sounds, the sound of the air conditioner or heater turning on, the smell of food from the cafeteria, birds flying by the classroom window, even the feel of our own clothing against our skin. People with ADD, however, are often hypersensitive to their senses, and they have trouble suppressing the sounds and sights of the environment—the sensory noise that surrounds us. The distractibility is likely due to the underlying mechanism of ADD, underactivity in the prefrontal cortex of the brain.

The prefrontal cortex has many inhibitory cells that signal other areas of the brain to settle down. It is supposed to send these inhibitory signals to the parietal lobes (our sensory cortex) so that we do not sense too much of the environment. However, when the prefrontal cortex is underactive, the parietal lobes bombard us with environmental stimuli. The prefrontal cortex also sends inhibitory signals to the brain's emotional centers in the limbic system. When this doesn't happen, people get distracted by their internal thoughts and feelings. For example, many of my patients tell me that they frequently feel irritated by their own clothing. Most people never feel their own clothing unless their attention is directed to it. When directed to think about the shoes on your feet, you can easily feel them, but since you don't need to pay attention to the feeling of your shoes, your brain blocks out the unnecessary sensation. People with ADD cannot do that. My daughter with Type 3 (Overfocused) ADD used to repetitively take off her socks if the seam was not perfectly aligned. ADD patients also routinely cut the tags out of their clothing. I remember the weekend my ex-wife (who had been diagnosed with ADD) moved into my apartment after our wedding. Unbeknown to me, she cut the tags out of all of my shirts. When I asked her why, she said she thought I would appreciate it. She hated how tags felt and always removed them from her clothing. As you can imagine, the hypersensitivity to touch can also cause sexual problems. Many people with ADD do not like to be touched, or they react negatively if touched the "wrong" way. In a similar way, sight sensitivity is a frequent problem. While it may not seem like much of an issue, seeing too much can cause problems in many situations. When driving, for example, it is important to focus on the road. Many people with ADD, however, see everything around them, becoming bombarded with visual stimuli. Reading a book also requires you to block out extraneous visual stimuli. Unfortunately, many people with ADD are unable to do this and they are frequently distracted by the movements around them.

Many people with ADD complain of being excessively bothered by sounds, especially the chewing sounds of others. I have several young patients who will not go to school because they are so bothered by the sounds that other students make. I once evaluated an inmate who told me that he got murderous thoughts when other inmates would drag chess pieces across the chess board while playing the game. The noise, he said, would make him crazy. Other patients have told me that they need white noise (such as that of fans) to block out the other sounds in the environment. My ex-wife used to sleep with a fan on in our room in order not to hear all of the other sounds in the house—whether it is 70 degrees out or 20 degrees out. I often hid under the covers to avoid the noise and the cold breeze from the fan.

Sensitivity to taste is another common problem. Many people with ADD will eat only foods with a certain taste or texture. Parents frequently complain that they have trouble finding foods their children will eat. One of my patients went through a two-year period where he would only eat burritos with peanut butter and bananas.

Organizational Problems (Space and Time)

Organizational struggles are also very common in ADD, specifically disorganization for space, time, projects, and long-term goals.

A common ADD trait, space disorganization is often seen early in the lives of ADD children. When you look at their rooms, closets, dresser drawers, desks, or book bags, you frequently see a disaster. Things are left half done, half put away, or dropped wherever. I used to tell my son that his room followed the second law of physics, entropy, in which things degrade from order to disorder. His room showed hyperentropy. I remember helping him clean his room on Sunday afternoons, but by Sunday evening it often looked a mess. Once, when he was in the third grade, I went to an open house at his school. All of the desks were in neat rows . . . except one. It was out of place with papers hanging out of it. My heart sank. I knew it was Anton's desk, and when I opened the desk's lid I saw his name.

Other people often complain bitterly about the disorganization, such as bosses, teachers, children, and spouses. I have received a number of letters from wives writing about their ADD husbands. "He'll tell you he's organized," they write, "but I am enclosing a picture of his office [filing cabinet, closet, or garage]. What do you think?" The pictures show spaces that are incredibly overstuffed and disorganized.

People with Type 3 ADD often appear very organized on the outside. They are often perfectly dressed, and parts of their living space may be very neat. For example, they may insist on perfect living rooms, but if you go into their drawers or their closets, you'll find a disaster. Similarly, time organization plagues people with ADD. They tend to be late and have trouble predicting how long things will take them to do. Often they will agree to do too many things, not realizing the time commitment involved. The chronic tardiness lands many ADD people in deep trouble. For example, they get fired from jobs for being late to work, not once, but on a regular basis. Many of my patients' spouses have told me that they have to lie in order to be on time for appointments or engagements. "If I tell her we have to leave at noon, invariably she won't be ready until 12:30 or 1 P.M. It makes me so mad! So in order for me not to feel so stressed out I tell her we have to leave at 11:00. She hasn't caught on yet."

ADD people often take a haphazard or disorganized approach to projects or chores, dramatically increasing the time it takes to complete them. For example, one of my patients planned to clean out the garage over the weekend. On Friday night he put half of the garage contents into the driveway, but then he started organizing the boxes that were inside the garage. Three weeks later the neighbors started to complain about the mess in the driveway. One of the college students I treat complained about spending excessive time on projects. When I asked him to explain the process of doing a project, it was clear that it had no beginning, middle, or end: He was working on multiple ideas that did not have any structure to them.

In addition, many people with ADD take a disorganized approach to their own lives. They frequently lack long-term goals and tend to live from crisis to crisis or problem to problem.

Difficulty with Follow-through

People with ADD frequently suffer from poor follow-through, lacking the staying power to see projects through to the end. They will do something so long as there is intense interest. In addition, they put things off until the very last minute—until the looming deadline generates enough stress to entice them to get it done. For example, if there is a term paper due in a month, they will put it off, put it off, and put it off until they are pushed to the wall of the deadline, working feverishly to finish, even if they have told themselves that this time they will get to their project early.

Often people with ADD have so many different interests, they will only do a project as long as long as it holds their curiosity. I once saw a college professor for evaluation. His wife sat in on the initial session. I asked him how many projects he started last year. He said, "I think about 300." His wife added in an irritated tone, "He only finished three, and none of them were for me."

Many people with ADD will complete 50 to 80 percent of their task and then go off to another project. They frequently get distracted by other things and fail to follow through with the task at hand. Many people with ADD pay late fees on bills, even though they had the money to pay the bill on time.

Poor follow-through affects many areas of life. Here are some examples:

- schoolwork—fails to turn in assigned work
- chores at home—things often put off until the very last minute or not done at all
- work—reports or paperwork not turned in on time
- finances—late charges paid, even when the money is there because bills were not paid on time
- and friendships—promises go unfulfilled.

Poor Internal Supervision

Many people with ADD have poor internal supervision. The prefrontal cortex (pfc) is the brain's chief executive because it is so heavily involved with forethought, planning, impulse control, and decision making. North Carolina neuropsychiatrist Thomas Gualtieri, M.D., succinctly summarized the human functions of the pfc: "the capacity to formulate goals, to make plans for their execution, to carry them out in an effective way, and to change course and improvise in the face of obstacles or failure, *and to do so successfully, in the absence of external direction or structure.* The capacity of the individual to generate goals and to achieve them is considered to be an essential aspect of a mature and effective personality. It is not a social convention or an artifact of culture. It is hard wired in the construction of the prefrontal cortex and its connections."*

When there are problems in this part of the brain, as is typical in ADD patients, exhibiting forethought is a constant struggle. The pfc helps you think about what you say or do before you say or do it. The pfc helps you, in accordance with your experience, select among alternatives in social and work situations. For example, a person with good pfc function is more likely to have a tempered, reasonable disagreement with a spouse. A person with poor pfc function is more likely to do or say something that will make the situation worse. Likewise, if you're a checkout clerk with good pfc function and a difficult, complaining person (who has poor pfc function) comes through your line, you are more likely to keep quiet or give a thoughtful response that helps the situation. If you have poor pfc function, you are more likely to do or say something that will inflame the situation. The pfc helps you problem-solve, see ahead of a situation, and, by learning through experience, pick between the most helpful alternatives. Effectively playing a game such as chess requires good pfc function.

*From John Ratey, M.D., editor, *The Neuropsychiatry of Personality Disorders* (Cambridge, MA: Blackwell Science, 1995).

This is also the part of the brain that helps you learn from mistakes. Good pfc function doesn't that mean you won't make mistakes. Rather, you won't make the same mistake over and over. You are able to learn from the past and apply its lessons. A student with good pfc function can learn that if he or she starts a long-term project early, there is more time for research and less anxiety over getting it done. A student with decreased pfc function doesn't learn from past frustrations and may tend to put everything off until the last minute. In general, poor pfc function leads people to make repetitive mistakes. Their actions are not based on experience, or forethought, but rather on the moment.

The moment is what matters. This phrase comes up over and over with my ADD patients. For many people with ADD, forethought is a struggle. It is natural for them to act out what is important to them at the immediate moment, not two moments from now or five moments from now, but now! A person with ADD may be ready for work a few minutes early, but rather than leave the house and be on time, she may do another couple of things that make her late. Likewise, a person with ADD may be sexually attracted to someone he just met, and even though he is married and his personal goal is to stay married, he may have a sexual encounter that puts that at risk. The moment was what mattered.

In the same vein, many people with ADD take what I call a *crisis management approach* to their lives. Rather than having clearly defined goals and acting in a consistent manner to reach them, they ricochet from crisis to crisis. In school, people with ADD have difficulty with long-term planning. Instead of keeping up as the semester goes along, they focus on the crisis in front of them at the moment—the next test or term paper. At work they are under continual stress. Deadlines loom and tasks go uncompleted. It seems as though there is a need for constant stress in order to get consistent work done. The constant stress, however, takes a physical toll on everyone involved (the person, his or her family, coworkers, employers, friends, etc.).

Assessing ADD

The hallmark assessment tool for ADD is a detailed history by an experienced clinician. I have found that a life history is the most reliable diagnostic tool. Of course, I use other things, such as checklists, brain-imaging studies, information from collateral sources (such as teachers and caregivers), and blood work, but I find that a good clinical history is essential to proper diagnosis. It is most helpful to take a biological, psychological, and sociological approach when evaluating any psychiatric, learning, or behavioral problem. If you look at problems in these three spheres you are likely to obtain the best possible evaluation and set the stage for proper treatment.

Bio-Psycho-Social Assessment of ADD

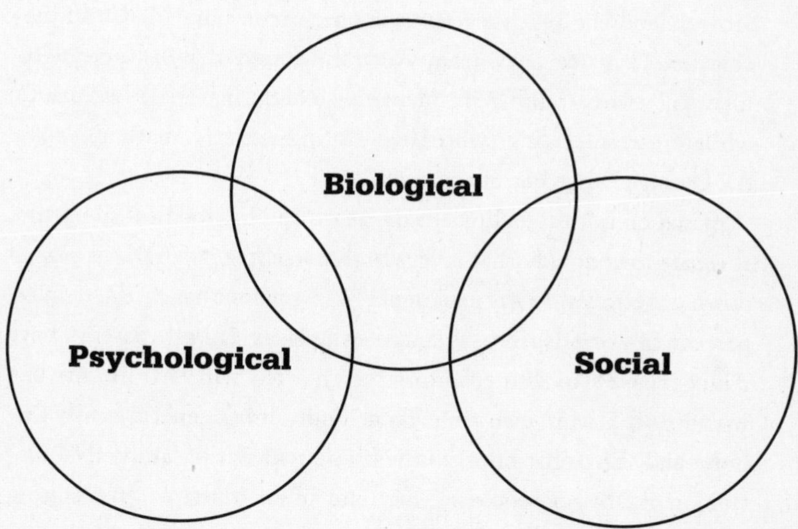

BIOLOGICAL FACTORS

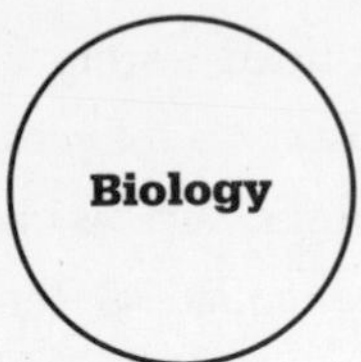

Genetics

Since ADD tends to run in families, an assessment should begin with a good family history starting with the grandparents from each side and learning as much as possible about the primary family members.

In the last decade scientists have made progress in understanding the genetics of ADD. The pioneering works of David Comings, Florence Levy, and others have clearly demonstrated a genetic component to this disorder. Specific gene sites implicated include the HLA on chromosome 6, the dopamine transporter gene on chromosome 5, and the D4 receptor gene on chromosome 11. Child psychiatrist Florence Levy from Australia found that 81 percent of identical twins (who share identical genetic material) had ADD, while fraternal twins (who have sibling genetic material) share ADD only 29 percent of the time.

Based on both my clinical experience and the medical literature, it is safe to conclude that a very high percentage of ADD is passed down genetically. In my experience, if one parent has ADD, then 60 percent of the offspring will have it as well. If both parents have ADD then 85 to 90 percent of the children will have it. Anyone who does this work over time has no doubt it is a genetic family disorder and that contributes to the high incidence of family dysfunction in ADD households. There are often multiple challenging people in an ADD family, not just one challenging child.

Head Injury

I have also seen other factors involved in causing ADD. One of the most common is unrecognized head injury, especially to the left front side of the brain. In my experience, many professionals and parents discount or ignore the impact of head injuries. They think that a person needs to have a significant loss of consciousness for a prolonged period of time in order for it to do damage. Our brain-imaging work, as well as the work of others, is disproving this notion. More on head injuries in Chapter XI.

Toxic Exposure

When the brain is exposed to a lack of oxygen or some toxic substance, it is much more likely to show symptoms of ADD. Lack of oxygen can happen with premature babies who have underdeveloped lungs, babies born with the cord wrapped tightly around their necks, and individuals after a drowning accident. Lack of oxygen causes a decrease in overall brain activity. Brain infections, such as meningitis or encephalitis, cause toxic inflammation in the brain and damage tissue. Clearly, fetal exposure to drugs, alcohol, and cigarettes also put a child at risk for ADD and learning disabilities. Often mothers who use these substances during pregnancy are medicating their own struggles with depression, ADD, or anxiety. The babies inherit vulnerabilities to these problems and in addition experience toxicity to their brains.

Medical Problems, Medications

Certain medical problems, such as thyroid disease, can look like ADD. An overactive thyroid gland may look like Type 1 ADD (feeling hyperactive and inattentive), while an underactive thyroid may look like Type 2 ADD (feeling lethargic and inattentive). Likewise, certain medications, such as asthma medications, can make people feel and look hyperactive and inattentive. It is important for your doctor to assess the impact of medical problems on behavior.

Hormonal Influences

Hormonal influences play a major role in ADD. ADD symptoms are generally worse around the time of puberty in both males and females. In females, ADD symptoms are also exacerbated in the premenstrual period and also around the time of menopause. A number of SPECT studies have shown an overall decrease in brain activity when estrogen levels are low. During perimenopause or menopause, many women who had only mild ADD before now look as if they have major ADD symptoms. Estrogen replacement, although controversial, appears to have a positive effect on brain function.

Drug Abuse

It is key to learn about drug abuse when assessing for ADD. While ADD and drug abuse commonly occur together, drug abuse can masquerade as ADD. New onset ADD symptoms at the age of 14, for example, may signal marijuana abuse. Many drug abusers are not honest (due to feelings of shame or the fear of being found out), so I will frequently order a drug screen to be sure. Drug screens are not foolproof, but I have found that just the act of ordering the drug screen is helpful. I generally say something like "I want to order a drug screen on you. I know you said that you weren't using drugs, but people who do use drugs often won't admit to it. I want to do a thorough evaluation of you and just want to make sure." If a person says, "I don't believe in drug screens. They are not reliable. I won't do it," that is generally a good indicator that he is using drugs. If he says, "No problem, I understand," and willingly goes for the test, then it is generally a sign that he is not using drugs. Of course, I have been fooled, so even if the patient agrees, I send the specimen to the lab.

Poor Diet

In the last thirty years our diet has changed dramatically. These days, children eat a diet high in simple carbohydrates (sugar, white bread, white-flour food products), poor in lean protein, and positively deficient in vegetables. Think about the great American breakfast. Morning time is often rushed especially when both parents work outside the home, and there is less time to fix a nutritious breakfast. Kids eat Pop-Tarts, sugar cereals, donuts, frozen waffles, or muffins. Gone are the days of sausage and eggs (protein), and sugar is in. Try to find bread in the store without sugar or forms of sugar (corn syrup, high-fructose syrup, etc.). In my local supermarket, out of about thirty brands of bread available, only one—a dark Russian rye bread—is made without any sugar.

Your diet provides the fuel for the brain's work. I have found that a diet high in simple carbohydrates makes attentional problems worse for most people, especially with people vulnerable to ADD. Most ADD children and adults simply do better on a high-protein, low–simple-carbohydrate diet (more on this later). A lack of protein causes a tremendous problem with focus throughout the day. If a person is vulnerable to ADD, a high-carbohydrate, low-protein diet will certainly make their symptoms worse.

Lack of Exercise

Exercise boosts blood flow to the brain. Unfortunately, children and teens get much less exercise than they did 20 years ago. With the advent of video and computer games children are spending more time indoors, doing activities which require little exertion. A sedentary lifestyle makes someone more prone to exhibit ADD symptoms.

PSYCHOLOGICAL FACTORS

Early Neglect and Abuse

Both physical and emotional neglect and abuse contribute to ADD. The brain needs nurturing and appropriate stimulation to develop properly. When a baby is neglected or abused, the brain cannot develop properly and is put at great risk for learning and behavioral problems. An extreme example of neglect occurred during the late 1980s when thousands of Romanian orphans were raised without affection, touching, or nurturing, even though they had food. Many of these children developed severe emotional, learning, and behavioral problems. Brain scans showed overall decreased activity in their brains. Without appropriate stimulation, the brain does not make the connections it needs to make. Emotional or physical abuse causes a rush of stress hormones and chemicals that poison a baby's or child's brain. Stress hormones damage the memory centers, and chronic stress causes the brain to become hyperalert, leading to severe distractibility and an inability to filter out extraneous stimuli.

Negative Self-Talk

Low self-esteem, self-doubt, and a lack of confidence can make some look as if they have ADD. Of course, having ADD makes one more prone to these problems. Negative self-talk often stems from having people talk in a negative way toward you, although this is not always the case. Type 5 (Limbic) ADD is often associated with excessive negativity.

Learned Helplessness

Psychologist Martin Seligman coined the term "learned helplessness" to describe what he saw in depressed patients. I often see this phenomena in people with ADD. Learned helplessness occurs when a person tries to do something important, such as study for school, but performs poorly. Then she tries again, but it doesn't work. She tries yet another time, but it still doesn't work. Finally she gives up. This demoralization contributes heavily to ADD symptoms and must be assessed.

SOCIAL AND SOCIETAL FACTORS

Social Situation

Evaluating the current family and social situation is essential to get a complete picture of a person. Who is she living with? What are the relationships like? How is the financial health of the family? Are there any physical or emotional challenges? Is there alcohol or drug abuse in the home?

ADD Is Increasing in the Population

ADD is increasing in the population, a fact that frightens me, and it should frighten you as well. When you look at the fallout from untreated ADD, our society may be in for a lot more problems, especially considering that ADD remains underdiagnosed and undertreated. Thirty years ago, teachers would typically have one or two Classic ADD kids in their classrooms. Now I hear them say they have three, four, or five of these kids. What is happening? Are we just better at recognizing ADD? Are societal influences causing more ADD symptoms? One answer comes from David Comings, M.D., a geneticist from the City of Hope Hospital in Los Angeles. In his book *The Gene Bomb* he postulates that as our society becomes more technologically advanced, we require students to stay in school longer to get the best jobs. The students who drop out of the educational system first are those with ADD and learning disabilities. (Remember, 35 percent of untreated people with ADD never finish high school.) If you drop out of school first, what behavior are you likely to engage in first? You guessed it: sex. I see a much higher percentage of teenage pregnancies in ADD girls. They do not think through the consequences of their behavior. Also, according to Dr. Comings, ADD women have their first baby on average at the age of 20. Non-ADD women have their first baby on average at the age of 26. ADD women tend to have more children. Non-ADD women tend to have fewer children.

There is a historical example of how this childbearing dynamic can change a population. I am of Lebanese heritage. Lebanon was first made a country in 1943, but had long-standing roots in the

Phoenician culture. At the time, in 1943, the country's population was approximately half Christian and half Muslim. The Lebanese parliament was set up as half Christian and half Muslim to reflect the population. At the time, however, the Christians were better educated than their Muslim counterparts. They tended to stay in school longer. They also tended to have fewer children. Thirty-two years later—in 1975, when civil war broke out in Lebanon—the country was only one third Christian and two thirds Muslim. Part of the reason for the civil war was the change in population dynamics. In thirty-two years, a generation and a half, the population showed a dramatic shift.

Let's bring this example closer to home. In 1972, renowned psychologist Thomas Auchenbauch performed a study to determine the incidence of learning and behavioral problems in children among the general population. At the time, using standardized instruments that he developed, he reported that 10 percent of the childhood population had learning or behavioral problems. A generation later, in 1992, he repeated the study using the same psychological instruments on basically the same population. He found a staggering difference: Eighteen percent of the childhood population now met the criteria for learning or behavioral problems. The incidence of problems had nearly doubled in a generation. Why?

Societal Contributions to ADD

I believe the geneticists have a big part of the answer. ADD parents are having more ADD children. There are other factors contributing to the rise of ADD and related problems in our society: dietary changes, excessive television watching, video games, and decreased exercise. Moreover, we are also better at diagnosing ADD. In addition to having improved psychological assessment tools, ADD has received repeated national exposure over the past ten years. It has been on the cover of *Time, Newsweek,* and *U.S. News & World Report.* Almost all of the talk shows have done programs on ADD, and there have been several national best-selling books. ADD has become part of movies, TV shows, courtroom dramas, and national legislation. We are at least better at thinking about it and talking about it. I alone lecture thirty to forty times a year to professionals. Over the last ten years we have seen strong interest in the medical and mental-health community to learn more about ADD and get beyond the myths and the hype of ADD.

As far as excess television is concerned, the research is very clear: Kids who watch the most TV do the worst in school. TV is a "no brain" activity. Everything is provided for it (sounds, sights, plots, outcome, entertainment), and the brain doesn't have to learn or make new connections. Like a muscle, the more you use your brain, the stronger it becomes and the more it can do. The opposite is also true: The less you work it, the weaker it becomes. Repeatedly engaging in "no brain" activities, such as TV, decreases a person's ability to focus. In addition, the pacing of TV has changed over the past thirty years. Thirty years ago a thirty-second commercial had ten three-second scenes. The same commercial in 2000 has thirty one-second scenes. We are being programmed to need more stimulation in order to pay attention.

Video games are another problem. I have seen that many ADD children literally become addicted to playing video games. They will play for hours at a time, to the detriment of their responsibilities, and go through tantrums and withdrawal symptoms when forced to stop. A recent study on brain-imaging and video games was published in the journal *Nature.* In the study, PET scans were taken while a group of people played action video games. The researchers were trying to see where video games worked in the brain. They discovered that the basal ganglia (where dopamine is produced in the brain) were much more active when the video games were being played than at rest. Both cocaine and Ritalin work in this part of the brain as well. The reason that cocaine is addictive and Ritalin is not is related to how each drug is metabolized. Cocaine has a powerful, immediate effect that stimulates an enormous release of the neurotransmitter dopamine. The pleasure this brings rapidly fades, leaving the addict wanting more. Ritalin, on the other hand, works slowly, inducing no high or pleasure from taking it and the effects stay around for a long time. Similarly, video games bring pleasure and focus by increasing dopamine release. The problem with them is that the more dopamine is released, the less neurotransmitter is available later on to do schoolwork, homework, chores, and so on. Many parents have told me that the more a child plays video games, the worse he does in school and the more irritable he tends to be when asked to stop playing.

I saw the negative effects of video games in my own house. Nintendo came into our home when my son was 10 years old. Initially, I thought that it was very cool. I never had exciting games like these when I was a child. But over the next few years I saw him spending more and more time with the video games and less time on his work. Moreover, he would become argumentative when he was told to stop playing. I decided that Nintendo had to go. We have all been better off since.

One cannot overlook the Internet as a potential source of serious problems for our children and ourselves. The Internet is such a valuable source of information. (I have several Web sites, which we are very proud of, at *www.amenclinic.com* and *brainplace.com.*) But the Internet is also filled with danger and time wasters. Because of the impulsivity and excitement-seeking nature of many people with ADD, they frequently visit sexually explicit sites, engage in racy conversations with others, and find ways to get into trouble. One of my patients thought she fell in love over the Net. She was seventeen years old when the story unfolded. She met a man from Louisiana in a chat room. They talked for hours over the Net, sent scanned photos, started talking over the telephone, and decided to marry after two months, even though they had never met in person. When I found out about it in therapy, I called a meeting with her parents. When she tried to break it off with this man, he threatened to kill her. We discovered that he had recently gotten out of prison for violent behavior. It's essential that parents supervise time children spend on the Net and that they put limits over the kinds of sites available. Recent studies have shown that the kids who spend the most time on the Net have the poorest social skills. Balance and supervision are the biggest keys.

I have become more concerned recently about a child's exposure to how computer and TV screens flash (or refresh themselves). If you look at a computer monitor or television screen through a video camera, you will see thick black lines quickly roll across the screen. TV and computer screens flash at different speeds, up to 30 flashes or cycles per second. Interestingly, this speed of flashing is similar to a concentration brain state. Your brain gravitates to that rhythm, and you tune in to whatever is drawing your attention—forced focus, so to speak. "Entrainment" is the technical term of this phenomena: Your brain picks up the rhythm in the environment. So if a light (or TV) flashes at a slow rate, one's brain picks up the slow rate and that person feels sleepy. If it flashes at a fast rate, you may feel energized or anxious. If your brain picks up a concentration flashing rate, you will focus on the TV or computer screen, even though you may not be at all interested in what's on it. Have you ever had the experience of watching TV even though you didn't want to—the feeling of being mesmerized or compelled to watch, even though you were bored with what was on? I have. The most recent example of mass entrainment occurred in late 1997 in Japan. Tens of thousands of Japanese children were watching the top-rated Nintendo cartoon *Pokémon.* During one scene there was an explosion in which red, white, and yellow lights flashed at approximately 4.5 cycles (or flashes) per second for several seconds. All of a sudden kids started to have seizures. Seven hundred and thirty Japanese children went to emergency rooms that night, reporting seizures. Most of the children had never had a seizure before. The 4.5 cycles per second happened to be a seizure frequency. That was a dramatic example, but I wonder what all of this exposure to computer flashing is doing to our children. As far as I know, no one is studying it, and we should be.

Video games and television have lead to another major contributor in the rise of ADD in our society: the lack of exercise. Exercise increases blood flow to all parts of the body, including the brain. As kids watch more TV and spend more time exercising only their thumbs with video games, they are becoming more sluggish and less attentive. Through the years I have seen a direct relationship between the level of exercise a person gets and the severity of their symptoms. I have seen a number of ADD professionals (such as physicians and attorneys) get through school by exercising two to four hours a day. I have also noted that when my ADD patients are playing sports, such as basketball, where there is intense aerobic exercise, they do better in school, without any change in their medication. Exercise is important on many levels, and we'll talk more about it later on.

Obtaining a bio-psycho-social evaluation gives clinicians the most complete picture. As we will see, it sets the stage for proper treatment.

Other Things to Look For in Assessing ADD

When ADD is present, these other problems should also be evaluated. Sometimes these problems are misdiagnosed as ADD, sometimes they occur with ADD.

Psychiatric/Adjustment Problems: Emotional and adjustment problems can masquerade as ADD, be a result of ADD, or occur together with ADD. Here are samples of the problems:

Adjustment Disorders or Family Problems: Temporarily, family problems or significant stress can cause a person of any age to have problems with concentration or restlessness. The difference between stress and ADD is history and duration of the difficulties. ADD is a long-standing problem that is relatively constant over time. The stress of long-term family problems can cause a child to look as though he or she has ADD. It must be determined, however, whether or not the serious family problems are a result of ADD in one or more of the family members.

Behavioral Problems Not Related to ADD: Some behavior problems have nothing to do with ADD. When parents have ineffective parenting skills, they can actually encourage difficult behavior in their children.

Depressive Disorders: Depression may be confused with ADD, especially in children. Depressive symptoms include poor memory, low energy, negativity, periods of helplessness and hopelessness, social isolation, along with sleep and appetite changes. Many of these symptoms are also found in ADD. History is the key to proper diagnosis. ADD symptoms are generally constant over time, while depression tends to fluctuate. Many people with ADD experience demoralization (from chronic failure) and may indeed look depressed when ADD is the primary problem. Depression and ADD often occur together.

Manic-Depressive Disorder: Manic-depressive or "bipolar" symptoms may be similar to ADD. Both experience restless, excessive talkativeness, hyperactivity, racing thoughts, and impulsivity. The difference is usually found in the severity, consistency, and course of the symptoms. ADD remains constant; bipolar disorder fluctuates from highs to lows. People who have ADD are consistently distractible, restless, and impulsive. People with bipolar disorder will have periods of those symptoms, but they often fluctuate with depressive episodes and periods of relative calm or normalcy. The manic highs of bipolar disorder are not experienced by people with ADD.

Anxiety Disorders: Anxiety disorders can also present similar symptoms to ADD, including restlessness, hyperactivity, forgetfulness, and an inability to concentrate. Again, the key to proper diagnosis is history. As with depression and bipolar disorder, anxiety disorders tend to fluctuate; ADD symptoms are generally constant. Moreover, having ADD can breed symptoms of anxiety or nervousness. When your mind turns off in the face of stress, it can cause nervousness and fear in work, family, and social situations. It is common for people with ADD to experience significant anxiety from underachievement. These disorders also commonly run together.

Obsessive-Compulsive Disorder (OCD): OCD is marked by a person with obsessions (repetitive negative thoughts) and/or compulsions (repetitive negative behaviors), which interfere with their lives. People with OCD get "stuck" or "locked in" to negative thoughts or behaviors. In my clinical experience, there is a high percentage of people with ADD who also have features of OCD, especially if there is significant alcohol abuse in their family backgrounds. The overfocused subtype of ADD has many features in common with OCD, and both disorders tend to respond best to antiobsessive antidepressants, such as Prozac, Paxil, Luvox, Anafranil, and Zoloft.

Tic Disorders, Such as Tourette's Syndrome: Tic disorders are more common among people with ADD. Tics are abnormal, involuntary motor movements, (blinking, shoulder shrugging, head jerking), or vocal sounds (throat clearing, coughing, blowing, and even swearing). Tourette's syndrome occurs when there are both motor and vocal tics that have been present for more than a year. Up to 60 percent of people who have Tourette's also have ADD, and 40 to 50 percent of people with Tourette's have OCD. There is a significant connection between ADD, OCD, and Tourette's.

History of Physical, Emotional, or Sexual Abuse: Abuse in any form can cause learning and behavior problems. Certainly they can also occur together. Many clinicians see an increased incidence of abuse occurring in families with ADD. The increased level of frustration, impulse control problems, and anger found in ADD families causes them to be more at risk. An accurate, detailed history is necessary to distinguish between abuse and ADD. People who have been abused present more clearly symptoms of posttraumatic stress disorder (PTSD), such as nightmares, fearfulness, a tendency to startle easily, flashbacks, feelings of numbness or emotional restriction. Yet, many people who have ADD feel they have a form of PTSD from the chronic dysfunction they have experienced.

Medical Factors: Medical factors also need to be considered in fully evaluating ADD:

- Gestational problems, such as maternal alcohol or drug use during pregnancy
- Birth traumas, such as oxygen deprivation or injury
- History of head trauma
- Seizure disorders
- Physical illness/disease, such as thyroid disease or lead exposure
- Severe allergies to environmental toxins or food
- Medications, such as asthma medications.

Learning/Developmental Problems: Learning disabilities occur in approximately 40 percent of people with ADD. Suspect the diagnosis of a learning disability whenever there is long-standing underachievement in school or at work. Medical evaluation and history, family and school history, and clinical observation best evaluate these disabilities. The diagnosis is confirmed by "psychoeducational" testing.

Psychoeducational testing evaluates three areas:

1. IQ and cognitive style (look for discrepancies between verbal and performance scores)
2. level of academic skill (standard achievement tests)
3. evidence of a specific learning disabilities or problems (with tests such as the Woodcock-Johnson Psychoeducational Battery).

TREATMENT FOR LEARNING DISABILITIES

The specific treatments for learning disabilities are beyond the scope of the book. When they occur, it is important for the school system to assist with an assessment for special services or special education to evaluate the need for alternative learning strategies and academic accommodations.

ADD THROUGHOUT THE LIFE CYCLE

Since ADD is best diagnosed through history over a long period of time, it is critical to understand the developmental course of ADD. Here's a look at ADD throughout the life cycle. It is important to note that ADD does not just appear in the teenage years or in adulthood. When you know what to look for, you can see that ADD symptoms have been present for most of a person's life.

Many ADD children are noted to be overly active in the womb. One mother told me that her unborn child kicked her so hard during the eighth month of pregnancy that he broke her ninth rib. (I wonder what that did for bonding!) Many are also difficult from birth: Many are colicky, fussy eaters, have a difficult time being comforted, are sensitive to noise and touch, and have eating and sleeping difficulties. As toddlers, they're often excessively active, mischievous, demanding, difficult to toilet train, and noncompliant with parental requests (like the terrible twos continued).

Most ADD children are not recognized as such until they go to school: In kindergarten or in first or second grade, schoolteachers often notice the difference between these children and others. Teachers have a large database of expected behavior, while many parents do not.

By the time they have entered school, hyperactive boys' problems with aggression, defiance, and oppositional behavior have often emerged. These problems often lead to social isolation and poor self-esteem.

The majority of ADD kids have varying degrees of poor school performance related to failure to finish assigned tasks, disruptive behavior during class, and poor peer relations. The time that these problems become apparent often relates to intelligence and the school setting. Often, the brighter the child, the later he or she is diagnosed. Up until that time, the child is likely to be labeled as an underachiever, willful, defiant, or oppositional.

As teenagers, current studies indicate that approximately 25–50 percent fully outgrow their symptoms by puberty. However, many do not outgrow their symptoms at puberty as previously thought, and they have difficulty with their family, school, and/or the community. The error occurred in part because most ADD children outgrow the hyperactive component before or at puberty. The problems with inattention and impulsivity remain, and tens of thousands of teenagers are taken off their medication just at a time when their defiant behavior is at its peak. I have seen that many teens experience serious school and social failure after the pediatrician or family doctor prematurely took them off their medication.

There is a high incidence of conflicts in ADD families, especially during the teenage years. These conflicts often center around failure to do schoolwork, problems completing routine chores, and difficulty being trusted to obey the rules. I have seen many teenagers sent away from home (to a residential treatment setting, boarding school, or relative's house) as a way for the family to survive the turmoil.

Many adults with ADD live lives of chronic frustration. Psychiatrists Henry Mann and Stanley Greenspan wrote the first article on ADD in adults in 1977. Yet, the medical community was very slow to recognize ADD in adults. It has only been since the late 1980s that professionals began talking about ADD beyond the adolescent years. Still, even now many professionals do not understand ADD in adults and often describe these people as having character problems, anxiety, depression, or even manic-depressive disorder. Their child ADD symptoms are assumed to have just melted away. Adults with ADD often come to our clinic with the following concerns:

- Concerns about a child with ADD. Most adults with ADD are only diagnosed after they bring their children in for evaluation. During a thorough history, the child psychiatrists ask about family history. Through these questions the light goes on for many people. Child psychiatrists are best at diagnosing this disorder, because they typically see a lot of children with ADD.

- Poor school/work performance caused by the following symptoms: deficient sustained attention to reading, paperwork, etc.; high susceptibility to boredom by tedious material; poor organization and planning; procrastination until deadlines are imminent; restlessness, trouble staying in a confined space (not a phobia); impulsive decision-making; inability to work well independently; failure to listen carefully to directions; frequent impulsive job changes; poor academic grades for ability; frequent lateness for work/appointments; or a tendency to misplace things frequently.
- Symptoms of trouble thinking clearly, generally poor self-discipline, moodiness, chronic anxiety, restlessness, substance abuse, uncontrolled anger, marital problems, sleep problems, financial problems, or impulsiveness.

There is also no question in my mind that ADD exists in the elderly and that it seriously handicaps many of them. I have diagnosed many elderly people with ADD, mostly after I have seen their children, grandchildren, or great-grandchildren. My oldest patient, Betty, was 94 when she came to see me. I had seen three generations of people in her family: her son, grandson, and great-granddaughter. When I asked her why she wanted to be evaluated, she said that she wanted to be able to finish reading the paper in the morning. ADD symptoms in the elderly cause social isolation, difficult behavior, and a higher incidence of cognitive problems. For decades geriatric psychiatrists have used medications like Ritalin to help sharpen cognitive skills. Perhaps they were, in part, treating the very high incidence of ADD in the elderly.

WATCH FOR THE WALL

Many bright children with ADD, especially Type 2 (Inattentive ADD), are not diagnosed until later in their development, if at all. They do fine for a while and then slam into failure: The Wall! Depending on intelligence, class size, and knowledge level of the parents, they may not have problems until third grade, sixth grade, ninth grade, or even college. I've treated some college professors who received good grades in graduate school but still had the majority of symptoms of the disorder. They state, however, that it took them four or five times the amount of time and effort to do as well as their peers.

My son, whose greatest difficulties were in the ninth grade, actually got straight A's in the sixth grade. He said, "In sixth grade, I knew everything that the teacher was talking about. It was easy. In ninth grade, I did not know as much and I couldn't bring myself to focus on all the material I needed to learn."

The Wall is different for each person with ADD.

CHAPTER 3

Looking into the ADD Brain

The Development of SPECT Imaging in Psychiatry

My work on ADD started in an unlikely place: at a military hospital in the middle of nowhere. The opportunities afforded me by the U.S. Army started me on a journey to explore the unorthodox concept of brain-imaging. I did my psychiatric training at Walter Reed Army Medical Center (WRAMC) in Washington, D.C. I had been an infantry medic in the early 1970s and the GI Bill helped to support me through college and medical school. WRAMC was (and is) the premier military hospital in the world. It is responsible for the medical care of soldiers, family members, and international political figures. After three years at WRAMC, I went to Honolulu, Hawaii, to do a child and adolescent psychiatry fellowship at Tripler Army Medical Center. Military training was very practical. Learning about combat psychiatry and taking care of soldiers and their families in times of crises did not leave one with the inclination to become married to any particular psychiatric dogma or tradition. We learned to use what worked, what was helpful, and what made a difference—right then and there.

After my training I was stationed at Fort Irwin, forty miles north of Barstow, in the Mojave Desert. Halfway between Los Angeles and Las Vegas, Fort Irwin was also known as the National Training

Center—the place where American soldiers were taught to fight the Russians (and later the Iraqis) in the desert. At the time, I was the only psychiatrist for 4,000 soldiers and an equal number of family members. It was considered an isolated assignment. There were problems with domestic violence, drug abuse (especially amphetamine abuse), depression, and ailments resulting from the stress of living in the middle of nowhere. I dealt with many people who suffered from headaches, anxiety attacks, insomnia, and excessive muscle tension.

Shortly after arriving at Fort Irwin, I went through the cabinets in the community mental health clinic to see what instruments and psychological tests my predecessors had left behind. To my delight, there was an old Autogen biofeedback apparatus that measured hand temperature. There was one lecture on biofeedback during my psychiatric training. The concept of biofeedback was fascinating: If you get feedback on body measures, such as hand temperature or heart rate, you can learn to change them through mental exercise and discipline. The problem with biofeedback, as I knew it at that time, was that the training was boring. The needles and dials on the machines were not interesting to patients. Nonetheless, the old machine was dusted off and we used it with patients who had migraine headaches. I taught them how to warm their hands, using only their imagination. It was fascinating to see how patients could actually warm their hand temperature, sometimes as much as 15 to 20 degrees. Hand-temperature training taught patients how to participate in their own healing process. In late 1987, six months after coming to Fort Irwin, I wrote a request to Colonel Knowles, our hospital commander, to buy the mental health clinic $30,000 worth of the latest computerized biofeedback equipment, including ten days of training for me in San Francisco. He laughed at me: He said that the Army didn't have the money and that when my assignment at Fort Irwin was over, the equipment would just end up in a closet somewhere, much like the equipment I had found. I dropped the idea but continued using the old temperature trainer. In May 1988, Colonel Knowles called me into his office. He asked if I had kept a copy of the biofeedback proposal. When I said yes, he authorized its funding. In the Army, if a unit does not spend its entire annual budget, they lose the unspent portion the next year. We had money left over, and the colonel wanted to make sure he spent it all. I was very excited: Great new equipment, and ten days in San Francisco!

The biofeedback training course in San Francisco at the Applied Psychophysiological Institute (API) changed my life. It was the most stimulating and intense learning experience I had as a physician. The ten-hour days went by in a flash. The new computerized biofeedback equipment was patient-friendly, interesting, and easy to learn. I learned how to help people relax their muscles, warm their hands (much faster than with the old equipment), calm sweat-gland activity, lower blood pressure, slow their own heart rates, and breathe in ways that promoted relaxation.

The lectures on brainwave biofeedback were the most amazing. I was taught that people could actually learn how to change their own brainwave patterns. What an exciting concept, being able to change your own mental state! I also learned about Dr. Joel Lubar's research at the University of Tennessee on brainwave underactivity in children with ADD. In published research using electroencephalograms (EEGs), Dr. Lubar demonstrated that ADD children had excessive slow brainwave activity in the front part of their brain, which worsened when they tried to concentrate. This diminished activity, when compared to a group of people without ADD, made perfect sense to me. Psychostimulants, such as Dexedrine and Ritalin, were the treatment of choice for calming hyperactive children and helping them concentrate. I was taught that these medications exerted a "paradoxical effect": a stimulant calming down a hyperactive child. Understanding Dr. Lubar's research meant that psychostimulants probably corrected the underactivity in the ADD brain—not a paradoxical effect, but rather a direct effect: stimulating the brain's frontal lobe so that the brain could calm and focus the person.

Dr. Lubar's work gave me a critical insight: the importance of looking at the brain in different thought states. He studied people with ADD at rest and while they were doing concentration tasks. After all, people with ADD have problems when they try to concentrate, not when they are at rest.

Dr. Lubar also demonstrated that many children can develop more normal brainwave patterns (and therefore improved focus and behavior) through brainwave biofeedback. In brainwave biofeedback, electrodes are placed on the scalp and connected to computerized biofeedback equipment. The computer screen shows the patient his or her own moment-by-moment brainwave patterns. By knowing these patterns, many patients can learn to change them to more normal, more focused patterns. When I first heard this I was interested but very skeptical: How can you change your brain? I started talking to other clinicians around the country doing this work who were getting exciting results. Why not change your brain? After all, if you can warm hand temperature by 20 degrees, why can't you increase the amount of focused brainwave activity?

When I returned to Fort Irwin, I tried everything I learned. I did biofeedback on almost all of the patients who came to see me. I loved it. My patients loved it. I also spent time each day doing it myself. I became a master at breathing with my diaphragm. I could slow my heart rate. And I could even warm my own hands over 15 degrees whenever I felt stressed. I also started to evaluate ADD children with EEG measures. Many of them demonstrated the same patterns that Dr. Lubar had written about. Many of them benefited from biofeedback training. I had to learn more.

In 1989 my commitment to the U.S. Army ended and I started a private practice in Fairfield, California. I bought my own biofeedback equipment and continued using it in clinical practice. Also, I became the medical director of the dual diagnosis unit (where patients had both substance abuse and psychiatric problems) at a local psychiatric hospital. I instituted the use of biofeedback throughout the hospital. My interest in biofeedback and evaluating brain function in ADD patients grew each year. In late 1990 and early 1991 it exploded.

In late 1990, Alan Zametkin, M.D., of the National Institutes of Health published an article in the *New England Journal of Medicine* on brain PET (positron emission tomography) studies in ADD adults. PET studies are sophisticated nuclear medicine studies that evaluate glucose metabolism, blood flow, and activity in the brain. His research showed that when ADD adults concentrate, there is decreased activity in the prefrontal cortex. There was quite a buzz in the medical community. This meant that ADD was real: It is a medical problem you can actually see. For many people this was a profound shift in thinking. I wasn't quite as excited as many of my colleagues. Dr. Lubar had virtually said the same thing many years earlier, using EEG scalp measurements. But I was excited about the developing new technology to help study our patients. Shortly after Dr. Zametkin's article appeared, I attended a lecture at the hospital given by Jack Paldi, M.D., a nuclear medicine physician in our community. He opened my eyes to brain SPECT imaging.

SPECT (single photon emission computed tomography), like PET, is a nuclear medicine study that evaluates brain blood flow and activity patterns. Dr. Paldi said that SPECT was easier to perform, less expensive, and involved less radiation than PET studies. He showed SPECT images of patients with depression, dementia, schizophrenia, and head trauma. He showed brain images before and after treatment. Unlike the PET researchers who felt that their technology was still very experimental, Dr. Paldi said that, in his opinion, SPECT was ready to be used clinically and it could provide useful diagnostic information for psychiatric patients. I was intrigued. When he offered physicians no-cost SPECT scans to try them out, I took him up on his offer. The same day of Dr. Paldi's lecture, I met Sally.

Sally, a 40-year-old woman, had been hospitalized for depression, anxiety, and suicidal ideas. In my clinical interview with her I discovered that she had many ADD symptoms, such as short attention span, distractibility, disorganization, and restlessness. She had an ADD son (a frequent tip in diagnosing ADD in adults). She had never finished college, despite having an IQ of 140, and she was employed below her ability as a laboratory technician. Since I had just heard Dr. Paldi's lecture and read Dr. Zametkin's paper, I decided to order a SPECT study on Sally. I called the University of Wisconsin, known for research in brain SPECT studies, and asked them how to perform the scans on an ADD adult. They gave us their protocol: a rest study, with the patient doing nothing, and then two days later a concentration study done while the patient performs a series of random math problems. Sally's concentration study was abnormal. At rest, she had good overall brain activity, especially in the prefrontal cortex. When she performed the math problems, she had marked decreased activity across her whole brain, especially in the prefrontal cortex! This correlated with Dr. Lubar's EEG finding and Dr. Zametkin's paper. With that information I placed her on low-dose methylphenidate (Ritalin). She had a wonderful response. Her mood was better, she was less anxious, and she could concentrate for longer periods of time. She eventually went back to school and finished her degree. No longer did she think of herself as an underachiever, but rather as someone who needs treatment for a medical problem. After seeing the SPECT pictures she said, "Having ADD is not my fault. It's a medical problem, just like someone who needs glasses." Seeing the pictures was very powerful for Sally. Watching her facial expression when she saw her own brain pictures led me to believe that SPECT may have a powerful application in decreasing the stigma many patients feel when they are diagnosed with "emotional, learning, or behavior problems." It makes them realize that these conditions are not just manifestations of a weak will or poor conduct. The scan and her response to medication changed the perception she had about herself.

With Sally's positive response to treatment fresh in my mind, I ordered more SPECT studies, especially on my most difficult patients. I found SPECT immediately useful in a number of different ways. I was able to "see" areas of good brain function and areas of compromised brain function. I could see areas of the brain that worked too hard and areas of the brain that did not work hard enough. I read everything I could on brain imaging, especially

Sally's SPECT Studies

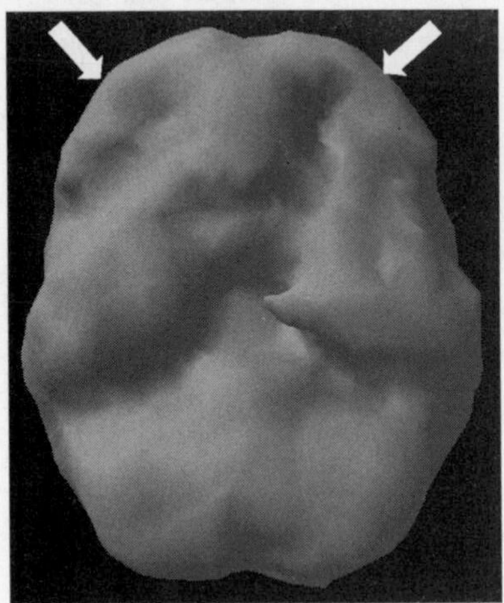

Underside surface of brain at rest (good prefrontal activity [arrows])

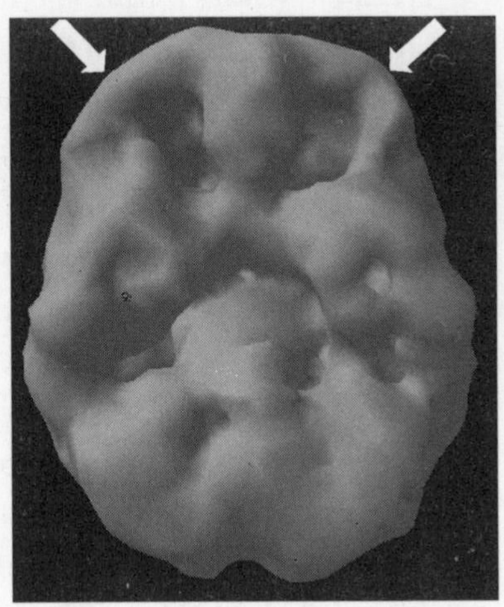

Underside surface view during concentration (marked dropoff of prefrontal activity [arrows])

SPECT studies. A number of my colleagues at the hospital where I worked also ordered SPECT studies on their patients. To my surprise, by early 1991 there was already a very large body of medical literature on SPECT imaging for neuropsychiatric indications.

At this point in the story it is important to understand a bit about SPECT technology. (I'll try to make it as painless and interesting as possible.) SPECT is a sophisticated nuclear medicine study that looks directly at cerebral blood flow and indirectly at brain activity (or metabolism). In this study, a radioactive isotope (which, as we will see, is akin to a beacon of energy or light) is connected to a substance that is readily taken up by the cells in the brain. A small amount of this compound is injected into the patient's arm vein, from which it runs throughout the bloodstream and is taken up by certain receptor sites in the brain. The patient then lies on a table for 14 to 16 minutes while a SPECT "gamma" camera rotates slowly around his head. The camera has special crystals that detect where the compound (signaled by the radioisotope acting like a beacon of light) has gone. A supercomputer then reconstructs 3-D images of brain activity levels. The elegant brain snapshots that result give a sophisticated blood flow/metabolism brain map. With these maps, physicians have been able to identify certain patterns of brain activity that correlate with psychiatric and neurological illnesses.

SPECT studies belong to a branch of medicine called nuclear medicine. Nuclear medicine uses radioactively tagged compounds (radiopharmaceuticals) that emit radiation in the form of gamma rays. The rays act like a beacon of energy or light shining from each location they go to. We detect those gamma rays with film or special crystals and record an accumulation of the number of rays that have been emitted in each area of the brain. The radioactive compounds are essentially tracking devices: They track the cells that are most active and have the most blood flow and those cells that are least active and have the least blood flow.

Nuclear medicine studies measure the physiological functioning of the body and can be used to diagnose a multitude of medical conditions: heart disease, certain forms of infection, the spread of cancer, and bone and thyroid disease. Brain SPECT studies help in the diagnosis of head trauma, dementia, atypical or unresponsive mood disorders, strokes, seizures, the impact of drug abuse on brain function, complex forms of ADD, and atypical or unresponsive aggressive behavior.

During the late seventies and eighties, SPECT studies were being replaced in many cases by the sophisticated anatomical CAT and later MRI studies. The resolution of those studies was far superior to SPECT as far as seeing tumors, cysts, and blood clots. In fact, they nearly eliminated the use of SPECT studies altogether. Yet, despite their clarity, CAT scans and MRIs could offer only images of a static brain and its anatomy; they gave little or no information on the activity in a working brain. It was analogous to looking at the parts of a car's engine without being able to turn it on. In the last decade it has become increasingly recognized that many neurological and psychiatric disorders are not disorders of the brain's anatomy but problems in how it functions.

Two technological advancements have encouraged the use, once again, of SPECT studies. Initially the SPECT cameras were single-headed, and they took a long time to scan a person's brain—up to an hour. People had trouble holding still that long, and the images were fuzzy and hard to read (earning nuclear medicine the nickname "unclear medicine"), and they did not give much information about the functioning deep within the brain. Then multiheaded cameras were developed that were able to image the brain much faster and with enhanced resolution. The advancement of computer technology also allowed for improved data acquisition from the multi-headed systems. The brain SPECT studies of today, with their higher resolution, can see into the deeper areas of the brain with far greater clarity and show what CAT scans and MRIs cannot: how the brain actually functions.

SPECT studies can be displayed in a variety of different ways. Traditionally the brain is examined in three different planes: horizontally (cut from top to bottom), coronally (cut from front to back), and sagittally (cut from side to side). What do physicians see when they look at a SPECT study? We examine it for symmetry and activity levels indicated by shades of color (in different color scales selected according to the physician's preference, including gray scales) and compare it to what we know a normal brain looks like. The images that accompany this book will be mostly two kinds of three-dimensional (3-D) images of the brain.

One kind is a *3-D surface image,* looking at the blood flow of the brain's cortical surface. These images are helpful for picking up cortical surface areas of good activity as well as underactive areas. They give insight into the effects of strokes, brain trauma, drug abuse, etc. A normal 3-D surface scan shows good, full, symmetrical activity across the brain's cortical surface.

The other kind is a *3-D active brain image,* which compares average brain activity to the hottest 15 percent of activity. These images are helpful for picking up areas of overactivity, as seen in active seizures, obsessive-compulsive disorder, anxiety problems, certain forms of depression, etc. A normal 3-D active scan shows increased

Normal 3-D Brain SPECT Studies

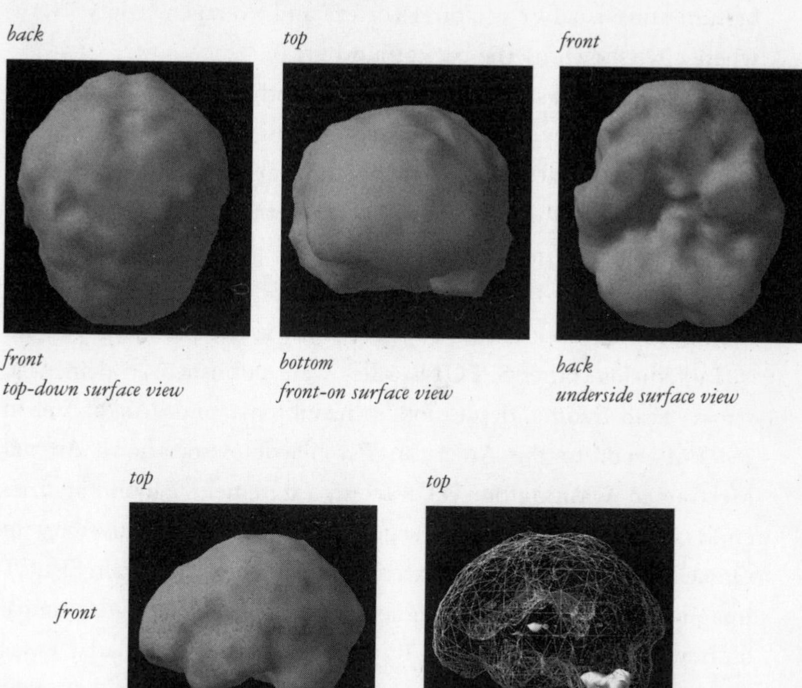

top-down surface view

front-on surface view

underside surface view

side surface view

side active view

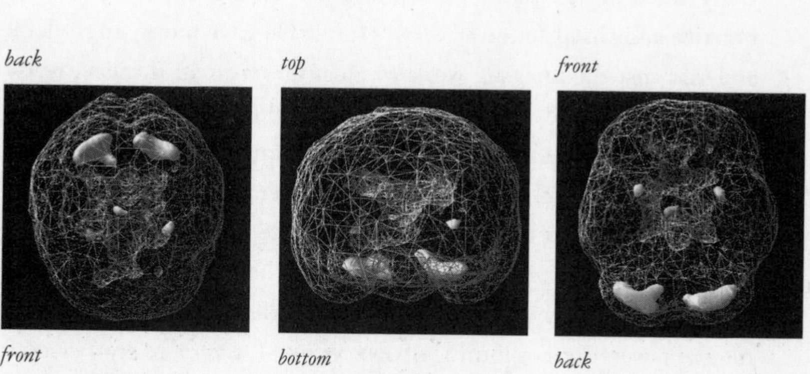

top-down active view

front-on active view

underside active view

activity (seen by the light color) in the back of the brain (the cerebellum and visual or occipital cortex) and average activity everywhere else (shown by the background grid).

Physicians are usually alerted that something is wrong in one of three ways: (a) they see too much activity in a certain area; (b) they see too little activity in a certain area; or (c) they see asymmetrical areas of activity, which ought to be symmetrical.

In the last four images the outline grid equals average activity in the brain, and the light color equals the most active 15 percent of the brain. The back is normally the most active part of the brain.

In addition, other SPECT studies were published on dementia, stroke, head trauma, depression, schizophrenia, and drug abuse. In 1992, I went to the American Psychiatric Association's Annual Meeting in Washington, D.C. To my excitement I found another child psychiatrist, Thomas Jaeger from Creighton University in Omaha, Nebraska, who had extensive experience with brain SPECT imaging. Dr. Jaeger and colleagues were presenting an all-day course on how to utilize brain SPECT imaging in child psychiatry. I was very excited. The day of the course, however, was my first sense that a storm was brewing in the brain-imaging world. I went to hear a lecture by Dr. Zametkin, who had led the PET research on ADD in adults. After the lecture I went up to him and told him that, partially based on his work, I was using brain imaging in my clinical practice and that I found it very helpful. He gave me an angry look and said that the imaging work was just for research: It wasn't ready for clinical use, and we shouldn't use it until much more was known about it. I protested, saying that it was immediately helpful. I had many cases in which it helped to direct therapy. He didn't want to hear it. I told him about the all-day course by Dr. Jaeger and his group. He said that he should go "crash their party and set them straight." Internally, I was very upset. Little did I know that that moment was the beginning of five years of a very rocky personal road. Dr. Jaeger's course that day, however, was wonderful. He showed all of the different ways SPECT could be applied in a clinical setting: with ADD, depression, bipolar disorder, head trauma, drug abuse, etc. In the program abstract Dr. Jaeger wrote, "Regardless of the initial diagnosis, patients who underwent brain SPECT prior to, or during, psychiatric hospitalization had markedly shorter stays than controls. As demonstrated by this clinical database (2,000 patients), brain SPECT may lead to more effective, shorter, safer, and less expensive diagnostic and treatment modes in children and adolescents with suspected neuropsychiatric illness."

When I returned home from the meeting, another storm was brewing. A local pediatric neurologist had started to complain to hospital officials about our use of brain imaging for psychiatric patients. He had called three or four researchers around the country (not Dr. Jaeger or other people who were using the technology clinically) who said that SPECT was not ready to be used clinically. There was a big meeting at the hospital. There was support by the hospital's medical director to continue to utilize the technology, but there was also dissent. I remember the meeting as if it were yesterday. Now, rather than being anxious, I was angry. "How can we not look at the brain?" I said. "Cardiologists look at the heart. Orthopedic doctors have bone X rays. We deal with the most complex organ in the body. How can we treat it without having any information on how it functions? We are the only medical specialists that never look at the organ we treat!" Even though we were allowed to continue ordering the studies, there was now an approval process and a feeling of controversy rather than collaboration.

By 1993, I had ordered several hundred SPECT studies on my patients, and I continued to find them helpful and fascinating. I started to lecture about the findings. I was asked to give grand rounds at local hospitals and even at the University of Colorado School of Medicine. I wrote a research article based on our findings with ADD children.

We performed brain SPECT studies on fifty-four medication-free ADD children and adolescents. We compared this group to eighteen medication-free children and adolescents who did not have ADD. The studies were performed at rest and while the patients were doing a concentration task. Sixty-five percent of the ADD children and adolescents diagnosed with ADD had significant decreased activity in the prefrontal cortex when they tried to concentrate, compared to only 5 percent of those who did not have ADD. Of the 19 ADD patients (34 percent) who did not suppress their prefrontal lobe activity with concentration, 12 (63 percent) had decreased prefrontal cortex activity at rest.

Soon a year had passed. This time Dr. Jaeger asked me to help teach the brain-imaging course at the 1993 American Psychiatric Meeting in San Francisco. That was the year the controversy became even more intense. When the program announcement came out, months before the meeting, a SPECT researcher from Dallas wrote to APA's program chairman asking how they could have such a controversial person (me) on their program. He said that I made exaggerated claims about what we could read on a SPECT image and that they should take me off the program. Dr. Jaeger phoned me and asked me if I had somehow made this doctor mad at me. I told him I didn't even know who he was. The program chairman sat in on our all-day course at the APA. Later he said he liked the course and didn't understand what this doctor had been so upset about. What I was seeing in the brain was real and changed the lives of many patients, but I was done with lecturing: I did not like the adversarial environment of those meetings and decided to keep a low profile, expecting others would do the research. Then, in April 1995, nine-year-old Andrew came into my clinic.

Andrew is a very special child. He is my godson and nephew. When he was young he was a happy, active child, but in the year and a half before he came to my clinic as a patient, his personality had changed. He appeared depressed. He had serious aggressive outbursts and he complained to his mother of serious suicidal and homicidal thoughts (very abnormal for a 9-year-old). He drew pictures of himself hanging from a tree or shooting other children. When he attacked a little girl on the baseball field for no particular reason, his mother called me late at night in tears. I told his mother to bring Andrew to see me the next day. His parents drove to my clinic, which was eight hours from their home in Southern California.

As I sat with Andrew's parents and then with Andrew, I knew something wasn't right. I had never seen him look so angry or so sad. He had no explanations for his behavior. He did not report any form of abuse. Other children were not bullying him. There was no family history of serious psychiatric illnesses. He had not sustained a recent head injury. And he had a wonderful family. Unlike most clinical situations in which I do not know what really goes on in a family, this family I knew. Andrew's parents were loving, caring, pleasant people. What was the matter?

The vast majority of my psychiatric colleagues would have placed Andrew on some sort of medication and had him see a counselor for psychotherapy. Having performed more than 1,000 SPECT studies by that time, I first wanted a picture of Andrew's brain. I wanted to know what we were dealing with. But with the hostility from my colleagues fresh in my mind, I told myself, *Maybe this is really due to a family problem that I just don't know about. Maybe this is a psychological problem.* (Incidentally, if you have good psychoanalytic training, you can find dirt in anybody's family.) I thought, *Maybe Andrew is acting out because his older brother is a "perfect" child who does well in school and is very athletic. Maybe Andrew has these thoughts and behaviors to ward off feelings of insecurity related to being the second son in a Lebanese family.* (I had personal knowledge of this scenario.) *Maybe Andrew wants to feel powerful and these behaviors are associated with issues of control.* Then logic took over my brain. Nine-year-old children do not normally think about suicide. Nine-year-old children do not normally think about homicide. I needed to scan his brain. If it was normal, then we could look further into the underlying emotional problems that might be present.

I went with Andrew to the imaging center and held his hand while he had the study performed. As his brain appeared on the computer screen, I thought a mistake had been done in performing the procedure. *Andrew had no left temporal lobe.* Upon quick examination of the complete study, I realized the quality of the scan was fine. He was indeed missing the function of his left temporal lobe. Did he have a cyst or a tumor? Had he had a stroke? I was scared for him as I looked at the monitor, but relieved that we had some explanation for his aggressive behavior. My research and the research of others had implicated the left temporal lobe in aggression. The next day Andrew had an MRI (an anatomical brain study), which showed a cyst (a fluid-filled sac) about the size of a golf ball occupying the space where his left temporal lobe should have been. I knew the cyst had to be removed. Getting someone to take this seriously proved frustrating, however.

That day I called Andrew's pediatrician in Orange, California, and told him of both the clinical situation and the brain findings. I told him to find the best person possible to take this thing out of his head. He contacted three pediatric neurologists. All of them said that Andrew's negative behavior was probably not in any way related to the cyst in his brain and they would not recommend operating on him until he had *real symptoms.* When the pediatrician told me this information, I became furious. *Real symptoms! I had a child with homicidal and suicidal thoughts who loses control over his behavior and attacks people!* I contacted a pediatric neurologist in San Francisco, who told me the same thing. I then called a friend of mine at Harvard Medical School, also a pediatric neurologist, who told me yet again the same thing. She even used the words "real symptoms." I said to her, "'*Real symptoms*'! I have a child with homicidal and suicidal thoughts who attacks people: What do you mean by 'real symptoms'?" "Oh, Dr. Amen," the neurologist replied, "when I say 'real symptoms' I mean problems like seizures or speech problems." Could the medical profession really not connect the brain to behavior? I was angry and appalled! But I wasn't going to wait until this child killed himself or someone else. I called the pediatric neurosurgeon Horhay Lazarette, M.D., at UCLA and told him about Andrew. He told me that he had operated on three other children with left temporal lobe cysts who were all aggressive. He wondered if it was related. Thankfully, after evaluating Andrew, he agreed to take it out.

Dr. Lazarette called me right after the surgery in April 1995. He said that he was so glad that I had referred Andrew to him. The cyst had put so much pressure on Andrew's brain that it had actually thinned the bone over his left temporal lobe. If Andrew had been hit near that part of his head with modest force—with a basketball, for example—it would have killed him. He said the pressure from the cyst might have killed Andrew anyway within six months. When Andrew woke up from the surgery, his mother told me, he smiled at her. He had not smiled at her for a year. Immediately after the surgery, his aggressive thoughts were gone and his temperament changed back to the sweet child he always wanted to be. Now, six years later, Andrew remains nonviolent, happy, and well-adjusted.

When I lecture and tell Andrew's story, tears still come to my eyes, even though I have told it hundreds of times. I was in Hawaii with Andrew on vacation last year. When we were on a boat, getting ready to snorkel, Andrew looked at me and said, "Uncle Danny, why did I have the cyst and had to go through all those problems?" Feeling a bit overwhelmed, I tenderly looked at Andrew and said, "We'll never really know why, but I think a part of the reason was for me. When I was able to help you, it gave me the courage to tell the world about my brain-imaging work without caring about all the people who criticized me. I have to tell everyone I know about it." He didn't fully understand what I was saying to him, but he accepted my response and we had a great time snorkeling.

With Andrew's experience in my mind, I found the inner strength to continue the work. There were too many children, teenagers, and adults like Andrew who had clear brain abnormalities whom our society was just writing off as bad human beings or, worse, ignoring until they had suffered terrible problems or hurt themselves or someone else. Only then would the medical community treat these unfortunate people. In 1995, I completed the training to obtain my own license in nuclear brain-imaging (which took 200 hours of nuclear physics and radiation safety and 500 supervised hours of reading scans and interacting with patients) and incorporated SPECT imaging into the day-to-day operations of my

Andrew's Missing Left Temporal Lobe (3-D Underside Surface View)

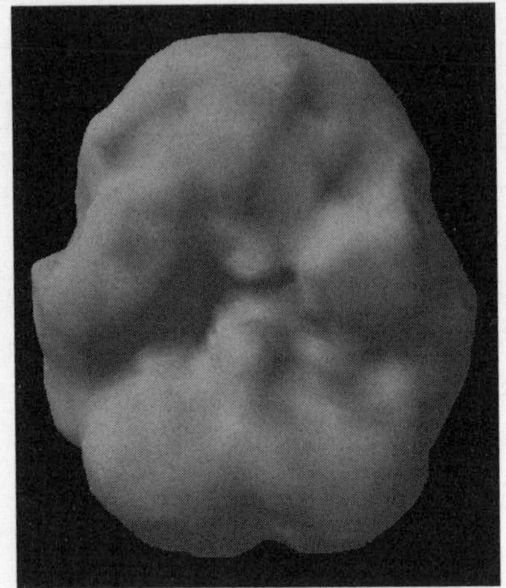

normal study

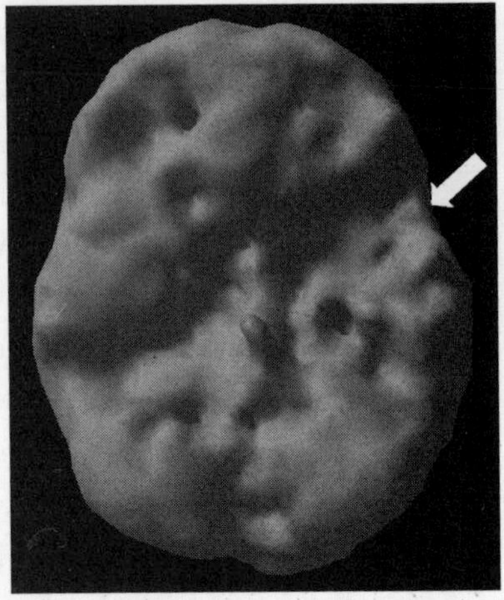

missing left temporal lobe

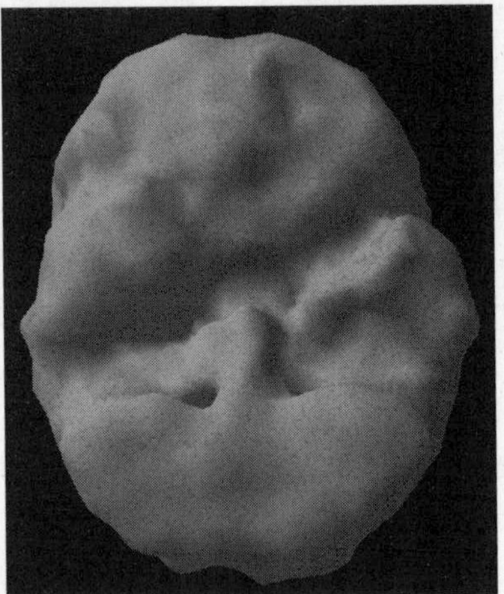

two years later (Notice improvement in left temporal lobe activity.)

clinic. As far as I knew, I was the only psychiatrist in the world who also had a brain-imaging component in his practice.

The struggles, however, were certainly not over. In 1996, I was invited to give the State-of-the-Art Lecture in Medicine to the Society of Developmental Pediatrics. The lecture generated a heated discussion. A pediatrician from the San Francisco Bay Area stood up and criticized my work. He said people quoted me and my brain-imaging research as a justification to give ADD children medication. I said that we give glasses to children who can't see. If you can see physical brain problems on SPECT with people who have ADD, doesn't it make sense to treat it? Shortly after the meeting, someone—I suspect this pediatrician—anonymously reported me to the California Medical Board.

In California, if you do anything in medical practice outside of the generally accepted standards of the community, you can have your licensed revoked. The law is meant to protect the public, but it can also stifle innovation. What I was doing with brain SPECT imaging was certainly different from what my colleagues were doing. For a year I answered questions, gave the medical board copies of research articles, hired an attorney, and appeared at interviews. Many times I felt like running away. With Andrew in my heart, I was able to weather that year. I am thankful that the investigator for the medical board was an intelligent man who listened to the facts. The first board reviewer, a psychiatrist who had no experience with brain-imaging, said that my practice was outside the standard of care. He said that there was never an indication for brain SPECT imaging. The investigator, who had done his homework, knew that the reviewer was wrong. He agreed to send my work to the departments of neurology and nuclear medicine at UCLA. Several months later the investigator read me the letter from the results of the UCLA investigation of my work. They said I was doing good medicine. It was innovative and appropriate. They hoped that I would continue the work and continue to publish the findings. The investigation was over. In fact today I am an expert reviewer for the California Medical Board.

Only a few years later the criticism has seemed to come full circle. I have presented the information in this book to thousands of medical and mental health professionals across North America: in medical schools, at national medical meetings and even recently at the prestigious National Institutes of Health. I have published much of this research in medical book chapters and journal articles. From 1997 to 1999, I published six peer-reviewed professional medical articles on brain SPECT imaging in psychiatry. I was honored by being asked to coauthor the chapter on functional brain imaging in the *Comprehensive Textbook of Psychiatry,* one of the most respected psychiatric texts in the world. In the spring of 1999, I was invited by the nuclear medicine community to give lectures at their meetings. Dr. Dennis Patton, the historian for the Society of Nuclear Medicine, introduced me at one of the meetings by saying that I was a pioneer in the brain-imaging field and that people would read my work for years to come. As I write this book I believe I have personally seen more functional brain images for behavioral reasons than any other living person. To date I have read about 10,000 studies. My clinic gets referrals from approximately 350 physicians in the Bay Area, around California, and the Western United States. This year alone my clinic has seen patients from Italy, Austria, Hong Kong, West Africa, Lebanon, Israel, Australia, and Canada. The price I have personally had to pay to do this work has been worth it many times over.

BRAIN BASIC TENETS

Here are some of the basic tenets my brain-imaging work has taught me in general:

- The brain is involved in everything you do, how you think, how you feel, how you act, and how well you get along with other people.
- The brain even determines the kind of person you are—the kind of mother, doctor, receptionist, husband, daughter, student, etc.
- When your brain works right, you work right.
- When your brain doesn't work right, it is very hard for you to be your best.
- There are things we can do to hurt our brains, such as injuries,

pollution (taking drugs, excessive caffeine, smoking, etc.), poor nutrition, and excessive stress.

- There are things we can do to optimize our brain function, such as proper nutrition, protection, and coping with stress.

Here are some examples of brain SPECT imaging. In order to appreciate the functional changes in ADD brains, it's helpful to look at more dramatic examples of brain dysfunction.

Lawrence had a stroke, and since then, his speech has been affected, he has problems with depression, and he has trouble with short-term memory.

Steven fell off a roof onto his head and fractured his skull. He was unconscious for several days. Since the accident, he has had problems with his temper, seizures, and impulse control.

Kathy has Alzheimer's disease. Over the last few years her memory has gotten progressively worse. She gets lost easily and she says inappropriate things to her loved ones.

Left-Sided Stroke (3-D Underside and Left-Side Surface Views)

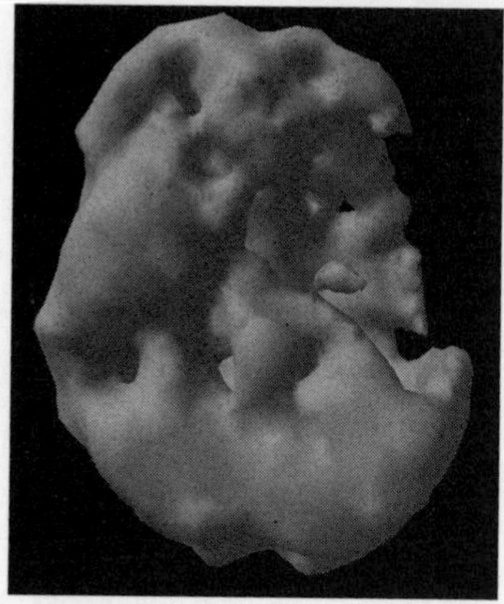

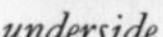

underside

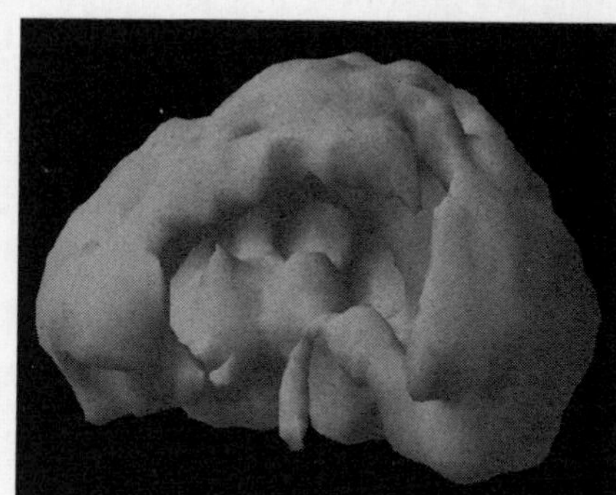

left side

Head Trauma (3-D Top-Down and Left-Side Surface Views)

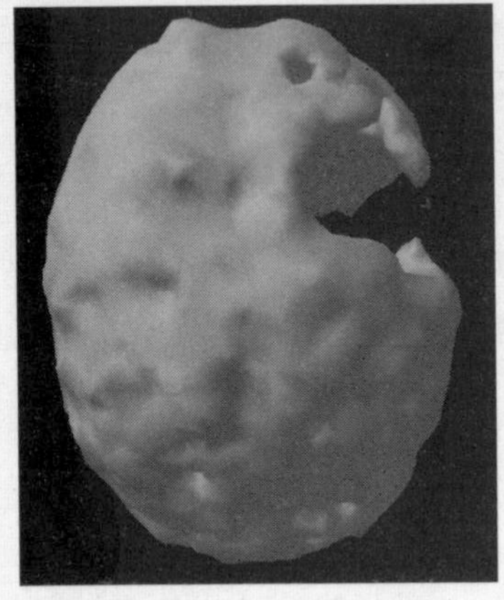

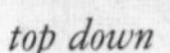

top down

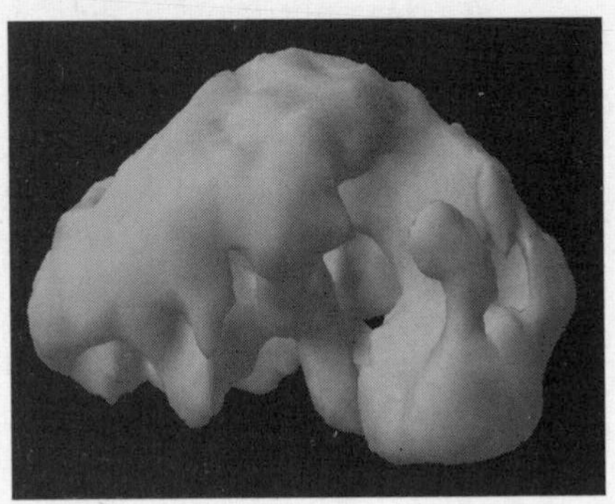

left side

Alzheimer's Disease (3-D Underside and Top-Down Surface Views)

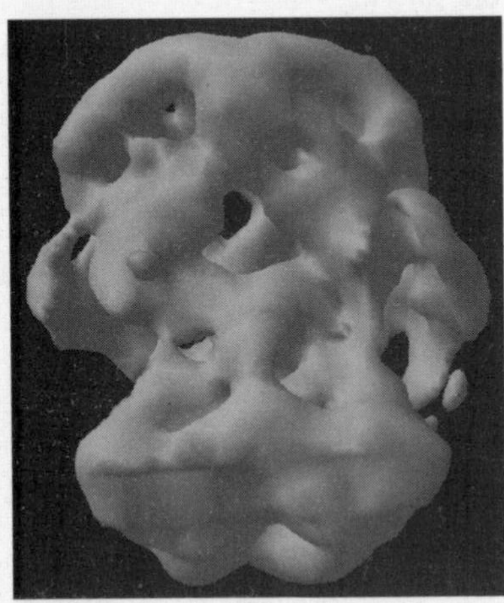

underside

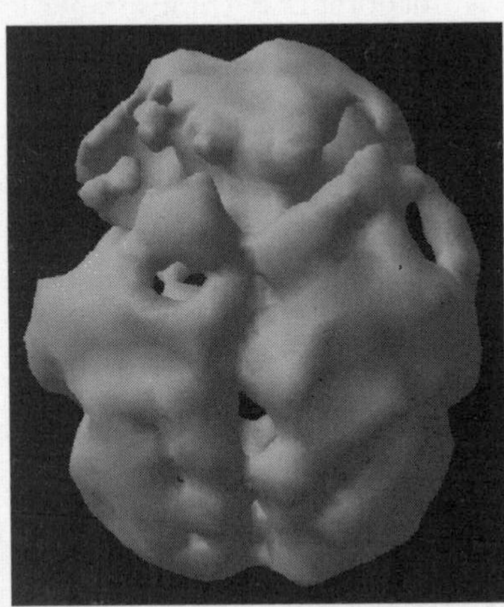

top down

Laura had been abusing alcohol heavily for ten years. She now complained of memory problems and trouble learning new information.

Due to my personal situation at home, throughout the brain-

Alcohol Abuse (3-D Underside and Top-Down Surface Views)

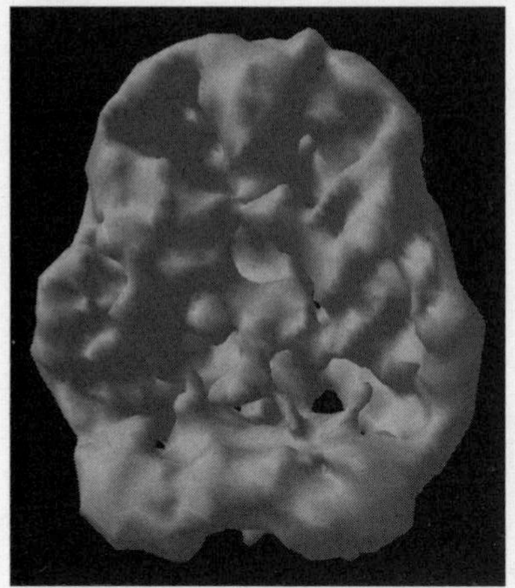

underside

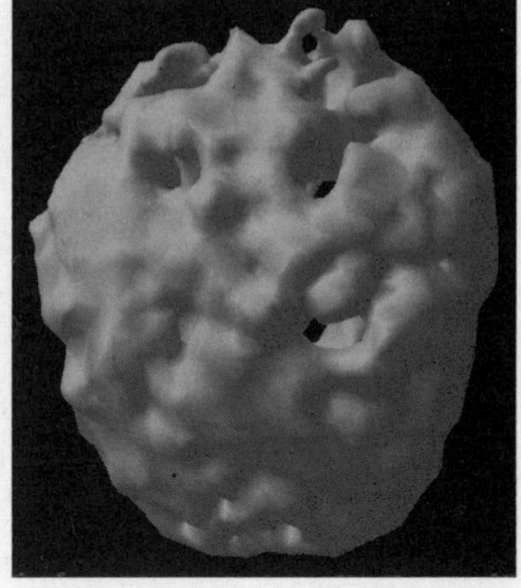

top down

imaging work I have always had a strong interest in ADD. Initially, as in Sally's case, I thought that ADD was primarily a problem of decreased activity in the prefrontal cortex. My 1993 study showed that 65 percent of ADD patients had decreased prefrontal cortex activity with concentration, but we soon saw other patterns, especially in our more complex patients. As our brain-imaging became better known across Northern California, then California, the West and later internationally through my book *Change Your Brain, Change Your Life* (New York: Times Books, 1999), the volume and complexity of our cases increased, as did our knowledge and database of scans. We found that there were a number of different brain systems involved. Here is a brief summary of the brain-imaging findings and symptoms for the different types of ADD that I saw. I will devote a chapter to each type with several examples for each.

TYPE 1: CLASSIC ADD

SPECT findings: a normal resting brain. During concentration, decreased activity in the underside and lateral prefrontal cortex with concentration.

Primary symptoms: inattentive, distractible, disorganized, hyperactive, restless, and impulsive.

This is the easiest pattern to spot. Almost all brain-imaging studies outside of The Amen Clinic have been done on this type of ADD. Clear prefrontal cortex deactivation can be seen on the scans. This pattern tends to be seen much more frequently in boys.

TYPE 2: INATTENTIVE ADD

SPECT findings: a normal resting brain. During concentration, a decreased activity in the lateral prefrontal cortex. Primary symptoms: inattentive, sluggish, slow-moving, low motivation, often bored; sufferers are often described as space cadets, daydreamers, couch potatoes.

This pattern tends to be seen more in girls.

TYPE 3: OVERFOCUSED ADD

SPECT findings: At rest and during concentration there is increased activity in the anterior cingulate gyrus. During concentration there is also decreased activity in the underside and lateral prefrontal cortex.

Type 1: Classic ADD (3-D Underside Surface View at Rest and with Concentration)

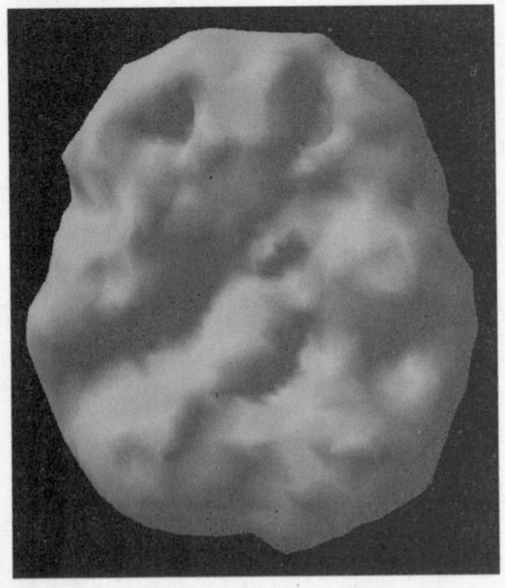

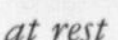

at rest

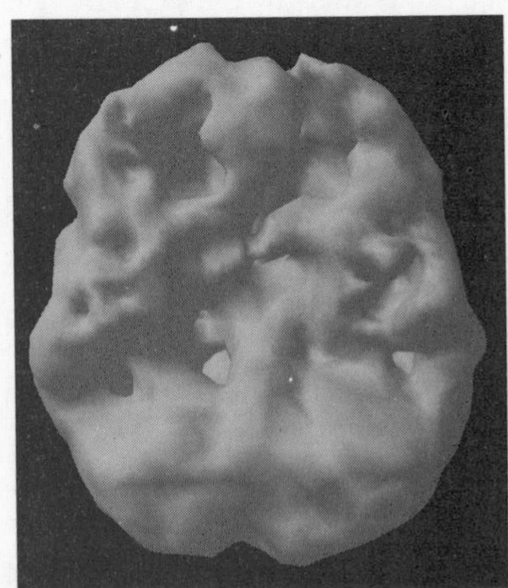

with concentration

Type 2: Inattentive ADD (3-D Underside Surface View at Rest and with Concentration)

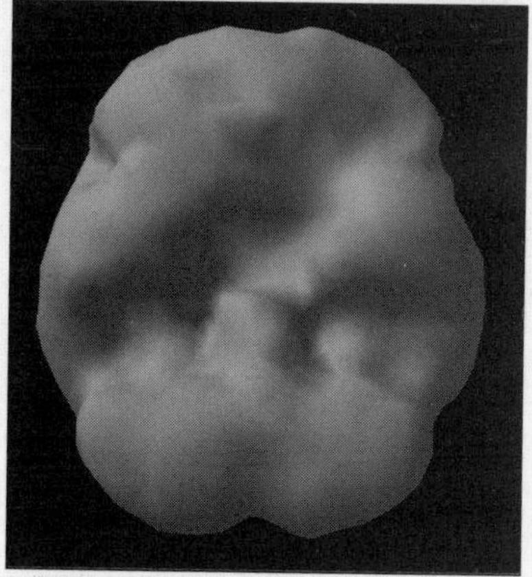

at rest
(full overall activity)

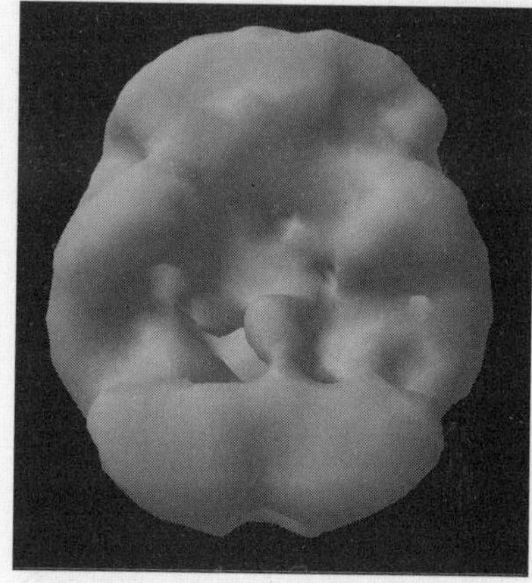

with concentration
(decreased lateral prefrontal cortex)

Primary symptoms: has trouble shifting attention; frequently gets stuck in loops of negative thoughts or behaviors; obsessiveness; excessive worrying; inflexibility; frequent oppositional and argumentative behavior.

This pattern tends to be seen more commonly in children and grandchildren of alcoholics. For personal reasons, families with alcohol-abuse histories were my research interest during training. This is a pattern I discovered within my first year of doing SPECT imaging.

TYPE 4: TEMPORAL LOBE ADD

SPECT findings: At rest and during concentration there is decreased (and infrequently increased) activity in the temporal lobes. During concentration there is also decreased activity in the underside and lateral prefrontal cortex.

Primary symptoms: inattentiveness, irritability, aggressiveness, dark thoughts, mood instability, learning problems, inattention, and impulsivity.

Type 3: Overfocused ADD (3-D Active Concentration View, Front On and Left Side)

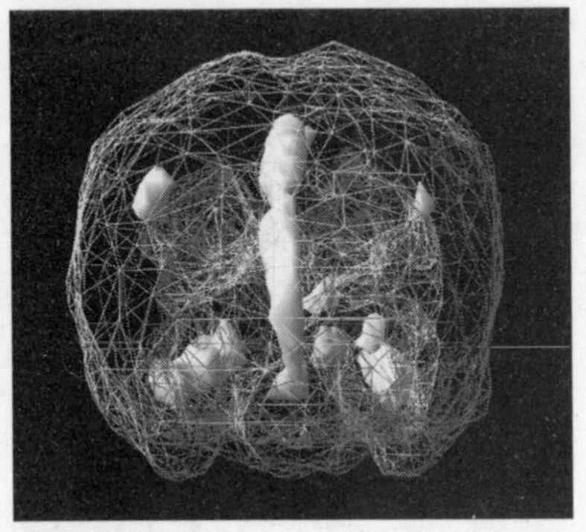

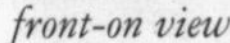

front-on view

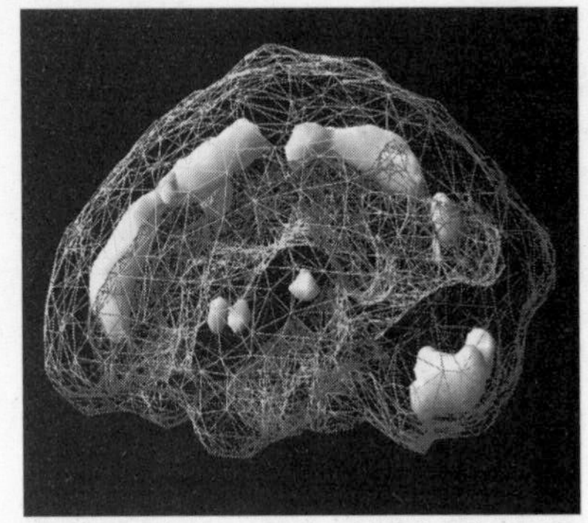

left-side view

A great number of my initial cases involved temporal lobe dysfunction. Early in my imaging education, I discovered how important the temporal lobes are in psychiatric illness, mood instability, violence, and learning disabilities.

Type 4: Temporal Lobe ADD (3-D Underside Surface Concentration View)

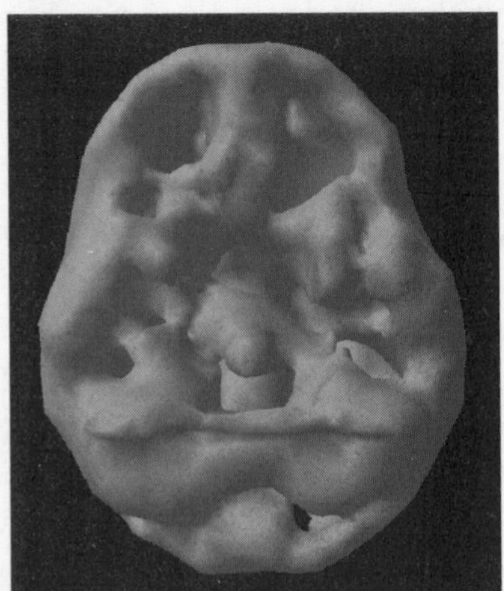

underside view

TYPE 5: LIMBIC ADD

SPECT findings: At rest there is increased deep limbic activity (thalamus and hypothalamus) and decreased activity in the underside and lateral prefrontal cortex. During concentration there remains increased deep limbic activity and decreased prefrontal cortex activity.

Primary symptoms: inattentiveness, chronic low-grade depression, negativity, "glass-half-empty" syndrome, low energy, and frequent feelings of hopelessness and worthlessness.

Some people say that Limbic ADD is really a combination of ADD and depression. That may be so, but we see this combination very frequently in our ADD patients and it leads us to specific treatments that seem best for this type.

Type 5: Limbic ADD (3-D Underside Active Concentration View)

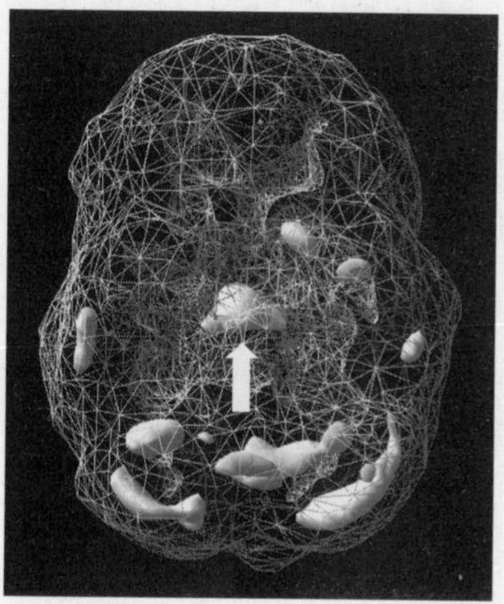

underside view

TYPE 6: "RING OF FIRE" ADD

SPECT findings: At rest and during concentration (often worse during concentration) there is patchy increased uptake across the cerebral cortex with focal areas of increased activity, especially in the left and right parietal lobes, left and right temporal lobes, and left and

Type 6: "Ring of Fire" ADD (3-D Top Down Active Concentration View)

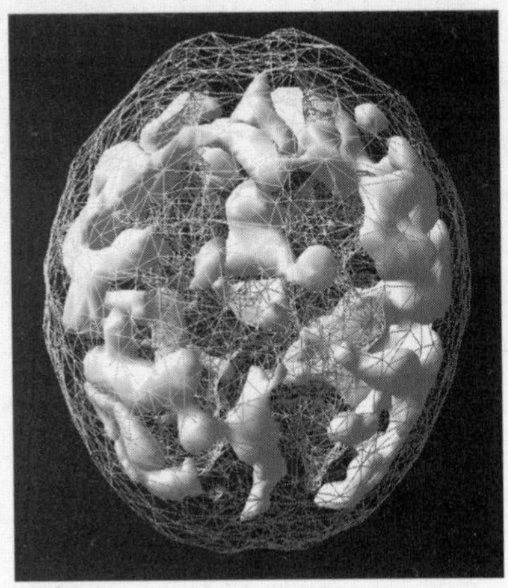

top-down view

right prefrontal cortex. In addition there is often increased activity in the cingulate gyrus.

Primary symptoms: inattentiveness, extreme distractibility, anger, irritablility, oversensitivity, moodiness, hyperverbal, and extreme opposition.

This is the last pattern I identified in my work. So many of our "really difficult cases" had this pattern in the brain. Initially, I did not have enough experience to see this pattern, but over time it became clear.

One of the main reasons we have been so successful in both our clinical and brain-imaging work is that they were done in concert, simultaneously, in a clinical setting. Being a neuroscientist who studied the brain as well as being a psychiatrist responsible for patient care put me in a unique position to understand what I was seeing in the scans of my patients. They kept me searching, asking questions, and looking for answers. The brain is truly the last frontier.

CHAPTER 4

The Amen Clinic ADD Type Questionnaire

The day-to-day use of functional brain-imaging in clinical practice is still, unfortunately, ten to fifteen years away. However, I have developed an instrument that allows others to take advantage of the information we have learned. Based on over 10,000 brain SPECT studies and over 15,000 patient evaluations, I have identified six different types of ADD. Through the years I have developed a clinical questionnaire to evaluate these ADD types without the use of functional brain-imaging. The Amen Clinic ADD Type Questionnaire is a 71-question self-test that evaluates the ADD syndrome and its six major types. This questionnaire has gone through many revisions, and while I'm sure it will go through more as we continue, it correlates remarkably well with SPECT imaging. We use this questionnaire as part of our evaluation at The Amen Clinic.

Self-report questionnaires have certain advantages and limitations. They are quick, inexpensive, and easy to score. One of the dangers is that people may fill them out as they want to be perceived. For example, some people mark, inaccurately, all of the symptoms as occurring frequently, in essence saying, "I'm glad to have a problem so that I can get help, be sick, or have an excuse for the problems I have." Some people are in total denial: They do not want to see any personal flaws and they do not check any symptoms as problematic, saying, "I'm okay. There's nothing wrong with me. Leave me alone." In our clinical experience, most people gauge themselves with reasonable accuracy. Self-report bias is one of the reasons that it is important to have another person fill out the questionnaire as well. This will give you and others a more complete picture.

This questionnaire is an invaluable tool to determine if ADD exists and, if so, which type. It provides the basis for specific effective treatment planning. It's not unheard-of to score as displaying several different types of ADD. A person may have more than one, and some people have three or four types.

It's important to note that this (or any) questionnaire is never meant to be used alone. It is not meant to provide a diagnosis. It serves as a guide to help people begin to identify problems and get further evaluation for them.

THE AMEN CLINIC ADD TYPE QUESTIONNAIRE

Please rate yourself (or the person you are evaluating) on each of the symptoms listed below using the following scale. If possible, also have someone else rate you or the other person (such as a spouse, lover, or parent). This is done to obtain a more complete picture of the situation.

0 Never
1 Rarely
2 Occasionally
3 Frequently
4 Very Frequently
NA Not Applicable

SELF OTHER

____ ____ 1. is easily distracted

____ ____ 2. has difficulty sustaining attention span for most tasks in play, school, or work

____ ____ 3. has trouble listening when others are talking
____ ____ 4. has difficulty following through (procrastination) on tasks or instructions
____ ____ 5. has difficulty keeping an organized area (room, desk, book bag, filing cabinet, locker, etc.)
____ ____ 6. has trouble with time, for example, is frequently late or hurried, tasks take longer than expected, projects or homework are "last-minute" or turned in late
____ ____ 7. has a tendency to lose things
____ ____ 8. makes careless mistakes, poor attention to detail
____ ____ 9. is forgetful
____ ____ 10. daydreams excessively
____ ____ 11. complains of being bored
____ ____ 12. appears apathetic or unmotivated
____ ____ 13. is tired, sluggish, or slow-moving
____ ____ 14. is spacey or seems preoccupied
____ ____ 15. is restless or hyperactive
____ ____ 16. has trouble sitting still
____ ____ 17. is fidgety, in constant motion (hands, feet, body)
____ ____ 18. is noisy, has a hard time being quiet
____ ____ 19. acts as if "driven by a motor"
____ ____ 20. talks excessively
____ ____ 21. is impulsive (doesn't think through comments or actions before they are said or done)
____ ____ 22. has difficulty waiting his or her turn
____ ____ 23. interrupts or intrudes on others (e.g., butts into conversations or games)
____ ____ 24. worries excessively or senselessly
____ ____ 25. is superorganized
____ ____ 26. is oppositional, argumentative
____ ____ 27. has a strong tendency to get locked into negative thoughts; has the same thought over and over
____ ____ 28. has a tendency toward compulsive behavior

____ ____ 29. has an intense dislike of change
____ ____ 30. has a tendency to hold grudges
____ ____ 31. has trouble shifting attention from subject to subject
____ ____ 32. has difficulties seeing options in situations
____ ____ 33. has a tendency to hold on to own opinion and not listen to others
____ ____ 34. has a tendency to get locked into a course of action, whether or not it is good for the person
____ ____ 35. needs to have things done a certain way or becomes very upset
____ ____ 36. others complain that he or she worries too much
____ ____ 37. has periods of quick temper of rages with little provocation
____ ____ 38. misinterprets comments as negative when they are not
____ ____ 39. irritability tends to build, then explodes, then recedes; is often tired after a rage
____ ____ 40. has periods of spaciness or confusion
____ ____ 41. has periods of panic and/or fear for no specific reason
____ ____ 42. perceives visual changes, such as seeing shadows or objects changing shape
____ ____ 43. has frequent periods of déjà vu (feelings of being somewhere before even though he or she has never been there)
____ ____ 44. is sensitive or mildly paranoid
____ ____ 45. has headaches or abdominal pain of uncertain origin
____ ____ 46. has a history of a head injury or a family history of violence or explosiveness
____ ____ 47. has dark thoughts, may involve suicidal or homicidal thoughts
____ ____ 48. has periods of forgetfulness or memory problems

____ ____ 49. has a short fuse or periods of extreme irritability
____ ____ 50. is moody
____ ____ 51. is negative
____ ____ 52. has low energy
____ ____ 53. is frequently irritabile
____ ____ 54. has a tendency to be socially isolated
____ ____ 55. has frequent feelings of hopelessness, helplessness, or excessive guilt
____ ____ 56. has lowered interest in things that are usually considered fun
____ ____ 57. undergoes sleep changes (too much or too little)
____ ____ 58. has chronic low self-esteem
____ ____ 59. is angry or aggressive
____ ____ 60. is sensitive to noise, light, clothes or touch
____ ____ 61. undergoes frequent or cyclic mood changes (highs and lows)
____ ____ 62. is inflexible, rigid in thinking
____ ____ 63. demands to have his or her way, even when told no multiple times
____ ____ 64. has periods of mean, nasty, or insensitive behavior
____ ____ 65. has periods of increased talkativeness
____ ____ 66. has periods of increased impulsivity
____ ____ 67. displays unpredictable behavior
____ ____ 68. way of thinking is grandiose or "larger than life"
____ ____ 69. talks fast
____ ____ 70. feels that thoughts go fast
____ ____ 71. appears anxious or fearful

THE AMEN CLINIC ADD TYPE QUESTIONNAIRE SCORING KEY

For each of the groups listed below, add up the number of answers that were scored as three or four and place them in the space provided. A cutoff score is provided with each type. Some people score positively in more than one group; some even score positively in three or four groups. Use the results to help guide you through the treatment sections of the book.

Type One: Classic ADD (Questions 1–23)

Meets the criteria for both the inattentiveness questions and the hyperactivity-impulsivity questions.

Inattentiveness questions 1–14: Six or more of a score of three or four is needed to make the diagnosis; more than four is suspicious for this type of ADD.

Hyperactivity-impulsivity questions 15–23: Six or more of a score of three or four is needed to make diagnosis; more than four is suspicious.

Inattentiveness score of three or four: ________

Hyperactivity-impulsivity score of three or four: ________

Type Two: Inattentive ADD (Questions 1–14)

Six or more of a score of three or four is needed to make the diagnosis; more than four is suspicious, but does not score six or more on the hyperactivity-impulsivity questions (15–23)

Inattentive ADD score of three or four: ________

Type Three: Overfocused ADD (Questions 24–36)

Meets the criteria for inattentiveness (six or more on questions 1–14) and also scores six or more on the overfocused questions.

Overfocused ADD score of three or four: ________

Type Four: Temporal Lobe ADD (Questions 37–49)

Meets the criteria for inattentiveness (six or more on questions 1–14) and also scores six or more on the temporal lobe questions.

Temporal Lobe ADD score of three or four: ________

Type Five: Limbic ADD (Questions 50–58)

Meets the criteria for inattentiveness (six or more on questions 1–14) and also scores five or more on the limbic questions.

Limbic ADD score of three or four: _________

Type Six: "Ring of Fire" ADD (Questions 59–71)

Meets the criteria for inattentiveness (six or more on questions 1–14) and also scores five or more on the Ring of Fire questions.

"Ring of Fire" ADD score of three or four: _________

PART 2

The Six ADD Types

CHAPTER 5

Type 1: Classic ADD

The sufferer:

Is easily distracted

Has difficulty sustaining attention span for most tasks in play, school, or work

Has trouble listening when others are talking

Has difficulty following through (procrastination) on tasks or instructions

Has difficulty keeping an organized area (room, desk, book bag, filing cabinet, locker, etc.)

Has trouble with time, e.g., is frequently late or hurried, tasks take longer than expected, projects or homework are "last-minute" or turned in late

Has a tendency to lose things

Makes careless mistakes, poor attention to detail

Is forgetful

Is restless or hyperactive

Has trouble sitting still

Is fidgety, in constant motion (hands, feet, body)

Is noisy, has a hard time being quiet

Acts as if "driven by a motor"

Talks excessively

Is impulsive (doesn't think through comments or actions before they are said or done)

Has difficulty waiting his or her turn

Interrupts or intrudes on others (e.g., butts into conversations or games).

When most people think about ADD, they think about Type 1: Classic ADD. Hyperactive, restless, impulsive, disorganized, distractible, and trouble concentrating are Type 1's hallmark symptoms. This type of ADD is usually evident early in life. As babies, Type 1 sufferers tend to be colicky, very active, and they are hard to soothe and hold (they wiggle a lot). They have less eye contact than other children their age and parents have a more difficult time bonding with these children. It is hard to bond with a child who is in constant motion, who struggles to get away when you try to hold her. The hyperactivity and conflict-driven behavior usually gets everyone's attention early. The children are restless, in constant motion, noisy, talkative, and demanding. They also seem to need constant excitement or to see someone get upset. In addition, many of the inattentive symptoms are present as well. These ADD children are usually the first ones to be diagnosed, because they bring a lot of negative attention to themselves. These children are hard to be around, especially for people who are sensitive to noise. Parents of hyperactive children frequently feel tired, embarrassed, angry, and overwhelmed. As a group, Type 1 ADD individuals have low self-esteem. Due to the hyperactivity, conflict-driven behavior, and impulsivity these children, teens, and adults are in trouble with someone nearly every day of their lives. The brain SPECT findings in Type 1 show normal brain activity at rest and decreased activity, especially in the prefrontal cortex (pfc), during a concentration task.

Here are four typical examples of Type 1 ADD (covering ages throughout the lifespan).

Joey

Mrs. Wilson brought Joey to see me when he was 7 years old. He had just repeated first grade. Since preschool, teachers had mentioned problems with Joey. They said he was restless, fidgety, impulsive, and unable to stay focused unless he was really interested. The school had tested his intelligence, which was high normal, and they tested his hearing and vision—also normal. Mrs. Wilson thought that the teachers weren't skilled enough to manage him, but she had to admit she was frequently frustrated with him at home. Ten minutes of homework would take him an hour of unfocused time. He started fights with his older brother and he had to be told to do things over and over. His bedroom was a perpetual mess, even right after it was picked up. He needed extra supervision, and dinnertime upset everyone because he wouldn't sit still long enough to eat. Joey had trouble getting to sleep at night because of his restlessness, and he was hard to get up in the morning. Mrs. Wilson said she had stopped taking him shopping with her because it was too much. Even at the age of seven, he would not stay close, he touched everything, and he asked for treats repeatedly. "He just has no impulse control," she told me. Mrs. Wilson had brought Joey to the pediatrician when he was four years old because of his hyperactivity, but the doctor said he would probably outgrow it in a year or two.

During the evaluation in my clinic, Joey was all over the place. He took books off my bookshelves and played with items on my desk without permission. He was in constant motion. His mother appeared upset by his behavior and constant motion. I gave him a computerized test of attention (Conner's CPT), which he scored very poorly on. He had a very impulsive, fast approach to the test. I diagnosed Joey with Type 1 ADD and spoke to Mrs. Wilson about treatment options. A SPECT series was performed to gather the most information possible before treatment.

We often do two SPECT studies for ADD and learning disabilities: one at rest and one a day or two later during a concentration task. We have found that ADD is not a disorder of a resting brain—people with ADD can rest just fine—but problems show up during a concentration task. The concentration test is similar to a heart stress test. Physicians often order an electrocardiogram (EKG) to get a baseline look at heart function, but if there are heart problems, physicians frequently order a stress EKG done while the person is exercising to bring out the most problems or vulnerabilities. I believe it is essential to do concentration or stress SPECT tests as well.

At rest, Joey's SPECT study showed good, full, symmetrical activity throughout his brain. Two days later, when he tried to concentrate, his SPECT test showed marked decreased activity in the underside of the prefrontal cortex. Typically, in our non-ADD group, when people try to concentrate they get increased activity in this part of the brain: Their brains help them focus by turning on the part of the brain that is largely responsible for focus and follow-through. Joey's brain, however, betrayed him. When he tried to concentrate, his prefrontal cortex shut down rather than on. As part of a research project, a third study was done with concentration on Adderall. Adderall significantly enhanced prefrontal cortex activity, allowing Joey to have access to the part of his brain that helps him with focus, follow-through, and impulse control.

Joey's SPECT Series: Rest, Concentration, and Concentration with Adderall (Underside Surface View)

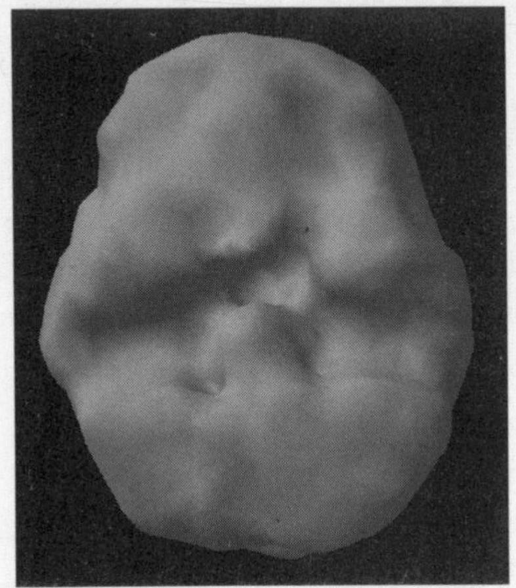

at rest
(good overall activity)

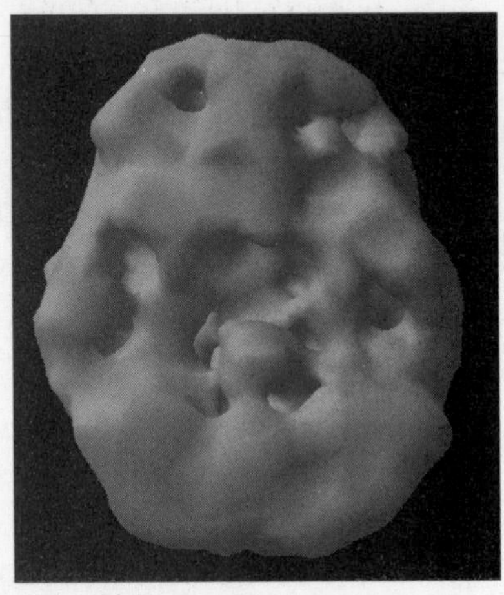

with concentration, no medication
(decreased pfc and temporal lobe activity)

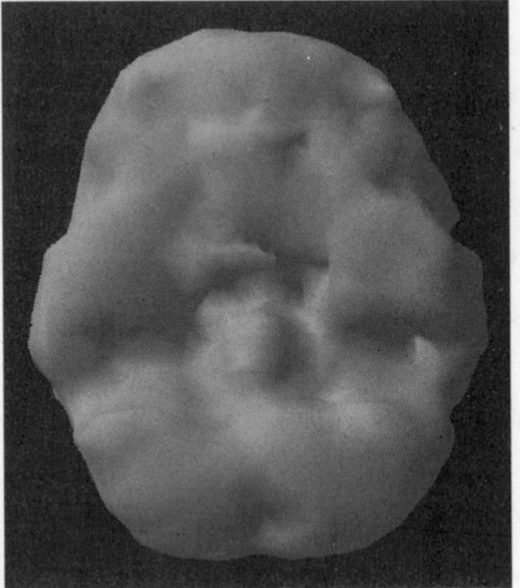

with concentration with Adderall
(overall improved activity)

With a low dose of Adderall, a higher-protein, lower-carbohydrate diet, and regular exercise, Joey had a nice response to treatment. He was more focused, more settled, and over the years, much more successful in school.

Joshua

Sixteen-year-old Joshua found himself in the vice-principal's office. He made an off-color comment in history class and refused to go the office when he was told to go by the teacher. A scene between Joshua and the history teacher ensued. A small, thoughtless comment turned into a big deal. He and his parents had to meet with the vice-principal, Larry. Fortunately, Larry's wife was a family counselor who was expert in ADD. Rather than lecture Joshua, he asked the parents questions and he took the time really to listen to their answers. Joshua had been diagnosed with ADD when he was 6 years old. Despite being a bright child, he had always been impulsive, restless, inattentive, and disorganized. He had been on Ritalin as a child, which helped his school performance and behavior. The parents and pediatrician took him off Ritalin at age 11. They thought everyone outgrew ADD by puberty, and Joshua was not as hyperactive as he once had been. Thinking back on it, his parents said that after fifth grade his school performance deteriorated and he definitely got into more trouble. Larry related to the family that many people with ADD never outgrow the disorder. If Joshua still had problems with impulsivity (obviously), inattention (the mother said homework took him all night to do), and restlessness (he still had trouble sitting still), then he needed another evaluation. Larry recommended the family to my clinic.

We see many, many teenagers like Joshua. As part of the evaluation he had a brain SPECT series, which showed normal activity at rest and markedly decreased activity in the prefrontal cortex during concentration.

Showing Joshua and the family the SPECT study was very helpful. Joshua could see that ADD is not some imaginary illness, not an excuse: It is a medical problem that needs treatment. He needed treatment just as someone needs glasses if they have problems seeing. When we were looking at the study, I asked Joshua if he ever woke up and planned to have problem behavior. Joshua's eyes looked down. He said, "No. I never want to get into trouble. I just say stupid things without thinking." I responded that he needed a better internal supervisor. I explained how the prefrontal cortex helps us think about what we say or do before we say something or do something. His prefrontal cortex needed help. I then showed him some before- and after-treatment SPECT images. His attitude was very positive. He wanted the best brain he could get. His initial treatment consisted of medication, a higher-protein, lower-carbohydrate diet, and intense exercise. With the help of treatment Joshua did very well. In the beginning he was very consistent with his medication, but less consistent with the diet and exercise. When he turned 18 he decided to go into the U.S. Air Force, which had been his lifelong dream. The Air Force, however, would not take Joshua while he was taking medication. He had to be off medication for at least a year. He told me that he really wanted to go off his medication so that he could go into the military. Having a lot of experience with this scenario, I told him he had three choices: He could forget about the military and stay on his medication; he could go off his medication and work hard on natural treatments; or he could just go off his medication, go into the military, and take his chances, but the odds were that the ADD symptoms would get him into trouble. He agreed to work hard at the natural treatments. He exercised intensely for thirty minutes every day. He ate better, eliminating sugar and simple carbohydrates, such as pasta, bread, potatoes, and rice. And he took 1,000 milligrams of L-tyrosine twice a day. He did very well on this combination and entered the Air Force a year later.

Gloria

I met Gloria (45 years old) when she brought her 21-year-old son to our clinic. He was having trouble in college. During the evaluation we had the parents fill out ADD questionnaires on themselves. Gloria scored very high on her questionnaire. She decided to make an appointment for herself. All of her life she had felt stupid. Even though she ended up finishing college, she was labeled a slow learner in elementary and junior high school. She felt that she had to try harder than everyone else. She needed more time to do her homework than her friends did. She often didn't go out on weekends because she was overloaded with schoolwork. Even now, chores around the house took her longer than she (or her husband) thought they should. Gloria complained of a long-standing sense of anxiety and restlessness. She did not go to movies. "I can't sit still for more than fifteen minutes at a time. Getting up all the time and walking around irritates others," she told me. She had problems with follow-through, and often had to pay late fees on bills. Her husband complained that Gloria was conflict-seeking. "Often I feel like she will just start problems," he said. "If we are having a nice day, she'll start to pick at me or bring something up from the past to be upset about. I don't think we have had a whole month in our twenty-five-year marriage without a fight." In addition, Gloria was disorganized. She told me that her closets were a "disaster area." "You have to wear a hard hat when you go in them" was her husband's comment. She was also frequently late.

As part of a family study, both Gloria and her son were scanned. They showed a similar SPECT pattern: healthy brain activity at rest, but poor activity in the prefrontal cortex during concentration.

Gloria had a nice response to treatment. She said her energy was better. She felt more focused and more effective in her day-to-day life. Her anxiety level settled down and she was able to sit through movies without having to get up, missing part of the plot. Her husband said that she was more relaxed, less negative, and less oppositional.

George

Eighty-seven-year-old George made an appointment at our clinic after he saw the improvement in his great-grandson after treatment. He told me that his grandson was just as he himself had been when growing up. He had made too many mistakes in life and wanted to understand why. He also wanted to be able to concentrate better.

He said, "I want to be able to read a book. I have never finished a book even though I like to read." George's family was thrilled when he agreed to an appointment. He had always been difficult. He never sat through a meal, getting up and sitting down several times. He frequently said impulsive things that hurt other people's feelings. No one wanted to go out to a restaurant with George. Invariably he would say something awful to the waitress about the service or the food and embarrass everyone. As part of a four-generational family study, I ordered a SPECT study on George. His study showed normal brain activity at rest with decreased prefrontal cortex activity during concentration. With a low dose of medication (Adderall), a change in his diet, and increased exercise, George felt like a new man. He told me a month later, "I have better energy. I'm more thoughtful and don't upset my family by saying stupid things. My memory appears better, and I can concentrate for the first time in my life. I finished three books this month!" Now six months later, George's family wants to spend more time with him. His grandson, also my patient, told me that Grandpa was easier to be around and that people were not on pins and needles anymore if they went out with him.

THE BRAIN AND TYPE 1 ADD

It appears that Type 1 ADD is caused by a relative deficiency of the neurotransmitter dopamine. Dopamine is a chemical heavily involved with attention span, focus, follow-through, and motivation. When its availability in the brain is low, people tend to struggle with Classic ADD symptoms. Too much dopamine causes people to get overfocused or stuck in negative thought patterns or behaviors. The stimulant medications appear to work by enhancing dopamine availability in the brain. Physician and brain-imaging researcher Nora Volkow from Brookhaven Laboratory in New York State studied the effects of methylphenidate and cocaine on the brain. She injected these substances tagged to a radioactive isotope and watched

Gloria's SPECT Studies (Underside Surface Views)

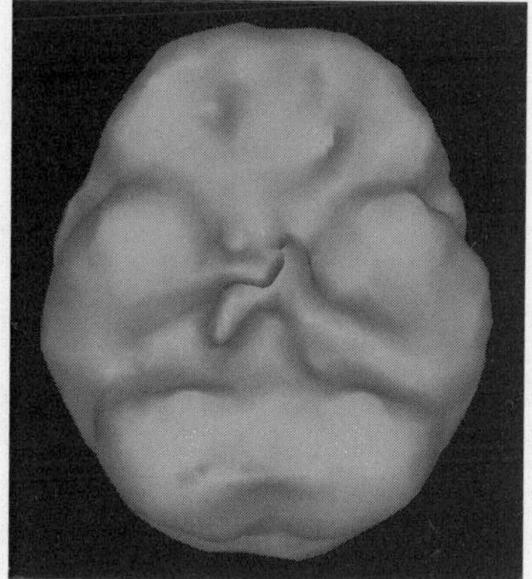

Rest
(good overall activity)

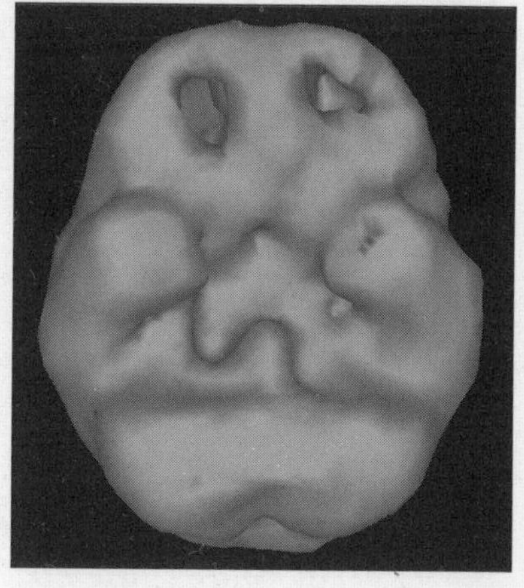

Concentration
(decreased prefrontal cortex activity)

Gloria's Son's SPECT Studies (Underside Surface Views)

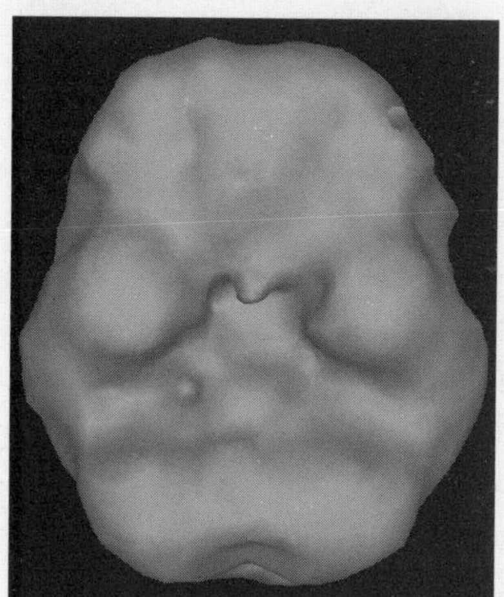

no meds
(overall decreased activity)

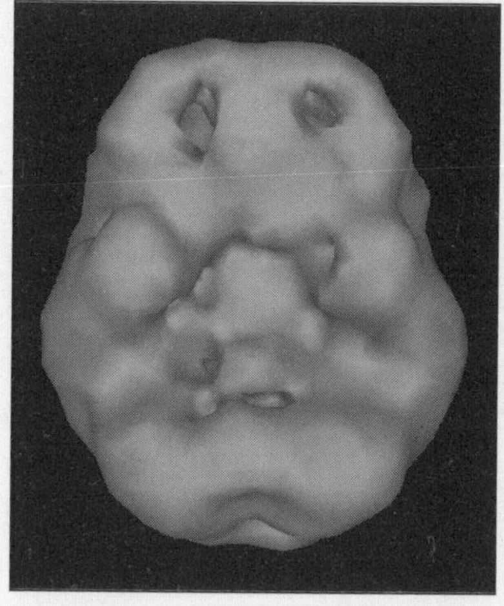

with Adderall
(overall marked improved activity)

George's SPECT Series: Rest and Concentration (Underside Surface View)

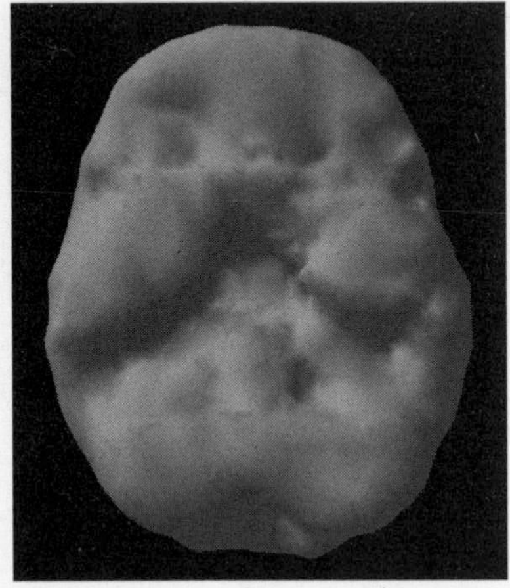

at rest
(good overall activity)

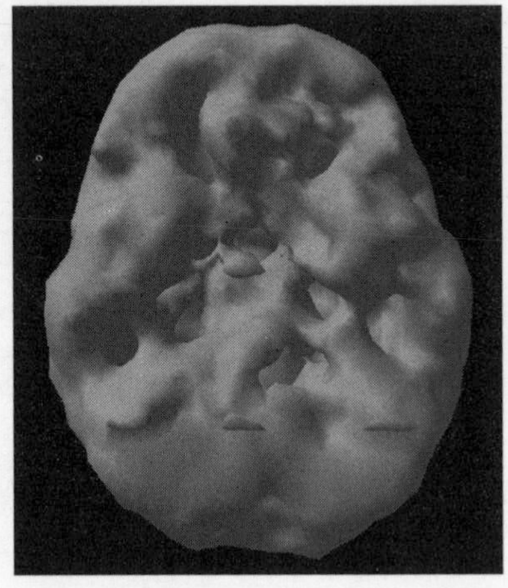

with concentration
(decreased pfc and temporal lobe activity)

where they worked in the brain. Both methylphenidate and cocaine worked in the same area of the brain: the head of the caudate nucleus in the basal ganglia (a structure deep in the brain). This is the same area found to be underactive in a number of ADD studies and may be one of the reasons many ADD adults abuse cocaine and methamphetamines. Dr. Volkow concluded in her study that the reason cocaine is addictive and methylphenidate is not is that cocaine is taken up very quickly in the basal ganglia, has a much more powerful effect in releasing dopamine (a high sensation), and is gone quickly (leading to withdrawal). Methylphenidate, on the other hand, is taken up much more slowly, has a weaker effect, and stays around longer (no withdrawal).

The caudate nucleus appears to be an important brain structure in psychiatry, and is involved in motivation, attention shifting, and anxiety control. When it is overactive, people have a tendency to be overfocused or obsessive. When it is underactive, people have trouble paying attention. There are many connections between the basal ganglia and prefrontal cortex. When there is low basal ganglia activity, there is not enough dopamine being produced to drive the prefrontal cortex. The result is primary ADD symptoms.

All of the brain-imaging research on ADD outside of The Amen Clinic has been on Type 1. The results consistently point to decreased prefrontal cortex activity, especially in the undersurface of the prefrontal cortex (often termed the inferior orbital prefrontal cortex) and the basal ganglia. Understanding how the key brain structures work helps in appreciating the havoc they can cause when they don't.

THE PREFRONTAL CORTEX (PFC)

Occupying the front third of the brain, underneath the forehead, the prefrontal cortex (pfc) is the most evolved part of the brain. It is divided into three sections: the dorsal lateral section (on the outside surface of the pfc), the inferior orbital section (on the front undersurface of the brain), and the anterior cingulate gyrus (which runs through the middle of the frontal lobes). The anterior cingulate gyrus, often considered part of the limbic system, is associated with shifting attention and is often involved with Type 3 (Overfocused) ADD. The dorsal lateral and inferior orbital pfc go by the term "executive control center" of the brain.

Overall, the pfc is the part of the brain that watches, supervises, guides, directs, and focuses your behavior. It contains "executive functions": time management, judgment, impulse control, planning, organization, and critical thinking. Our ability as a species to think, plan ahead, use time wisely, and communicate with others is heavily influenced by this part of the brain. The pfc is responsible for behaviors that are necessary for you to act appropriately, focus on goals, maintain social responsibility, and be effective.

The pfc—especially the inferior orbital pfc—helps you think about what you say or do before you say or do it. It enables you, in

The Prefrontal Cortex

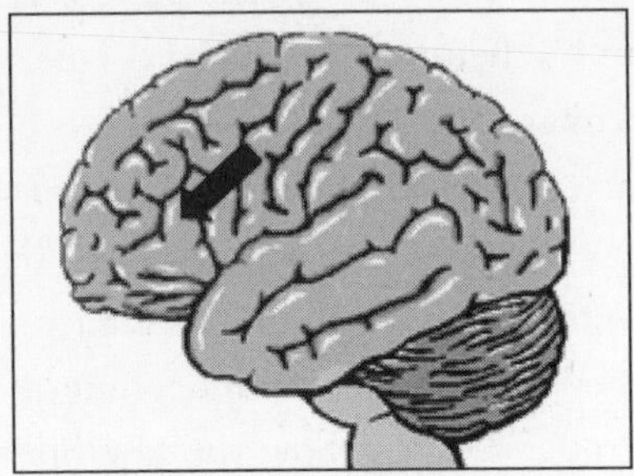

dorsal lateral prefrontal cortex (outside view)

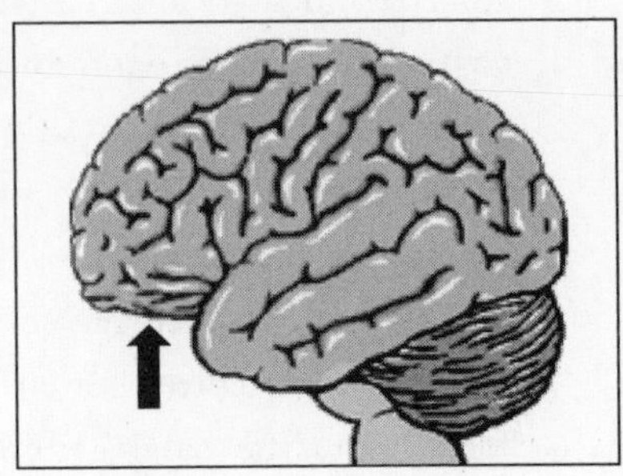

inferior orbital prefrontal cortex (outside view)

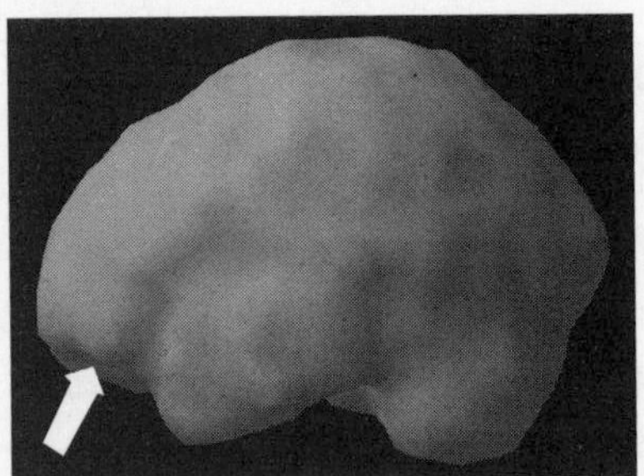

3-D side surface view (dorsal lateral prefrontal area)

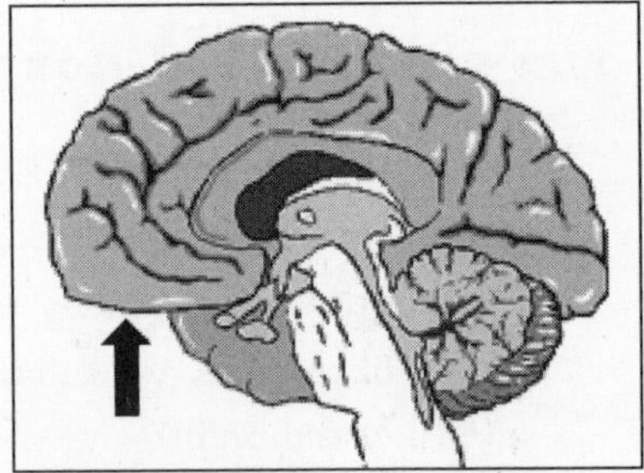

inferior orbital prefrontal area (inside view)

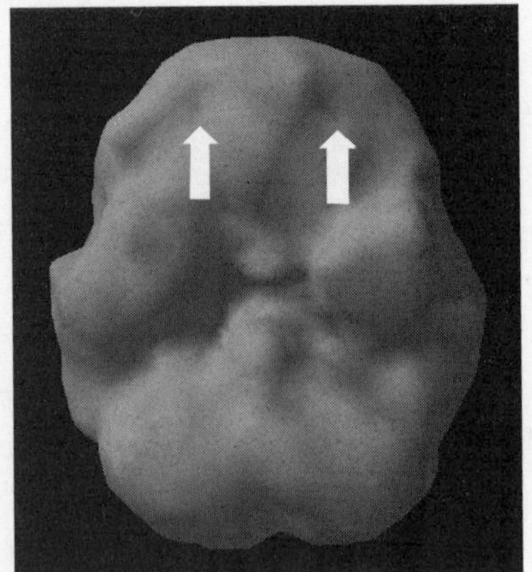

3-D underside surface view (inferior orbital prefrontal area)

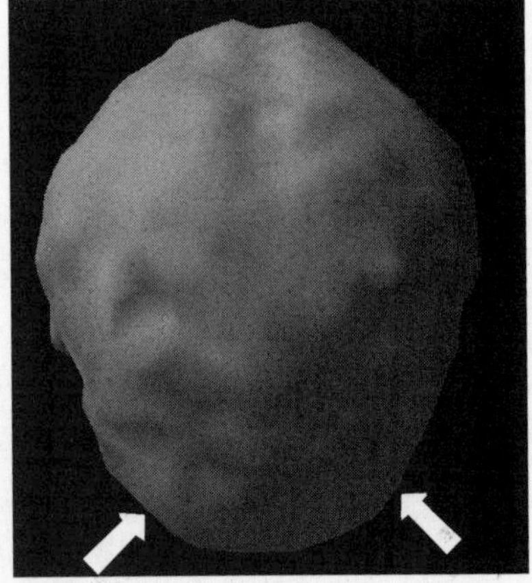

3-D top-down surface view (prefrontal area)

accordance with your experience, to select actions among alternatives in social and work situations.

The pfc (especially the dorsal lateral pfc) is also involved with sustaining attention span. It trains your mind to focus on important information while filtering out less significant thoughts and sensations. Attention span is required for short-term memory and learning. The pfc, through its many connections within the brain, keeps you on task and allows you to stay with a project until it is finished. The pfc accomplishes this by sending quieting signals to the limbic and sensory parts of the brain. In the face of a need to focus, the pfc decreases the distracting input from other brain areas, inhibiting rivals for our attention. However, when the pfc is underactive, less of a filtering mechanism is available and distractibility becomes common.

The pfc—especially the dorsal lateral pfc—enables you to feel and express emotions: to feel happiness, sadness, joy, and love. Distinct from the more primitive limbic system (responsible for mood and libido) the prefrontal cortex translates the feelings of the limbic system into what we think of as higher emotions, such as love, passion, or hate. Underactivity or damage in the pfc often leads to a decreased ability to express thoughts and feelings.

Thoughtfulness and impulse control are also heavily influenced by the pfc. The ability to think through the consequences of behavior is essential to every aspect of human life. Without forethought, it would be awfully difficult to choose a good mate, interact with customers, deal with difficult children, spend money, or drive on the freeway. In all of those kinds of situations, consistent, thoughtful action and inhibition of impulse behavior hold the keys to success.

Within the pfc as a whole, problems in the dorsal lateral prefrontal cortex often lead to decreased attention span, distractibility, impaired short-term memory, decreased mental speed, apathy, and decreased verbal expression. Problems in the inferior orbital cortex often lead to poor impulse control, mood control problems (due to its connections with the limbic system), decreased social skills, and impaired control over behavior.

Test anxiety, along with social anxiety, also may be hallmarks of problems in the pfc. Situations that require concentration, impulse control, and quick reactions are often hampered by pfc problems. Tests require concentration and the retrieval of information. Many people with pfc problems experience difficulties in test situations because they have trouble activating this part of the brain under stress, even if they have adequately prepared for the test. In a similar way, social situations require concentration, impulse control, and dealing with uncertainty. Pfc deactivation often causes a person's mind to "go blank" in conversation, which leads to being uncomfortable in social situations.

Problems in the pfc lead to the organization of daily life spiraling into chaos while internal supervision goes awry. People with pfc problems exhibit problems with impulse control, doing things they later regret. They also experience impaired attention span, distractibility, procrastination, poor judgment, and difficulty expressing themselves.

When men have problems in this part of the brain, their emotions are often unavailable to them and their partners complain that they do not share their feelings. This can cause serious problems in a relationship because of how other people interpret the lack of expression of feeling. Many women, for example, blame their male partners for being cold or unfeeling, when it is really a problem in the pfc that causes a lack of being "tuned in" to the feelings of the moment.

The basal ganglia are a set of large structures toward the center of the brain. Involved with integrating feelings, thoughts, and movement, they also help shift and smooth motor behavior. In our clinic we have noticed that the basal ganglia are involved with setting the body's idling and anxiety levels and modulating motivation. The basal ganglia tend to be underactive in Classic ADD.

The integration of feelings, thoughts, and movement occur in the basal ganglia. This is why you jump when you're excited, tremble when you're nervous, freeze when you are scared, and get

The Basal Ganglia System

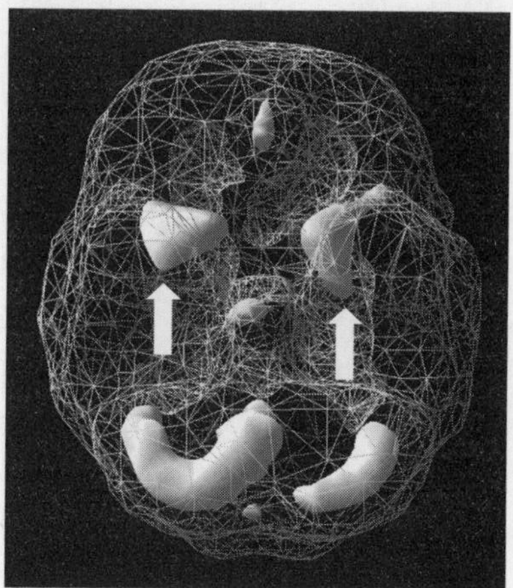

3-D underside active view

tongue-tied when the boss is chewing you out. The basal ganglia allow for a smooth integration of emotions, thoughts, and physical movement. When there is too much input, they tend to lock up and do not allow a smooth transition. When the basal ganglia are *over*active (as we have seen in the case of people with anxiety tendencies or disorders), people are more likely to become immobile (in thoughts or actions) in stressful situations and have a tendency to freeze up. When the basal ganglia are *under*active (as in this type of ADD), a stressful situation often moves a person to action. People with ADD are frequently the first ones on the scene of an accident. They respond to stressful situations without fear. I know, for example, that one of my friends who has Type 1 ADD is a lot quicker at responding to crises than I am. (I have naturally overactive basal ganglia.)

Shifting and smoothing fine motor behavior is another basal ganglia function and is essential to handwriting and motor coordination. Many children and adults who have ADD have very poor handwriting. Their writing often looks choppy or sloppy. In fact, many teens and adults with ADD print rather than write in cursive. They find printing easier because it is not a smooth motor movement but rather a start-and-stop motor activity. Many people with ADD also complain that they have trouble getting their thoughts out of their head and onto paper, a condition called finger agnosia. We know that the medications that help this type of ADD, such as the psychostimulants Adderall, Ritalin, and Dexedrine, work by enhancing the production of the neurotransmitter dopamine in the basal ganglia. It is often amazing how these medications improve handwriting and enhance a person's ability to get their thoughts out on paper in an easier way. In addition, many people with ADD say that their overall motor coordination is improved with these medications.

Reversing the low pfc and basal ganglia activity in Type 1 ADD is the therapeutic goal. We'll learn more about that later.

CHAPTER 6

Type 2: Inattentive ADD

The sufferer:

Is easily distracted

Has difficulty sustaining his or her attention span for most tasks in play, school, or work

Has trouble listening when others are talking

Has difficulty following through (procrastination) on tasks or instructions

Has difficulty keeping an organized area (room, desk, book bag, filing cabinet, locker, etc.)

Has trouble with time, for example, frequently late or hurried, tasks take longer than expected, projects or homework are "last minute" or turned in late

Has a tendency to lose things

Makes careless mistakes, with poor attention to detail

Is forgetful

Daydreams excessively

Complains of being bored

Appears apathetic or unmotivated

Is tired, sluggish, or slow-moving

Is spacey or seems preoccupied.

The second most common type of ADD is Type 2: Inattentive ADD. Unfortunately, many of these people never get diagnosed. Instead they are labeled slow, lazy, spacey, or unmotivated. While Type 1 people bring negative attention to themselves with their hyperactivity, constant chatter, and conflict-driven behavior, inattentive ADD folks tend to be quiet and distracted. Rather than cause problems in class, they are more likely to daydream or look out the window. They are not often impulsive and are less likely to blurt out inappropriate things. They are frequently thought of as couch potatoes who have trouble finding interest or motivation in their lives. Girls seem to have this type as much or more than boys.

As in Type 1 (Classic) ADD, dopamine is generally considered the neurotransmitter involved in inattentive ADD—although, in this case, its imbalance is felt by another area of the brain.

Read the following four examples of Type

2 ADD. Seeing what these people went through and how they were helped gives a clear picture of the nature of inattentive ADD.

Sara

Eight-year-old Sara was brought to our clinic by her mother and father. They were worried about her inability to pay attention. A few minutes of homework often took her three to four hours, with her parents upset at her for taking so long. She appeared spacey, internally preoccupied, and generally in her own world. Her room was usually very messy. She had poor social skills and often ignored children her own age whom her parents arranged to come over to the house to be her playmates. Even though she did not have a defiant attitude at home, she often simply did not do what was asked of her. She said that she had forgotten or didn't hear the request. Her teacher said that she appeared to be a smart child but performed far below her potential. Her mind wandered in class and she had to be reminded to pay attention. She frequently made silly mistakes on tests and homework. Her handwriting was awful. Hearing and vision tests checked out normal, as did thyroid studies done by the pediatrician and tests for learning disabilities done by the school psychologist. She had all the hallmarks of Type 2 Inattentive ADD, but the parents were hesitant to start treatment, and wanted further evaluation. We did a SPECT study to evaluate her brain function. Clinically she appeared to have Inattentive ADD. I certainly could have started treatment without a SPECT study, but I honored the parents' request: If it had been my child, I, too, would have wanted to know how her brain worked before I started treatment.

Sara's SPECT study showed marked decreased activity when she tried to concentrate, especially in the prefrontal cortex. I prescribed a high-protein, low-carbohydrate diet (her diet before the evaluation had been almost entirely carbohydrates), regular exercise, and a regimen of 500 mg of L-tyrosine twice a day. Sara's schoolwork and behavior improved within the first week of starting this regimen. Whenever Sara strayed from her treatment, she again became spaced-out and inattentive.

Chris

Ten-year-old Chris was diagnosed as mentally retarded at age 6. He was a slow learner and now read at only the first-grade level. After testing Chris, the school psychologist said that he had only limited potential. His parents were very upset with the prognosis given by the school psychologist because at home they saw flashes of real intelligence. They also saw problems: For example, his room tended to be very disorganized, even though the parents tried to help him. Chris had a low energy level and frequently had to be called several times before he would answer. A local neurologist ordered a brain MRI, EEG, and blood tests, all of which were normal.

A friend of Chris's mother was a patient at our clinic and suggested that she have Chris evaluated by us. Reviewing his tests, I saw that Chris had a low IQ, but also that the psychologist had noted that Chris had been very inattentive during the test. In talking to Chris, I found that I had to work hard to make eye contact with him. He gave only limited answers to my questions and seemed easily distracted by the things in my office. I ordered a

Chris's Concentration SPECT Study on and off Adderall (Underside Surface View)

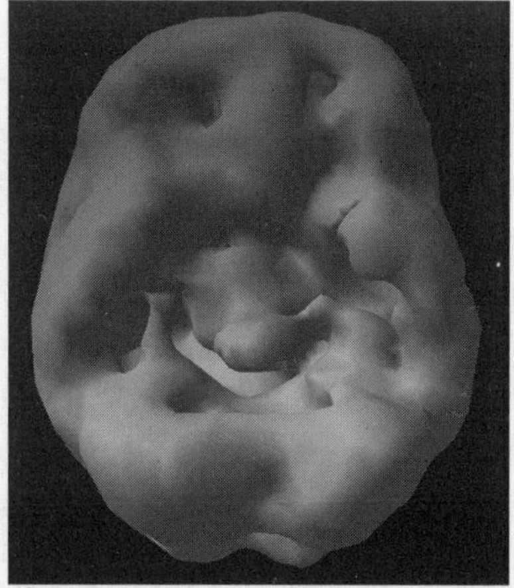

with no medication

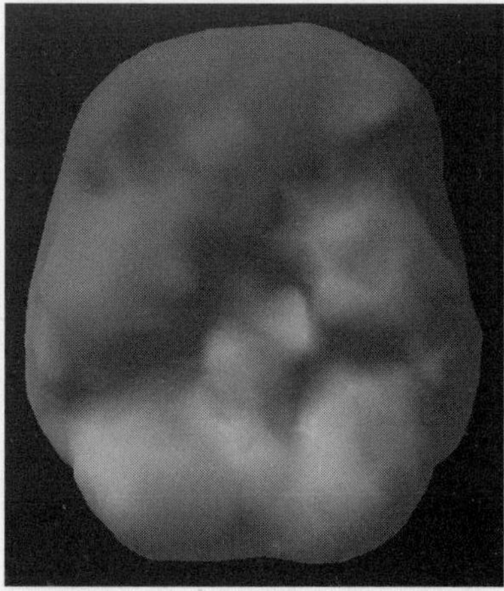

with Adderall

SPECT study to understand how his brain worked. I believe that all children diagnosed with mental retardation need a functional brain-imaging study. Overall, Chris had very poor blood flow in his brain, especially in the prefrontal cortex. I scanned him again on Adderall to see if it would have a positive effect. On Adderall he had significantly more activity in his brain. Almost immediately the parents noticed a difference in Chris. He was more talkative, more energetic, and more responsive. The next year he picked up three grade levels in reading. A year later, IQ tests were redone and found to be in the normal range. Today, Chris is happy and performing well in school. Prior to treatment, Chris's brain was in darkness. Now, with treatment, the lights have been turned on: It was as if we had given a blind person sight.

Allison

My 18-year-old niece, Allison, is the kind of teenager whom most parents can only dream about. She has always been sweet, responsible, easygoing, organized, and self-motivated. Yet, several years ago she began to appear stressed and depressed. She was staying up to 1 or 2 o'clock every morning studying for classes. She had trouble remembering what she studied and she frequently had to reread material because distracting thoughts would get her off track. As I learned about Allison's problems I became concerned. Allison had never performed very well in school, but she usually got B's because of the great effort she expended. In fact, in the eighth grade she won a Presidential Scholar Award—not for grades but for effort. Secretly her parents thought that she just wasn't as intelligent as some of the other teens at her college prep school. They thought, however, that her diligence would help her be successful in life. When I talked with her at a family Christmas gathering, I saw a stressed-out teen at risk of depression.

Allison had been part of my normal control group when we first started to do scans in 1990. Seeing her struggle, I had went back and looked at her prior scan. Compared to when I first looked at her brain with the experience of only about 50 scans, I now had the experienced eyes of someone who had seen about 5,000 studies. Her old scan looked very underactive. In fact, it looked as if she had had some toxic exposure. I then remembered that her mother had taken Bendectin when she was pregnant with Allison. Bendectin was the antinausea medication that was given to pregnant mothers who had severe morning sickness. Unfortunately for many, Allison included, Bendectin was found to cause learning problems in some children and was pulled from the U.S. market. Over Christmas vacation in 1997, I asked Allison to get another SPECT study. Her SPECT study was virtually identical to the one seven years earlier. It showed markedly decreased activity overall, especially in the prefrontal and temporal lobes (areas involved with concentration and memory). With this information I rescanned Allison on Adderall. I wanted to see if a stimulant medication would help her brain activity. The follow-up scan was amazing. On one dose of 15 milligrams of Adderall one hour before the next scan, her brain normalized: It became much more active overall. The medication enhanced the activity in her prefrontal cortex and temporal lobes, giving her access to the parts of her brain involved in concentration and memory, access she did not have prior to the medication. Allison's learning struggles had nothing to do with her intelligence. The underactivity in her brain was limiting the access she had to her own memory and ability to concentrate. I told Allison that she would have to rethink herself. Until then, she had felt that she wasn't as smart as her friends and that she would have to limit her goals. With this new information and enhanced brain activity, who knew what she would be able to do? After the Christmas vacation, when she went back to school, she said that learning was much easier. She started bringing home tests with A's on them. When she went to biology class, she said she understood concepts for the first time. Before the Christmas vacation they started discussing genetics, which she said was way over her head. After vacation, on her new treatment program, she said that the material was clear and easy to understand. Four months after her scans, she got straight A's for the first time ever. She repeated the feat on her next three report cards. She has a com-

Allison's Concentration SPECT Study Before and After Treatment with Adderall (Underside Surface View)

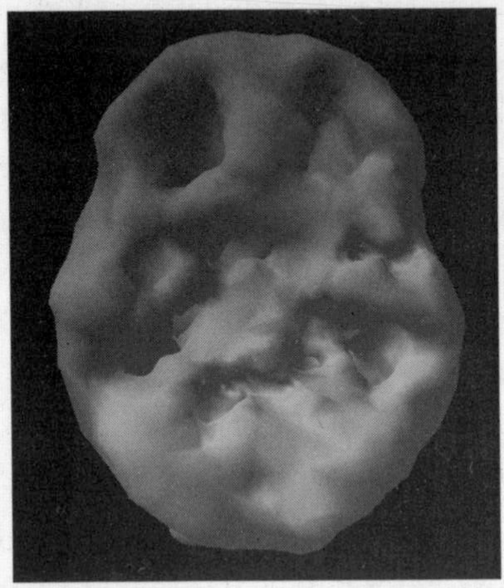

no medication
(poor prefrontal and temporal lobe activity)

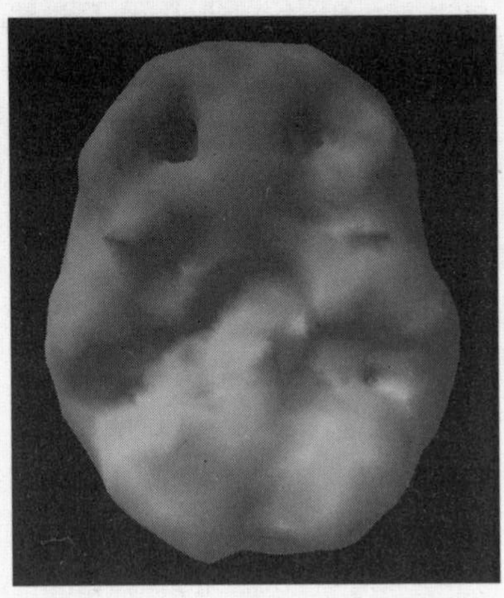

with Adderall
(marked overall improvement)

pletely different perception of herself—one that fits her reality of being smart, competent, and able to look forward to a bright future. She wants to be a geneticist.

Gary

Gary, age 29, came to see me because he had trouble living independently. His parents were still supporting him. Despite his high intelligence, he underachieved in school. Teachers said he didn't care and needed to try harder. He appeared unmotivated, tired, and off in his own world. Even his girlfriend had trouble getting his attention. Even though he worked at several odd jobs and was good at carpentry, he did not make enough money to pay all of his bills. Employers fired him for being late to work or not coming back from lunch on time. Gary's father told him to "get his stuff together" or he would not help Gary anymore.

Even though many people would call Gary lazy, I suspected a medical problem. Gary had symptoms consistent with Type 2 (Inattentive) ADD. Rather than being hyperactive, he appeared underactive. He was spacey, easily distracted, inattentive, and lethargic. His brain SPECT study showed marked decreased activity in the prefrontal cortex when he tried to concentrate. I placed him on a low dose of stimulant medication (Adderall), a higher-protein, lower-carbohydrate diet, and regular, intense exercise. Over the next two years he was able to become more effective in his day-to-day life.

Jenna

Jenna, a 57-year-old artist, was referred to The Amen Clinic by her psychiatrist. She complained of trouble concentrating, distractibility, "fuzzy thinking," disorganization, low energy, difficulty reading, and feelings of life being overwhelming. Facing the day was frightening for her. She would become frozen and panicked by daily tasks, such as opening the mail. She has a beautiful house, but there were piles everywhere. Many of her friends said that she was "too creative" to be organized and focused. Her doctor had tried her on a small dose of Ritalin, which had a significant positive effect on her symptoms. He wanted to send her for a second opinion and for brain-imaging studies to clarify the diagnosis and better target treatment.

Clinically, Jenna was diagnosed with Type 2 (Inattentive) ADD. Two SPECT studies were performed as part of her workup. The first study, performed without any medication, showed marked decreased activity, especially in her prefrontal cortex. The second study was performed several days later after she took a dose of Adderall. With medication there was significant overall improvement throughout her whole brain, especially in the prefrontal cortex.

On Adderall she feels much better. "I feel like I have access to much more of my own brain," she told me, which indeed the SPECT study verified.

Initially, Jenna was very afraid of medication. She wanted to deal with her problems in a "natural" way. In fact, she had tried different diets, exercise, and meditation, with little effect. On medication, she feels more focused, and more organized, with more consistent energy and more brain power. She still exercises, eats right, and meditates to help keep her brain healthy. She has asked me who the

Jenna's Concentration SPECT Study on and off Adderall (Underside and Left-Side Surface Views)

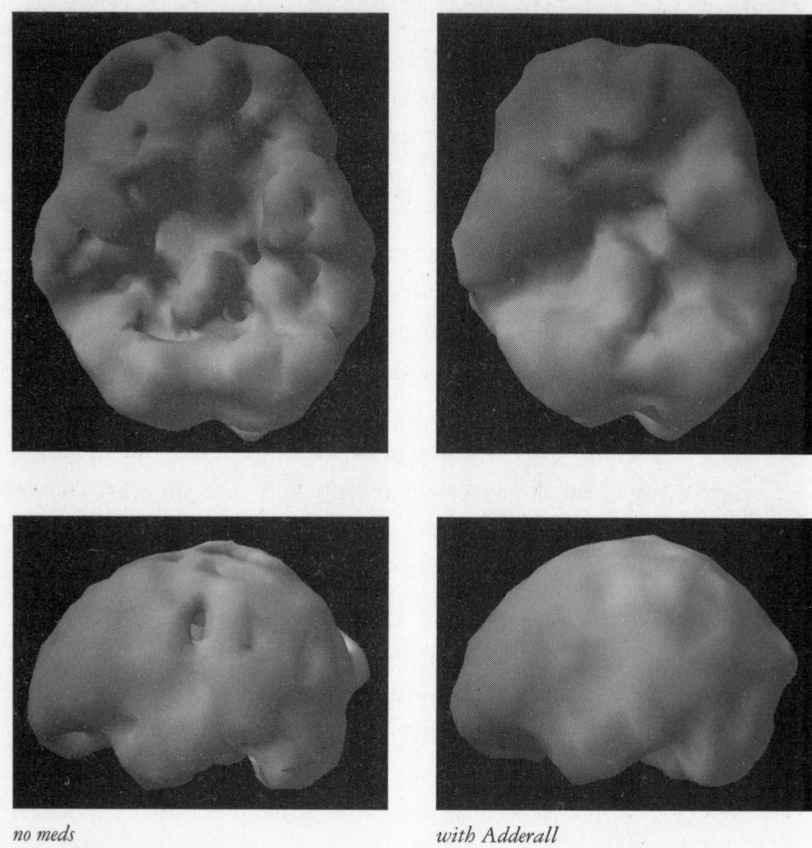

no meds
(overall decreased activity)

with Adderall
(overall marked improved activity)

natural Jenna is, the one with the underactive brain, or the one with the normal-looking brain. My bias is that she is really herself when her brain works right. Since our first visit in 1998, Jenna has referred most of her family to me, because they struggle with very similar issues.

Type 2 ADD is usually very responsive to treatment. As the case studies illustrate, it is often possible to change the whole course of a person's life if the disorder is properly diagnosed and treated.

CHAPTER 7

Type 3: Overfocused ADD

The sufferer has ADD core symptoms, plus:

Worries excessively or senselessly

Is oppositional and argumentative

Has a strong tendency to get locked into negative thoughts, having the same thought over and over

Has a tendency toward compulsive behaviors

Has a tendency to hold grudges

Has trouble shifting attention from subject to subject

Has difficulties seeing options in situations

Has a tendency to hold on to his or her own opinion and not listen to others

Has a tendency to get locked into a course of action, whether or not it is good for him or her

Needs to have things done a certain way or becomes very upset

Is criticized by others for worrying too much.

In my experience Overfocused ADD is the third most common type of ADD. Overfocused ADD patients have all of the core ADD symptoms plus tremendous trouble shifting attention and a tendency to get stuck or locked into negative thought patterns or behaviors. This type of ADD can have devastating effects on families. It is frequently found in substance abusers and in children and grandchildren of alcoholics.

I discovered Overfocused ADD early in my brain-imaging work. Due to personal reasons, I did extensive research on children and grandchildren of alcoholics during my residency training years. When my brain-imaging work began, I discovered excessive activity in the anterior cingulate gyrus in many of these patients. The anterior cingulate gyrus is the brain's gearshift. It allows a person to shift from thought to thought or idea to idea. When it is overactive, people have a tendency to get stuck or locked into negative thoughts and behaviors, and this was a common trait I discovered among the children and grandchildren of alcoholics.

At the time I started my brain-imaging work, there were several studies in this field that suggested that there was overactivity in the anterior cingulate gyrus in patients who had obsessive compulsive disorder (OCD). In 1991 a SPECT study reported that Prozac decreased activity in the anterior cingulate gyrus in patients with OCD. I saw this same hyperactivity in the anterior cingulate gyrus in many patients who did not have OCD. But I noticed a common behavioral thread with OCD patients. My patients with hyperactive anterior cyngulate gyri had trouble shifting attention: They would get locked or stuck in patterns of thought or behavior, and there was a certain cognitive inflexibility evident in many of their symptoms. This can give rise to many different symptoms, but the underlying mechanism, trouble shifting attention, remains. The anterior cingulate area of the brain is heavily innervated with serotonin neurons, and, as with OCD patients, we have also found that serotonergic medications seem to be the most helpful in this disorder.

Tammy

Tammy was in fourth grade when she first came to our clinic. Tammy was a stubborn child. If she did not get her way, she would throw mammoth tantrums that could go on for hours. In addition, Tammy was shy around other people, worried a lot, and was having problems in school. She would stare at her work for long periods of time. She craved perfection in her schoolwork, and as a result her papers showed evidence of many erasures. Tammy was distracted easily and had trouble sitting still. While Tammy's attention could easily be diverted from some things, she held on to hurts. If a friend said something she didn't like, her parents would hear about it for weeks. Another child psychiatrist diagnosed Tammy with ADD and put her on Ritalin. But the Ritalin aggravated her, making her moody, irritable, and even more anxious. Tammy's brain scan showed that her anterior cingulate gyrus was very overactive. It was clear from a brain biology perspective that she had trouble shifting

The Anterior Cingulate Gyrus

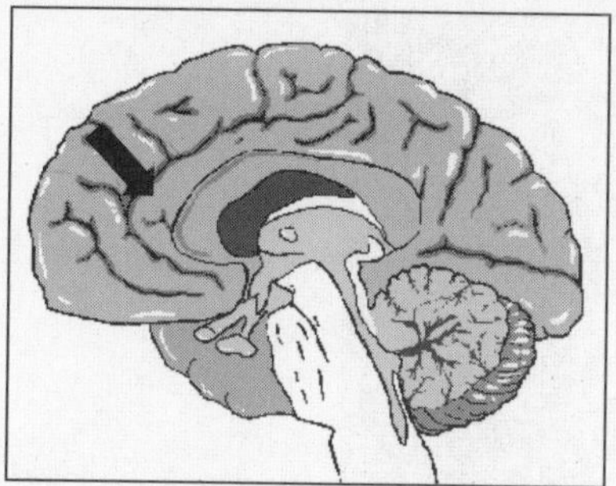
cingulate gyrus

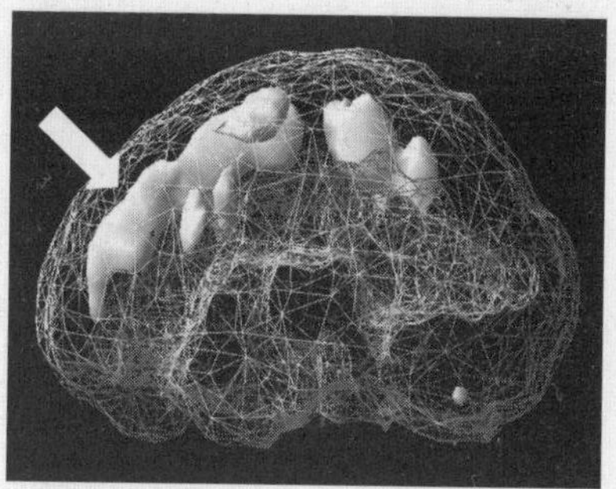
3-D side active view

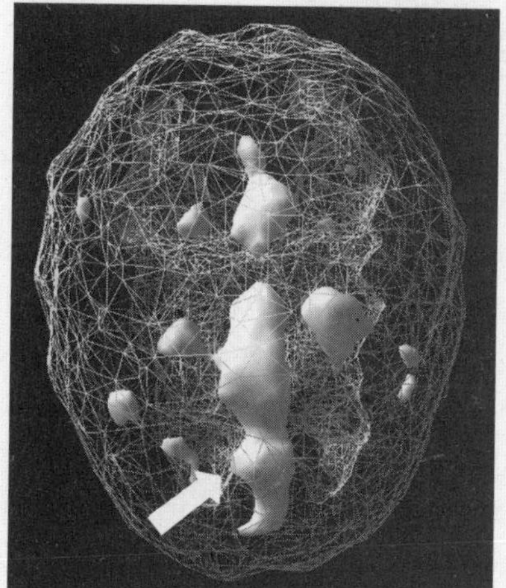
3-D top-down active view

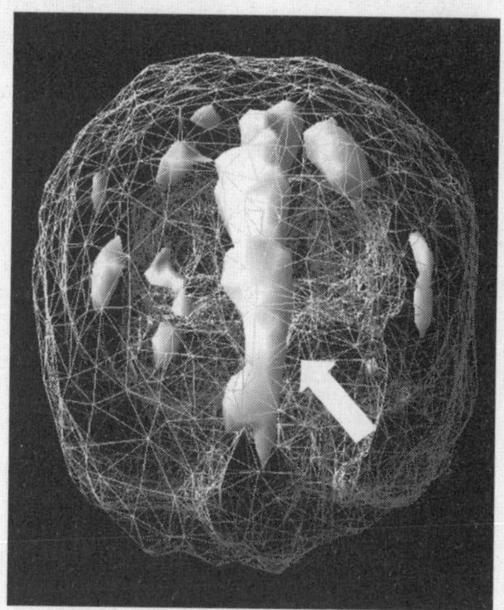
3-D front-on active view

her attention. She needed a calmer cingulate if she was going to improve. Given her poor prior response to medication, the parents and I initially decided to try an herbal approach to treatment. I placed her on St. John's wort (a seratonin booster) and had her engage in a daily exercise program. In addition her parents had to learn to be very firm and prevent her from arguing or opposing them. It took two months for all of the interventions to work together, but they had a significant positive impact on her behavior and academic ability.

Tammy's Concentration SPECT Study (Top-Down Active View)

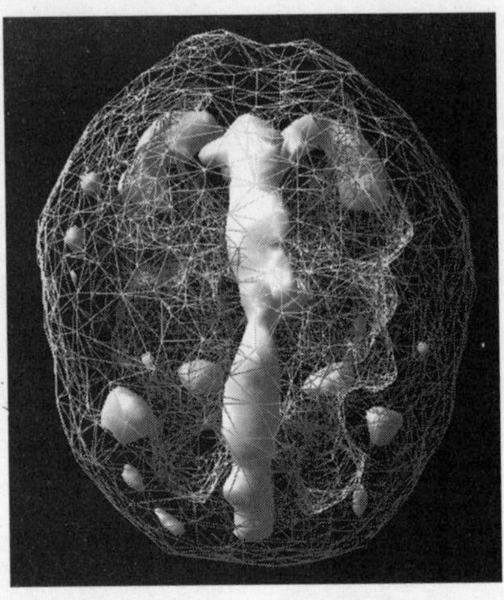

Mark

Mark, 14 years old, was evaluated for anger outbursts and defiant behavior. Psychotherapy and parent training were ineffective. Dietary interventions did nothing. Depakote, Ritalin, Dexedrine, and Wellbutrin had no more success. Prozac made him *more* aggressive. We were all frustrated, including Mark. His parents were ready to send him away to a residential treatment center. The stress on their family was just too much. I ordered a SPECT study. His SPECT study revealed marked hyperfrontality (his anterior cingulate gyrus and lateral prefrontal cortices were very overactive). Mark was unable to shift his attention. He was unable not to be difficult. I placed him on Risperdal, one of our new, novel antipsychotic medications. He was clearly not psychotic—he wasn't delusional or hallucinating—but we have found this class of medications helpful for this severe hyperfrontality. He had a dramatic response. He was more compliant, happier, and no longer aggressive. One week after I started Mark on Risperdal, his mother came to my clinic, even though she didn't have an appointment. As I walked into the waiting room to greet a patient, I saw her. I wondered why she was there. I smiled at her and she immediately came over to me,

Mark's Concentration SPECT Studies, Before Treatment and at One and Six Months After Treatment with Risperdal (Top-Down Active View)

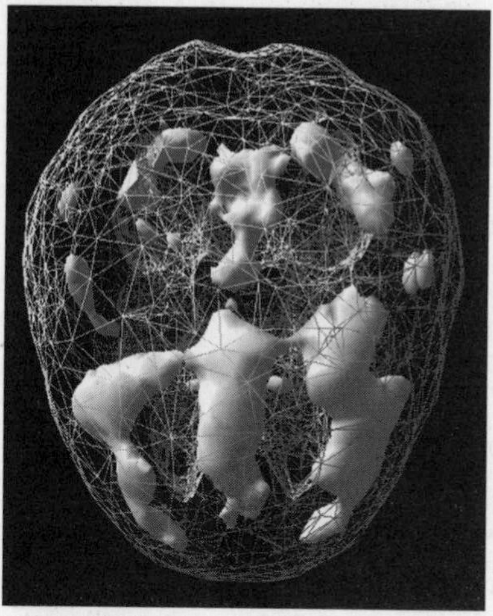

before treatment
(note marked hyperfrontality)

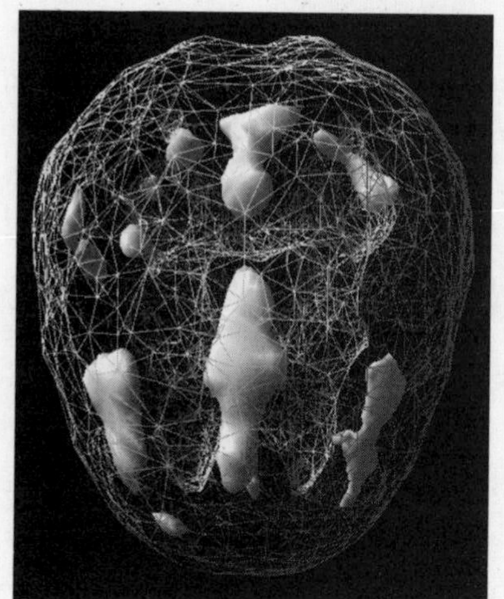

one month later
(mild decrease in hyperfrontality)

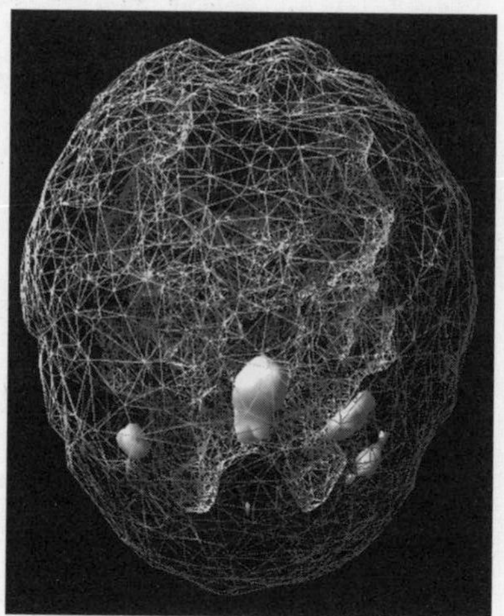

six months later
(marked decrease in hyperfrontality)

grabbed me, and gave me a big hug. She said, "Thank you so much. I have my son back. Mark is doing so much better!" I felt pretty good that day. As the improvement held, I did two follow-up studies; one study was done a month later, the next one was six months later. There was a progressive calming of the hyperfrontality.

Brandon

Sixteen-year-old Brandon was one of the more difficult children I have treated in my practice. He was negative, surly, argumentative, and oppositional, and would throw long tantrums when he did not get his way. He did poorly in school. He would not cooperate with teachers, and he did not get along with other students. The parents were at their wits' end when they brought Brandon to see me.

Brandon was very opposed to seeing a psychiatrist. "I'm not crazy," he announced to his parents, "and I'm not going to talk to any shrink, so don't waste your money." From the clinical history it was obvious to me that Brandon had anterior cingulate problems. He held true to his word that he wouldn't talk to me, so for a number of months I spent most of my time with Brandon's parents. Brandon refused to take medication and he was threatening to run away from home. The parents and I felt that Brandon might need a residential treatment center where he could get intensive treatment over nine months to a year.

Before I sent Brandon to treatment, however, I ordered a scan to evaluate his brain function and partly to help convince him of the biological need for treatment. Surprisingly, Brandon agreed to the scan without his usual fuss. He was curious and had seen the brain images around our clinic. Brandon's SPECT scan was one of the most abnormal studies that I had ever seen. His anterior cingulate gyrus was on fire. His frontal lobes were completely overactive as well. It looked as if he had three large racing stripes running down the middle of his prefrontal cortex.

As I explained the SPECT results to Brandon, he actually seemed to listen to me for the first time. He asked questions, seemed inter-

Brandon's Concentration SPECT Study (Top-Down Active View)

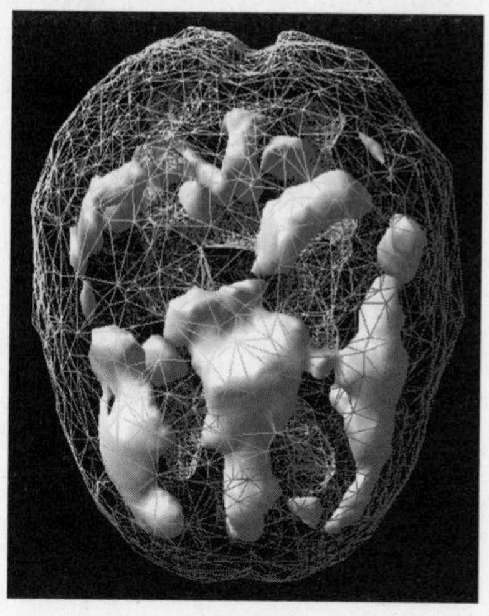

ested, and asked to see both healthy and dysfunctional brains. By the end of our appointment he had agreed to try some medication. He also agreed to exercise on a regular basis. The scan seemed to help him shift to a more open emotional place. I placed him on 20 milligrams of Prozac. Three weeks later I had a follow-up appointment with Brandon. I walked to my waiting room, wondering what I would see. I was used to having bad interactions with Brandon. To my surprise Brandon stood up when he saw me, shook my hand, and said, "It's nice to see you again, Dr. Amen. How are you?" My mouth dropped open. I thought to myself, *Where is Brandon? Who is occupying his body? Someone must have performed a brain transplant on him.* Brandon and his parents came back to my office and told me that about a week after taking the Prozac, Brandon's whole demeanor started to change. He woke up in a pleasant mood. He was more cooperative and even asked if he could help around the house. The tantrums were gone and he was a joy to live with. Over the next several months Brandon's improvement held firm, but he was still having trouble focusing in school. At that point I added a very small dose of Adderall, a psychostimulant medication, to help him focus. It was the missing piece of the puzzle and Brandon's schoolwork improved as well.

The first time I saw Brandon's improvement, I wondered, "Who is he really?" What was Brandon's character? What was his soul really like? Over time I learned that Brandon really was a charming, sweet young man who had been trapped inside the circular hell of his brain's inflamed anterior cingulate gyrus. When his anterior cingulate gyrus and his brain worked right, Brandon was able to work right as well.

Sarah

Sarah, 28, was referred by her therapist because she had failed the bar exam six times. Even though Sarah had graduated from law school, the therapist felt that Sarah had attention deficit disorder because she had trouble with attention span, was distractible, and had poor impulse control.

Sarah had grown up in an alcoholic home. She struggled with periods of depression and obsessive thinking. Many of the people who knew her thought she was selfish, because if things did not go Sarah's way she would get angry. She was rigid, frequently argumentative (while she was growing up her parents told her that she would make a good lawyer because of her tendency to argue), held grudges, and often worried about insignificant matters. Just before the evaluation, Sarah was nearly arrested for an incident on the freeway in which she chased down another driver who had accidentally cut her off. Whenever she took traditional ADD medications, however, she got worse. She overfocused on trivia and became more irritable. To my eye, Sarah had symptoms consistent with Overfocused ADD.

I placed Sarah on Effexor, which is a stimulating antidepressant that increases serotonin, norepinephrine, and dopamine neurotransmitters. Sarah began to feel better within three weeks. She felt more focused, less worried, and more relaxed. Her friends noticed that she was more flexible and didn't always have to have things her way.

Phil

At the age of 67, Phil was an unhappy, lonely man. He had been divorced three times and his children did not talk to him. Even though he had been somewhat successful in business, he didn't enjoy his life. He was argumentative and negative and worried excessively. He hated to be alone but tended to be rigid, oppositional, and unpleasant whenever he was around others. Anything that did not go his way caused fierce outbursts. He came to see me after his grandson had been helped in my clinic. I ordered two SPECT studies on Phil as part of a family study we were doing. He had significant decreased activity in his prefrontal cortex during concentration and marked increased cingulate activity on both studies. After seeing his scans and listening to his family history, it was clear to me that Phil suffered from Type 3 ADD. He had a deficiency in serotonin and dopamine, causing the brain abnormalities in his prefrontal cortex and cingulate gyrus, which also caused his difficult behavior.

I treated Phil with a combination of medication, dietary interventions, and exercise. It was wonderful to see the difference. Phil became more relaxed, more positive, less argumentative, and more able to love. His children noticed the difference within several weeks and started to enjoy being around him.

GILLES DE LA TOURETTE'S SYNDROME (TS)

TS is a tic disorder that is frequently associated with Type 3 (Overfocused) ADD. Characterized by both motor and vocal tics lasting more than a year, TS provides the bridge between the basal ganglia and two seemingly opposite disorders: ADD and obsessive-compulsive disorder (OCD). Motor tics are involuntary physical movements such as eye blinking, head jerking, shoulder shrugging, and arm or leg jerking. Vocal tics typically involve making involuntary noises such as coughing, puffing, blowing, barking, and sometimes swearing (corprolalia). TS runs in families and there have been several genetic abnormalities found in the dopamine family of genes. SPECT studies, by my clinic and others, have found abnormalities in the basal ganglia of the brains of TS patients. There is a high association between TS and both ADD and OCD. It is estimated that 60 percent of people with TS have ADD and 50 percent of people with TS have OCD. On the surface it would appear that these are opposite disorders: People with ADD have trouble paying attention, while people with OCD pay too much attention to their negative thoughts (obsessions) or behaviors (compulsions). In looking further at both ADD and OCD patients clinically, I have found a high association of these diseases in the two groups' family histories.

DIFFERENTIATING TYPE 3 (OVERFOCUSED) ADD FROM OCD AND OCPD

I am frequently asked how I differentiate people with this type of ADD from people who have obsessive compulsive disorder (OCD) or obsessive compulsive personality disorder (OCPD). That is easy. All three groups have overfocused tendencies (anterior cingulate issues), but people with Type 3 (Overfocused) ADD also have longstanding core ADD symptoms: short attention span, distractibility, spotty organization, poor follow-through, and poor internal supervision. People with OCD have clear obsessive thoughts and/or compulsive behaviors, such as repetitively checking locks or hand washing. People with OCPD have difficult personality traits—such as emotional rigidity, an "anal" need for sameness, the need to have their way, and compulsive cleanliness—but generally do not have core ADD symptoms. In fact, they usually have the opposite of ADD symptoms: They are overorganized, always on time, never say something impulsively, and must follow through with every task.

CHAPTER 8

Type 4: Temporal Lobe ADD

The sufferer has ADD core symptoms, plus:

Has periods of quick temper or rages with little provocation

Misinterprets comments as negative when they are not

Has a tendency to become increasingly irritable, then explode, then recede, and is often tired after a rage

Has periods of spaciness or confusion

Has periods of panic and/or fear for no specific reason

Imagines visual changes, such as seeing shadows or objects changing shape

Frequent periods of déjà vu (feelings of being somewhere before even though he or she has never been there)

Is sensitive or mildly paranoid

Experiences headaches or abdominal pain of uncertain origin

Has history of a head injury or family history of violence or explosiveness

Has dark thoughts, may involve suicidal or homicidal ideas

Has periods of forgetfulness or memory problems

Has a short fuse or periods of extreme irritability.

Type 4 (Temporal Lobe) ADD is commonly associated with severe behavioral problems. It is often seen in people with ADD who have problems with temper, mood instability, learning disabilities, and memory problems. Under your temples and behind your eyes, the temporal lobes seem to be responsible for mood stability, memory, learning, and temper control. People with Temporal Lobe ADD show decreased activity in the temporal lobes, along with reduced blood flow to the prefrontal cortex during concentration tasks. Associated with domestic violence and suicide, this type of ADD can ruin a family. I saw this type of ADD early in my brain-imaging work, especially with our most difficult patients, and I began to see a correlation with previous head injuries.

Kris

The second brain SPECT study that I ever ordered was on Kris. By age 12, Kris had a long history of emotional outbursts, excessive activity level, short attention span, impulsiveness, problems in school, untruthfulness, and aggressive behavior. These problems had not gone unnoticed. At age 6, Kris was placed on methylphenidate (Ritalin) for hyperactivity. It only made him more aggressive and gave him visual hallucinations; it was stopped. After he attacked a boy at school when he was 8 years old, Kris was admitted to a psychiatric hospital in Alaska, where his father was stationed in the military. He was given the diagnosis of depression and started on the antidepressant desipramine (Norpramin). It didn't help either. At the young age of 12, Kris and his parents had already been through several years of largely ineffective psychotherapy with a psychiatrist/psychoanalyst.

Kris' behavior escalated to the point where he became more aggressive and uncontrollable at home. When he once again attacked another child at school he was readmitted to a psychiatric hospital.

I was on call the weekend Kris was admitted to the hospital. To connect with my patients on the child psychiatry ward, I often played football with them. That day Kris was on my team. He cheated in every single play. When we were on defense, in between plays he would move the ball three steps back and look at me with an expression that said, "Are you going to yell at me like my mother does?" I decided not to yell at Kris but rather to scan his brain to get some clues as to why he acted the way he did. I refused to play his ADD game of "get the adult angry." (See page 180.) Kris's brain SPECT study was very abnormal at rest, showing marked decreased activity in the left temporal lobe. It was 40 percent less active than his right temporal lobe. On top of that, when Kris performed the concentration task there was marked decreased activity in the prefrontal cortex.

Given the temporal lobe problems, I placed Kris on the anticonvulsant medication carbamazepine (Carbatrol) as a way to normalize his temporal lobe. Within a month he was a dramatically different child. He was more compliant, more social, and much more pleasant to be around. On the day he was discharged from the hospital, I was on call again. I gathered my patients and we played football with Kris once again on my team. He didn't cheat. Instead

Kris's SPECT Pictures

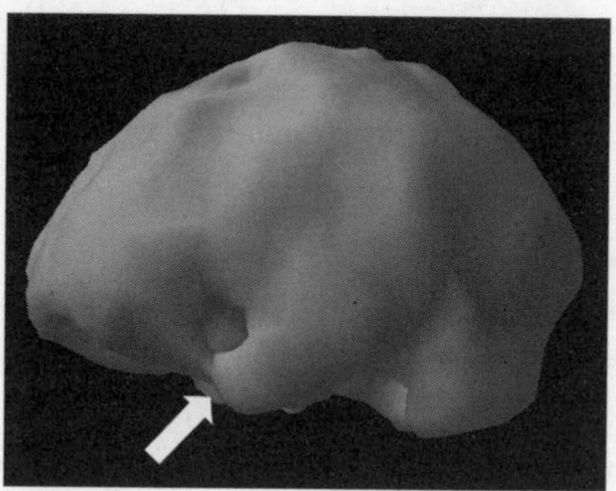

left-side surface view (arrow points to decreased activity in the left temporal lobe)

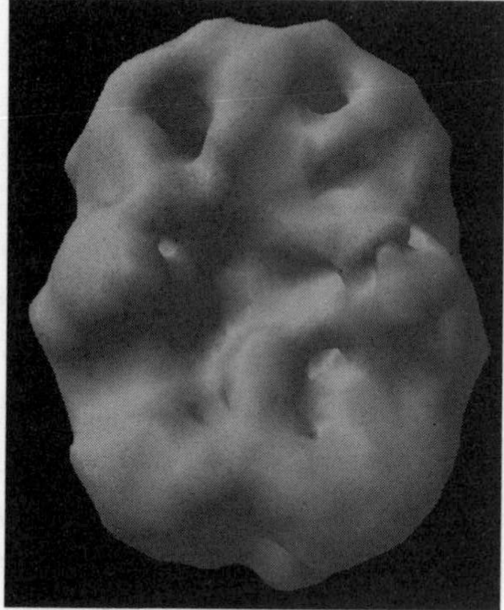

underside surface view at rest (mild decreased prefrontal and left temporal lobe)

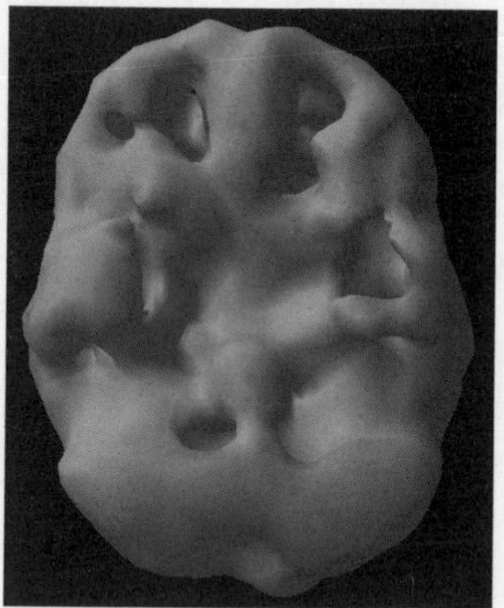

underside surface view with concentration (marked decreased prefrontal and left temporal lobe)

he talked to me about what we were going to do in the game. His conflict-driven behavior had changed to something effective and goal-directed.

When Kris went back to school, his behavior was much better but he still struggled academically. Due to the fact that he had two problems (the left temporal lobe disorder and prefrontal cortex shutdown), I added the stimulant medication magnesium pemoline (Cylert). This helped his attention span, and his schoolwork improved dramatically. The positive response to treatment held for nine years. He recently graduated from high school. Before his graduation, I gave a lecture to the teachers at his school. Kris saw me in the hallway and came over to introduce me to five of his friends.

What do you think would have happened to Kris if he hadn't received appropriate treatment? It is likely that he would have found himself in the California Youth Authority, juvenile hall, a residential treatment facility, or multiple psychiatric facilities. I get upset when I think of all the children like Kris who never get the help they need. They get labeled as bad, willful, defiant children who need more punishment, rather than what I see as the truth: children with medical problems who need treatment.

THE TEMPORAL LOBES

The temporal lobes have largely gone unnoticed. They are rarely talked about in psychiatric circles, and even most neurologists do not speak about the rich contribution they make to who we are and what we experience in life. Until we were able to map activity in the temporal lobes, their function remained mysterious. Professionals basically relegated them as armrests for the brain. The brain-imaging work we have done clearly shows that the temporal lobes play an integral part in memory, emotional stability, learning, temper control, and socialization.

On the dominant side of the brain (the left side for most people), the temporal lobes are intimately involved with understanding and

The Temporal Lobes

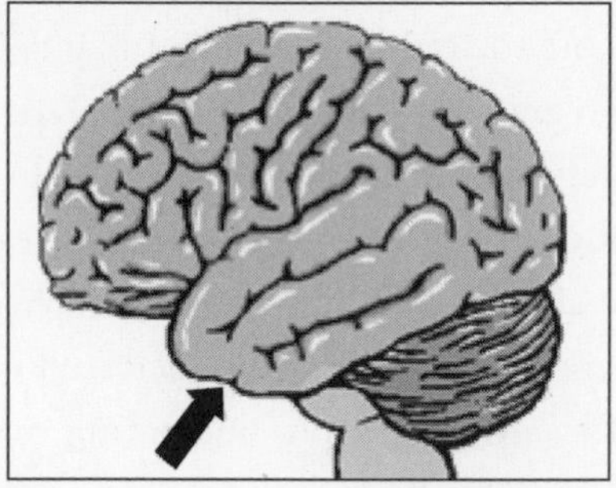

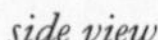

side view

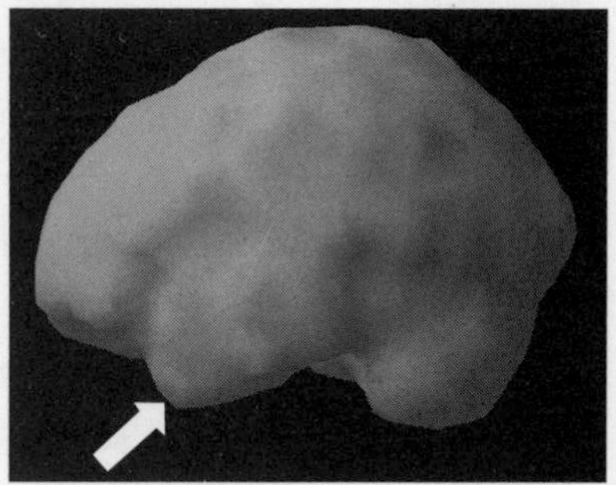

3-D side surface view

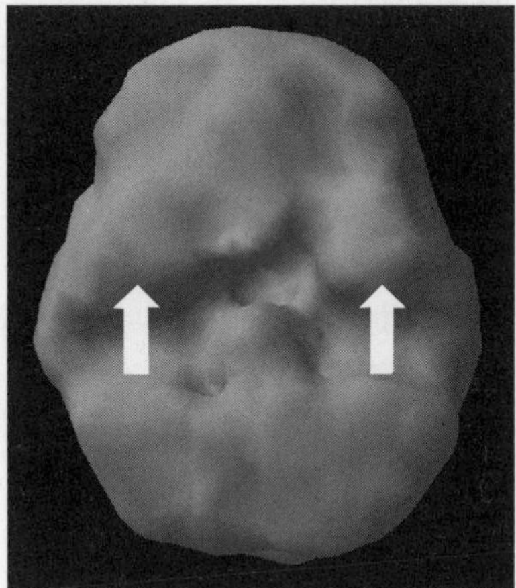

3-D underside surface view

processing language, intermediate- and long-term memory, complex memories, the retrieval of language or words, emotional stability, and visual and auditory processing.

Language is one of the keys to being human. It allows us to communicate with other human beings and it allows us to leave a legacy of our thoughts and actions for future generations. Receptive language, being able to receive and understand speech and written words, requires temporal lobe stability. The ability to accurately hear your child say, "I love you, Daddy," or to listen and be frightened by a scary story is housed in this part of the brain. The dominant temporal lobe helps to process sounds and written words into meaningful information. Being able to read in an efficient manner, remember what you read, and integrate the new information relies heavily on the dominant temporal lobe. Problems here contribute to language struggles, miscommunication, and reading disabilities.

Through our research we have also found that optimum activity in the temporal lobes enhances mood stability, while increased or decreased activity in this part of the brain leads to fluctuating, inconsistent, or unpredictable moods and behaviors.

The nondominant temporal lobe (usually the right) is involved with reading facial expressions, processing verbal tones and intonations from others, hearing rhythms, appreciating music, and visual learning.

Recognizing familiar faces, facial expressions, and voice tones and intonations is critical to social skill. Being able to tell when someone is happy to see you, scared of you, bored, or in a hurry is essential for effectively interacting with others. A. Quaglino, an Italian ophthamologist, reported on a patient in 1867 who, after a stroke, was unable to recognize familiar faces despite being able to read very small type. Since the 1940s more than one hundred cases of prosopagnosia (the inability to recognize familiar faces) have been reported in the medical literature. Patients who have this disorder are often unaware of it (right hemisphere problems are often associated with neglect or denial of illnesses) or they may be ashamed of being unable to recognize close family members or friends. Most commonly, these problems were associated with right temporal lobe problems. Results of current research suggest that knowledge of emotional facial expressions is inborn, not learned. (Infants can recognize their mothers' emotional faces.) Yet, when there are problems in this part of the brain, social skills can be impaired.

The temporal lobes help us process the world of sight and sound, and give us the language of life. This part of the brain allows us to be stimulated, relaxed, or brought to ecstasy by the experience of great music. The temporal lobes have been called the "interpretive cortex," as it interprets what we hear and integrates it with stored memories to give interpretation or meaning to the incoming information. Strong feelings of conviction, great insight, and knowing the truth have also been attributed to the temporal lobes.

Temporal lobe abnormalities occur much more frequently than previously recognized. The temporal lobes sit in a vulnerable area of the brain: the temporal fossa, a cavity behind the eye sockets and underneath the temples. The front wall of the cavity includes a sharp, bony ridge (the wing of the sphenoid bone), which frequently damages the front part of the temporal lobes in even minor head injuries. God would have done well to put bumper guards on that ridge. Since the temporal lobes sit in a cavity surrounded by bone on five sides (front, back, right side, left side, and underside) they can be damaged from a blow to the head at almost any angle.

As with other brain problems, temporal lobe problems come from many different sources: genetic inheritance (you can get these problems from your parents), toxic or infectious exposure, and head

Model showing the base of the skull

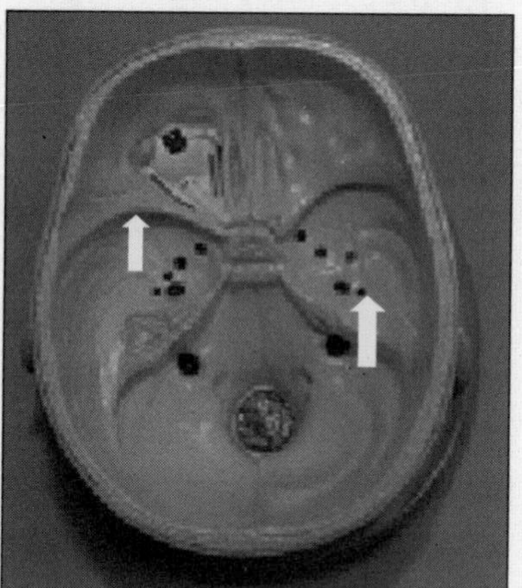

(The thick arrow points to the temporal fossa, where temporal lobe sits; the thin arrow points to the sharp wing of the sphenoid bone.)

injuries. In my clinic we will ask you five times whether or not you ever had a head injury. (It amazes us how often people forget they have had head injuries!) My intake paperwork will ask you if you've ever had a head injury. My historian, who people see before seeing me, asks this question. The structured computer testing we do asks this question. If I see that patients answer no, no, and no to this question, I'll ask them again. If they say no for the fourth time, I'll ask them, "Are you sure? Have you ever fallen out of a tree or off a fence or dived into a shallow pool?" It is not uncommon for people to say, "Oh, that's right—now I remember." One man, after saying no four times to this question, said, "Oh, yeah, I fell out of a second-story window. I forgot." Other patients, after saying no four times, have told me about falling out of cars, going through car windshields, falling off porches five feet onto their heads, falling off balconies or down staircases, etc. Your brain is very soft and your skull is very hard. Your brain is more sophisticated than any computer we can design, and you cannot just drop a computer and expect things will be okay. By virtue of their placement within the skull, the temporal lobes, prefrontal cortex, and cingulate gyrus are the most vulnerable brain areas to damage.

Jake

Jake, age 65, came to see me from Mississippi. His wife heard me on national television and she was sure he had a temporal lobe problem. He was moody and aggressive and had memory problems. Jake complained of hearing bees "buzzing" (even though no bees were around) and of having a short fuse. "The littlest things seem to set me off. Then I feel terribly guilty," he said. When Jake was fifteen years old he was in a diving accident in which he hit his head on the board and was unconscious for several minutes. After the accident he developed problems in school and with his temper. His brain SPECT study showed me that many of Jake's problems came from the poor activity in both the front and back of the left temporal lobe (a pattern frequently seen in head injuries) and in his prefrontal cortex. I placed him on Depakote (an antiseizure medication known to stabilize activity in the temporal lobes) and Adderall, along with the other Type 4 suggestions given later. When I spoke to Jake and his wife three weeks later, they were very pleased. The temper outbursts had stopped completely and he felt more focused and energetic. Six years later, his temper remains under control.

TEMPORAL LOBE PROBLEMS

Common problems seen with left temporal lobe abnormalities include aggression, dark or violent thoughts, sensitivity to slights, mild paranoia, word-finding problems, auditory processing problems, reading difficulties, and emotional instability.

The aggressiveness often seen with left temporal lobe abnormalities can be expressed externally or internally (aggressive thoughts toward oneself.) Aggressive behavior is complex, but in a large study performed in my clinic on people who had assaulted another person or damaged property, more than 70 percent had left temporal lobe abnormalities. It seems that temporal lobe damage or dysfunction makes a person more prone to irritable, angry, or violent thoughts. One patient of mine with temporal lobe dysfunction (probably inherited, as his father was a rage-a-holic) complains of frequent, intense violent thoughts. He feels shame over having these thoughts and didn't understand where they came from. "I can be walking down the street," he told me, "and someone accidentally brushes against me, and I get the thought of wanting to shoot him or club him to death. These thoughts frighten me." Thankfully, even though his SPECT confirmed left temporal lobe dysfunction, he has good prefrontal cortex function so he is able to supervise his behavior and maintain impulse control over these terrible thoughts. In a similar case, Misty, a 45-year-old woman, came to see me for anger outbursts. One day someone accidentally bumped into her in the grocery store and she started screaming at the woman, which was the reason she came to see me. "I just don't understand where my anger comes from," she said. "I've had sixteen years of therapy and it is still there. Out of the blue, I'll go off. I get the most horrid thoughts. You'd hate me if you knew." In her history, she had fallen off the top of a bunk bed when she was 4 years old. She was unconscious for only a minute or two. The front and back part of her left temporal lobe was clearly damaged. A little bit of Depakote was very helpful to calm the monster within.

Internal aggressiveness often expresses itself in suicidal behavior. In a study from our clinic, we saw left temporal lobe abnormalities in 62 percent of our patients who had serious suicidal thoughts or actions. After I gave a lecture about the brain in Oakland, a woman came up to me in tears. "Oh, Dr. Amen," she said, "I know my whole family has temporal lobe problems. My paternal great-grandfather killed himself. My father's mother and father killed themselves. My father and two of my three uncles killed themselves and last year my son tried to kill himself. Is there help for us?" I had the opportunity to evaluate and scan three members in her family. Two had left temporal lobe abnormalities and Depakote was helpful in their treatment.

In terms of suicidal behavior, one very sad case highlights the involvement of the left temporal lobes. For years I wrote a column in my local newspaper about the brain and behavior. One column was about temporal lobe dysfunction and suicidal behavior. A week or so later a mother came to see me. She told me that her twenty-year-old son had killed himself several months before and she was grief-stricken over the unbelievable turn of events in his life. "He was the most ideal child a mother could have," she said. "He did great in school. He was polite, cooperative, and a joy to have around. Then it all changed. Two years ago he had a bicycle accident. He accidentally hit a branch in the street and was flipped over the handlebars, landing on the left side his face. He was unconscious when an onlooker got to him, but shortly thereafter came to. Nothing was the same since then. He was moody, angry, easily set off. He started to complain of 'bad thoughts' in his head. I took him to see a therapist, but it didn't seem to help. One evening, I heard a loud noise out front. He had shot and killed himself on our front lawn." Her son might well have been helped if someone had recognized that his "minor head injury" had likely caused temporal lobe damage and that anticonvulsant medication may well have prevented his suicide.

In addition to aggression, we have seen people with left temporal lobe abnormalities be more sensitive to slights and even appear mildly paranoid. Unlike people with schizophrenia, who can become frankly paranoid, temporal lobe dysfunction often causes a person to think others are talking about them or laughing at them when there is no evidence for it. This sensitivity can cause serious relational and work problems.

Being able to read, integrate, and remember what you read is an essential skill in the modern-day world. Reading and language-processing problems are common when there is dysfunction in the left temporal lobe. Nearly 20 percent of the U.S. population has difficulty reading. Our studies of people with dyslexia (underachievement in reading) often show underactivity in the back half of the left temporal lobe. Dyslexia can be inherited or it can be brought about after a head injury, damaging this part of the brain.

In our experience, left temporal lobe abnormalities are more frequently associated with externally directed discomfort (such as anger, irritability, or aggressiveness), while right temporal lobe abnormalities are more likely associated with internal discomfort (anxiety and fearfulness). The left-right dichotomy has been particularly striking in our clinic population. One possible explanation is that the left hemisphere of the brain is involved with understanding and expressing language; as a result, when the left hemisphere is damaged, a person can express discomfort. When the right or nondominant hemisphere is involved, the discomfort is more likely expressed nonverbally.

Nondominant (usually right) temporal lobe problems more often involve social skill problems, especially in the area of reading and recognizing facial expressions and voice intonations. Mike, age 30, illustrates the difficulties we have seen when there is dysfunction in this part of the brain. Mike came to see me because he wanted a date. He had never had a date in his life and was very frustrated by his inability to meet and successfully ask a woman out. During the evaluation Mike said he was at a loss as to what his problem was. His mother, who accompanied him to the session, had her own ideas. "Mike," she said, "misreads situations. He has always done that. Sometimes he comes on too strong; sometimes he is withdrawn when another person is interested. He doesn't read the sound of *my* voice right either. I can be really mad at him and he doesn't take me seriously. Or he can think I'm mad when I'm nowhere near mad. When he was a little boy Mike tried to play with other children, but he could never hold on to friends. It was so painful to see him get discouraged." Mike's SPECT showed marked decreased activity in his right temporal lobe. His left temporal lobe was fine. The intervention that was most effective for Mike was intensive social skills training. He worked with a psychologist who coached him on facial expressions, voice tones, and proper social etiquette. He had his first date six months after coming to the clinic.

Abnormal activity in either or both temporal lobes can cause a wide variety of symptoms including abnormal perceptions (sensory illusions), memory problems, feelings of déjà vu (the sensation that you have been somewhere before even though you haven't), jamais vu (not recognizing familiar places), periods of panic or fear for no particular reason, periods of spaciness or confusion, and preoccupation with religious or moral issues. Illusions are also very common temporal lobe symptoms. Common illusions include:

- seeing shadows or bugs out of the corners of the eyes
- seeing objects change size or shape (One patient would see lamp posts turn into animals, which would then run away; another patient would see figures move in a painting.)
- hearing bees buzzing or static from a radio
- smelling odors or getting odd tastes in the mouth
- feeling bugs crawling on one's skin or other skin sensations.

Unexplained headaches and stomachaches also seem to be common in temporal lobe dysfunction.

Moral or religious preoccupation is a common symptom with temporal lobe dysfunction. I have a little boy in my practice who, at age 6, made himself physically sick by worrying about all of the people who were going to hell. Another patient spent seven days a week in church, praying for the souls of his family. He came to see me because of his morally indignant outbursts directed at his family. Another patient came to see me because he spent hours focused on the "mysteries of life" and could not get any work done. All of these patients had temporal lobe abnormalities.

Hypergraphia, a tendency toward compulsive and extensive writing, has also been reported in temporal lobe disorders. Some of my temporal lobe patients spend hours and hours writing. One patient, who moved to another state, used to write me twenty- and thirty-page letters, detailing all of the aspects of her life. As I learned about temporal lobe hypergraphia and had her treated with anticonvulsant medication, her letters became more coherent and concise. Many people with temporal lobe problems have the opposite of hypergraphia: They are unable to get words out of their heads. One of the therapists in my office, a wonderful public speaker, could not get the thoughts out of his head to write his book. On his scan there was decreased activity in both of his temporal lobes. On a very small dose of Depakote his ideas were unlocked and he could now write for hours at a time.

Memory problems have long been one of the hallmarks of temporal lobe dysfunction. Amnesia after a head injury is frequently due to damage to the inside aspect of the temporal lobes. Brain infections also cause severe memory problems. Harriet came to see me from New England. She was a very gracious 83-year-old woman who had lost her memory fifteen years earlier during a bout of encephalitis. Even though she remembered events before the infection, she could only remember small bits and pieces of them after the accident. An hour after she ate, she would feel full but forget what she ate. Her daughter heard me lecture in Burlington, Vermont, and told her to come see me. Harriet said, "I left my brain to the local medical school, hoping my problems would help someone else, but I don't think they'll do anything with my brain except give it to medical students to cut up. Plus, I want to know what the problem is. And write it down: I won't remember what you tell me!" Harriet's brain showed marked damage in both temporal lobes, especially on the left side, as if a virus had gone to that part of her brain and chewed it away.

Jenny

Jenny, 16, tried to kill herself the night before I first met her. Her boyfriend had just broken up with her. He told her that he was tired of the fights she started with him. She told him that she would kill herself if he left. When he started to leave, she took a knife and cut her wrist. He called the police. At that time Jenny was also having problems in school. Many of Jenny's teachers said she was not living up to her potential and that she needed to try harder. Jenny and her parents fought constantly. Whenever they asked her to do something around the house she would fly into a rage. Over the last year she had broken a window and put several holes in walls and doors.

Much was explained by the fact that at the age of 8, Jenny had fallen off her bike facefirst onto the cement. She had lost consciousness for about ten minutes. Since the accident, she had complained of headaches and vague abdominal pain. Her pediatrician told her mother that it was just stress. Jenny was also overly sensitive to perceived slights, saw shadows that were not there, had periods of anxiety with little provocation, and had trouble with reading and memory.

Jenny had Temporal Lobe ADD, one of the most difficult behavioral types of this disorder. She had trouble with inattention and impulse control. She was also conflict-seeking and underachieved in school. In addition, she had specific temporal lobe symptoms, such as headaches and abdominal pain, illusions, periods of anxiety for little reason, hypersensitivity to others, and memory and reading problems. One of the hallmarks of Temporal Lobe ADD is aggression. She had both external aggression (toward others and objects) and internal aggression (toward herself: the suicide attempt). Her brain SPECT study showed decreased activity in the prefrontal cortex (giving her trouble concentrating) and decreased activity in her left temporal lobe (probably from the head injury that predated the onset of many symptoms). I placed her on the anticonvulsant Neurontin, which stabilized her mood instability and temper, and Adderall, which helped her attention span and impulsiveness. In addition, she changed her diet and exercised every day. Six years later she remains much better. She has just finished college and has been in a stable relationship for two years.

Omar

Omar, 32, was sent to our clinic by his defense attorney after he had been arrested for felony spouse abuse. On six occasions in the last four years Omar had assaulted his wife. On the last occasion he broke her ribs and left arm. His explosions seemed to come out of the blue.

His wife said that some days he woke up "different." On certain days he had headaches and was overly sensitive, and nothing his wife did was right. All his life he had a frank expression of the core symptoms of ADD: impulsiveness, disorganization, short attention span, etc. Despite his problems, he had risen to be a top salesperson in his company and was now in a management position. Due to his explosive rage, he had attended psychotherapy and an anger management class, but it didn't make much difference. He also had seen a psychiatrist who had diagnosed him with ADD and given him Ritalin. The Ritalin made him feel speedy and irritable.

Anyone who assaults another person should have a brain scan, and Omar's case illustrates this. His SPECT study showed decreased activity in both of his temporal lobes and in the prefrontal cortex. He was placed on Neurontin and Adderall and given the dietary and exercise advice for this type. Over the next three months I adjusted his medication dosages and his temper cooled while his abil-

Omar's Concentration SPECT Study Before and After Treatment with Depakote (Underside Surface View)

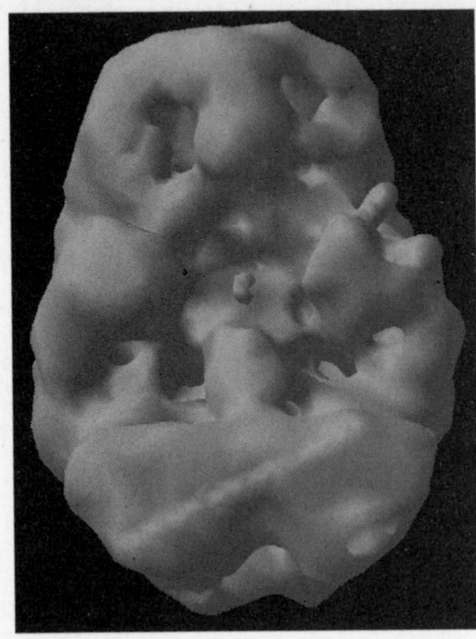

with no medication
(poor prefrontal and temporal lobe activity)

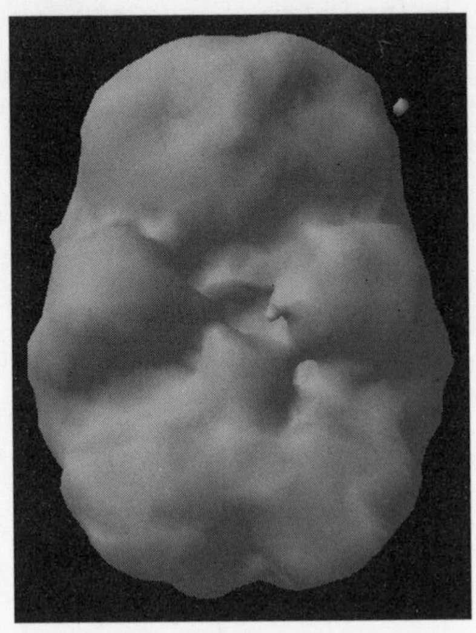

with Depakote
(marked overall improvement)

ity to focus and organize himself improved. The scans were used in his court case. As part of the plea agreement, Omar had to do community service and see a psychiatrist every month for five years. If he dropped out of treatment, he would be taken to prison.

Frequently, stimulants such as Ritalin or Adderall make this ADD type worse if they are given without anticonvulsant medication to stabilize temporal lobe function. They cause people to be irritable and sometimes more aggressive. Stabilizing the temporal lobes with anticonvulsant medications such as Depakote, Neurontin, or Tegretol can literally rescue a life from despair, hatred, and self-loathing. After the temporal lobes are treated, a stimulant medication may be very helpful for concentration.

Jacob

Since his mother was a drug addict and unable to care for him, Jacob lived with his grandparents. Jacob was exposed to drugs in utero. When I saw him at the age of 6, he was hyperactive, very impulsive, and easily distracted. Moreover, he struggled with learning and had severe temper problems. His pediatrician had diagnosed him with ADD and put him on the psychostimulant Cylert. Four days after starting the Cylert, he had visual hallucinations and became much more irritable. The pediatrician referred Jacob to me. A SPECT evaluating his temporal lobes showed drug damage still evident from his in utero exposure. It was no surprise when I saw overall decreased activity in his brain, especially in the area of the left temporal lobe. Jacob's temper improved on the anticonvulsant carbamazepine (Carbatrol). When his temporal lobes had stabilized, I started him on Adderall to help his attention span. A year later he is much better.

John

John, a 79-year-old contractor, had a long-standing history of alcohol abuse and violent behavior toward his family. Almost all of the abuse occurred when he was intoxicated. As a boy he had been described as hyperactive, slow in school, and impulsive. At age 79, John underwent open-heart surgery. After the surgery he had a psychotic episode, which lasted days. His doctor ordered a SPECT

John's Concentration SPECT Study (Left-Side Surface View)

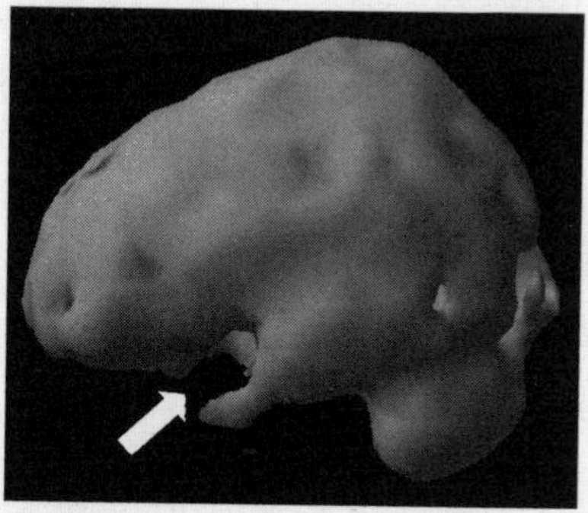

left-side surface view
(Note marked area of decreased activity in the left frontal and temporal region.)

study as part of his evaluation. The study showed marked decreased activity in the left outside frontal-temporal region, a finding most likely due to a past head injury, and decreased activity in his prefrontal cortex. When the doctor asked John if he had ever had any significant head injuries, John told him about a time when he was 20 years old. While driving an old milk truck that was missing its side rear mirror, he put his head out of the window to look behind him. His head struck a pole, knocking him unconscious for several hours. After the head injury he had more problems with his temper and memory. Despite a family history of alcohol abuse in four of his five brothers, he was the only one with aggressive behavior. He was placed on Neurontin and Adderall. His behavior was much more even and he was able to focus better than he had even when he was a child.

Neil

Neil, a 17-year-old male, was diagnosed with attention deficit/hyperactivity disorder (ADHD) and left temporal lobe dysfunction (diagnosed by EEG) at the age of 14. Before then (from grades one to eight) he had been expelled from eleven schools for fighting, frequently cut school, and had already started drinking alcohol and using marijuana. He had a dramatically positive response to 15 milligrams of methylphenidate (Ritalin) three times a day. He improved three grade levels of reading within the next year, attended school regularly, and had no aggressive outbursts. His grandmother (with whom he lived) and his teachers were very pleased with his progress. However, Neil had a negative emotional response to taking medication. He later said that taking his medication, even though it obviously helped him, made him feel stupid and different. Two years after starting his medication, he decided to stop it on his own without telling anyone. His anger began to escalate again, as did his drinking and marijuana usage. One night, while he was intoxicated, his uncle came over to his home and asked Neil to help him "rob some women." Neil went with his uncle and forced a woman into her car and made her go to her ATM and withdraw money. The uncle and Neil then raped the woman twice. He was apprehended two weeks later and charged with kidnapping, robbery, and rape.

I was asked by Neil's defense attorney to evaluate Neil. I agreed

Neil's Rest, Concentration, and Concentration with Treatment SPECT Study (Underside Surface View)

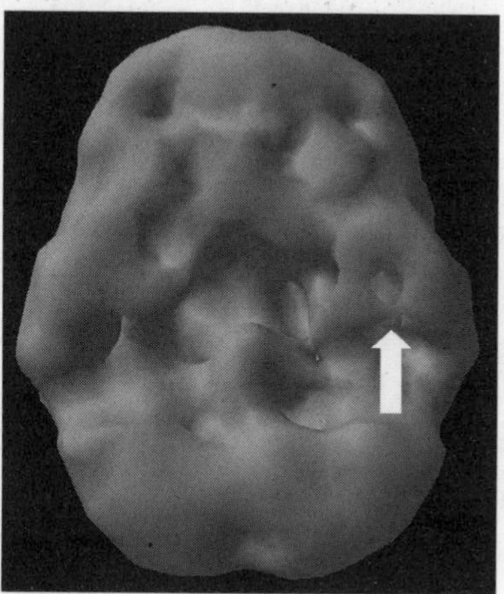

at rest
(mild decreased prefrontal cortex and left temporal lobe [arrow])

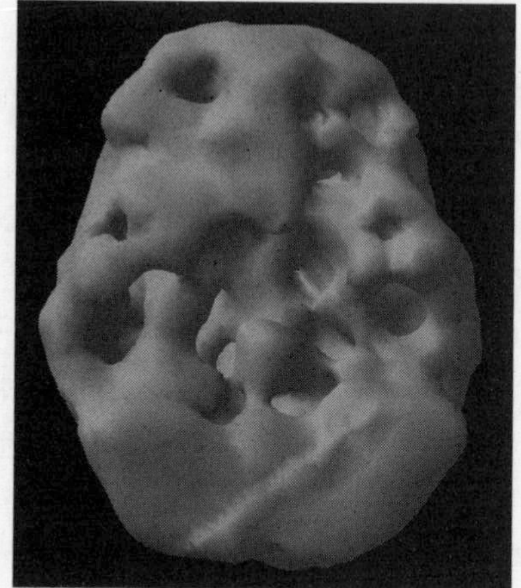

with concentration
(marked overall decreased activity)

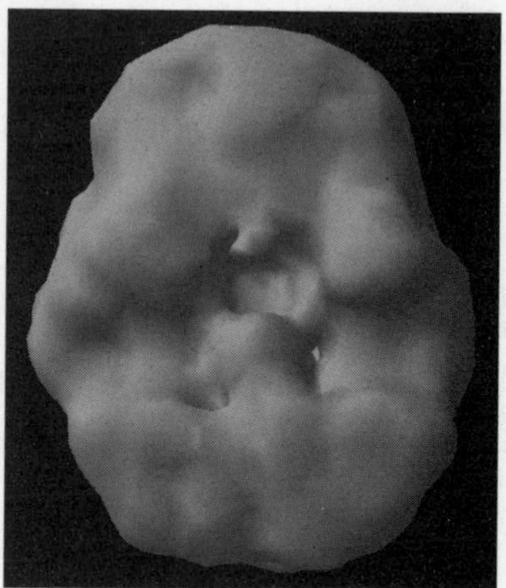

with concentration with methylphenidate
(overall improved perfusion)

with the clinical history of ADD and suspected left temporal lobe dysfunction as well because of the chronic aggressive behavior and abnormal EEG. I ordered a series of brain SPECT studies: one at rest, one while he was doing a concentration task, and one on methylphenidate. The rest of the study showed mild decreased activity in the prefrontal cortex and the left temporal lobe. While performing a concentration task, there was marked suppression of the prefrontal cortex and both temporal lobes. The third scan was done one hour after taking 15 milligrams of methylphenidate. This scan showed marked activation in the prefrontal cortex and both temporal lobes.

After understanding the history and reviewing the scan data, it was apparent that Neil already had a vulnerable brain that was consistent with long-term behavioral and academic difficulties. His substance use might have further suppressed an already underactive prefrontal cortex and temporal lobe, diminishing executive abilities and unleashing aggressive tendencies. It is possible that with an explanation of the underlying metabolic problems and brief psychotherapy on the emotional issues surrounding the need to take medication, this serious problem might have been averted. In prison he was placed on pemoline and valproic acid, and he has had no aggressive outbursts for the past two years.

DIFFERENTIATING TYPE 4 (TEMPORAL LOBE) ADD FROM TEMPORAL LOBE EPILEPSY (TLE)

It can be challenging to differentiate Type 4 (Temporal Lobe) ADD from temporal lobe epilepsy. Both disorders are due to abnormal activity in the temporal lobes and both are helped with anticonvulsant medication. Temporal lobe ADD may be a combination of a variant of temporal lobe epilepsy that is comorbid with ADD. In order for the diagnosis to be Temporal Lobe ADD, there needs to be long-standing core ADD symptoms in addition to the temporal lobe symptoms. Many people with TLE do not have ADD symptoms and so would not fall into the Temporal Lobe ADD category.

CHAPTER 9

Type 5: Limbic ADD

The sufferer has ADD core symptoms, plus:

Moodiness
Negativity
Low energy
Frequent irritability
A tendency to be socially isolated
Frequent feelings of hopelessness, helplessness, or excessive guilt
Lowered interest in things that are usually considered fun
Sleep changes (too much or too little)
Chronic low self-esteem.

Type 5 (Limbic) ADD is where ADD and depression intersect each other. The ADD core symptoms are present in addition to negativity, moodiness, sadness, low energy, and decreased interest in life. On SPECT we see decreased prefrontal cortex activity both at rest and during a concentration task, and we see too much activity in the deep limbic or emotional center of the brain. Depression looks similar on SPECT. There is decreased activity in the prefrontal cortex (especially on the left side) at rest, but unlike Limbic ADD it improves with concentration. In order to fully understand Limbic ADD, we must gain a comprehensive picture of the deep limbic system.

The deep limbic system lies near the center of the brain. Considering its size—about that of a walnut—it is packed with functions critical to human behavior and survival. From an evolutionary standpoint, this is one of the oldest parts of the mammalian brain

The Deep Limbic System

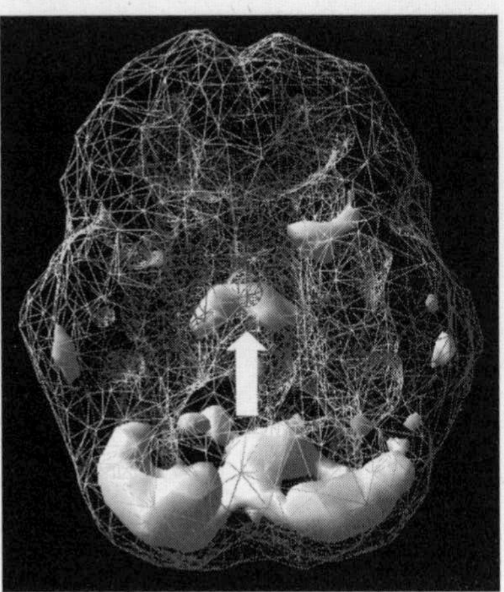

3-D underside active view

that enabled animals to experience and express emotions. It freed them from behavior and actions dictated by the brain stem, found in the older reptilian brain. The subsequent evolution of the surrounding cerebral cortex in higher animals, especially humans, gave the capacity for problem solving, planning, organization, and rational thought. Yet, in order for these functions to occur, one must have passion, emotion, and the desire to make it happen. The deep limbic system adds the emotional spice, if you will, in both positive and negative ways.

This part of the brain is involved in setting a person's emotional tone. When the deep limbic system is less active, there is generally a positive, more hopeful state of mind. When it is heated up, or overactive, negativity takes over. This finding surprised us at first. We thought that excessive activity in the part of the brain that controlled emotion might correlate with enhanced feelings, not negative ones. But we noticed, again and again, that when this area was overactive on SPECT, it correlated with depression and negativity. It seems that when the deep limbic system is inflamed, painful emotional shading results. New research on depression from other laboratories around the world has borne this out.

By providing emotional shading, the deep limbic system provides the filter through which you interpret the events of the day. It tags or colors events, depending on your emotional state of mind. When you are sad, with an overactive deep-limbic system you are likely to interpret neutral events through a negative lens. For example, if you have a neutral or even positive conversation with someone whose deep limbic structure is overactive or "negatively set," he or she is likely to interpret the conversation in a negative way. Emotional tagging of events is more important than it seems at first: In fact, it is critical to survival. The emotional charge we give to certain events in our lives drives us to action (such as approaching a desired mate) or causes avoidance behavior (withdrawing from someone who has hurt you in the past).

The deep limbic system, along with the deep temporal lobes, has also been reported to store highly charged emotional memories, both positive and negative. If you have been traumatized by a dramatic event, such as being in a car accident or watching your house burn down, or if you have been abused by a parent or a spouse, the emotional component of the memory is stored in the deep limbic system of the brain. Likewise, if you have won the lottery, graduated magna cum laude, or watched your child's birth, those emotional memories are stored here as well. The total experience of our emotional memories is responsible, in part, for the emotional tone of our mind. The more our experience is on balance stable and positive, the more positive we are likely to feel. The more trauma in our lives, the more emotionally set we become in a negative way. These emotional memories are intimately involved in the emotional tagging that occurs.

The deep limbic system also affects motivation and drive. Hyperactivity in this area is associated with lowered motivation and decreased drive, which is often seen in depression. The deep limbic system, especially the hypothalamus, controls the sleep and appetite cycles of the body. Healthy sleep and appetite is essential to maintaining a proper internal milieu, and both of these components are often a problem with limbic abnormalities.

The deep limbic structures are also intimately involved with bonding and social connectedness. When the deep limbic system of animals is damaged, they do not properly bond with their young. For example, mother rats with damaged deep limbic structures will drag their offspring around the cage as if they were inanimate objects. They would not feed and nurture the young as they would normally do. In people, this system affects the bonding mechanism that enables you to connect with others on a social level. As anyone who has ever moved to a new and unfamiliar place can attest, your ability to do this successfully in turn influences your moods.

The deep limbic system directly processes the sense of smell, the only sense that has so direct a connection. (The messages from all the other senses are sent to a "relay station," the thalamus, before they are sent to their final destinations in different parts of the brain.) Considering this, it is easy to see why smells can have such a powerful impact on our feeling states.

Research has demonstrated that females, on average, have a larger deep limbic system than males. This gives females several advantages and disadvantages. Due to their larger deep limbic brains, women are more in touch with their feelings and are generally better able to express their feelings than men. They have an increased ability to bond and be connected to others (which is why women are the primary caretakers of children: There is no society on earth in which men are the children's primary caretakers). Females have a more acute sense of smell, which is likely to have developed from an evolutionary need for the mother to recognize her young. Having a larger deep limbic system leaves a female somewhat more susceptible to depression, especially at times of significant hormonal changes such as the onset of puberty, before menses, after the birth of a child, and at menopause.

The deep limbic system, especially the hypothalamus at the base of the brain, is responsible for translating our prevailing emotional state into physical feelings of relaxation or tension. The front half of the hypothalamus sends calming signals to the body through the parasympathetic nervous system. The back half of the hypothalamus sends stimulating or fear signals to the body through the sympathetic nervous system. The back half of the hypothalamus, when stimulated, is responsible for the fight-or-flight response. The deep limbic system and the prefrontal cortex have an intimate connection, serving as a switching station between emotion and rational thought. This allows us to integrate both rational and emotional information into our decision making. Without this integration, we'd be creatures of pure logic or pure emotion—and hamstrung either way.

DEPRESSION VERSUS LIMBIC ADD

Due to the similarities between the two conditions, it can be hard to distinguish between depression and Limbic ADD: After all, both diseases demonstrate similar symptoms and even somewhat similar SPECT results. Developmental history seems to be the most helpful tool in helping clinicians decide. Depression tends to be a cyclic illness. It may be associated with some of the core symptoms of ADD, but not in an ongoing developmental pattern. The cognitive symptoms (core ADD symptoms) are only present when the depression is present. By contrast, in ADD one can see symptoms for a prolonged period of time, often back to childhood.

There are subtle SPECT differences. Depression is seen on SPECT as decreased activity in the left prefrontal cortex *at rest* correlated with increased limbic activity. When a depressed person tries to concentrate, however, activity in the prefrontal cortex usually increases. Limbic ADD, on the other hand, tends to show decreased prefrontal cortex activity *during concentration* in conjunction with increased limbic activity

Barry

Barry, 70, came to my clinic for help with a short attention span, poor memory, decreased energy, terrible disorganization, and trouble finishing projects. Barry also complained of problems sleeping, frequent negative thoughts, excessive guilt, and a tendency to isolate himself. His doctor felt that he was depressed, but the antidepressants Prozac and Zoloft only made him feel worse. His great-grandson had just been diagnosed with attention deficit disorder and got significant benefit from treatment. Barry's great-grandson reminded Barry of himself when he was a little boy. Maybe there was still time for him to get help. . . .

Barry had symptoms consistent with limbic ADD. His brain SPECT study showed the characteristic decreased activity in the prefrontal cortex plus increased activity in the limbic system. Barry needed supplements of DL-phenylalanine and L-tyrosine, the amino acid building blocks for norepinephrine and dopamine, the two neurotransmitters implicated in this type of ADD. Within two weeks Barry noticed a significant benefit. He felt more focused, had better physical and mental energy, and was more positive and more social.

Barry's Concentration SPECT Study (Underside Active View)

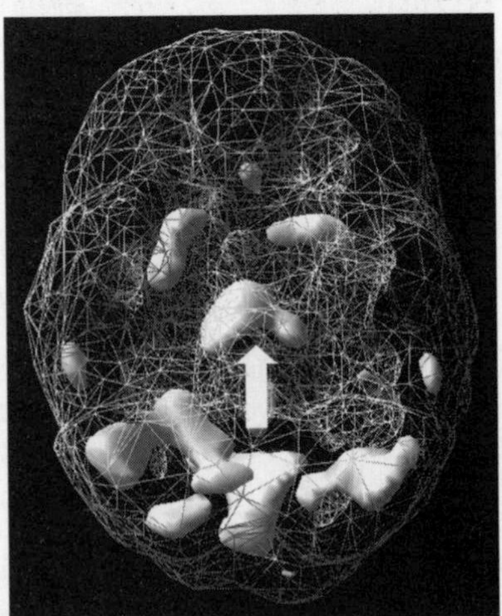

Charity

Charity was 37 when she first came to my clinic, brought in by her husband, a local minister. Both she and her husband wanted help with Charity's negativity, low energy, poor organization, irritability, and short attention span. She also had a poor appetite and trouble gaining weight. Charity was also very distractible and sensitive to touch. She cut tags out of her shirt and could only be touched by her husband when she was in the mood. Her family physician tried her on Paxil and Celexa, but they seemed to make her symptoms worse.

Charity had had struggles in school since she was a little girl. She was a quiet, sad child who tended to be in trouble for her messy room. Homework was torture for her. Her long-standing symptoms of short attention span, distractibility, disorganization, and poor follow-through were consistent with an ADD diagnosis. In addition, the symptoms of negativity, social isolation, low libido, and poor energy put the ADD into Type 4. Initially, Charity wanted to try a "more natural treatment" than prescription medication. I placed her on DL-phenylalanine and L-tyrosine along with The Zone Diet and intense aerobic exercise. Within several weeks Charity felt much improved. Her appetite was better, she was able to gain a few pounds, and she felt more focused and less distracted. Her husband said she was like a new person. Her libido also improved.

Doug

Seventeen-year-old Doug was brought to our clinic by his parents. He was failing in school, despite his high intelligence. Even before his appointment he started to talk about feeling hopeless and suicidal. He was socially isolated, didn't find pleasure in activities other teens enjoyed, and had negative thought patterns. He smoked marijuana as a way to feel more relaxed and less depressed. He had always struggled in school with a short attention span and distractibility, and he was, as he put it, "the master of procrastination." He had been seen in psychotherapy and had had tutors through the years, but these interventions did not make much difference. The family doctor put Doug on Prozac, but it only made him less motivated.

Seeing the situation as serious, I ordered a SPECT series. Doug had decreased prefrontal cortex activity at rest that worsened with concentration, increased deep limbic activity, and decreased activity in the back half of the temporal lobes, a finding common among marijuana users. I showed Doug his scan and encouraged him to stay away from the marijuana as it was probably damaging his brain. I told him the damage would probably get much better if he stopped. In addition, I put him on Wellbutrin to stabilize his mood, plus a small dose of Adderall to help him with energy and focus, and encouraged him to change his diet and get more exercise.

Within two months Doug was feeling much better. He was less negative and more optimistic, focused, and positive about school. He decided to take the California High School Proficiency Examination for his high school equivalency diploma. By the age of 20 he earned his A.A. degree and is now attending a California university.

Doug's case is not unusual. Many people use illegal drugs as a form of self-medication. They have an underlying mood disorder, some type of ADD or anxiety disorder, and use drugs as a means to feel better, more normal. Without proper treatment it is very hard for them to give up the substance abuse.

Stacey

At the age of 15, Stacey was failing school. She had two D's, two F's, and a C. She had been cutting classes, smoking cigarettes, and arguing with her parents. To make matters worse, she had recently become sexually active and had just had an abortion before she came for an evaluation at the clinic. Despite being a bright child, she had always struggled in school. Homework took forever to do, and she frequently did not turn it in. She had poor handwriting and was easily distracted, impulsive, and disorganized. As time went on, she was becoming more negative, irritable, and isolated.

After a full evaluation it was clear to me that Stacey had Limbic

Stacey's Concentration SPECT Study (Underside Active View)

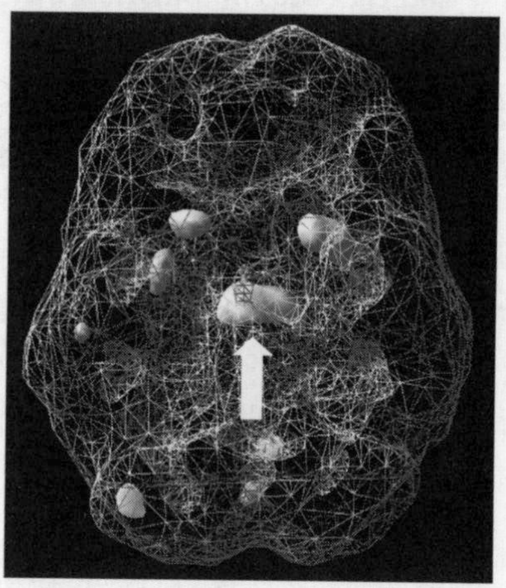

ADD. A SPECT study confirmed the diagnosis. Initially, I tried her on a purely supplemental approach: DL-phenylalanine and L-tyrosine. They were not effective. But she did have a nice response to Wellbutrin, a stimulating antidepressant. Within two weeks her mood brightened, her attention span improved, and she even stopped smoking. (Wellbutrin has been approved by the FDA to help people stop smoking.)

Sonny

Thirty-eight-year-old Sonny was brought to see me by her husband. Frequently overwhelmed, irritable, and negative, she had trouble keeping up with her work at home and constantly complained of being tired. She had a very poor appetite and did not sleep well. She had little interest in sex and was growing ever more distant from her husband and family. She had barely graduated from high school. She tended to fall asleep whenever she read. Her husband had read about ADD and found our clinic on the Web. She took our interactive ADD test on the Web and found it was likely that she had Limbic ADD. After evaluating her, I agreed. I gave her the options of antidepressant medication or the amino acid supplements. We started with the supplements and a diet and exercise regimen. After three weeks she said that the combination was very helpful for her. She could tell within half an hour if she cheated on the diet. She said, "It's amazing to me that food is as powerful as a drug. When I eat right I feel good. When I don't eat right I feel bad." Her libido improved, as she felt better emotionally and physically.

Limbic ADD is often responsible for failed marriages. The low sexual interest, tiredness, feelings of being constantly overwhelmed, and lack of attention to detail often cause marital conflict. Treating Limbic ADD can literally save families and change a person's life.

CHAPTER 10

Type 6: "Ring of Fire" ADD

The sufferer has ADD core symptoms, plus:

Is angry or aggressive

Is sensitive to noise, light, clothes, or touch

Has frequent or cyclic mood changes (highs and lows)

Is inflexible, or rigid in thinking

Insists on having his or her own way, even when told no multiple times

Has periods of mean, nasty, or insensitive behavior

Has periods of excessive talkativeness

Has periods of excessive impulsivity

Exhibits unpredictable behavior

Displays grandiose or "larger than life" thinking

Talks fast

Has the sensation that thoughts go fast

Appears anxious or fearful.

Ring of Fire" ADD gets its name from the physiology underlying the disease as seen on SPECT scans. Rather than having the typical underactive prefrontal cortex activity that is seen in Type 1 and Type 2 ADD, these patients have brains that are on balance hyperactive and disinhibited. People with "Ring of Fire" ADD have too much brain activity across the whole cerebral cortex, especially in the cingulate gyrus, parietal lobes, temporal lobes, and prefrontal cortex. In a brain scan it looks like a ring of hyperactivity around the brain. At The Amen Clinic we look at the 3-D active scans in blue (average activity) and red (the most active). In this type of ADD the ring of red reminded me of a band of fire surrounding the brain—fire that burns the person within and anyone with whom he comes into contact.

Jared

Jared was diagnosed with ADD at the age of 8. He was hyperactive, restless, impulsive, hyperverbal, moody, and oppositional. His parents brought him to the pediatrician on the recommendation of the teacher. In succession, he was tried on three stimulant medications (Ritalin, Dexedrine, and Cylert), but they all made him worse: Each made him more moody, irritable, and talkative. His parents stopped the medication and refused to bring him back for help. Every bad thing that happens to untreated ADD children happened to Jared. He dropped out of school in ninth grade. He started using drugs and alcohol at age 14. His parents threw him out of the house at age 16 because of his temper and drug use. He had trouble with the law. Drinking alcohol often sparked fits of violence, even though he said the alcohol made him feel better. From the ages of 18 to 20 he was arrested ten times for violent behavior, all when he was intoxicated. It wasn't until Jared was arrested for armed robbery that he came to my clinic.

On the night of the last crime Jared started drinking at about 10:00 P.M. He drank a fifth of peach schnapps chased by 40 ounces of malt liquor. He then raced a friend down the freeway, crashing his car and fleeing the scene on foot. A short while later he flagged down a cab driver. At exactly 12:10 A.M. he pointed a loaded gun at the cab driver's head and demanded all his money. He got $25. The next morning, after sobering up, he turned himself in to the police.

Jared's defense attorney called me to discuss the case. He wondered if the ADD diagnosis would help his defense. I said I didn't think it would help but wondered why, if Jared really had ADD, the stimulants made him worse and why he continued to drink despite all of the terrible problems it caused him. Since he seemed to be aggressive only when he drank, I decided to scan him both sober and drunk.

The first SPECT study was performed when Jared was clean and sober. The second study was performed after he consumed a fifth of peach schnapps, followed by 40 ounces of malt liquor (the same brands he had drunk on his last night of crime). The sober study revealed marked overactivity in the "Ring of Fire" pattern (hot zones in the cingulate gyrus, the right and left lateral prefrontal cortices, the right and left parietal lobes, and the left and right temporal lobes). These findings are often associated with anxiety, cyclic mood tendencies, and irritability.

For the alcohol study, Jared's blood alcohol level was 0.2g/dl(%)—double what is legally drunk in most states. This study showed an overall dampening effect on the hyperactive areas of the brain (prefrontal, parietal, and temporal lobes), with only the cingulate gyrus showing excessive activity, although significantly less activity than in the nonalcohol study. In addition, the right and left prefrontal cortex was now significantly underactive, as were the left and right temporal lobes.

Given Jared's marked brain hyperactivity in a sober state, along with his report that he felt more relaxed when he drank, it was not unreasonable to assume that he may have been using alcohol as a way to self-medicate—a way to settle down his brain and feel more comfortable. Unfortunately, by self-medicating, he was inducing his brain to violence. The intoxicated pattern in his brain—increased anterior cingulate activity, abnormal left temporal lobe activity, and decreased prefrontal cortex activity—is the triad of symptoms that have been found in violent patients. In trying to ease the underlying abnormalities in his brain, he drank himself into a violent state.

Jarred is a textbook example of "Ring of Fire" ADD. He had all the hallmark symptoms, including irritability, hyperactivity, excessive talking, overfocus, extreme oppositional behavior, and cyclic periods of calm alternating with intense aggressiveness.

Psychostimulant medication, such as Ritalin, frequently makes "Ring of Fire" ADD patients more worried, more irritable, and more negative. "Ring of Fire" ADD is often helped with either anticonvulsant medication or new antipsychotic medications such as Risperdal or Zyprexa. A high-protein, low-carbohydrate diet is often helpful as well. The amino acid GABA often has an overall

Jared's SPECT Series off and on Alcohol (The top four images are 3-D active views: Notice that the "Ring of Fire" is calmed by alcohol. The bottom two images are 3-D surface views: Notice that alcohol crashes brain activity, especially in the prefrontal cortex and temporal lobes.)

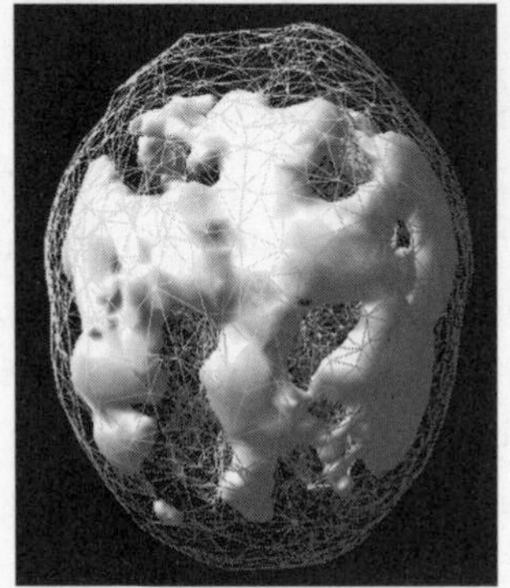

no alcohol, *top-down view*

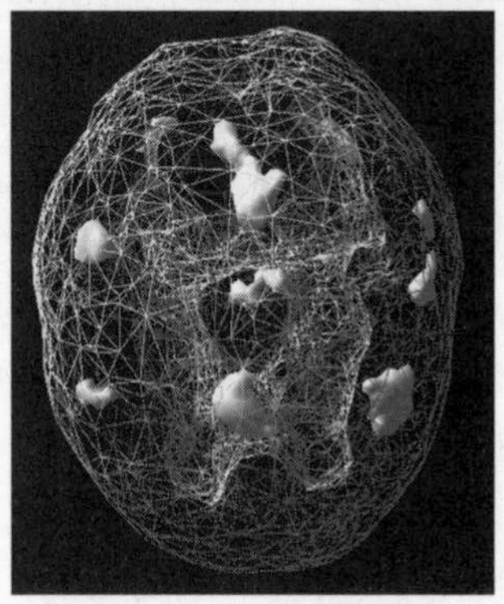

intoxicated, *top-down view*

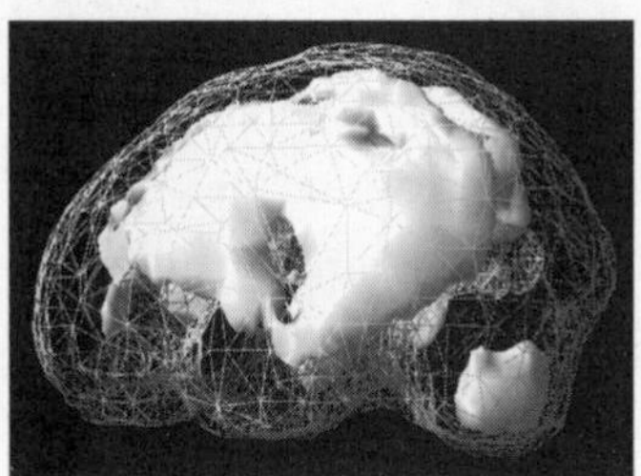

no alcohol, *left-side view*

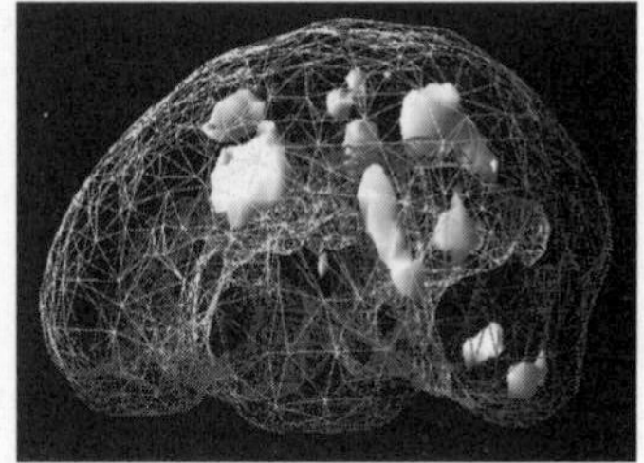

intoxicated, *left-side view*

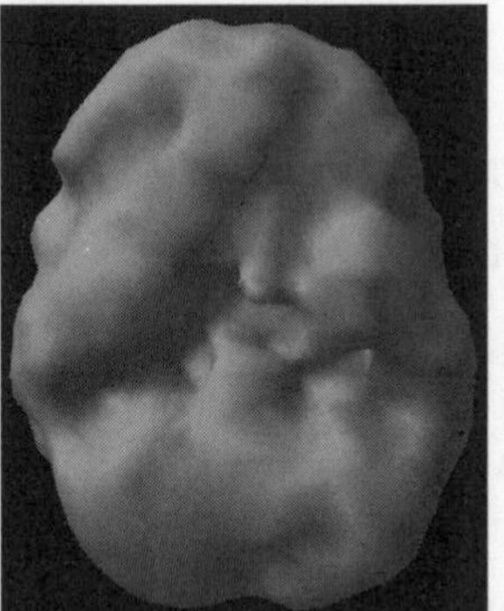

no alcohol, *undersurface view*

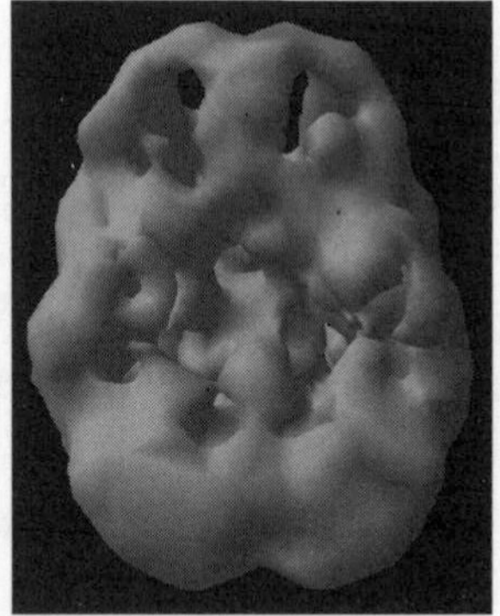

intoxicated, *undersurface view*

calming effect on the cortical hyperactivity. St. John's wort and SSRI antidepressants such as Prozac or Zoloft (medications that increase serotonin) often make this type much worse.

In looking at the SPECT scans for this pattern, we see a number of abnormalities that seem to explain the symptoms. "Hyperfrontality," a term for the combined findings of increased anterior cingulate activity and increased left and right lateral prefrontal cortex activity, is associated with severe overfocused symptoms, such as worrying, obsessiveness, oppositional behavior, and cognitive inflexibility. Distractibility and hypersensitivity to the environment (extreme sensitivity to sound, touch, taste, smells, and sights) are marked by *increased parietal lobe activity.* The parietal lobes contain the brain's sensory cortex, which when overactive causes a person to be hypersensitive to incoming information. *Increased lateral temporal lobe activity* often causes problems with mood instability and rages. In many ways, the "Ring of Fire" is every type of ADD rolled into one! This is the most intense ADD type.

Casey

Casey was described by his teacher as a sweet, endearing boy who tries very hard and always does his best. She also said that even though he does worry too much and gets upset if he makes a mistake, he works with enthusiasm and is a super student.

That's when he is on his medication. Without it he is a horror to be around. Unmedicated, Casey is cruel, combative, angry, and obnoxious. He has temper tantrums and is violent. He has difficulty following rules set by his teacher and will often argue with her or just refuse to obey instructions. At home it's just as bad. He is afraid of new situations and usually reacts to change by covering his ears to block out the new experience. At The Amen Clinic he was so paralyzed, he couldn't even flush the toilet. He has difficulty following instructions that his mother gives. Casey often replies to an order by saying things like "I hate you," "I wish you were dead," and "I want to kill you." Occasionally he dispenses with words entirely, choosing instead to lash out with his fists.

Casey's Concentration SPECT Study (Top-Down Active View)

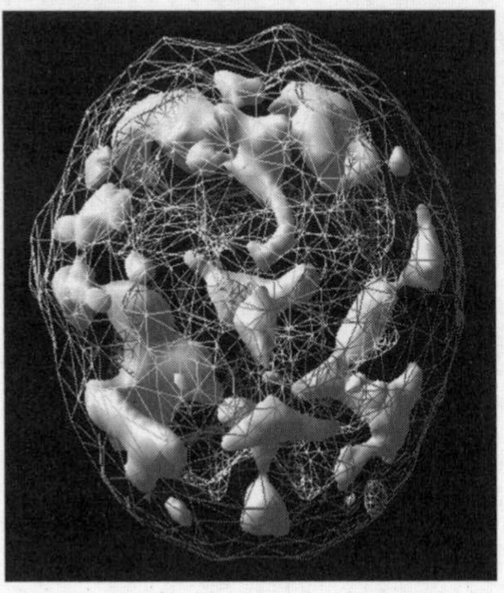

There was no question that Casey needed a SPECT scan as part of his evaluation. The scan showed an overactive brain with increased activity in both prefrontal cortex, both parietal lobes, and the anterior cingulate gyrus. Casey needed Risperdal (a new, novel antipsychotic medication that we have found to be helpful for this pattern) to tame the "Ring of Fire" and then Ritalin to treat the underlying core ADD symptoms. Ritalin by itself had made Casey worse, but in combination with a full treatment program, it helped Casey become who he *really* is. The changes in his behavior while on the medications have been vast. The effects of treatment were best summed up by his fourth-grade teacher when she said, "This year I have only seen two incidents of misbehavior and both times were days he had missed his medication."

Ronny

Ronny was 9 years old when his mother brought him to The Amen Clinic. His mother first sensed that something was wrong when, at ten months old, he would begin screaming for no apparent reason. Throughout kindergarten he often hid in the cupboards. Even when he wasn't in a cupboard, he refused to participate in class. From the second grade on, he would experiment sexually with several boys. He became obsessed with sex. As Ronny grew up, he became increasingly oppositional and would scream and throw temper tantrums when asked to do something. Right before his initial evaluation his behaviors became even more worrisome. He threatened to kill himself when his mother tried to take a knife away from him. Ronny's SPECT study showed the "Ring of Fire" pattern. Before Ronny came to the clinic, he had been on Ritalin, which had made him more irritable and aggressive. Seeing his scan, the doctor in my clinic put him on Depakote (an anticonvulsant medication often helpful with the "Ring of Fire" pattern). After some improvement in his behavior, we did a second SPECT study. His second study, performed on Depakote, was calmer overall, but his prefrontal cortex was underactive. Once Adderall was added to his regimen, he was better able to focus. On his current medication his mood is much better, he has a more even temper, and he is less distractible. His oppositional behavior has diminished, and through parent training, exercise, and dietary interventions he continues to improve.

Ronny's Concentration SPECT Study (Top-Down Active View)

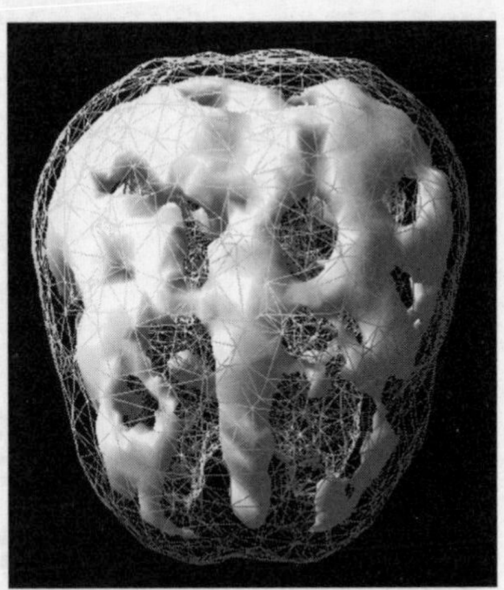

Guy

Nineteen-year-old Guy came to the clinic because he was having problems controlling his temper. He has always had a bad temper and was constantly getting into fights, but they were just that: minor fistfights. That all changed ten months before he first came to The Amen Clinic. He got in a fight with someone from a gang. In that fight he took several blows to the head from a pair of numchucks and went to the hospital with a concussion. While he was in the ER of the hospital he got into *another* fight, this time with a police officer, and was once again hit in the head several times, this time with a mag flashlight. Since the incidents of that night ten months before he came to the Clinic, Guy has even less control over his temper, especially around figures of authority. He had always taken umbrage at authority figures, but now he had no control over his temper around them. "He also experienced an increase in dark thoughts. When angry, his impulses have turned homicidal. This disturbed Guy, who said, "I definitely don't want to hurt anybody or take someone's life, but my thoughts say something different. I just don't understand my own brain anymore." At about the same time Guy began to think about suicide. He even knew how he

Guy's Concentration SPECT Study (Top-Down Active View)

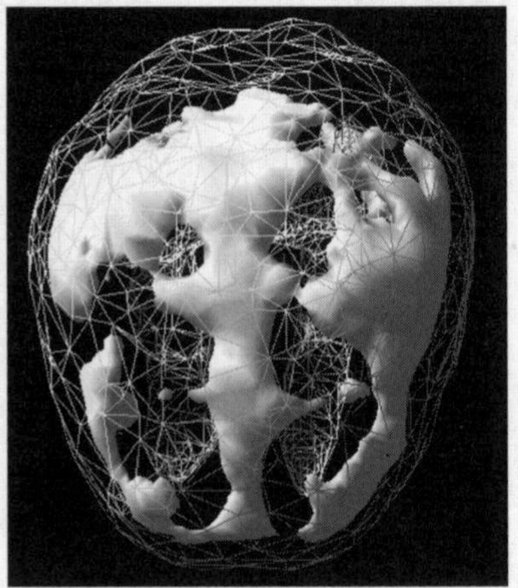

would do it: with a shotgun "to make sure it was over." He didn't think he'd ever try to kill himself, but the thought hadn't even crossed his mind until his head trauma ten months earlier. His relationships with the people in his life also changed. He would cut people out of his life on a whim: "My way or the highway," he said.

Guy has a new son, and that's what brought him to The Amen Clinic. His scan showed the "Ring of Fire" pattern. With a combination of medication (an anticonvulsant, Neurontin, and a stimulating antidepressant, Effexor), diet, therapy, and exercise, he has improved greatly. He is less depressed and has control over his temper, and his attention span has improved.

THE PARIETAL LOBES

One brain system not discussed yet is the parietal lobes, located toward the back top of the brain. Also called the sensory cortex, the parietal lobes process the sense of touch. When this part of the brain is too active, as is often the case in "Ring of Fire" ADD (and to a lesser extent the other types as well), people become hypersensitive to their environment: They tend to see too much, feel too much, and sense too much. Distractibility is especially heightened in these patients.

DIFFERENTIATING TYPE 6 ("RING OF FIRE") ADD FROM BIPOLAR DISORDER

Child psychiatrist Thomas Jaeger from Creighton University in Omaha, Nebraska, has also done pioneering work with brain SPECT imaging. Early in his work he noticed that children and teenagers with bipolar disorder (what used to be known as manic-depressive illness) had a patchy pattern of increased activity across the cortical surface of the brain. Below is an image of a bipolar patient during a manic episode. Manic episodes are characterized by a cluster of the following symptoms: inflated self-esteem, hyperactive behavior, fleeting attention span, extreme impulsivity (such as in sexual matters or by foolish spending), increased energy, decreased need for sleep, and oftentimes psychotic thinking. "Ring of Fire" ADD is very similar to this in both its symptoms and brain pattern. However, patients with bipolar disorder do not have the underlying core symptoms of ADD. In addition, their symptoms appear and disappear in a cyclic fashion. If the core ADD symptoms are present over a prolonged period of time, "Ring of Fire" ADD must be suspected. Frequently we see both patterns. The ADD core symptoms are present over time, but the mood problems occur in a cycle. Some doctors would argue that there are really two separate conditions at work: both ADD and bipolar disorder. We see the "Ring of Fire" pattern so commonly in our ADD patients that we feel it is a distinct ADD type and are comfortable describing it as a discrete disorder.

Differentiating "Ring of Fire" ADD from bipolar disorder is generally difficult in children and easy in adults. In children bipolar disorder resembles severe ADD. Bipolar children tend to be cyclic in their mood and behavior problems. They have times when they are awful, irritable, and aggressive, and they have times when

Bipolar Brain

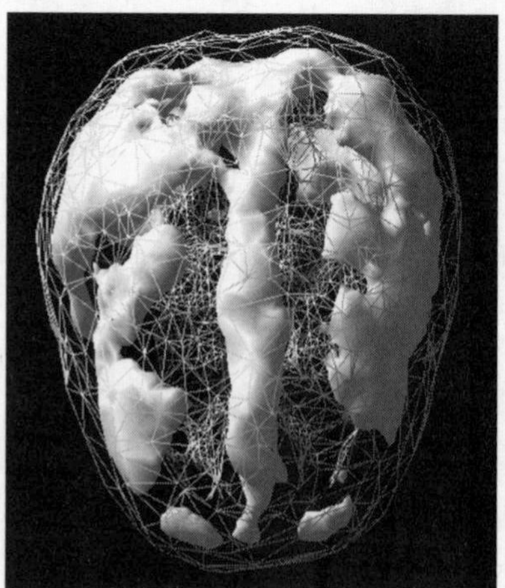

3-D top-down active view

things are relatively normal. "Ring of Fire" ADD kids tend to have problems on a more consistent basis. Adults with bipolar disorder have manic episodes, while people with "Ring of Fire" ADD do not. Their behavior tends to be consistent over long periods of time. One can have both "Ring of Fire" ADD and bipolar disorder, and some studies suggest that as many as half of the people with bipolar disorder also meet the criteria for ADD.

CHAPTER 11

Soft Brain, Hard Skull

Head-Trauma–Induced ADD

One of the most common causes of ADD outside of genetics is head trauma, especially to the left prefrontal cortex. Our brain-imaging work has taught us that head injuries are more important than most physicians have previously believed. SPECT shows areas of damage not seen in anatomy studies like CAT scans or MRI. With SPECT we can see contra-coup injuries (opposite parts of the brain damaged by the same injury) and old injuries (even damage from birth or forceps deliveries). Why are head injuries so important? Some basic brain facts will clear that up.

- *Your brain is involved with everything you do.* How you think. How you feel. How you act. And how well you get along with other people. How your brain works is intimately involved with determining the kind of person you are.
- *Your brain is very complex.* Did you know you have 100 billion nerve cells, or neurons? Every one of your neurons is connected to hundreds and even thousands of other neurons. You have more connections in your brain than there are stars in the universe. Your brain is more intricate, delicate, and complicated than any computer that we can imagine.

- *Your brain is soft.* It is similar in consistency to soft butter or a raw egg. When I was a little boy working in my father's grocery store, I used to see cow brains in little white cups. The cow brains, like human brains, were so soft that they took on the shape of the cup.
- *Your skull is hard.* Inside your skull there are many ridges, rough areas, and sharp, bony ridges.
- *Your brain is in a closed space.* When you experience a blow to the head, there is no place for the brain to go. It ends up slamming against the walls, ridges, and sharp, bony edges of your skull, ripping small blood vessels, causing micro-hemorrhaging (bleeding) and, over time, small areas of scar tissue.
- *Consciousness is controlled by structures deep in the brainstem.* The brain stem may not be injured in a head trauma, but there may be a significant injury to the cortex or surface of the brain, with no loss of consciousness.

Our experience with ADD tells us that when the left prefrontal cortex is injured, people have more ADD-like symptoms. The injuries can be from any cause: a damaging forceps delivery; a fall down a couple of stairs or off a bicycle, head-banging as a child; a blow during a fight, a rape, or a robbery; or a motor vehicle accident. Because of higher levels of activity and impulsivity, people with ADD have more head injuries, which may make it hard to determine the original cause of the problematic symptoms.

Frequently patients and their parents forget about head injuries, even though they might have been very significant. We will ask a patient five times whether or not they have had a head injury.

Due to its location, the prefrontal cortex and temporal lobes are especially susceptible to head injuries. Many people do not fully understand how head injuries—sometimes even "minor" ones, in which no loss of consciousness occurs—can alter a person's character and ability to learn. We see head injuries so often on the SPECT studies we order in our ADD patients that we are tempted to add a seventh type of ADD: Head Injury ADD. Post–head injury symptoms often consist of attention problems, memory difficulties, and decreased energy and motivation. In head injury–induced ADD, the symptoms follow a significant head injury and frequently look like one of the types of ADD. If the injury just affected the prefrontal cortex, it can look like Type 1 or Type 2. If the injury affected the prefrontal cortex and temporal lobes (common because of the location of the temporal lobes) it can look like Type 4. If the injury damaged the anterior cingulate gyrus, it can look like Type 3. The treatment depends on the clinical picture. We have seen anticonvulsants help to stabilize temporal lobe symptoms and stimulants help prefrontal cortex symptoms.

Brain damage from a head injury has a number of causes. After a head injury, blood vessels may tear or break near the area of injury, causing bleeding, inflammation, and scarring. The blood vessel disruption decreases blood flow to an area, preventing the delivery of nutrients and the disposal of toxins. In addition, rotational and shearing effects can also occur from the force of an injury. After an injury the body's defense system goes into action. Recent studies have indicated that the immune system may release substances that are actually toxic to brain cells.

Brian

When Brian was 7 years old he rode his bike full speed into the corner of a brick column. He was wearing a helmet, but it cracked under the force of the blow. He was unconscious for about half an hour. His parents did all of the right things, including taking him to the emergency room to have a CAT scan done. The emergency-room physician just said to watch him. No one said to watch for problems in behavior or learning. After the injury, the mother noted changes, subtle at first and then more drastic. By the age of 12, Brian was moody, emotional, irritable, and struggling in school. When he finally came for evaluation at age 16, he was almost failing in school and had just started to experiment with drugs.

Brian's SPECT study showed clear decreased activity in the left

Brian's SPECT Study (Left-Side Surface View)

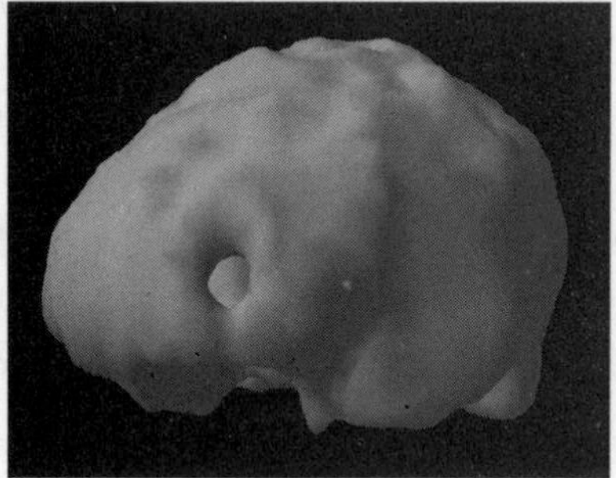

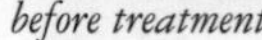

before treatment

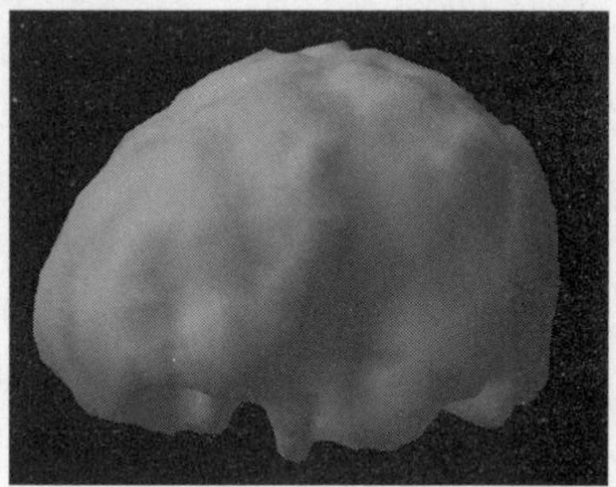

after treatment

lateral prefrontal cortex, underneath the scar from the bicycle accident. His treatment plan included a small dose of Adderall and brainwave biofeedback over his left prefrontal cortex. The biofeedback was so effective that within eight months he was able to perform in school and at home at a high level without the medication.

Danielle

Danielle, age 9, was a sweet, loving child who was doing well in third grade and getting along well with other children. Over Christmas break, while going with her older brother to a family party, she was in a car accident. Danielle had been using a seat belt; nevertheless, the left side of her head slammed against the rear side window. She was only briefly unconscious. Over about eight weeks Danielle's behavior began to change. She became negative, irritable, and oppositional. She blurted out in class and she had trouble paying attention to her work at school. Homework was a chore, where before it had been easy for her. Over the next year she lost most of her friends because she started trouble with them or said things that hurt their feelings.

A year after the accident, Danielle's mother knew that there was something seriously wrong. She brought Danielle to a counselor, who thought the problem was psychological—an emotional vestige of the accident. Her pediatrician thought Danielle was just being oppositional and recommended a tough-love approach. Reluctantly the pediatrician diagnosed her with ADD and tried Ritalin, but it didn't help very much: In fact, it only seemed to make her more moody and aggressive. By the age of 14, when she came to our clinic for evaluation, Danielle was failing in school and had many behavioral problems at home. I suspected that her problems were the result of physical damage to her brain from the accident, and her SPECT study bore that out. She showed marked decreased activity in the prefrontal cortex and temporal lobes. I placed her on a small dose of Neurontin to stabilize her temporal lobes and Adderall to help her to focus. The medication evened out her mood and improved Danielle's focusing ability, allowing her to be more successful in school and more pleasant to be around.

Wes

Wes was 54 years old when he sought help. He was depressed, suicidal, and lethargic, and had a very short attention span. His volatile temper, a problem for his whole life, had cost him two marriages and any shred of closeness with his children. Now he had just broken up with his girlfriend of two years and was facing a very lonely life. Wes told me that he had done well in school until the eleventh grade. That was the time that he was in a car accident with a teenage friend. The friend had been drinking and had lost control of the car. Wes wasn't wearing a seat belt and his head cracked the windshield. Before the accident he had been a good student with dreams of going to Stanford, but the next semester he did very poorly. He gave up the idea of going to a top-rung university, saying, "I couldn't pay attention anymore. My mind was always wandering off task." Wes had job security because he worked in his father's business, but he and his father fought constantly. His father wanted him to be on time and stay the whole day. Wes frequently took off and didn't finish the tasks assigned to him.

Wes's SPECT series was very abnormal. He had decreased activity over the vertex (top) of the brain and decreased prefrontal cortex

Wes's SPECT Series

At Rest | *With Concentration*

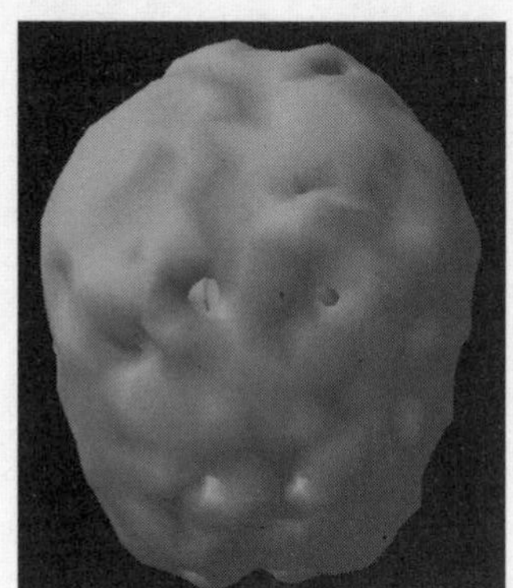

top-down

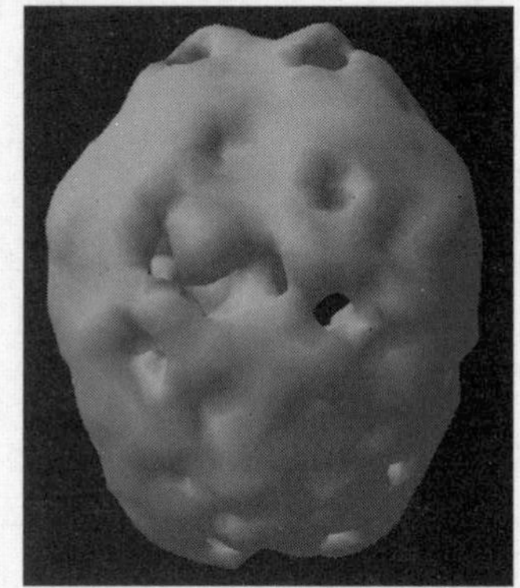

top-down

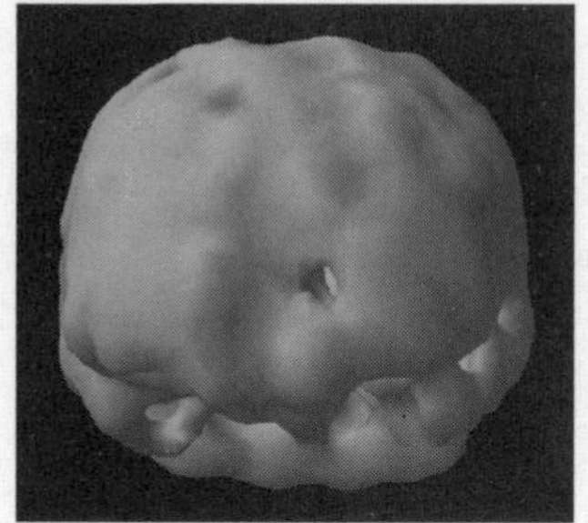

front-on

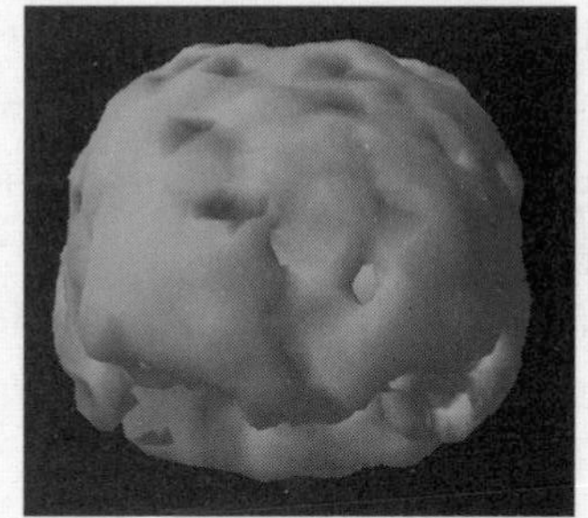

front-on

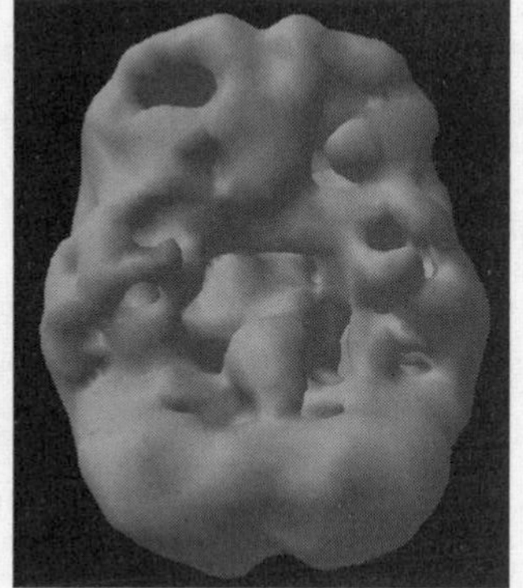

underside

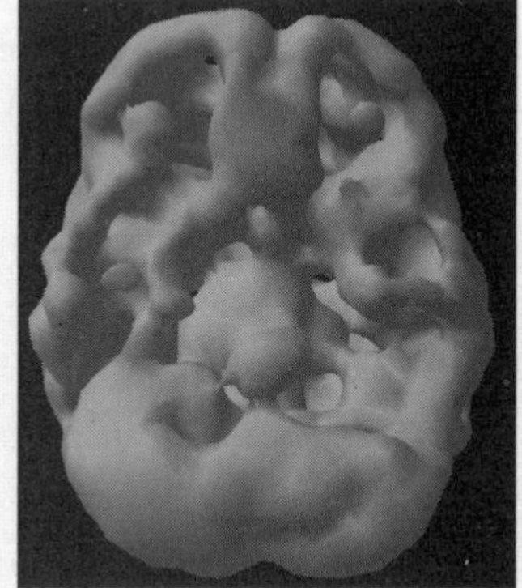

underside

and temporal lobe activity, especially on the left side of the brain. With concentration, there was further overall decreased activity. Seeing the scan helped Wes understand why he had the struggles he did. On a combination of anticonvulsant and stimulant medication and biofeedback over the left prefrontal and temporal lobe regions, his mood, temper, and attention span stabilized. His girlfriend returned when she realized he was dealing with a medical problem, as opposed to just being a difficult person.

Alecia

At the age of 22, Alecia tripped and fell facedown on a slick, rain-soaked ramp at college. She slid fifteen feet before her head struck a concrete wall. She was dazed for most of the day, nauseated for a week, and had a headache for a month. A year later she was referred to me by a therapist who had been seeing her for temper problems. She also had trouble thinking clearly and had to drop out of school. She had energy problems, problems with goal setting, and trouble organizing herself, in addition to spending money foolishly. On SPECT there was marked decreased activity in her prefrontal cortex (especially in the prefrontal pole) and temporal lobes.

Sal

Sal was referred to my clinic by his marital therapist. Sal and his wife had a relationship filled with conflict, tension, and turmoil. Sal's wife complained that he was inattentive, selfish, and incapable of expressing feelings. Sal was a marginally successful attorney who had trouble keeping clients. Like his wife, they found him aloof and seemingly uninterested.

Sal's problems began in high school. During his senior year Sal had four concussions playing football—two on the same night! Sal went to college but played football only for a year: With all the time he now had to spend studying, he just didn't have the room in his schedule. After college it took him three years to get into law school. He was persistent but not as sharp as he had been in the early years of high school.

Alecia's SPECT Study (with Concentration)

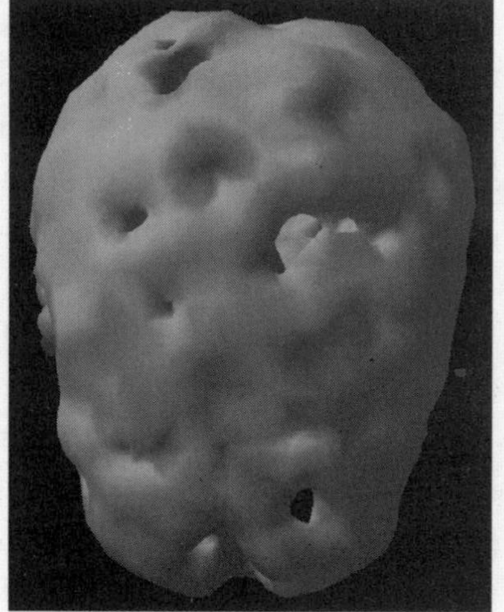

top-down

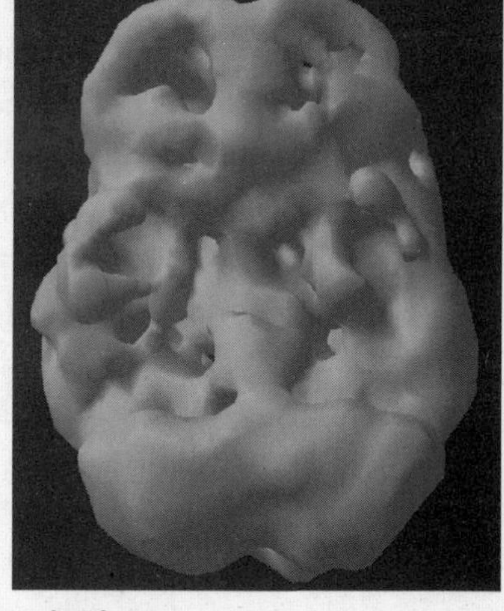

underside

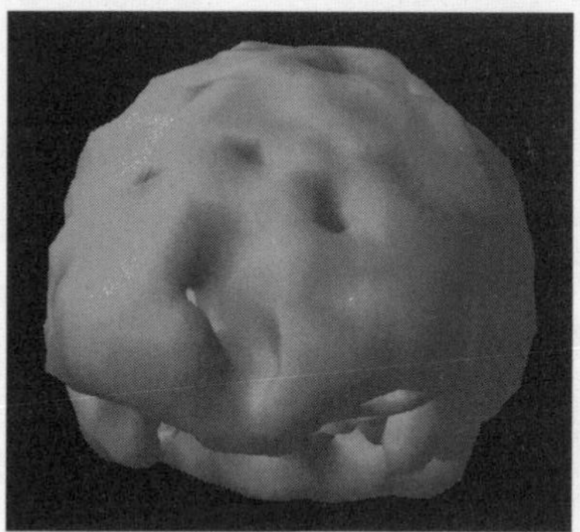

front-on

I suspected that the football head injuries were important in explaining his current symptoms. His SPECT study showed very specific damage to his left prefrontal cortex and left temporal lobe in a pattern consistent with head injury. The outside of the left prefrontal cortex (called the dorsal lateral prefrontal cortex) is the expressive language area of the brain. In Sal's case it had suffered damage and taken with it his ability for empathy and expressive language. I diagnosed him with alexythymia, a disorder in which people do not have access to their own feelings. Sal cared about his wife, but no amount of therapy helped him to express his feelings. He didn't understand feelings: When people talked about feelings, it was like a foreign language to him.

On a combination of an anticonvulsant medication and biofeedback over his left prefrontal cortex, Sal, to his wife's delight, became more expressive and more empathic.

Head injuries, depending on the areas affected, can result in different ADD types. ADD symptoms subsequent to head injuries often respond to the same treatments as do the specific ADD types. My SPECT work has taught me how devastating head injuries can be and how important it is to protect your head and the heads of children. After seeing these scans, I would not let my children hit soccer balls with their heads, play tackle football, or snowboard without a helmet. Instead, I encourage my own kids to play tennis, golf, and Ping-Pong, and to run track and row.

Sal's SPECT Study (with Concentration)

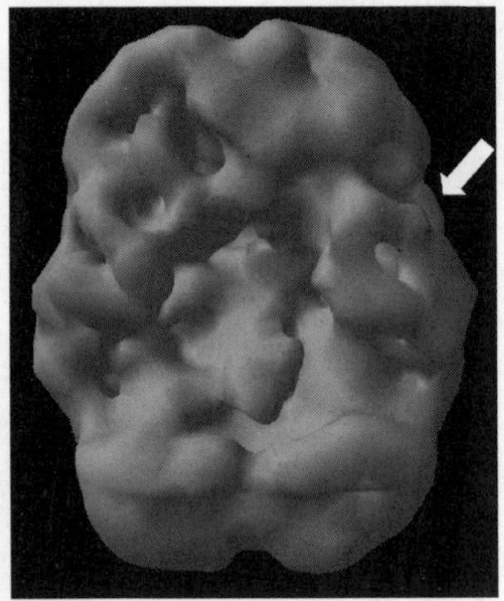

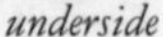

underside

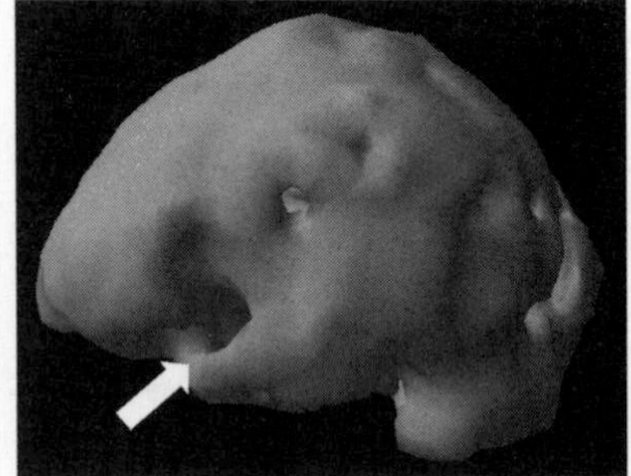

left side

CHAPTER 12

ADD in Families

SPECT Studies Across Generations

ADD is a generational disorder, meaning that ADD in a family significantly influences the development of each member. The level of influence is often determined by which parent has ADD, whether it is the father or mother. ADD mothers often have a more negative impact on children than ADD fathers. In addition, ADD influences parenting, job choices, creativity, family moves, and legal issues. Here are four examples of ADD across generations.

Celina, Samuel, and Laura

Before she came to see me, Celina, 36, had been depressed for ten years, following the birth of her first child. Her symptoms included significant irritability, crying spells, sleeplessness, and weight loss. She also had problems concentrating and she was unable to manage her two children. Her condition was brought to a crisis when she attempted suicide after separating from her husband. She was initially seen by a psychiatrist, who started her on medication for depression, but it had little effect. Then she came to see me. I treated her with psychotherapy and a different antidepressant. The treatment helped her feel more positive and less irritable, but several months later she decided that she "should be stronger than the depression" and took herself off the medication. Her depression worsened, but she was resistant to restarting her medication: "I don't want to have to rely on medication to feel well," she said.

In an effort to demonstrate to Celina that her depression was, at least in part, biological and that her medication was an important part of treatment, I ordered a brain SPECT study. The results surprised me. Celina's SPECT study revealed marked decreased frontal lobe activity and increased activity in her limbic system, which fit with her underlying depression. However, it showed striking overactivity in the anterior cingulate portion of her brain as well. As we have seen, this finding is often seen in people who tend to get stuck in negative thought or behavioral patterns.

With this information I asked her more directly about obsessive thoughts and compulsive symptoms. In fact, Celina was a perfectionist at home and had obsessive negative thoughts. She tearfully remarked, "You mean my husband was right when he said it was strange that I had to have all the shirts buttoned a certain way and put just so in the drawer."

She then told me about her 8-year-old daughter, Laura, who had inflexible rituals. Before Laura would enter a new room, she would run a finger under her nose and lick her lips. She also became obsessed with locking doors and would frequently lock her brother and sister out of the house.

Another psychiatrist was seeing Celina's 10-year-old son, Samuel, for school and behavior problems. He was diagnosed with ADD, but the stimulant medication he took had little effect on him. Samuel also had some obsessive traits: Once he got a thought in his mind, he was unable to let it go. He would follow Celina around the house for two and a half hours, asking her the same questions she had already answered.

We did a brain SPECT study on both children. They showed the same overactivity in the cingulate gyrus as their mother did. In light of their brain scans, the overfocusing tendency they all had was no surprise.

In addition to the overfocus problems, Celina deactivated her

Celina's, Laura's, and Samuel's SPECT Results (Top-Down Active View, All with Overactivity in the Anterior Cingulate Gyrus)

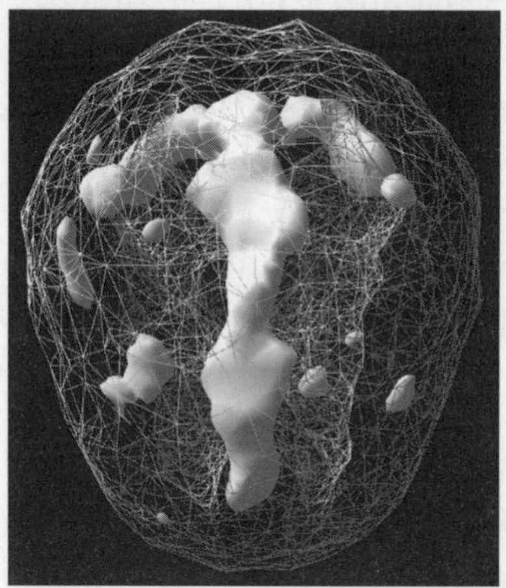

mother

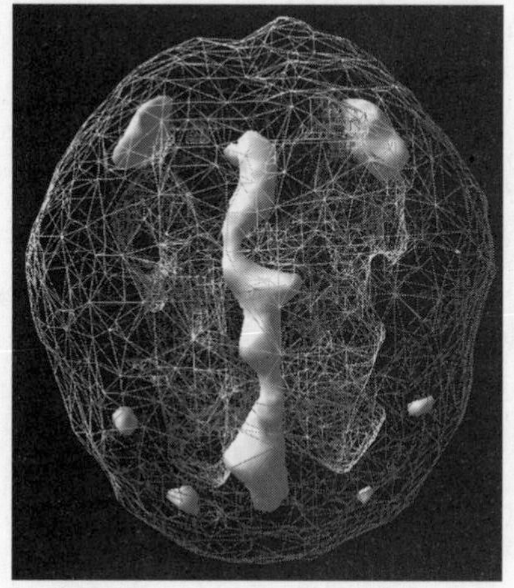

daughter

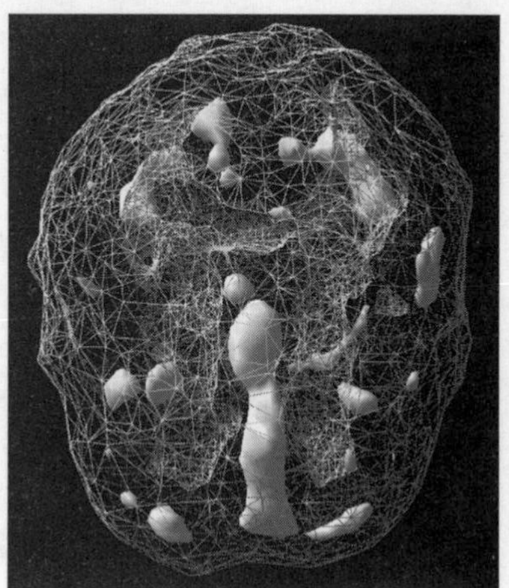

son

frontal lobes when she tried to concentrate, as did Samuel. As a result, Celina had been labeled an underachiever in school and had difficulty completing projects. Laura, on the other hand, activated her frontal lobes and did not have any school or concentration problems.

Based on this information, Celina was placed on the antidepressant Prozac to decrease her depression and obsessive and compulsive tendencies, and on Adderall to help with concentration. She had a dramatically positive response. She said that it was the first time in ten years that she felt "herself." The SPECT study further convinced her that her condition had biological underpinnings: It was not her fault or the result of a weak will. This realization allowed her to take her medication for a longer period of time.

Samuel's psychiatrist used the SPECT results to add Prozac to the stimulant medication. Within several weeks Samuel's behavior normalized and he had a remarkable improvement in school. He even made the honor roll for the first time in his life. Several months later Laura was also placed on Prozac and her ritualistic behavior markedly diminished. In this family the generational quality of ADD stands out. The mother's brain dysfunctions and depression contributed to the anxiety and behavior problems in her children, and the abnormal brain metabolism in the children added to their difficult behavior, further stressing the mother. The family dynamics improved significantly after the mother and the children were treated with the appropriate medication and psychotherapy.

When I first submitted this family's case study to a medical journal, one of the reviewers said that it was absurd for me to correlate family dynamics to brain studies. I think it is absurd *not* to. The functions of our brains have a dramatic effect on how we feel and how we interact with the world.

Tim, Pam, Paul, and Karen

Paul, age 20, came to see me because he was having trouble finishing his senior year at UC Berkeley. He was having trouble completing term papers, he could not focus in class, and he had little motivation. He began to believe that he should drop out of school to go work for his father. He hated the idea of quitting school so close to graduation, and so he came to see me on a referral from a friend. Paul told me that he had bouts of depression for which he had been ineffectively treated. Paul's brain SPECT study was consistent with both depression and ADD. He had a wonderful response to a combination of antidepressant and stimulant medications. He finished college and got the kind of job he wanted.

When Paul's mother, Pam, saw what treatment had done for her son, she came to see me for herself. As a child she had had trouble learning: Even though she was very artistic, she had little motivation for school and her teachers labeled her an underachiever. Later, as an adult, Pam went back to school and earned her degree in elementary-school teaching. In order to student teach, however, she had to pass the National Teacher's Exam. She failed four times. Pam was ready to give up and try a new avenue of study, but Paul's improvement gave her hope that there might be help for her. She had a brain study quite similar to Paul's, and she responded to the same combination of medication. Four months later she passed the National Teacher's Exam.

With two successes in the family, the mother then sent her 19-year-old daughter, Karen, to see me. Like her brother, Karen was a bright child who had underachieved in school. At the time she came to see me, she lived in Los Angeles and was enrolled in a broadcast journalism course. She complained that learning the material was hard for her. She was also moody, restless, easily distracted, impulsive, and quick to anger. Several years earlier she was treated for alcohol and amphetamine abuse. She said that the alcohol settled her restlessness and the amphetamines helped her to concentrate. Karen's brain SPECT study was very similar to her brother's and mother's. Once on medication, she could concentrate in class. Karen's level of confidence increased to the point where she could go and look for work as a broadcaster, something she had been unable to do previously.

The most reluctant member of the family to see me was the father, Tim. Even though Pam, Paul, and Karen told him that he should see me, he balked at the idea. He said, "There's nothing wrong with me; look at how successful I am." But his family knew differently. Even though Tim owned a successful grocery store, he was reclusive and distant. He got tired early in the day, he was easily distracted, and he had a scattered approach to work. His success at work stemmed, in part, from the good people who took his ideas and made them happen. Tim enjoyed high-stimulation activities and loved riding motorcycles, even at the age of 55. Looking back, Tim had done poorly in high school and barely passed college, even though he had a very high IQ. Tim's wife finally convinced him to see me. Their relationship was on the rocks due to Tim's difficulty communicating. She felt that he didn't care about her. He told me that by evening he was physically and emotionally drained.

During my first session with Tim, he told me that he couldn't possibly have ADD because he was a success in business. But the more questions I asked him about his past, the more lights went on his head. At the end of the interview I asked him, "If you really do have ADD, given what you've already accomplished, I wonder how successful you could be if we treat it." Tim's brain study showed the pattern for classic ADD. When he tried to concentrate, the frontal lobes of his brain shut down.

Tim had a remarkable response to Ritalin. He was more awake during the day, he accomplished more in less time, and his relationship with his wife dramatically improved. In fact, they both said they couldn't believe that their relationship could be so good, after all the years of distance and hurt.

Phillip and Dennis

Nine-year-old Phillip was frightened when the police came to his school to talk to him. His teacher had noticed bruises on his legs and arms and called Child Protective Services. He wasn't sure if he should tell them that his father, Dennis, had beaten him up, or if he should say that he fell down a flight of stairs or something like that. Phillip did not want to get his dad into trouble and he felt responsible for the beating he had received. After all, he thought, his father had told him ten times to clean his room and for some reason unknown to Phillip he hadn't done it. Phillip and his father often fought, but it had never been apparent to people outside the home. Phillip decided to tell the truth, hoping that it would somehow help.

Indeed, Phillip's family did get help. The court ordered the father to undergo a psychiatric evaluation and counseling for the family. The father was found to have a short fuse. He was impulsive and explosive in many different situations. He had begun to have problems with aggressiveness after he sustained a head injury in a car accident six years earlier. His wife reported that when Phillip was first born, the father was loving, patient, and attentive, but after the accident he was irritable, distant, and angry.

In family counseling sessions I noticed that Phillip was restless, active, impulsive, and defiant. The interaction between Phillip and his father was the most troubling. I doubted that counseling alone would be helpful. In an effort to understand further the biology of this family's problems, I ordered brain SPECT studies on both Phillip and Dennis.

Phillip and his father had abnormal SPECT scans. The father showed an area of decreased activity in his left temporal lobe near the temple, probably a result of the car accident. Phillip's SPECT study revealed decreased activity in the front part of his brain when he tried to concentrate—a finding consistent with his impulsive, hyperactive, and conflict-driven behavior.

After taking a history, watching the family interact, and reviewing the SPECT studies, it was clear to me that Phillip's and his father's problems were, in large part, biological. I placed both of them on medication. The father was put on an antiseizure medication to calm his left temporal lobe, and Phillip was placed on a stimulant medication to increase activity in the front part of his brain.

Once the underlying biological problems were treated, the family was able to benefit from psychotherapy and begin to heal the wounds of abuse. In counseling sessions Phillip was calmer and more attentive and the father was able to learn how to deal with Phillip's difficult behavior.

Whenever child abuse occurs, it is a severe tragedy. It may become an even worse tragedy, however, if people ignore the underlying brain problems that may be contributing to the abusive situation. Too often we rush to separate families before healing the problems that caused the trouble in the first place. In this case and in many others, it is often the negative interaction between a difficult child and an aggressive, impulsive parent that leads to the problem: negative interactions that may have a biological basis to them. In these cases it's no one's—and certainly not the child's!—"fault." To be effective in helping these families, it is very important to understand the underlying biological or "brain" contribution to the problem. It is *never* appropriate to place or leave a child in an abusive situation. However, if the family dynamic can be made to function properly, we can avoid compounding the problems.

Jack and Monica

Jack and Monica had been married eleven years and had two children, ages 6 and 9. Both parents were physicians: Jack was an emergency-room doctor, and Monica an internist. They came to see me from 300 miles away because of chronic marital problems. While there had been recent talk of divorce, they wanted to salvage the marriage for the sake of their children. Jack had been diagnosed with ADD (not uncommon among emergency physicians) by a local psychiatrist several years before they came to my clinic. Jack was disorganized, impulsive, inattentive, distractible, and forgetful. He did not follow through on his promises. He was also bad in business and frequently did not do the paperwork necessary to get reimbursed for his services. Unfortunately, Jack did not have a positive response to Ritalin or Dexedrine. The medications made him moody and irritable.

Monica was angry. She blamed every problem in their marriage on Jack's ADD. There was chronic conflict and tension, exacerbated by the behavior of their youngest child, Matthew. He was hyperactive, impulsive, aggressive, and defiant. It seemed that, with their busy schedules and constant stress, the couple could never connect in a positive way.

During my first session with the couple, I sensed that Monica had an anterior cingulate problem. She talked about the same point over and over, held grudges from long ago, worried, and tended to argue automatically with everything that came out of Jack's mouth. When I asked about Monica's family, she told me about her father, who won first prize for overactive anterior cingulate symptoms. He was a physician with whom she shared an office. Monica described him as angry, rigid, and compulsive. If things didn't go his way, he'd throw things, and he must have talked about how managed care was ruining medicine at least five times a day. With such a history, I thought it might be a good idea to scan both Jack and Monica—even Monica's dad, if he'd let me. Jack and Monica readily agreed. Monica said that if she was part of the problem, she wanted to know about it.

Jack's scan showed decreased activity in the prefrontal cortex and temporal lobes. The temporal lobe problems were probably making the stimulants ineffective. I placed Jack on Aricept, a memory-enhancing medication used for Alzheimer's disease that I have also found helpful for ADD adults who complain of memory problems. In addition, Jack exercised intensely, changed his diet, and also took L-tyrosine for focus.

Monica's scan showed marked hyperactivity in the anterior cingulate gyrus. No doubt she was faced with a tough marriage, but her overactive cingulate was not helping her have the needed flexibility to roll with the regular ups and downs of living in an ADD family. I started her on St. John's wort and exercise.

In addition, I saw their son Matthew. He had Type 3 (Overfocused) ADD and oppositional defiant disorder. He had decreased prefrontal cortex activity and too much activity in the anterior cingulate gyrus, a combination of Mom and Dad. I started him on St. John's wort and Adderall and worked with his parents on developing the parenting skills needed for him. The parent training was a boon to the family. Up to that point they had just used their parenting style differences as another way to disagree.

Over about six months the family began to heal. There were fewer fights, more loving interactions, and a deeper understanding of the underlying problems. Jack became more focused and his memory was better. Monica became more flexible and able to let go of hurts. Matthew settled down and was becoming happier and more cooperative. After two years I finally got to meet Monica's father. He came to a lecture I gave near his home. After the lecture he came up to me and thanked me for helping his children. He asked if I was doing any family studies. When I said yes, he volunteered for a scan. To no one's surprise, least of all Monica's, he had a very overactive anterior cingulate gyrus. He agreed to take St. John's wort and exercise regularly. Within several weeks Monica e-mailed me, thanking me on behalf of three generations for making life less stressful. She said her father was more relaxed, more flexible, and not talking about managed care.

ADD in all its types can affect multiple generations. Understanding family history in light of the ADD types can bring healing and hope for generations of families to come.

CHAPTER 13

Self-Medication, Self-Pollution

ADD and Substance Abuse

Drug and alcohol abuse are very common among teenagers and adults with untreated ADD. One study by psychiatrist Joseph Biederman and his colleagues at Harvard University indicated that 52 percent of untreated ADD adults abuse drugs or alcohol. The drugs that they choose to abuse are alcohol and marijuana to settle the internal restlessness they feel, and cocaine and methamphetamines to feel more energetic and focused. Nicotine use (cigarettes, cigars, and chewing tobacco) is much more common in people with ADD, as is the intake of large amounts of caffeine. Nicotine and caffeine are mild stimulants. People with ADD rarely abuse heroin, other opiates, painkillers, or tranquilizers, such as Valium. They are generally not stimulating enough to be of much benefit.

A common myth in the lay community is that the use of medication to treat ADD children somehow predisposes them to drug abuse in later life. The theory is that giving children or teens medicine to help them with the challenges ADD poses to their daily lives somehow teaches them to abuse substances later on. This theory is false. Both my clinical experience and research show that, in fact, the opposite is true: *Treating ADD* decreases *drug or alcohol abuse later on.*

Many people with ADD self-medicate (treat their underlying

problems) with substances as a way to feel more focused, more together, less anxious, less depressed, less overwhelmed, and just generally better. Despite the advantages, substance abuse is always bad medicine. Rather than helping, substance abuse makes the ADD symptoms much worse over time. Brain-imaging work has taught us just how harmful drug abuse is to brain function. Cocaine, methamphetamines, alcohol, marijuana, nicotine, and caffeine decrease brain activity over time, sometimes significantly. When an ADD teen uses alcohol to settle the internal restlessness she feels, she's applying a bandage to a wound that will only fester. One study done by Dr. Ismael Mena at UCLA showed that cocaine addicts had 23 percent less brain activity overall compared to a group of people who had never used drugs. Cocaine addicts in the study who also smoked had 45 percent less activity in their brains. In short, the smokers did not have access to nearly half their brains.

In my clinical experience, people with Type 1 (Classic) ADD and Type 2 (Inattentive) ADD tend to abuse stimulants, such as cocaine and methamphetamines; people with Type 3 (Overfocused) ADD tend to abuse alcohol more frequently; people with Type 4 (Temporal Lobe) and Type 5 (Limbic) ADD tend to be marijuana and stimulant abusers; and people with Type 6 ("Ring of Fire") ADD tend to abuse alcohol and marijuana.

Cindy

Cindy, 42, came to our clinic because she was abusing methamphetamines. She had failed a number of treatment programs and was being prevented from seeing her three children because of her drug problems. In addition, she had just lost the third job in a year because of tardiness and poor performance.

Cindy was depressed. She wanted help but felt stuck and out of control. Cindy had begun abusing drugs during high school and been off and on them since then. "When I use speed I feel clear and have energy and focus. I hate coming down and I hate that I have to break the law." It was clear that Cindy had Type 1 (Classic) ADD. As a child she was described as hyperactive, restless, impulsive, disorganized, and thrill seeking. She took Ritalin for a brief period of time, but her parents felt uncomfortable giving her medication. They told her that she needed to try harder in school.

When Cindy learned that adults can have ADD, it gave her hope to seek treatment. I changed her diet, gave her supplements, and put her on Wellbutrin, a stimulating antidepressant, often helpful for Type 1 ADD. Due to California law, I could not prescribe Adderall or Ritalin: It is illegal to give a substance abuser a controlled medication, even though it may be the best treatment. Over the first four months there were many ups and downs, but Cindy stayed with the program and is now four years sober, employed, and able to see her children on a regular basis.

Jim

Jim is a tragic story. He was a close friend of mine when I was in the military. At the age of 36 he shot and killed himself. At his funeral his mother told me the following story.

As a child, Jim had been like three boys in one. He was hyperactive, impulsive, and had a hard time sitting still. During the elementary-school years, Jim had trouble with his behavior in class and on the playground, and his mother was frequently called to school. As a teenager he got into minor skirmishes with the law and began using alcohol and marijuana. He barely graduated from high school. "He only graduated because I made him stay at his desk until his homework was done," his mother told me.

During the Vietnam War, Jim was drafted and spent two years in the Army, where he and I met. He was often in trouble with his commander. He had a number of disciplinary actions for insubordination and drug abuse. After his discharge, he got a job with the local sheriff's office, but he was fired two years later for stealing a shot glass at a local bar when he was drunk. He married and had a child. Unfortunately, his marriage could not stand his emotionally erratic, often intoxicated behavior. After his wife left him, his alcohol consumption increased. He got married two more times with the same disastrous results. After he had been fired from a job, in the same year that his last wife left him, and while drunk, he shot and killed himself.

Looking back on Jim's life, through the eyes of a child psychiatrist, I have no doubt he had had ADD. When we were together he was fun and impulsive, but I often had to keep him focused, and I worked hard to keep him out of trouble. Inside he was a very loving and giving man. He just couldn't be consistent. The alcohol settled his restlessness but ruined his life.

Jose

In a highly publicized Bay Area case, Jose, a 16-year-old gang member, was arrested after he and another gang member beat another teenager nearly to death. They were charged with attempted murder. One evening, when they were in an intoxicated state (from both alcohol and heavy marijuana usage), they approached a boy wearing a red sweater walking his dog across the street. They asked him, "What colors do you bang?" (referring to gang affiliation). When the boy said he did not know what they were talking about, Jose replied, "Wrong answer." You see, Jose's gang claimed the color red. The two gang boys started hitting and kicking their victim repeatedly until he was unconscious. Other gang members described pulling Jose off the boy because "once he started he didn't stop." They were worried he would kill the boy.

The public defender ordered neuropsychological testing on Jose, which found frontal lobe dysfunction and evidence of ADD, depression, and learning disabilities. The psychologist suggested a resting and concentration SPECT series for independent verification. The SPECT series was significantly abnormal. Both studies showed marked increased activity in the anterior cingulate gyrus, consistent with problems shifting attention. At rest, his SPECT also showed mildly suppressed prefrontal cortex activity. While doing a concentration task, Jose showed marked suppression of the prefrontal cortex and both temporal lobes, consistent with types 1, 3, and 5 ADD, learning disabilities, and aggressive tendencies.

Jose had a long history of problems shifting attention. He was

Jose's SPECT Results
(Left-Side Active and Underside Surface Views)

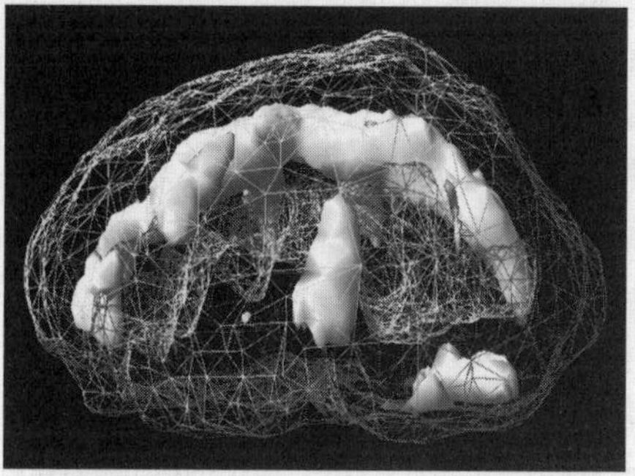

3-D active side view
(marked increased cingulate activity)

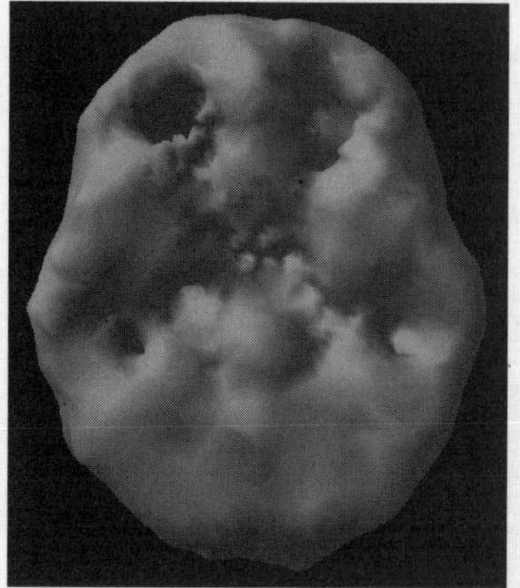

at rest
(mild decreased prefrontal cortex activity)

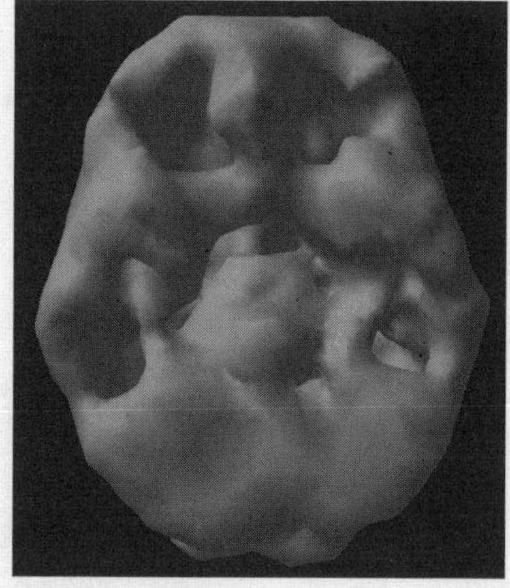

with concentration
(marked decreased prefrontal cortex and temporal lobe activity)

described by others as "brooding," argumentative, and oppositional. "Once he got a thought in his head," his father said, "he would talk about it over and over." In prison he was placed on Zoloft (a serotonergic antidepressant to calm his cingulate) and Cylert (to activate his prefrontal cortex). He felt calmer, more focused, and less easily upset.

David

A friend of mine came to visit me from another state. He said that he had growing trouble concentrating and that his energy was low. I knew he smoked three packs of cigarettes and drank at least three pots of coffee every day. For a long time I suspected he had ADD (he underachieved in school, did impulsive things, and could never sit still) and that he was medicating himself with the stimulant affects of caffeine and nicotine. But he was the CEO of a very successful corporation and not used to taking advice, even from people he knew cared about him. I told him about ADD and said that it would be a good idea to treat it and stop self-medicating. He didn't want to take medication, he told me. Didn't I have a natural treatment for it? A bit amazed, I said, "You *are* doing the natural treatments for ADD—caffeine and nicotine. They'll kill you eventually. My medication is more effective, and when it is used properly, it doesn't kill anyone."

I felt SPECT images of his brain might help him see the reality

David's Concentration SPECT Study (Underside Surface View)

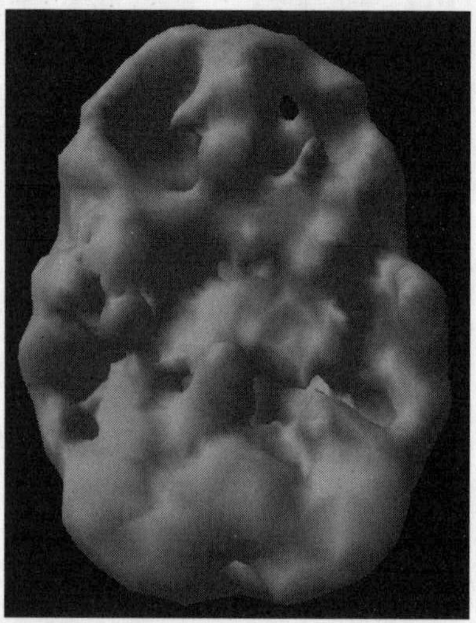

marked overall decreased activity, especially in prefrontal cortex and temporal lobes

of the situation and encourage him to stop. Even I was surprised by how bad his brain looked. He had marked decreased activity across the whole cortex, especially in the areas of the prefrontal cortex and temporal lobes. I told my friend that he needed to find another way to stimulate his brain. If he didn't stop the caffeine and nicotine, he wasn't going to have much of a brain left to enjoy his success. He took my advice for a few weeks, but shortly after he returned home he went back to his old ways. I couldn't get through to him—even with his frightening brain scans. Even though I recommended that he try brain stimulants, such as Ritalin or Adderall, he wanted to treat his ADD naturally—with exactly those drugs that were making the problem even worse.

SUBSTANCE ABUSE AND ADD TREATMENT ISSUES

ADD treatment issues are often complicated by substance abuse. As mentioned, as many as half of ADD adults have substance abuse issues. Yet, many physicians feel very uncomfortable prescribing controlled substances like Ritalin or Adderall to people who have addiction problems. In my experience these medications are rarely abused by people with ADD, but one must be careful with this population. In the state of California it is illegal to give controlled medication to someone who has a substance abuse problem. This law puts the physician and ADD patient in a precarious situation. For types 1 and 2 ADD, stimulants are the treatment of choice, and they may be the only intervention that works. If we cannot give patients the most effective treatment, they may not be able to stay away from the substances they abuse to self-medicate. It's a catch-22.

In my practice I weigh the pros and cons of each intervention. If I am going to treat someone who is actively abusing drugs, I will not use a stimulant medication until they are in a treatment program and have shown a prolonged commitment to sobriety. Instead I'll prescribe stimulating antidepressants, supplements, and dietary interventions.

CHAPTER 14

The Games ADD People Play

"Let's Have a Problem"

"I Bet I Can Get You to Yell at Me or Hit Me"

"My Thoughts Are More Terrible Than Your Thoughts"

"It's Your Fault"

"No, No Way, Never, You Can't Make Me Do it"

"I Say the Opposite of What You Say"

"I Say the First Thing That Comes to Mind"

"Let's Call It Even"

"Fighting as Foreplay"

Many people with ADD unconsciously, based on brain-driven (not will-driven) mechanisms, play ADD games as a way to boost adrenaline and stimulate their frontal lobes. These games just seem to happen. No one plans for them to happen. Most ADD people deny that they engage in these behaviors. However, I have seen these games in my own family, and I've heard about them from my patients for many years. Let's look at each of these games in depth.

"LET'S HAVE A PROBLEM"

Without enough stimulation, the brain looks for ways to increase its own activity. Being mad, upset, angry, or negative has an immediate stimulating effect on the brain. Whenever you get upset, your body produces increasing amounts of adrenaline, which stimulates heart rate, blood pressure, muscle tension, and, yes, brain activity. Many people with ADD pick on others to get a rise out of them, to get them upset, to make them crazy. All too often, family members of my patients tell me they are tired of the problems in their families. They say, "I'm so tired of fighting with my brother [sister, mother, father, son, daughter, etc.]. Why does there have to be this turmoil? Can't he [she] be happy with peaceful coexistence? Does he [she] have to fight? He [she] always has to have a problem!"

Joshua and Betsy were married for three years before they entered marital counseling. Betsy forced Joshua to get help. He didn't see any problems and initially refused to see the therapist, but Betsy was beside herself. It seemed to her that they fought nearly all the time. She never felt at peace, never felt that they could have an evening or weekend during which Joshua didn't complain about something. Even though Joshua was successful in his own business, he frequently complained about his employees. Betsy, who also worked with him, saw that he would regularly select an employee to pick on or engage in some kind of battle. After an extensive intake interview, the therapist saw Joshua's conflict-seeking behavior as only one of his many ADD symptoms, including disorganization, distractibility, and impulsivity. She referred Joshua for a psychiatric evaluation and worked with the couple on strategies to recognize and stop this destructive game.

Rosemary and Chrissy, mother and 16-year-old daughter, constantly fought. It didn't seem to matter about what: It could be curfew, clothes, music, tone of voice—whatever. I met Chrissy when she was brought to our clinic for evaluation because of troubles at school. During the initial interview with Chrissy and her parents, I watched the two females go after each other. The tone between them was contentious, mutually irritating, and on edge. The father wearily told me, "This is how they live at home. Everything is an issue. Everything is a problem. They both hold on to their own positions and cannot let go. It's as if they have to irritate each other. I often don't want to come home because I know I'll have to listen to their battles." In the evaluation process Chrissy was diagnosed with overfocused ADD (school struggles, inattention, impulsivity, restlessness, and oppositional and argumentative behavior), as was her mother, who had grown up in an alcoholic home, struggled in school, and complained of low energy, disorganization, procrastination, and forgetfulness. After they were both treated for overfocused ADD, the tension diminished dramatically. The need for conflict diminished and everyone felt less stressed and more comfortable at home.

"I BET I CAN GET YOU TO YELL AT ME OR HIT ME"

A similar game to "Let's Have a Problem" is "I Bet I Can Get You to Yell At Me or Hit Me." Many people with ADD are masterful at getting others to scream, yell, spank, and basically fly out of control. They get others so upset that they cannot help but lose it. These negative behaviors provide quite an adrenaline rush but frequently lead to serious negative consequences, such as divorce, fights at school, unemployment, and even abuse. Again, the game is unconscious, not planned. It seems as if the ADD person senses the most vulnerable issues for others, and they work on them until there is an explosion.

Bonnie had been diagnosed with Inattentive ADD at age 12. The only treatment she received was medication, which she took sporadically. Now, at age 15, she was struggling in school and had problems with her parents at home. She also fought with a number of her teachers. On top of all this, the parents were furious at the school because one of the teachers had yelled at her to shut up and sit down in class a number of months earlier. The teacher was disciplined by the school for the outbursts, but she said that she just couldn't take Bonnie's lack of respect and disruptive behavior. During Bonnie's initial evaluation in our clinic, her father cried, saying, "I never thought I would have such negative feelings and behaviors toward my own child. I just start screaming at her, because she says terrible things. She knows every hot button I have, and I feel like she intentionally pushes them on a regular basis. Sometimes I understand why parents abandon their children. They just can't take the negative feelings, the lack of respect, and the constant fighting."

Jesse, age 6, had parents who did not believe in spanking. They were well-educated people who discussed how they would raise their child even before he was born. Yet, even though they didn't want to use spanking, they often found themselves on the edge of losing control. They yelled more than they wanted to, and they found themselves using physical punishment on impulse because they would get so frustrated with Jesse's misbehavior. Jesse was impulsive and seemed driven to turmoil. Ironically, the parents found out that when they yelled or spanked him, his behavior would be better for a while. The mother told me, "If we have a bad morning at home, he has a good day at school. If we have a kind, loving morning at home, then he seems to have a bad day at school." I diagnosed Jesse with Classic ADD: He had the full cluster of symptoms. Besides treating him medically, I worked with his parents on effective parenting strategies. I warned them that as soon as they stopped yelling at Jesse, he would get worse for several weeks. It was as if he were going through adrenaline withdrawal. The parents' yelling, screaming, and hitting were stimulating to him, and he, unknowingly, used their anger to feel more alert, which is why he did better in school if they had a bad morning at home.

Evan and Alexa, ages 15 and 12, were a brother and sister at war. Evan was diagnosed with Classic ADD when he was ten years old and Alexa had only recently been diagnosed with Overfocused ADD. The parents brought them to our clinic for medication and family therapy evaluations. The siblings seemed to be masterful at upsetting each other. They had been at odds for as long as anyone could remember. On one occasion—the one that precipitated the referral—Evan, came into Alexa's bedroom to borrow a CD. Alexa screamed at him to get out. When Evan refused, she threw a speaker at him. Evan attacked her, leaving bruises all over her body.

It is essential to stop playing both "Let's Have a Problem" and "I Bet I Can Get You to Yell at Me or Hit Me" if an ADD person is to live happily with others. When I teach parents, siblings, and spouses to become less reactive and not to feed the need for adrenaline with anger, the ADD person may initially get *worse.* It seems as though the ADD person goes through withdrawal when others become more understanding or more tolerant, at least initially. When the ADD person can no longer get the adrenaline anger rush, he'll go after it full force, escalating the outrageous behavior. But if a parent, sibling, or spouse can remain nonreactive for a long enough period of time, the conflict-driven behavior usually diminishes significantly. Nevertheless, they will periodically test the "nonreactive skill" of the people in their environments by seeking intense emotional reactions. Others have to remain on guard to keep these negative behaviors away.

"MY THOUGHTS ARE MORE TERRIBLE THAN YOUR THOUGHTS"

Psychiatrist and brain-imaging specialist Mark George at the National Institutes of Health demonstrated, in a landmark study, that negative thoughts have a stimulating effect on the brain. Using functional brain-imaging studies, he looked at brain activity while people were thinking about something neutral, something positive, and something awful. The neutral thoughts did not change brain activity. The positive thoughts cooled overall brain activity, especially in the limbic area of the brain—certainly not good for ADD folks, who have poor brain activity to begin with. The negative thoughts, however, brought brain activation, especially in the limbic areas (making them more depressed) and in the prefrontal cortex (helping them focus).

Clinically, I have seen that many ADD people seem to be experts at picking out the most negative thoughts possible and staying focused on them for prolonged periods of time. It is almost as if they need the negativity to have the mental energy to function. When I started to talk about this idea to colleagues at my clinic, Jonathan, a marriage, family, and child therapist who has ADD, said, "I think I do that myself. I wake up thinking about the most horrific things that could happen during the day. I feel anxious, but it motivates me to get up and get moving."

You have probably noticed the people who play this game at work: If ten good things and one bad thing happen, most of their thoughts are focused on the bad thing. These are the people who complain, gossip, find fault, undermine, and pit people against each other. In meetings they disagree and find fault. As managers, they are often the ones who notice the negative much more than the positive.

The negativity often associated with ADD frequently ruins lives. Few people are drawn closer to people who are negative, complaining, or filled with anxious thoughts. Many ADD people who unknowingly play this game end up isolated, lonely, depressed, and even more negative. People who are isolated from others have a higher incidence of both physical and emotional problems.

Some time ago, one of the physicians who worked in my office went through a period during which he was one of the most negative human beings I had ever met. He always had a sour look on his face. Every time I saw him he complained nonstop about office procedures and personnel. He was negative with patients. He hadn't exhibited this behavior when I hired him. I found myself avoiding him in the hallway and feeling frustrated by his behavior. After several weeks of this behavior I told him to come into my office. He started the meeting by complaining about a front-office issue without first wanting to know why I asked to see him. Immediately I stopped him, saying, "I don't know what is going on with you, but something is different. You complain nonstop about nearly everything. People are avoiding you and patients don't want to see you anymore." The doctor then told me that he had ADD and that he had decided to stop his medication a month ago. He didn't know why he had stopped it, but when he started taking it again, the negativity problem subsided.

Many people with ADD who play the game of "My Thoughts Are More Terrible Than Your Thoughts" end up isolated. Be careful with negativity. This is a damaging and dangerous game.

"IT'S YOUR FAULT"

Another common game played by many people with ADD is "It's Your Fault." This may be the most dangerous ADD game of all. In it the ADD person reasons that he or she has little, if anything, to do with the problems in his or her own life. Any problem is someone else's fault. Frequently, I hear that these people do not perform properly at school, at work, or within their families because of "the lousy boss," "the ineffective teacher," or "the mean brother [or sister]." This game can completely ruin a life. Whenever you blame someone else for the problems in your own life, you become a victim of that other person and you have no power to change anything. Without a sense of personal power, people often feel overwhelmed and hopeless.

Billie Jean came into my office blaming nearly everyone in her life. Her husband mistreated her, her children neglected her, her boss was mean to her, and her doctor (not me, thankfully) didn't take her seriously. When she was late to an appointment, it was because of traffic; when she missed a payment, it was because she hadn't gotten her mail. There was an excuse for everything. Gently, I started to ask her what she could do to make these situations better—with her husband, children, job, and everyone else in her life. This process was critical for her emotional health. Unless she took responsibility for her emotions and reactions, she would always be at the mercy of others. Her tendency to blame was a way to feel angry and entitled so that she could use that anger as a stimulant. Eliminating blame and asking herself, "What can I do to make the situation better?" was one of the most important parts of her healing process.

Watch out for the "It's Your Fault" game. It may ruin your life.

"NO, NO WAY, NEVER, YOU CAN'T MAKE ME DO IT"

Opposition also increases adrenaline in the ADD brain. Many people with ADD, especially Type 3, tend to be argumentative and oppositional with people in their lives. These negative behaviors often cause tension and turmoil in families, in relationships, or at work. Many parents tell me they are tired of arguing with their children. This game has one simple rule: I ask you to do something, and you say no. I frequently ask my patients: "How many times out of ten, when your mother [father, teacher, boss] asks you to do something, will you do it the first time without arguing or fighting?" Many of my patients tend to look down at the floor when I ask this question. They quietly say, "Not many times, maybe two or three times out of ten." I then ask them why. They tell me they have no idea why they do it, that it is not their goal to be oppositional.

I had a very interesting session recently. I saw a 10-year-old boy for the first time. He came into my office with his mother. He immediately sat down on my blue leather couch and put his shoes on it. (That doesn't bother me: I figure that if you see difficult kids, you have to have an office that will stand up to them). The shoes on the couch bothered his mother, however. She told him to put them down. When he refused, she put them down on the floor. He immediately put them back up on the sofa. She looked at me in frustration and then moved her son's feet back on the floor. He put them up. She put them down. He put them up again. She put them down again and slapped his leg. This went on and on. I watched to see the interaction between them. He wanted his way. She was determined not to give in, but she engaged in the same repetitive ineffective behavior. She would have done better by cutting the oppositional behavior right away and give an immediate, unemotional, but firm consequence. After about ten minutes of this behavior I asked the boy if it was his plan to upset his mother. He said no. Then I asked him why he had to do the opposite of what she wanted. He said, like so many of these kids do, "I don't know."

The unconscious game of "No, No Way, Never, You Can't Make Me Do It" can isolate a person. The level of opposition drives others away, causing them to make negative judgments about you. While writing this book, I went to Israel to speak at an international ADD conference. At the conference I had the pleasure to spend time with a family who had come to see me in California. The 11-year-old boy had been depressed when he came to my clinic. Through his history and our scans we were able to diagnose him properly, put him on the right medication, and help the family with the right behavioral strategies. He made a wonderful improvement. The child and his mother joined my daughter and me on a trip to Jerusalem. The souvenir shops caught the boy's attention. He wanted a chessboard. The mother said no. He asked again. She said no again. This went on for about thirty minutes. I watched. Finally the boy asked me how he could get his mother to get him a chessboard. I said, "You don't want to hear my answer." He said he really wanted my help. I told him (with his mother listening), "If your mom gets you what you want after she has already told you no fifteen times, then she is teaching you to get your way by irritating other people. You'll be difficult and no one will want to be with you, because you will have to have your way." He put his hands over his mother's ears so she wouldn't hear any more of my advice. Later he said, "Dr. Amen, you are right. I don't like people who are pests. I'll try not to be one."

You cannot let people badger you or irritate you into getting their way. If you allow this game to work, it sets up serious social problems. No one likes someone who argues with everything they say or opposes them most of the time.

"I SAY THE OPPOSITE OF WHAT YOU SAY"

Here's another destructive ADD game. Let's call it "I Say the Opposite of What You Say." This game is similar to "No, No Way, Never, You Can't Make Me Do It," but it involves speech more than behavior. The people who play this game take a position opposite to that of the other person in the conversation. For example, if your spouse complains that you do not listen to him or her, you deny it and then say that he or she does not listen to you. If a parent tells a child to clean his messy room, he or she is likely to say that the room isn't messy. If a person takes a view on a political position, you will take the opposite position (even if it is against what you really believe). The need for opposition seems to be more important than the truth. The back-and-forth disagreement brings more adrenaline, stress, and irritation to the table. Watch out for this game. It pushes people away from you.

It seems to me that politicians in the United States and abroad are masters at this game. I have often thought that many politicians have ADD. If a Democrat has a good idea, the Republicans will automatically put it down; and if a Republican offers a helpful plan, the Democrats will automatically look for ways to shoot holes in it. Cooperation is so foreign to the political process it is a wonder anything gets done. Unfortunately, this same dynamic happens in many ADD homes.

"I SAY THE FIRST THING THAT COMES TO MIND"

Many of my patients struggle with the game of "I Say the First Thing That Comes to Mind." I have heard a number of my patients say, "I am brutally honest." They wear this trait as if it were a badge of courage. I usually reply to them that brutal honesty is usually not helpful. Relationships require tact.

Recently, I walked out into my waiting room to greet an 8-year-old patient. I was about ten minutes late for the appointment. When she saw me she said, "Well it's about damn time." Her mother looked horrified and apologized for the little girl's comment. Living in an ADD household, I knew comments like that were just part of the terrain.

This game causes many, many problems. When you just say the first thing that comes to mind, you can hurt someone's feelings, infuriate a customer, or give away secrets that were entrusted to you. One of my patients was charged with bringing a friend to a surprise party in the friend's honor. On the way to the party my patient inadvertently started talking about how much fun the party would be. It was only when he saw the look on his friend's face that he figured out he had ruined the surprise.

"LET'S CALL IT EVEN"

Many people with ADD play a deflection game titled "Let's Call It Even." In this game, whenever someone else has a complaint or criticism, the player also adopts that complaint as his or her own. For example, if a husband is unhappy that the house isn't clean, his wife (the player) complains that he doesn't help enough. If a wife complains that her husband doesn't listen enough, the husband will complain about the same thing. If a sibling says that her sister goes into her room and takes things, the sister will say she does that because her sister does it too.

"FIGHTING AS FOREPLAY"

Many couples whom I have seen through the years have described a fascinating ADD game I call "Fighting as Foreplay." In this game there is an intense fight, then a period of making up, which includes making love. The swing of emotions is quick and dramatic. One minute you are fighting, talking about divorce and ready to leave the relationship, the next moment you are making wild, passionate love and feeling blissful. It's confusing to the participants but makes some biological sense. The fight is needed for stimulation. Once stimulated, you are ready for love.

All of these games are very destructive in ADD relationships. The first step in eliminating these games is to notice them. The treatment guidelines given in parts III and IV of this book will go over ways to get out of the games ADD people play.

CHAPTER 15

The Impact of ADD on Relationships, Families, School, Work, and Self-Esteem

ADD impacts all aspects of life. In this chapter I'll list some of the most common complaints patients and their families bring into my office.

RELATIONSHIPS

For a child, teen, or adult, ADD often has a negative impact on a person's ability to interact with others. Here are some of the reasons:

Social Isolation

Many people with ADD have failed in relationships so many times in the past that they don't want to experience the pain anymore. They avoid relationships or they make excuses to be by themselves.

Teasing

People with ADD are often teased by others. Their behavior brings negative attention to themselves. Additionally, the impulsivity and conflict-driven nature causes them to tease others, sometimes to the point where the other person becomes very upset.

Fighting

Fighting is typical for many people with ADD. It may be related to impulsivity (saying things without thinking), stimulation-seeking behavior, misperceptions, rage outbursts, and chronically low self-esteem. The fighting leads to chronic stress for the person with ADD and those in his or her family.

Misperceptions

Misperceptions often cause serious problems in relationships. Often the parent or spouse of an ADD person has to spend an inordinate amount of time correcting misperceptions that lead to disagreements.

Distractibility

Due to distractibility, conversations are often cut short or left incomplete, leaving the other person feeling unimportant. When a person is distracted, he or she may miss large chunks of conversations and may unconsciously fill in missing pieces with negative information.

Problems Taking Turns

The ADD person's need to have what they want right away often causes problems in situations in which they need to take turns, such as in conversations or games.

Speaking Without Thinking

This is perhaps the most damaging problem with ADD in relationships. Just because a person has a thought doesn't mean that it is accurate or that he or she even necessarily believes it. Many people with ADD just say what comes to mind. They then get stuck in defending those statements, causing further problems.

Problems Completing Chores

Even though the person with ADD wants to finish what he or she starts, distractibility gets in the way, and many things may be left half done. This leads to many resentments, arguments, and frustrations felt by others.

Difficulty Playing or Being Quiet

Often the level of activity or noise created by the ADD person causes frustration and irritability in others.

Sensitivity to Noise

At the same time the ADD person may also be sensitive to noise. They often need to escape from others to feel calm or peaceful inside.

Sensitivity to Touch

When the person is sensitive to touch, they often shy away from affection. This can harm a relationship, especially if the person's partner wants or needs affection.

Excessive Talking

Sometimes people with ADD talk for self-stimulation. There is an internal drive to go on and on. This may irritate others, who feel that they cannot get a word in the conversation.

Lack of Emotional Expression

The partners of some ADD people complain that there is little talking or emotional expression in the relationship. "He {She} seems turned off when he comes home" is a common complaint. Often parents will ask their children about their day and the only response they'll get is "Fine" or "Okay." These kids are often called nonelaborators.

Disorganization

This causes problems in a relationship because the ADD person often doesn't live up to his or her part of the chores or agreements.

High-Risk Taking/Thrill Seeking

This type of behavior worries the parents, partners, or friends of the ADD person. Friends often feel pressured to go along with dangerous behavior, causing a rift in the relationship.

Easy Frustration/Emotionalism/Moodiness

Many family members of ADD children, teens, and adults have told me that they never know what to expect from the ADD person. "One minute she's happy, the next minute she's screaming" is a common complaint. Small amounts of stress may trigger huge explosions.

Tantrums/Rage Outbursts

Some studies have reported that up to 85 percent of people with ADD have rage outbursts, often with little provocation. After this occurs several times in a relationship, the parent, partner, or friend becomes "gun shy" and starts to withdraw from the person. Untreated ADD is often involved in abusive relationships.

Low Self-Esteem

When people do not feel good about themselves, it impairs their ability to relate to others. They have difficulty taking compliments or getting outside of themselves to truly understand the other person. The brain filters information coming in from the environment. When the brain's filter (self-esteem) is negative, people tend to see only the negative and ignore any positive. Many partners of ADD people complain that when they give their partners a compliment, the latter find a way to make it look as if they have just been criticized.

Looking for Turmoil

This is a common complaint of people living with someone who has ADD. They say that the person looks for trouble. Rather than ignoring a minor incident, he or she focuses on it and has difficulty letting it go. Things in an ADD house do not remain peaceful for long periods of time.

Chronic Anxiety or Restlessness

As mentioned above, ADD people often feel restless or anxious, causing them to search for ways to relax. They may use excessive sex, food, or alcohol to try to calm themselves. I treated one man who had had sex with his girlfriend over 500 times in the last year of their relationship. She left him because she felt that their relationship was only based upon sex.

Failure to See Others' Needs

Many people with ADD have trouble thinking of anyone but themselves. Blind to the emotional needs of others, they are often labeled spoiled, immature, or self-centered.

Failure to Learn from the Past

Often people with ADD engage in repetitive, negative arguments with others. They seem not to learn from the interpersonal mistakes from the past and repeat them again and again.

Chronic Procrastination

The ADD person often waits until the very last minute to get things done (paying bills; buying birthday, anniversary, or Christmas gifts; etc.). This may irritate those around them who feel the need to pick up the loose pieces.

FAMILIES

ADD often causes serious problems in families. I have seen "caring" families fall apart because of the turmoil caused by having an ADD child. I have also seen many couples who "truly loved each other" divorce because of the stress of one or both partners having ADD. Many of the issues listed in the previous section apply here. Here are several other important issues to consider:

Drive Toward Turmoil

ADD children and teenagers are often experts at getting their parents to yell at them. As I mentioned above, the ADD person often has decreased activity in their frontal lobes. They "unconsciously" seek stimulation to feel more awake or alert. In a family, this takes on many forms, such as temper tantrums, noise, and high activity.

Parental Splitting

ADD kids may also be skilled at getting their parents to fight with each other. Splitting parental authority gives children and teenagers too much power and increases the turmoil. Often the scenario is that the mother will blame the father for being "too absent" or "too harsh," and the father will blame the mother for being "too inconsistent" and "too soft." Of course, this goes both ways. I have seen many couples separate, in part to stop the turmoil they lived in at home.

Negative Expectations

In families with an ADD child, teen, or adult there is often the expectation that there will be problems. As a result, people begin to avoid each other. For example, a woman recently told me she expected that her ADD husband wouldn't wash the dinner dishes as he had promised. Before he even had a chance to do them, she resentfully cleaned them. She was angry at him for the rest of the night, even though she hadn't given him a chance to be helpful.

Feelings of Parents

Denial: "There's nothing wrong with the child! He only needs more time, more attention, more discipline, more love, a better teacher, a better school, a firmer mother, a father who is more available." These are common excuses parents make to deny that any problem exists. Admitting that there is a problem is often so painful that many parents go years and years without seeking help. Denial can seriously harm a child's or teen's chances for success!

Grief: There is often a grieving process that occurs in a family with an untreated ADD person. The parents or spouse often feel the loss of not having a "normal" child, teen, or spouse and end up feeling very sad that the situation is not as they expected it would be.

On Guard: For many parents, living with an ADD child is like being in a war zone. They have to be constantly on guard that the child won't run out into the street, break something at the store, or run off at a park. This chronic watchfulness causes much internal tension for parents.

Guilt: Guilt is a significant issue for many people who live with those who have ADD. The turmoil that an ADD child, teen, or adult causes often brings on bad feelings. Parents or spouses are not "supposed" to have bad feelings toward people they love and so end up burdened by feelings of guilt. In the treatment section I'll discuss how to break the cycle of guilt.

Anger: Anger at teachers, doctors, day care workers, and the other parent is common in parents with an ADD child. The levels of frustration are so high in these families that people look for someone at whom to blow off steam.

Envy: "Why can't we have normal kids? We didn't do anything to deserve the turmoil. It's not fair."

Blame: "You spoil him. How's he ever going to learn if you do everything for him?" "You're too soft on her." "You never say a kind word to him." "If only you would be home more: Then we wouldn't have these problems with her." Blame is very destructive and rarely if ever helpful. Yet, it is all too common in ADD families.

Isolation: "Everyone thinks I'm a bad parent. No one else has these problems. I can't go anywhere with him, I'm stuck at home." Feelings of isolation are very common. Many parents of ADD children feel that they are the only ones in the world who have these problems. Joining a support group can be very helpful for these people.

Bargaining: "Maybe she'll be OK if we put her in a new school." "Maybe if we put him in outside activities, his attitude will improve." "Maybe if I leave his father, we'll all feel better." Many parents of ADD children attribute their problems to outside forces and feel that making radical lifestyle changes will help. Without the right treatment, however, these changes are rarely helpful.

Depression: "I'm a failure as a parent. I've failed my child. I have no business raising children. I should go to work and leave him with a sitter. I'm so tired that I can't do this anymore." The physical and emotional drain of having an ADD child can often trigger a significant depression. Watch your moods.

Sibling Issues

Children with ADD often irritate their siblings to the point of causing tears, anger, or fights. Siblings develop negative feelings toward the ADD child because they are often embarrassed by the child's outrageous behavior at school or with friends.

Since ADD, for the most part, is a genetic disorder, it is more likely that siblings may also have features of ADD. Having two or more members of a family with untreated ADD can completely disorganize the family.

Oftentimes in families with an ADD child, there is an identified "good" child and a "bad" (ADD) child. Because the parents' self-esteem is so damaged by having an unrecognized ADD child, they will often avoid the ADD child to focus a lot of positive energy on the other child and think that they are more "perfect" than they really are. This causes resentment in the ADD child. It also causes the "perfect" child to subvert any progress that the ADD child might make. Corey and Sarah were an example of this "sibling subversion."

Corey, 9, had a severe case of ADD. He would throw three-hour temper tantrums, had problems nearly every day in school, and was chronically noncompliant with his mother. Six-year-old Sarah, with long, curly red hair, was her mother's angel. She could do no wrong. With treatment, Corey began to improve significantly. But in therapy Corey told me that his little sister was "flipping him off" with her middle finger. When he told his mother, she did not believe him, saying, "Sarah wouldn't do that, she's too sweet." I told the mother to watch them secretly when they were playing together. Sure enough, Sarah was using her middle finger to drive Corey crazy. She was having difficulty losing her place in the family as the "perfect" child, and she had a stake in Corey remaining a problem.

Feelings of Brothers and Sisters

Embarrassment: Just as parents are blamed by neighbors for the unacceptable behavior of their child, so brothers and sisters are often held responsible or ridiculed by their peers for the actions of their ADD sibling.

Anger: An ADD child can evoke intense emotions in his or her brother or sister.

Resentment: A sibling may feel very resentful at being labeled "weirdo's sister" or having a child come up and say, "Hey, do you know what your brother did?"

Put-upon: Siblings feel urged to include the ADD child in their play and free-time activities. He or she often has few friends of their own and it's natural for parents to seek relief.

Guilt: Like parents, siblings often feel guilty about emotions they harbor. They care deeply in spite of the behavior they live with.

Out of Control: Brothers and sisters find it difficult to engage the ADD child in play without constant struggles over rules and issues of control. They may strike out at the ADD child as a result of being constantly frustrated.

Jealousy: Siblings often question the double standards that exist in the rules that they are governed by. Although his or her behavior doesn't warrant it, the ADD child is often rewarded as a way of pacifying him or her at the time.

SCHOOL

Whether for children, teenagers, or adults, ADD has a powerful negative impact on a person's ability to do well in school. Except for classes that are small or highly interesting, many people with ADD have significant problems. Here is a list of common school problems.

Restlessness

The hyperactivity that often accompanies ADD in childhood causes obvious problems: The child is restless, out of his or her seat, irritating other kids (not to mention the teacher), and causing turmoil and disruption in his or her path. In teens and adults, the restlessness of ADD often distracts others in class who notice the constant movement (e.g., legs shaking and shifting body posture in seats).

Short Attention Span and Distractibility

Having a short attention span and being easily distracted affects nearly every aspect of school. This will affect a student's ability to follow teachers in lectures, participate in small groups, and perform consistently on tests. The short attention span often causes the ADD students' attention to wander while reading or performing class assignments, causing them to take an inordinate amount of time to finish tasks. Distractibility also may get ADD students in trouble, as they tend to be in everyone else's business.

Impulsiveness

Impulsiveness causes serious school problems. Blurting out answers in class, responding impulsively on quizzes or tests, and saying things without thinking are typical. I've treated many people with ADD who were "tactless" in how they responded to their teachers or professors. One teenager said to her teacher, "You're a lousy teacher! I don't know why you explain things like that, but the other teachers know how to explain things a lot better than you do." All of us have had that thought about certain teachers at one time or another. Most people, however, would never blurt out a statement like that because it would hurt the teacher's feelings and harm their relationship. But with ADD, the mouth is often engaged before the brain.

Procrastination

Many people with ADD wait until the last minute to complete their tasks for school. If it isn't the night before, they cannot get their brain upset enough to get their work done. Many parents have told me about the constant fights they have with their children or teens about starting projects early and working on them over time, rather than the night before. Many adults have told me that they never did term papers on time or they used amphetamines the night before the work was due to get it done. Procrastination in school caused the work to be done poorly or left undone or incomplete.

Trouble Shifting Attention

As I mentioned above, there is a group of people with ADD who have trouble shifting their attention from one thing to another. They have a tendency to get "stuck" or overfocus. This characteristic can be particularly troublesome in school. For these students, taking notes is often a disaster. Note taking requires constant shifts in attention: from teacher to paper to teacher to paper, etc.

Forgetfulness

This symptom often upsets the parents and teachers of ADD students. Forgetting to bring home books, leaving clothes at school, and not turning in homework assignments are common complaints.

Learning Disabilities

Learning difficulties and disabilities are very common in people with ADD. It is essential to recognize and treat these disabilities if a student is going to perform at his or her potential. Common disabilities are writing disabilities (getting thoughts from the brain to the paper), reading disabilities (shifting or reversing letters or numbers), and visual- and auditory-processing problems (trouble accurately hearing what was said).

Unusual Study Habits

Many people with ADD have unusual study habits. Most need a very quiet place to study. I know someone who used to sit in her car under a streetlight to study. She needed an environment that was absolutely quiet and free from distractions. Other people with ADD need noise in order to study. Some people have told me they need the TV or radio on or some other sort of noise to keep themselves focused.

Timed Situations

Timed testing situations spell disaster for those with ADD. Whether it is short math exercises, classroom writing tasks, or testing situations (standardized and otherwise), the time pressure these situations engender can paralyze those with ADD.

WORK

Bill, 32, had just been fired from a job he loved. He knew it was his fault, but he just couldn't organize his time to do the work that was expected. He missed deadlines, drifted off in meetings, and was often late to work. His wife was going to be furious. This was the third job he had lost in their three-year marriage. As a child, Bill had taken Ritalin for troubles in school, but he was taken off the medication when he was a teenager. His doctor told him that all kids outgrow the problems he was having. That was bad advice. At the age of 32, Bill still suffered from the effects of ADD.

Untreated ADD significantly affects the workplace. It costs employers millions of dollars every year in decreased productivity, absenteeism, and employee conflicts. Untreated ADD cuts throughout the adult population. It remains vastly underdiagnosed, at a great cost to our economy.

There is a positive side to ADD in the workplace. For example, people with ADD often are high in energy, enthusiastic, full of ideas, creative, and bursting with energy. If they surround themselves with people who organize them and manage details, they can be very successful. In my clinical practice, I treat many highly successful ADD executives. Unfortunately, many people with ADD are not fortunate enough to be in positions that maximize their strengths and minimize their weaknesses. These folks often have serious problems at work. Here are some of the difficulties that people with ADD are likely to have at work:

The Harder They Try, the Worse It Gets

Research has shown that the more ADD people try to concentrate, the worse it gets for them. As we've seen from SPECT images, the brain regions responsible for concentrated thinking turn off, not on. As the pressure to perform increases, they often fall off in their work. When this decreased performance is interpreted as willful misconduct, serious problems arise. I once treated a man with ADD who was employed as a ship welder. He told me that whenever his boss put pressure on him to do a better job, his work got worse—even though he really tried to do better. When the boss told him that he liked his work, he became more productive. In supervising someone with ADD, it is much more effective to use praise and encouragement than pressure.

Distractibility

Distractibility is often evident in meetings. People with ADD tend to look around the room, drift off, appear bored, forget the conversational direction, and interrupt with extraneous information. Their distractibility and short attention span may also cause them to take much more time to complete their work than their coworkers, just as it did with homework when they were schoolchildren.

Forgetfulness

Forgetfulness is common in ADD and a serious handicap on the job. Just a few examples, such as missed deadlines, forgotten reports, and steps gone undone, illustrate how serious ADD on the job can be.

Impulsivity

A lack of impulse control can get ADD people fired. They may say inappropriate things to supervisors, other employees, or customers. I once had a patient who was fired from thirteen jobs because of his trouble controlling his mouth. Even though he wanted to keep several of the jobs, he couldn't stop himself from blurting out whatever he was thinking before he had a chance to process the thought. Impulsivity also leads to poor decision making. Rather than thinking a problem through, impulsive people act without the necessary forethought. Similarly, ADD people have trouble going through the established channels at work. Their impulsive nature emboldens them to go right to the top to solve problems, rather than work through the system. This may cause resentment in their coworkers and immediate supervisors. Impulsivity may also lead to such problem behaviors as lying and stealing. I have treated many ADD people who have carried the shame and guilt of these behaviors.

Conflict Seeking

Many people with ADD are in constant turmoil with one or more people at work. They seem "unconsciously" to pick out people who are vulnerable to verbally spar with. Conflict-driven behaviors have a tendency to embarrass others, further alienating the ADD sufferer from his or her colleagues. Conflict may follow the ADD person from job to job.

Disorganization

Disorganization is a hallmark of ADD, and it can be particularly damaging in the workplace. Often when you look at the person's work area, it is a wonder they can work in it at all. They tend to have many piles of "stuff"; paperwork is often hard for them to keep straight; and they seem to have a filing system that only they can figure out (and only on good days).

Late to Work

Many people with ADD are chronically late to work because they have significant problems waking up in the morning. I've had several patients who bought sirens from alarm companies to help them wake up. Imagine what their neighbors thought! They also tend to lose track of time, contributing to their tardiness.

Start Many Projects, but Finish Few

The energy and enthusiasm of people with ADD often pushes them to start many projects. Unfortunately, their distractibility and short attention span impairs their ability to complete these undertakings.

One radio station manager told me that he had started over thirty special projects the year before but completed only a handful of them. He told me, "I'm always going to get back to them, but I get new ideas that get in the way."

I also treat a college professor who told me that the year before he saw me he had started three hundred different projects. His wife finished the thought by telling me he had only completed three.

Moodiness and Negative Thinking

ADD tends to cause moodiness, anxiety, and negativity. In addition to the stimulating effects of negative thinking, ADD people often have many experiences with failure, so they come to expect it. Their "sky is falling" attitude has a tendency to get on the nerves of coworkers and can infect the work environment.

Inaccurate Self-Assessment

People with ADD poorly judge their own ability. I've seen situations in which they overvalue themselves and think they are better at their jobs than they really are. Alternately, I've had patients who persistently devalue important assets that they have.

Switches Things Around

ADD causes people to switch things around. This happens with letters or numbers, even phrases or paragraphs. You can imagine the problems this can cause at work. Innumerable wrong numbers, misunderstood documents, and inaccurate calculations are just some of the problems that may result. I once treated a billing clerk who had reversed the amounts on bills she sent out, costing her employer over $12,000. I had to meet with the employer to convince him that ADD was a real phenomenon and that the employee was not trying to sabotage his business.

Tendency Toward Addictions

People with ADD have a tendency toward addictions, such as food, alcohol, drugs, even work. Drug or alcohol addictions cause obvious work problems. Food addictions cause health and self-image problems that can affect work. Addiction to work is also a serious problem, because it causes burnout and family problems that eventually show in the workplace.

Spends Excessive Time at Work Because of Inefficiency

The symptoms of ADD frequently cause a person to be inefficient on their job. This causes many people with ADD to put in overtime that managers consider excessive, resulting in a poor job evaluation or firing. To avoid these problems, many people with ADD take their work home in order to finish it.

SELF-ESTEEM

By the age of 6 or 7, ADD often has a significant negative impact on self-esteem. Here are some of the reasons why:

Frequent Conflict

ADD sufferers have been in conflict with their parents, friends, and teachers over and over for years. This causes them to develop negative "self-talk" patterns and low self- esteem.

Negative Input

The difficult behavior associated with ADD often elicits negative input from others. "Don't do that." "Why did you do that?" "Where was your head?" "What's wrong with you?" "Your brother doesn't act like that!" "You'd do better if you would try harder." "Shame on you!" These are phrases many ADD children hear on a regular basis. Constant negative input wounds a child's self esteem.

Inaccurate Self-Assessment

As mentioned above, people with ADD often judge their own ability poorly. They often devalue their strengths and positive attributes, focusing only on their failures.

Chronic Failure

Most people with ADD have had many failure experiences in life, school, relationships, and work. These disappointments set them up to expect further failure. Whenever a person expects that they will fail, they don't try their best or they don't try at all. Moreover, an expectation of failure causes crippling damage to one's self-image.

Negative Bonding

ADD often causes negative bonding with parents. Bonding is critical to the emotional health of human beings. Yet, by the time many ADD children are school age, they have such a negative relationship with their parents that they learn not to care about other people. This sets them up for societal problems. Without bonding, people don't consider the feelings of others. A person so conditioned has no problem hurting others to get what he or she wants.

A Sense of Being Damaged

Due to the many problems that ADD people have experienced throughout their lives, they often have a sense that they are different from others and that they are "damaged."

Tantrums/Rage Outbursts

As I mentioned above, there is a high incidence of rage outbursts among people with ADD. The sense of being out of control wounds the person's self-esteem, making him question why anyone would value someone so volatile.

Negative Thinking Patterns

Thought patterns are the manifestation of self-esteem. Due to difficult past life experiences, many people with ADD have a tendency to think negatively. They frequently distort situations to make them out to be worse than they really are. They tend to overgeneralize, think in black-and-white terms, predict bad outcomes, label themselves with negative terms, and personalize situations that have little personal meaning. Teaching the ADD person to talk back to negative thoughts is essential to helping them heal.

POINTS TO REMEMBER:

ADD is a neurobiological disorder with
serious psychological and social consequences.

Children, teens, adults, and parents need to know:
It's not their fault.
They didn't cause it.
There is hope.

Parents, spouses and family members with ADD family members
need information. Children, teenagers, and adults
with ADD need good treatment.

PART 3

The Amen Clinic's ADD Brain Enhancement Program

CHAPTER 16

Enhancing ADD Brain Function

Effective Interventions for Treating ADD Types, Including Diet, Exercise, Medications, Supplements, and Behavioral Interventions

The Amen Clinic's ADD Brain Enhancement Program is geared toward optimizing brain function. The program includes diet, exercise, supplements, medications, neurofeedback, and behavioral interventions. Certainly, not everyone needs all treatments, but I believe that it is important for people to know all the options available and the pros and cons of each.

Most people in America have their ADD treated with medication alone. However, research studies by Dr. James Satterfield of Oregon show that medication by itself does not make a lasting difference. To get the best results, patients need interventions in a number of areas. ADD patients need strategies geared toward enhancing brain function and improving their skills at home, in school, at work, and in society at large.

ADD has clear biological roots and serious psychological and social consequences when left untreated. I often use the following computer analogy with my patients: In order for a computer to effectively run any program, its hardware must be sufficient. It must have enough RAM, disk space, and processing speed. Trying to run complex programs on an old computer just won't work. Yet, many people with ADD do not have enough RAM (short-term memory), disk space, or processing speed in their brains because of the underactivity in the prefrontal cortex and temporal lobes. To run programs effectively, you must first optimize the hardware—the brain. But once a computer's hardware is optimized, it still has programming needs. Many people with ADD, because of their hardware (brain) problems, never fully loaded the programs (information) they needed. Once the brain is optimized, it is important to input strategies that help people with ADD be more effective in their family, school, work, and social relationships.

In Chapter 2, we discussed how important it was to assess ADD in a bio-psycho-social fashion. Treating ADD is best done in the same way. It is essential to optimize the ADD brain (biology), the mindset of an ADD person (psychology), and the interactions between the ADD person and the world (social). Ignoring any of these factors can cause treatment failure. Here is a brief summary of ADD treatments. Many of them are expanded in subsequent chapters.

Effective ADD Treatment

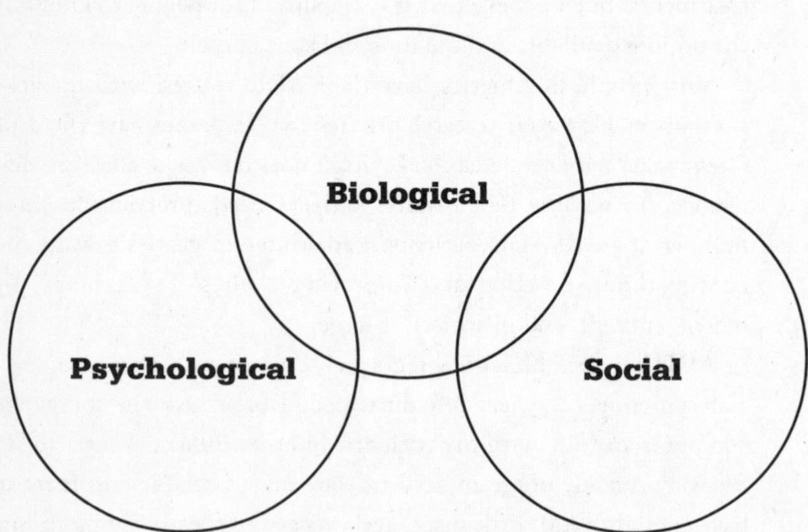

BIOLOGICAL INTERVENTIONS

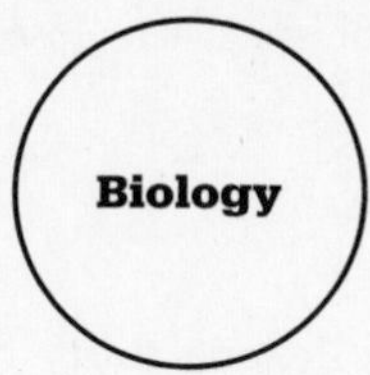

Eliminate Anything Toxic

Toxic substances can cause and exacerbate ADD-like symptoms. (For example, marijuana use can make some people appear as though they have Type 2 [Inattentive] ADD). Eliminate anything toxic to your brain. Given that more than 50 percent of ADD teenagers and adults have or have had problems with drug or alcohol abuse, treatment for abuse is essential in healing ADD.

Caffeine and nicotine have been shown in brain studies to decrease overall blood flow to the brain, in turn making ADD symptoms worse over time. In addition, in my experience both nicotine and caffeine decrease the effectiveness of medication and supplement treatments and increase the number of side effects people have from medication. "But I feel so focused after my coffee in the morning," you say. In the short run caffeine makes you feel more focused. It works much like Ritalin and Adderall. Unfortunately, caffeine also decreases brain blood flow and over time can make the ADD symptoms worse. If possible, also stop any medications that contribute to ADD symptoms.

Protect Your Head

As Chapter 11 clearly showed, head injuries can cause severe ADD-like symptoms. I have found that people who have ADD are more prone to head injuries due to their impulsive nature. Head injuries can take a mild case of Type 2 (Inattentive) ADD and turn it into a severe Type 4 (Temporal Lobe) ADD. Do everything you can to prevent these injuries. Wear your seat belt. Do not engage in activities, no matter how adrenally rewarding they are, if they put you at more risk for head injuries. Make kids wear their helmets when riding bikes, snowboarding, or rollerblading. My 13-year-old daughter knows that if she rides her bike without a helmet, she loses her bike-riding privileges for a month.

Dietary Interventions

This is no small recommendation! As my colleague Barry Sears, Ph.D. (author of *The Zone*), says, "Food is a powerful drug. You can use it to help mood and cognitive ability or you can unknowingly make things worse." All ADD types, except Type 3 (Overfocused) ADD, do better on a higher-protein, lower-carbohydrate diet: the exact opposite of the way that most people eat. I will explore dietary interventions for ADD types in Chapter 17.

Intense Aerobic Exercise

All ADD types benefit from intense aerobic exercise, especially Types 1, 2, 3, and 5. Exercise boosts blood flow to the brain. Exercise also increases serotonin availability in the brain, which has a tendency to calm anterior cingulate hyperactivity—especially important for Type 3. Tryptophan, the amino acid building block for serotonin, is a relatively small molecule. It does not compete well against the larger amino acids in attempting to cross the blood/brain barrier. With intense aerobic exercise the large muscles use up the available supply of bigger amino acids, decreasing the competition for tryptophan. As a result, it crosses more readily into the brain.

I recommend that my patients exercise for 30 to 45 minutes at least five times a week. A fast walk is sufficient, but not a stroll. Whatever exercise you choose, it needs to be intense enough to raise your heart rate.

Avoid Prolonged Exposure to Video or Computer Games

To my own patients I recommend an absolute maximum of 30 to 45 minutes a day spent playing computer or video games. These games are more than just unhelpful: I think they are in fact harmful to many vulnerable ADD brains. Over the past several years two of my patients had seizures while playing video games—patients who had never had seizures before. It is a phenomenon called photophobic seizure, as happened to 730 children in Japan a few years ago while they were watching the Nintendo *Pokémon* cartoon. I have another patient who becomes violent after playing video games. Granted, these cases may be extreme, but I cannot see much good that comes from playing these games, and I believe they have the potential to harm. My best advice is to limit the exposure.

Medication

Medication is an emotionally loaded issue for many people. There is a lot of controversy in this area. After doing brain-imaging work for the past ten years in addition to practicing psychiatry for the past twenty, I have no doubt that medication can be very helpful for many patients. In fact, withholding medication from some patients is downright neglectful. Medication is the best-studied and most effective treatment for ADD. Having said that, medication *alone* is generally bad treatment. Unfortunately, most people get medication by itself without any of the help needed for the psychological and social aspects of ADD. Medication for each ADD type will be discussed in Chapter 18.

Supplements

Even more controversial than medication is using natural supplements for ADD. There is very little if any research behind using supplements with this disorder. However, my clinical experience has shown that supplements can be helpful when used properly. I worry that people spend billions of dollars on these treatments with little regard to effectiveness or, more importantly, side effects. Because supplements are "natural," people think of them as innocuous. In my experience that's just not true. I am not opposed to natural supplements; in fact, I often recommend them. I am opposed to a person being ineffectively treated and dead-set against someone putting him- or herself at risk. Be sure you know what you are taking when you try a supplement. A rational, balanced approach to both medication and supplement treatment is the best medicine. Supplement treatment for ADD will be discussed in Chapter 19.

Neurofeedback

A very exciting biological treatment for ADD is neurofeedback. With neurofeedback electrodes placed on the scalp, electrical brain activity is measured, and the information is fed back to the patient. Both the patient and the doctor can recognize areas of increased and decreased activity. Neurofeedback, like biofeedback, is based on the principle that if one knows the activity in a certain bodily function, then one can learn to enhance or optimize the activity therein. Neurofeedback for each ADD type is discussed in Chapter 20.

Sleep Strategies

Sleep disturbances are very common in people with ADD. Many have trouble falling asleep at night and awakening in the morning. Sleep deprivation can worsen ADD symptoms in that it leads to decreased brain activity. Proper sleep is essential for brain function. Effective strategies for getting up and going to bed are given in Chapter 23.

PSYCHOLOGICAL INTERVENTIONS: EDUCATION

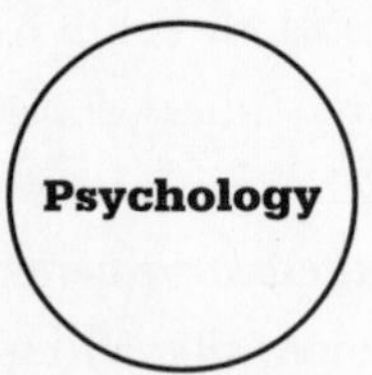

Education about ADD—its impact on home, school, family, and the self—is the first step in treatment. Accurate information empowers you to get the best help. Robert Pasnau, M.D., past president of the American Psychiatric Association, said that coping requires three things: information, self-esteem, and a sense of control. Education has a powerful effect on each of those three criteria, and obtaining accurate information is the critical first step.

Correcting Automatic Negative Thoughts

Negativity is one of the hallmark features of ADD. As I've said, many people with ADD use negative thoughts as a form of self-stimulation, but this habit predisposes them to depression and isolation. In Chapter 24, I will teach you how to identify and rid yourself of the negative thoughts (I call them ANTs—automatic negative thoughts) that invade your life.

Targeted Psychotherapy

For many people with ADD, there are a number of psychological issues that need to be addressed. Without the proper biological treatment, psychotherapy can be a fruitless and frustrating experience for both the therapist and the patient. I have consulted with many ADD patients who have been in psychotherapy for years without much benefit. When they were placed on the right medication or supplements and diet, however, psychotherapy brought about dramatic improvement in just several weeks. I am not dismissing psychotherapy as a necessary component of treatment for children, teens, and adults with ADD. It is often very helpful. It does, however, need to be in combination with the right biological treatment. The following are some psychotherapy themes that are essential in dealing with the ADD patient.

Breaking Up Erroneous Belief Patterns

Many people with ADD may have erroneous, negative beliefs that sabotage their chances for success in the present. For example, they may believe that they'll fail in school (because that was their experience before they were treated), so they will not try. Or they may believe that they are doomed to have poor relationships (again, because that was their experience before treatment), so they will engage in the same repetitive behaviors that impair their ability to relate to others. Once medical treatment is successful, it is also important to correct these beliefs, because beliefs drive behavior. Too often these predictions become self-fulfilling prophecies.

Adrianne never played cards. As a child and teenager, she had trouble learning card games because her attention span was so short. When she did manage to play, her impulsiveness led her into bad decisions. She often lost. As an adult, she avoided social situations in which card games were played. After beginning medication she still avoided playing cards until she began talking about this in therapy. When she made the connection between ADD and her underlying belief about card games, she was able to challenge herself to try again. She surprised herself. Not only did she quite like playing cards, but she was also rather good!

The emotional trauma of having ADD, and all that it entails, leaves many people with intense anxiety. I often have my patients undergo EMDR (eye movement desensitization and reprocessing) therapy to help them deal with the emotional pain of the past. EMDR is a specific treatment for patients who have post traumatic stress disorder, and I have found it helpful for many of my ADD patients. In EMDR the therapist has the patient move his or her eyes back and forth while a traumatic event is remembered. The therapist takes the patient through a series of steps to help relieve the trauma and rid the patient of the underlying beliefs associated with it. Traumas (such as the emotional wreckage left by ADD) often hinder people from moving their lives forward. EMDR is a powerful way to deal with the psychological fallout of struggling for years with untreated ADD.

Accept the Need for Biological Intervention

Biological interventions, such as medication, often become a psychotherapy issue. Many people do not want to believe that there is anything wrong with them. Taking medication or supplements may make them feel, in some way, defective. It is critical to talk about these feelings, for when they are ignored, patients often begin to skip taking their medicine. Those sorts of feelings also perpetuate negative self-esteem.

Justine was an example of this. At age 22 her life was falling apart. She had taken Ritalin as a teenager and it was very helpful for her. However, in the twelfth grade a friend teased her about the medication, and she stopped it. Within the next year she was arrested twice for shoplifting, started using drugs, and dropped out of high school. The next four years were nothing but trouble. After she saw a special on television about adult ADD, she remembered how helpful the medication had been for her and she sought help. Once she began taking Ritalin again, her life turned around.

Coaching for ADD

One of the most helpful psychological treatments for ADD is personal coaching. Coaching helps a person develop good "internal supervision skills." Coaching involves using another person (a coach) to help you set goals and develop the specific skills needed to meet those goals. I have seen it be very powerful for people with ADD, who, as a group, tend to struggle with issues of goal setting, organization, planning, and consistent performance. In Chapter 26, Jane Massengill (the coach for The Amen Clinic) and I will give you a step-by-step guide to ADD coaching.

Focused Breathing

I have found diaphragmatic breathing quite helpful for my ADD patients. This breathing technique lessens temper outbursts and anxiety while improving impulse control and clarity of thought. It is easy to learn and when practiced will help you feel in much better control of your own feelings and behavior. This will be discussed in Chapter 25.

Self-Hypnotic Reprogramming for Success

Many people with ADD have been programmed—in a sense "hypnotized"—into believing they can't change the problems that are holding them back. This negative belief system must be dispensed with in order to bring about lifelong change. In Chapter 27, world renowned mind-body physician Emmet Miller, M.D., and I will give readers a set of instructions to make their own (or their child's) self-hypnotic audiotape. Using this tape can help rewrite the negative emotional script in their minds. When my patients take the time to make this tape and listen to it regularly, they feel more aware, more focused, more goal oriented, and more positive.

SOCIAL INTERVENTIONS: SUPPORT

Obtaining support for yourself and your family is critical. Many people who have ADD or who have it in their family feel isolated and alone. A community of similar people can provide much needed and irreplaceable support. In addition, by interacting with other families on the same journey, you can share a wealth of ideas on coping strategies for specific situations. For over a year I wrote a column in the ADD support section of Prodigy, the online computer service, and I was privileged to see the support that these people found among each other. After I had been writing the column for about six months, I wrote a letter to the ADD group about the turmoil I had at home with my ADD son, who could not get up in the morning. The next morning I logged on to find seventeen e-mails from other people giving me suggestions on how to cope. There is no substitute for that kind of support.

There are many ways to get support for ADD: For example, virtually all of the online computer services have support-group sections for a wide variety of problems, including ADD. Prodigy, America Online, CompuServe, along with many Internet news groups, provide many opportunities for support, information, and interaction. The Internet is a wonderful resource for the very latest information. Look under ADD in the search functions of these services. *A word of caution: Anyone can write on the Internet, so be sure to check out the information you obtain with your personal physician.* I once treated a person who used high doses of a cough syrup to treat ADD on the suggestion of a Web site. He became psychotic and lost his job and his marriage over the bad advice.

Join a local community support group. There are support groups for ADD all over the country. They can be a source of great information. Here are some numbers to contact to get more information:

CHADD Children [and Adults] with ADD
(800) 233-4050
8181 Professional Place #201
Landover, MD 20785
Web site: www.chadd.org

The Kitty Petty Institute
(650) 329-9443
410 Sheridan Avenue
Palo Alto, CA 94306-2020
(415) 329-9443

LDA (Learning Disability Association of America)
4156 Library Road
Pittsburgh, PA 15234-1349
(412) 341-1515
Fax (412) 344-0224
www.ldanatl.org

If there are no effective support groups in your area, get online.

There are numerous toll-free numbers offering bits of information, guidance, and suggestions for adults with ADD and learning disabilities. Despite the useful services that these toll-free numbers provide, many people are confused about exactly what information they can expect to receive. The following resource list, compiled by the National Adult Literacy and Learning Disabilities Center, is designed to give an overview of what information the following organizations give to their callers:

Equal Employment Opportunity Commission (EEOC) 1-800-669-4000. EEOC voice mail directs calls from 7 A.M. to 5:30 P.M. Eastern Time (Monday to Friday). Operators accept orders for publications, fact sheets, posters, and a resource directory for people with disabilities, including learning disabilities. They do not answer questions relating to employment but can give referrals to local EEOC offices, 1103 Kenwood Rd., Bldg. 5, Cincinnati, OH 45242.

HEATH Resource Center, 1-800-544-3284. The National Clearinghouse on Postsecondary Education for Individuals with Disabilities (HEATH Resource Center) has information specialists available from 9 A.M. to 5 P.M. Eastern Time (Monday to Friday) who provide resource papers, directories, information on national organizations, and a resource directory for people with learning disabilities, 1 Dupont Circle NW, #800, Washington, DC 20036.

Job Accommodation Network, 1-800-526-7234, has a free consulting service from 8 A.M. to 8 P.M. Eastern Time (Monday to Thursday) and 8 A.M. to 5 P.M. Eastern Time (Friday) that provides information on equipment, methods, and modifications for persons with disabilities to improve their work environment. All information is specific to the disability, including learning disabilities, P.O. Box 6080, Morgantown, WVA 26506.

National Literacy Hotline, 1-800-228-8813, has a 24-hour bilingual (Spanish/ English) operator service that provides information on literacy/education classes, GED testing services, and volunteer organizations, as well as a learning disabilities brochure.

Orton Dyslexia Society (ODS), 1-800-222-3123, has a 24-hour voice mail service that receives information requests. From 8:30

A.M. to 4:30 P.M. Eastern Time (Monday to Friday) at (410) 296-0232, ODS staff direct people to appropriate materials about issues of dyslexia. Referrals for testing and tutors, branches of ODS, and workshops and conferences.

Parenting and Family Strategies

As we have seen, ADD is a chronic, stressful medical condition that affects every member of a family. Intervening at a family level is essential to having a happy, healthy family life. In addition, I think of parent training as a primary intervention for ADD children and teenagers. These children are often the most challenging for parents, and parents need superior skills to help their children thrive. Parenting and family strategies are found in Chapter 21.

School Strategies

Children, teens, and young adults spend more than a third of their lives in school or working on schoolwork. Understanding ADD in a school situation and learning proper strategies for intervention is an essential part of treatment. Thirty-five percent of untreated ADD teens never finish high school. I have heard it said that graduating from high school is the number one predictor of how a person will do in life. Chapter 22 lays out school intervention strategies for people with ADD.

Interpersonal Strategies

Making and keeping friends is difficult for many people with ADD. It is estimated that at least half of all children and teens with ADD have problems with their peers, and up to 75 percent of adults have interpersonal problems. Social skill training enhances the effectiveness of ADD treatment. Social skill treatment often includes:

- teaching communication skills, including active listening (repeating back the information and feelings you hear before you respond)

- providing an environment for successful peer contacts and positive experiences (Encourage the ADD person to invite peers over to the house to spend time together.)
- increasing knowledge about appropriate behavior (Look for situations to teach the child about helpful social behavior; discussing interactions that are seen on TV or in stores can be very helpful.)
- teaching self-monitoring and internal dialogue techniques. (These include techniques that teach people to question what they do before they do it, to stop and think through the consequences of their behavior before they act in a certain way.)
- searching for areas of social competence (sports, karate, music) and giving the ADD person healthy doses of these activities, and
- diligently working on decreasing aggressive behavior at home and school; (aggressiveness is one of the strongest predictors of peer rejection).

A good place to start social skill training is with the siblings at home. I believe it is essential to expect siblings to be civil and act appropriately with each other. Many psychologists say, "Let the children work out their own problems; don't interfere." I disagree. Remember what happened to Cain and Abel when their parents didn't intervene? In sibling relationships, clearly state that you expect them to treat each other with respect. When they are positive and appropriate with each other, notice and praise them. When they are inappropriate, condescending, aggressive, or mean with each other, discipline them. When parents lay out the ground rules, siblings are much more likely to get along with each other, which may translate into their behaving more appropriately with others.

CHAPTER 17

Dietary Interventions for ADD Types

I was recently in central Oregon, lecturing to mental-health professionals about ADD. When I walked into the large lecture hall, my heart sank. On a table in the back of the room were boxes and boxes of muffins, donuts, bagels, and cinnamon rolls. I thought to myself, *Oh, no, Daniel. You have to be really good this morning or no one will be able to pay attention in about half an hour.* High simple-carbohydrate foods—of which typical breakfast foods are a prime example—are terrible for concentration. Foods that are filled with sugar or substances that rapidly break down to sugar cause a quick rise in blood sugar. An insulin release that lowers blood sugar below normal levels follows soon thereafter, making people feel tired, spacey, confused, and inattentive. Give people a lot of sugar (or substances like bread that are easily broken down to sugar) in the morning and they will act as if they have ADD. I started my lecture talking about the food in the back. "The food in the back is a good example of what parents unknowingly do to make kids struggle in school. Most children start the day with muffins, donuts, Pop-Tarts, bagels, cinnamon rolls, and sugary cereals. They get virtually no protein in the morning. No wonder teachers complain that half their kids can't concentrate. In order for children or adults to focus, they need to have nutritious food that enhances energy and concentration. Especially for people with ADD, the solution is a higher-protein, lower-carbohydrate diet." A better breakfast for the group would have been cheeses, hard-boiled eggs, or whole-grain bagels with cream cheese. I finished my lecture by saying, "If you want to concentrate this afternoon and have good energy until dinnertime, have no simple carbohydrates at lunch. No bread, no pasta, no potatoes, no rice, and no sugar. Have something like a stir fry without the rice, a Cobb salad, or a cheeseburger without the bun." Many people who took my suggestions about lunch came up to me at the end of the day saying how amazed they were by their energy and concentration.

Dietary interventions are important in treating all types of ADD. Food can be used like medicine. It can have a powerfully positive effect on cognition, feelings, and behavior, but it can have a negative effect as well. In fact, the right diet can decrease the amount of medication needed. However, the wrong diet will do the opposite. In 1992, Joseph Egger reported in the British medical journal *Lancet* that 116 of 185 hyperactive children had a positive response to a low-allergen diet (higher in protein and lower in simple carbohydrates) supplemented by calcium, zinc, magnesium, and vitamins. Over and over in my clinical practice I have found that diet matters.

When I can convince my patients to eat this way, they notice better mood stability, better focus, less distractibility, more mental stamina, and less drowsiness in the late morning and midafternoon. Here are strategies geared toward using food as a positive force in ADD treatment.

ADD FOOD INTERVENTIONS

For the purpose of creating an ADD-friendly diet, we'll divide food into four groups: water, protein, carbohydrates, and fat.

Water

The human body is two thirds water. Water is an essential part of every function in the body, including brain blood flow and cell function. Necessary for proper metabolism, water helps transport nutrients and waste products in and out of cells. Without enough of it, the body struggles to function properly. An abundance of it gives cells the opportunity to work right. Be sure to drink adequate amounts of water every day. Nutritionists recommend at least 8 eight-ounce glasses a day. Avoid substances that dehydrate the body, such as caffeine (which causes increased urination) and alcohol (one of the main reasons people get hung over after getting drunk).

Proteins

Proteins are essential to life. They are involved with immune system function, muscle mass, the enzymes driving the chemical reactions of life, hormones, and the creation of neurotransmitters to make the brain function smoothly. When proteins are consumed, the body breaks them down to their constituent parts, called amino acids. Some amino acids are essential, because they have to come from the diet, and some are nonessential, because they can be made from protein stores in the body. In addition, there are two types of proteins, complete and incomplete. Complete proteins such as those found in meat, fish, poultry, cheese, eggs, dairy, and soybean products such as tofu and soymilk contain substantial amounts of all of the essential amino acids. Incomplete proteins have only some of the essential amino acids. They are found in a number of foods, most notably grains, legumes, nuts, and leafy green vegetables.

HEALTHIEST FORMS OF PROTEIN

Chicken
Turkey
Very lean cuts of beef
Fish, especially salmon and tuna (farm-raised, especially)
Low-fat cottage cheese
Low-fat string cheese
Milk
Soy-based food products
Protein powder.

Carbohydrates

Carbohydrates come from plant-based foods. Milk and milk products are the only foods derived from animals that contain significant amounts of carbohydrates. There are three types of carbohydrates: sugar, simple carbohydrates, and complex carbohydrates. The most basic carbohydrate, sugar, is a simple molecule used for energy. Sugar also goes by the names of fructose (fruit sugar), sucrose (table sugar), lactose (milk sugar), corn syrup, and glucose. Sugar passes rapidly from the stomach to the bloodstream. When the pancreas notices a rise in blood sugar, it releases the hormone insulin to drive the sugar into the body's cells. Paradoxically, a high sugar load can cause an overproduction of insulin that has the effect of lowering blood-sugar levels below optimal levels. When that happens, people feel tired, sluggish, and inattentive. Simple carbohydrates are sugar molecules connected by an oxygen molecule. They include products made from refined or white flour, such as pasta, bagels, and white bread, and such staples as potatoes, rice, and cereals. Simple carbohydrates easily break down to sugar in the stomach and rapidly enter the bloodstream, just a little slower than sugars. Complex carbohydrates, such as vegetables, whole grains, and beans, have more complex chemical bonds and take a longer time to break down in the stomach. Their higher quantity of fiber and water further slows the rate at which they are absorbed. In choosing carbohydrates for your or your child's diet, select more complex carbohydrates such as fruits, vegetables, peas, beans, and whole grain products, as opposed to sugar or simple carbohydrates. Complex carbohydrates are less likely to provoke an overproduction of insulin and the tired, inattentive feelings that produces. In addition, they are filled with fiber, vitamins, and minerals—all essential ingredients for your health.

HEALTHIEST FORMS OF CARBOHYDRATES

Fruits that tend to be especially good are apricots, oranges, tangerines, pears, grapefruit, apples, and kiwi.

Vegetables (avoid large amounts of carrots due to high sugar content)
Beans, especially black beans and kidney beans
Whole grains, no white bread or bread with added sugar (You'll have to search for good bread.)

Fats

In the last fifteen years a lot of attention has been focused on decreasing fat in the diet. Yet, fat is an essential ingredient in the body. Fat is necessary for normal brain development, making it an essential ingredient during infancy and childhood. Fats come from both animal and plant sources.

Fats are composed of building blocks called fatty acids. There are three types of fatty acids: saturated, polyunsaturated, and monounsaturated. *Saturated fatty acids* are found primarily in animal products, including dairy items, such as milk, cream, butter, and cheese; and fatty meats like beef, lamb, and veal. The fat marbling you can see in beef is composed of saturated fat. Some vegetable products, such as coconut oil and vegetable shortening, are also high in saturated fatty acids. The liver uses saturated fatty acids to produce cholesterol, especially LDL, or bad cholesterol, which clogs arteries. However, saturated fatty acids are also the basis for many hormones.

Polyunsaturated fatty acids are found in the greatest abundance in corn, soybean, safflower, and sunflower oils. Polyunsaturated fatty acids tend to lower both bad (LDL) and good (HDL) cholesterol.

Monounsaturated fatty acids are found in vegetable and nut oils, such as olive, peanut, and canola oil. An essential subgroup of these fats, omega-3 fatty acids, are found almost exclusively in coldwater fish, such as salmon, tuna, and mackerel. Monounsaturated fatty acids tend to raise HDL or good cholesterol.

Each of these three types of fat plays an essential role in the body. The ratio of these types of fat in your diet directly impacts how effectively your cells function.

The brain is a unique organ in that more than half of its weight is composed of fat. Nearly one third of that fat consists of the long-chain omega-3 fatty acid known as docosahexaenoic acid (DHA). This particular essential fatty acid must be part of your diet and is required, not for only maintaining healthy nerve synapses, but also for the development of new brain pathways. It has been shown in rodent studies that diets high in DHA increase the levels of both dopamine and serotonin in the frontal cortex.

HEALTHIEST FORMS OF FATS

Olive oil
Canola oil
Grapeseed oil
Avocados
Nuts, such as Brazil nuts, macadamia nuts, almonds, cashews, and pistachios
Fish oil

In using food as medicine, it is important to maintain a proper balance between proteins, carbohydrates, and fat. Many people with ADD have too many simple carbohydrates in their diet. Not only does this aggravate ADD symptoms, it upsets the body's metabolic balance.

All ADD types, except Type 3 (Overfocused) ADD, do better on a higher-protein, lower-carbohydrate diet. That's the exact opposite of the way that most people eat.

SIMPLE STEPS TO ADD DIETARY SUCCESS

1. **Eat three meals a day and one or two snacks.** Breakfast is important. It gives fuel for the morning and increases metabolism and blood flow. Make sure there is some form of protein in the morning (such as lean meat, cheese, cottage cheese, eggs, nuts, or protein powder). Snacks are also important to help maintain good energy and concentration.
2. **Eat protein at each meal.** (As we have seen protein is found in meat, eggs, cheese, nuts, and beans.) Protein contains the amino

acid building blocks for neurotransmitters in the brain. Protein is essential to a "concentration diet."

3. **Increase the amounts of complex carbohydrates in your diet.** (These are found in vegetables and whole grains.) Complex carbohydrates break down slower in the gut more readily than simple carbohydrates. They do not cause an overproduction of insulin and generally do not cause a drop in blood sugar. Carrots have a high sugar content, so they should be used only in small amounts.
4. **Watch fruit and fruit juice intake.** Most people think that they can have an unlimited amount of fruit and fruit juices. Most fruits are very high in natural sugar (fructose), which can have the same effect on blood sugar as sugar straight out of a box. Fruit is better than fruit juices because of the extra vitamins and fiber you get, but you can overdo fruit and feel sluggish and mentally slowed down. Good choices are apricots, oranges, tangerines, pears, grapefruit, apples, and kiwi. Avoid grapes, dates, and bananas, as their sugar content seems to be the highest.
5. **Reduce or eliminate most simple carbohydrates.** (This includes bread or pasta made with white flour, white rice, white potatoes, sugar, corn syrup, honey, and candy.) At the same lecture I mentioned at the beginning of the chapter, a therapist came up to me during the break with this story. He said, "I'm so glad you mentioned the sugar. I used to be a very angry person; sometimes I would even scare my family. It made me feel terrible. I even took anger management classes, but they didn't seem to help. When I eliminated the sugar in my diet, I noticed almost an immediate reduction in outbursts, plus I felt more energetic, lost weight, and was much more focused." His personal experience was the same as my clinical experience.
6. **Increase the amounts of omega-3 fatty acids in your diet.** (Sources include large coldwater fish, such as tuna and salmon, as well as walnuts and Brazil nuts.) More on this in Chapter 19.

Here is a list of suggestions to help implement these dietary strategies:

Things Good for Breakfast

Omelets with lean meats, cheese, or vegetables
Eggs and lean sausage
Whole-grain cereal (low or no sugar: Kashi cereals have no sugar.)
Cottage cheese and fruit
Cottage cheese and minute steak
Whole grain bagels and cream cheese
Oatmeal (high in fiber and also contains gamma linolenic acid, an essential fatty acid)

(Avoid sugar, e.g., sugar cereals, doughnuts, Pop-Tarts, waffles and pancakes with syrup, and cinnamon rolls.)

Things Good for Lunch

Stir-fry (vegetables and lean meat, no rice)
Cobb salad (no sugar in the salad dressing)
Caesar salad with chicken breast (no sugar)
Tuna salad
Sandwiches made with lean protein and multigrain bread
Sandwiches made with 100-percent natural peanut butter and a sugar-free spreadable 100-percent fruit jam

(Avoid sugar and simple carbohydrates, e.g., white bread, french fries, breaded onion rings or meat, potato chips, potatoes [unless eaten with the skin] and ketchup.)

Things Good For Dinner

Salad
Lean protein, such as beef, chicken, pork, lamb, fish (highest in Omega-3) fatty acids
Vegetables

(Avoid sugar and simple carbohydrates, e.g., white bread, french fries, breaded onion rings or meat, potato chips, potatoes [unless eaten with the skin], and ketchup.)

Balanced Fast Foods

Wendy's chili

Jack-in-the-Box Chicken Fajita Pita sandwich

McDonald's Egg McMuffin (balanced between protein and carbohydrates)

Snacks

Sugar-free ice cream

Cream cheese and celery

Deviled eggs

Olives

Natural peanut butter and celery

Nuts, especially Brazil Nuts (high in omega-3 fatty acids).

Homemade beef jerky (This is my personal favorite. Take flank steak and slice it thinly with the grain; put a little salt, pepper, and garlic powder on the meat, and then put it in a dehydrator. It is cheap, very tasty, and the kids like it a lot.)

Fruits such as apricots, oranges, tangerines, pears, grapefruit, apples, and kiwi, but eat them in conjunction with some form of protein.

Use these guidelines especially at the times you (or your child) needs to focus. A Twinkie snack before studying guarantees more problems with attention span. If you want to have pasta, bread, cinnamon rolls, or sugar ice cream, have it at a time that you don't need to focus, such as on the weekends or before bed.

Eating with these guidelines will stabilize blood sugar, lower cholesterol, decrease your appetite, help you to lose weight, and improve concentration and energy.

TYPE 3 (OVERFOCUSED) ADD

Type 3 (Overfocused) ADD is associated with low serotonin and dopamine levels. As a result, a higher-protein, lower-carbohydrate diet (which enhances focus) may cause people with Overfocused ADD to fixate even more on the things that bother them. Remember, the problem in this type is not that they can't pay attention; it is that they can't *stop* paying attention. Dietary interventions for this type are geared toward increasing serotonin and dopamine. Tryptophan (or L-tryptophan) is an essential amino acid found in abundance in all protein-rich foods. It would therefore seem reasonable to assume that if you ate a high-protein diet, you would increase tryptophan levels. However, the opposite is true. When you eat a high-protein diet, tryptophan, a relatively small amino acid, cannot muscle its way into brain cells in the presence of other, more robust amino acids. The result is lowered tryptophan levels in the brain. On the other hand, carbohydrate-containing foods, such as pastas, potatoes, bread, pastries, pretzels, candy, and popcorn, increase L-tryptophan levels in the brain. In 1972, Dr. John Fernstrom and Dr. Richard Wurtman from MIT published their landmark study on carbohydrates and brain serotonin levels in the journal *Science.* The researchers showed that the protein and carbohydrate content of food had a significant impact on the production of serotonin. They found that cerebral serotonin and dopamine levels can be raised by eating a diet balanced between carbohydrates and protein. Many people unknowingly trigger cognitive inflexibility or mood problems by eating diets low in L-tryptophan. The high-protein, low-carbohydrate diets that I recommend for the other types of ADD make people with cingulate problems worse.

Eating for Type 3 ADD needs balance. A diet high in simple carbohydrates (doughnuts, pasta, french fries, apple pie) will help you feel more positive and more flexible, but it will not help your energy level or ability to focus (or weight!). Type 3 ADD needs a balanced between carbohydrates and protein—for example, sausage and cheese with pasta; apple pie only after some protein at dinner; french fries with a hamburger patty; and meat pizza with a thin crust.

Diet matters. Pay attention to it.

CHAPTER 18

Medication for ADD Types

Most people associate ADD treatment with medication and medication alone. While medication is an important component of effective ADD treatment, it cannot be used in a vacuum. Giving a patient a pill with no social or psychological support can be as bad as withholding treatment entirely. However, it is just as irresponsible to deny a patient appropriate medication because of a bias. Healing ADD requires involvement in the patient's life. It requires caring, follow-up, and attention. Ignoring the patient's need for social, psychological, or biological intervention can only lead to failure.

In the midst of all the controversy about psychoactive drugs, we would do well to remember that ADD is a *neurobiological disorder*. Effective treatment depends upon biological intervention. Sometimes the other biological therapies discussed in this book (supplements, neurofeedback, exercise, etc.) can replace the need for medication. But sometimes medication is a must. It can be lifesaving.

Whenever medication is started or considered, it's essential to have clear goals in mind for its use. Appropriate ADD medication treatment goals include:

- increasing attention span and learning
- decreasing distractibility

- decreasing restlessness or high activity levels
- decreasing impulsiveness and increasing thoughtfulness
- decreasing irritability
- increasing motivation
- improving overall functioning at school, at work, at home, in relationships, and within the self.

Medication needs to be targeted to each individual ADD type. The wrong medication can make things worse. ADD treatment in this country has focused almost exclusively on brain stimulants. When these don't work (or when they make the patient worse), the ADD person is labeled nonresponsive and written off, or the drugs themselves are said to be ineffective, harmful, or "just a way of medicating bad behavior." In recent years, medical treatment of ADD has gotten a bum rap. The fault lies not with the concept of giving medicine to people with ADD, but with giving people with ADD *the wrong medicine.*

Misdiagnosis can cause serious problems, making an ADD person suffer even more. Inappropriate diagnosis can affix an inaccurate label to a child's perfectly healthy personality. ADD is *not* overdiagnosed: In fact, I think it's underdiagnosed. However, I have no doubt that misdiagnosis runs rampant throughout the health care community. People with ADD are being missed; people without ADD are being mistreated; and the reputation of effective ADD medications is being dragged down, with terrible consequences for the people who truly need them. It's time that the health care community recognizes that ADD is not a simple disorder and takes a serious look at how it is treated.

Ineffective treatment is not innocuous. When treatments fail, individuals and families get discouraged. Aside from the personal cost to the patient of this discouragement, a failed healing program can lead to the ADD remaining untreated. The costs for that are unimaginably high for both the individual and society at large. It's been my clinical experience that the earlier treatment is effective, the more people are willing to follow through with it.

TYPE 1 (CLASSIC) ADD & TYPE 2 (INATTENTIVE) ADD

The best-known medications, stimulants, are the first-line medications for treating Type 1 and Type 2 ADD. Our current understanding of these medications is that they increase dopamine output from the basal ganglia and increase activity in the prefrontal cortex and temporal lobes. The following is a table that analyzes the currently available stimulant medications:

Generic name	Brand name	Milligrams a day/ available strengths	Times a day	Notes
amphetamine salt combination	Adderall (sustained release)	5–80/ 5, 10, 20, 30	1–2	My personal favorite. I start with Adderall because it lasts longer and is gentler as it wears off. Also, the tablets are double-scored. This makes it easy to quarter them and fine-tune the dose.
methylphenidate	Ritalin Methylin	5–120 5, 10, 20	2–4	Watch for rebound when it wears off.
methylphenidate sustained release	Ritalin SR (sustained Metadate	10–120/ 20 Metadate comes in 10 mg tablets as well.	1–2	Many say it's erratic in its effect. I find that many doctors underdose it. It is only 50–60% bioavailable, which means you have to give more to get the same effect as regular Ritalin.
methylphenidate sustained release	Concerta	18–54/ 18, 36 mg	1	Once-a-day dosing is a clear advantage for many.
dextroamphetamine	Dexedrine, Dextrostat	5–80 5, (10 generic only)	2–4	Watch for rebound when it wears off.
dextroamphetamine slow-release caps	Dexedrine, Spansules (sustained release)	5–80 5, 10, 15	1–2	Seems more reliable than Ritalin SR.
pemoline	Cylert	18.75–112.5 (up to 150 for adults) 18.75, 37.5, 75	1–2	Routine liver screening is essential. Lasts longer than regular-release Ritalin or Dexedrine. I use Cylert last because of the liver toxicity issue.

Contrary to popular belief, these are very safe medications. The PDR lists 60 milligrams as the top dosage for Ritalin and 40 milligrams as the top dosage for Adderall and Dexedrine. The maximum safe dose is much higher. Many clinicians, like myself, feel the recommended doses are too low for some individuals. A study performed at Harvard indicated that adults, on average, needed about a milligram of methylphenidate per kilogram of body weight per day. So if someone weighs 70 kilograms (about 150 pounds), he or she will need on average 70 milligrams a day. With Cylert it is very important to monitor liver function tests. Two to three percent of people taking Cylert develop a chemical hepatitis. For this reason, I usually reserve Cylert as my last choice.

It is essential not to take stimulants with citrus juices (orange, grapefruit, lemon) or anything with citric acid in it. (Read the labels: Citric acid is used in many things as a preservative). It tends to lessen the effect of medication. Likewise, decrease caffeine intake when taking a stimulant. Caffeine and stimulants together overstimulate the nervous system.

ADDERALL AND CONCERTA: THE DRUGS OF CHOICE FOR TYPE 1 AND TYPE 2 ADD

Adderall and Concerta, my drugs of choice for types 1 and 2 ADD, have several important advantages. They last longer than regular-release Ritalin and Dexedrine—between five and seven hours for Adderall and ten and eleven hours for Concerta, versus only two to four hours for regular-release Ritalin and Dexedrine. They are generally given once or twice a day. Giving a higher dose of Adderall in the morning than in the evening has been shown in one study to help increase the duration of effectiveness. In one study, teachers preferred Adderall to Ritalin by 70 percent. Patients, parents, and teachers say that Adderall and Concerta are smoother when they take effect and smoother when they wear off.

Another reason that I prefer Adderall is that the manufacturer has made it in four strengths: 5, 10, 20, and 30 milligrams. The tablet is double-scored so that it can be halved and quartered to fine-tune the dose. Because of the ability to break tablets, the daily cost of Adderall is generally less than the other stimulant medications, and patient compliance is enhanced. Also, the number of pills one has to take is generally less with Adderall.

The number of pills a patient takes a day can be a very important issue. For example, Ritalin comes in 5-, 10-, and 20-milligram tablets. Let's say that a person is taking 15 milligrams three times a day—a fairly typical ADD dose. The person will end up taking three 5-milligram tablets three times a day, or nine tablets a day. Some people get upset about taking this many tablets, feeling that it reflects on how messed up they must be. An equivalent dose of Adderall is 15 milligrams twice a day. Since Adderall comes in 5-, 10-, 20-, and 30-milligram tablets, the patient takes half of a 30 milligram tablet twice a day. Taking half a tablet twice a day does not have the same emotional impact as nine tablets a day.

Adderall and Concerta do not always work. Often when they don't work, Ritalin or Dexedrine may. I go through each of the stimulants until I find the best one for my patients.

Here is a list of common questions about stimulant medications in general.

1. *What are the indications for stimulant medications?*
Stimulant medications have several uses in medicine. Most commonly, they are prescribed for ADD. They are also used for narcolepsy (sudden sleep attacks), as an adjunctive treatment for depression, in chronic obesity, and to help thinking, concentration problems, and appetite problems in the elderly.

2. *How can stimulant medications help?*
They can improve attention span, decrease distractibility, increase the ability to finish tasks, improve the ability to follow directions, decrease hyperactivity and restlessness, and lessen impulsivity. Frequently, handwriting improves with this medication. Schoolwork, homework, and overall work performance often improve signifi-

cantly, while aggression and stubbornness decrease. Listening and communication skills show improvement, along with a decrease in conflict-seeking or stimulation behaviors.

3. *How long does the medication last? What is the usual dosage?*

Ritalin and Dexedrine usually last three to four hours, but in some people they last as little as two and a half hours or as long as six hours. There is a slow-release form of Ritalin that lasts six to eight hours and may help you or your child avoid taking a late-morning or noontime dose. However, the slow-release form of Ritalin has a reputation for being somewhat erratic. For some people it works great; for others it's lousy. Often you just have to try it to see. A new form of slow-release methylphenidate, Concerta, was released in late 2000. It lasts from ten to eleven hours and appears so far to be more reliable than the slow-release form of Ritalin. The slow-release form of Dexedrine is reliable. Adderall acts like a slow release preparation and usually lasts about six to seven hours. It also tends to be smoother in onset of action and when wearing off.

In addition to weekday morning doses, I usually prescribe medication for my patients in the afternoon and on weekends. During those times people with ADD still need to do work, homework, or housework and interact with other people.

Everyone is different in his or her need for medication. Some people need small doses (2½ to 5 milligrams) of stimulant medication twice a day; some need it four or five times a day (of regular release). Others need larger doses (15 to 20 milligrams). I have found that response often does not correlate with body weight or age. Trial, supervision, and observation are the keys to finding the right dose.

4. *How will the doctor monitor the medication?*

In my practice, I initially see patients every couple of weeks until we find the right medication and dosage. During appointments I ask about progress (at home, school, and work) and check for any side effects of the medication. I'll keep a check on weight and height and occasionally check blood pressure. When Cylert is used, it is critical to check blood work for liver function before starting the medication, and every couple of months thereafter. In addition, I often ask teachers to fill out follow-up rating scales to help me gauge the effectiveness of the medication. For adults, I often ask that their spouses come to the appointments so that I can get another opinion on the patients' progress.

5. *What side effects can these medications have?*

Of all the medications I prescribe, stimulants, in my opinion, are the safest. I have never had to hospitalize a patient for a bad side effect, and I have never had a side effect that did not go away once we stopped the medication.

Any medication can have side effects, including allergies to the medication, which are usually exhibited by rashes. Because each patient is different, it is important to work together with your physician to find the best medication with the fewest, least bothersome side effects. The following list may not include rare or unusual side effects. Talk to your doctor if you or your child experience anything unusual after starting the medication.

Common side effects

These often go away after about two to three weeks or if the dosage of the medication is lowered. As the medication wears off, there may be a rebound effect where the hyperactivity or moodiness becomes worse than before the medication was started. Dosage adjustment usually helps rebound.

Lack of appetite. Encourage a good breakfast, and afternoon and evening snacks; give medication after meals rather than before. Some children and teens become hungry near bedtime. Unfortunately, some parents think that their child's hunger is no more than a manipulative ploy to stay up later, and they engage the child or teen in a battle. The medication really does affect appetite. If the child or teen is hungry later on and they did not have much to eat at dinner, it is often a good idea to give them a late-evening meal or snack. For some people a lack of appetite is a significant problem and the medication may need to be changed or adjusted. Some of my patients use nutritional supplements, to make sure they get enough calories and nutrients.

Trouble falling asleep. Some people experience insomnia. If they do, I either give them a lower dose in the late afternoon or eliminate the last dose. In cases where there are problems when the last dose is eliminated, I may try giving a small dose of the stimulant right before bedtime. This works especially well for the hyperactive group. The medication settles them down so that they can go to sleep. For insomnia, I often recommend a concoction of 6 ounces of warm milk with a tablespoon of vanilla and a teaspoon of sugar or honey. This seems to have a nice sedating effect for many people.

Headaches or stomachaches. Patients may complain of headaches or stomachaches. These typically go away after several weeks. Tylenol and ibuprofen (Advil) seem to be helpful for the headaches, and taking the medication with food often decreases the stomach problems.

Irritability, crankiness, crying, emotional sensitivity, staring into space, loss of interest in friends. Some patients experience moodiness and minor personality changes. These side effects often go away in a week or two. If they don't, the medication often needs to be changed, maybe to an antidepressant.

Less Common Side Effects

Tics. Some patients develop tics (such as eye blinking, throat clearing, head jerking) on the medication. If that happens, it is important to discuss it with your doctor. Sometimes the tics go away on their own; sometimes higher doses of the medication may improve the tics; and sometimes the medication has to be stopped. If the stimulant is very helpful, I may add another medication (such as clonidine or risperidone) along with the stimulant to help with the tics.

A complicating factor with tics is that a high percentage of patients with tic disorders, such as Gilles de la Tourette's syndrome (manifested by having both motor and vocal tics), have ADD. Sometimes it is hard to know if the medication caused the tics or if the tics were already present but worsened with the medication.

Slowed growth. There used to be a concern about stimulants stunting growth, but the long-term studies show that even though they may slow growth for a period of about a year, in the long run children usually catch up to where they should be.

Rapid pulse or increased blood pressure. If a patient notices chest pain or a heart flutter, it is important to notify the physician immediately.

Nervous habits. Picking at the skin, stuttering, and hair pulling can sometimes occur with these medications.

But keep in mind that the side effects of having untreated ADD are immeasurably worse that those caused by the medication!

6. *What could happen if this medication is stopped suddenly?*
There are no medical problems due to stopping the medication suddenly. A few people may experience tiredness, irritability, moodiness, trouble sleeping, or increased hyperactivity for a few days if they have been on daily medication for a long time. Often it is better to stop the medication gradually (over a week or so).

7. *How long will the medication be needed?*
There is no way to know how long a person may need to take the medication. The patient, doctor, parent, teacher, and spouse need to work together to find out what is right for each person. Sometimes

the medication is only needed for a few years, and sometimes it is needed for many years. Medication is an essential treatment for ADD, and until patients outgrow it (as sometimes happens) or find an alternative therapy that works (such as neurofeedback), they need to remain on the medication. Untreated ADD is a serious disorder and the goal of treatment should be to eliminate its effects, not get off medication.

8. *Does this medication interact with other medications?*
It is a good idea to check with your doctor before mixing any prescription medications. Make sure he or she knows every medicine—including over-the-counter preparations and dietary supplements—that you are taking. When stimulants are used with tricyclic antidepressants, an occasional side effect may occur, such as confusion, irritability, hallucinations, or emotional outbursts. Sometimes, however, combining stimulants with certain antidepressants can be a powerfully positive treatment. I have done this in many patients without any ill effects, but remember that everyone is different.

It is not a good idea to combine stimulants with nasal decongestants (such as medications that contain pseudoephedrine or related medications), because rapid pulse or high blood pressure may develop. If nasal decongestion is severe, it is better to use a cortisone nasal spray.

Many patients with ADD become cranky or more hyperactive on antihistamines, such as Benadryl. If medicine for allergies is needed, use one of the antihistamines that does not enter the brain, such as Claritan. Check with the pharmacist before taking any over-the-counter medication.

9. *Does this medication stop working at puberty?*
No! For most people it continues to work into adulthood. If it does lose its effectiveness, the dose may need to be increased; alternately, switching to another stimulant may be helpful. However, for the vast majority of people with ADD, medication does not stop working at puberty despite what physicians used to tell parents.

10. *Why does this medication require a special prescription? (This information varies from state to state.)*
    Prescriptions for Adderall, Concerta, Ritalin, and Dexedrine require special prescriptions known as "triplicates" that must be filled within fourteen days of the time the prescription is dated. (Cylert does not have this requirement.) Adderall, Concerta, Ritalin, and Dexedrine are controlled medications. Some adults have been known to abuse them, but this is rare. In fact, the research shows that children who are adequately treated for ADD have a much lower percentage of drug abuse as teenagers and adults than those kids with ADD who were never treated with medication. In my experience, this medication does not cause illegal drug use or addiction!

11. *What if my child or I have problems remembering to take the medication?*
    Remembering to take medication three times a day can be difficult, even for people who do not have ADD. Forgetfulness is a common symptom of ADD, and when the medication has worn off, the person is fully ADD again. If forgetfulness is a chronic problem, don't assign blame or be upset. Look for solutions. Here are two I recommend: Try switching to a slow-release form of the medication, or get an alarm system (such as a digital watch that has five alarms) to help you remember.

12. *What about the negative news media reports on these medications?*
    It is critical to get your medical information from your doctor, not from sensational talk-show hosts. Many people have erroneous ideas about stimulant medication. If you hear things that worry you, check with your doctor before making any decisions.

For a period of a year, I kept a log of comments my patients told me after I started them on stimulant medication for types 1 and 2 ADD. These medications can turn a person's life around. Here are some of the comments:

"I experienced an increased awareness of the world around me. I saw the hills for the first time when driving to work. I saw the bay when I crossed over the bridge. I actually noticed the color of the water!"

"A dramatic difference! I am really amazed."

"I experienced a 180-degree difference in my attitude."

"I left your office a skeptic. I came back converted."

"My husband said he doesn't have a knot in his stomach anymore."

"I look at my children and say 'Aren't they cute,' rather than complaining about them."

"I could enjoy the moment. My thoughts are calmer, quieter, easier to live with."

"I could sit and watch a movie for the first time in my life."

"I am able to handle situations where I used to be hysterical. I am able to see when I'm starting to overreact."

"The lens on my life is much clearer."

"I was tremendously overscheduled. No sane person would do that!"

"It amazes me that a little yellow pill [5 milligrams of Ritalin] can take me from wanting to jump off the bridge to loving my husband and enjoying my children."

"It is like being given sight!"

"I'm not running at train-wreck speed."

"For the first time I felt in charge of my life."

"I'm better able to keep things in perspective."

"I used to think I was stupid. It seemed everyone else could do more things than me. I'm starting to believe that there may be intelligent life in my body."

"My appetite is more normal."

"I sleep much better. Can you believe I'm taking a stimulant and it calms me down?"

"I'm out of the damned black hole I was in."

"I used to be the kind of person who would go walking by myself in downtown Detroit at 2 A.M. Now on the medication I would never do something so stupid. Before I just wouldn't think about the consequences."

"Now I can give talks in front of groups. Before, my mind would always go blank. I organized my life around not speaking in public. Now my brain feels calmer, clearer."

"I feel like I think everyone else feels."

"I'm not as intimidated by others like I used to be."

"My husband may not be as happy as before I was on medication. Now I can think and he doesn't win all of the arguments. I'm going to have to retrain him to not always expect to get his way."

"I'm not losing my temper."

"It's like waking up after being asleep your whole life."

"Night and day!"

"I feel totally in control of my life."

"Six months ago there was no way I would drive on LA freeways. Now I can drive on them no problem."

"I can't stand useless confrontation when I used to thrive on it!"

When stimulant medications do not appear to work for types 1 or 2 ADD, I may try the stimulating antidepressant medication listed under Type 5 (Limbic) ADD. I occasionally use blood-pressure medications, such as clonidine or guanfacine. These blood-pressure medications have been found to help hyperactivity, aggressiveness, and impulsivity. They do not much help the attentional symptoms. Mixing them with a stimulant medication can produce excellent results. I should stress that these are not my first choices and should be used only with careful medical supervision.

Clonidine and guanfacine are also used as primary treatments for tic disorders such as Gilles de la Tourette's syndrome. When I use clonidine in addition to a stimulant medication, I will order a screening EKG. There have been several reports that this combination may cause problems, even though personally I have found it to be an effective, safe combination. These medications have also been used to treat insomnia, which is very common in ADD.

Generic name	Brand name	Milligrams a day/ available strengths	Times a day	Notes
clonidine	Catapres	0.05–0.6/ 0.1, 0.2, 0.3 tabs and patches	1–2	Watch rebound hypertension and sedation.
guanfacine	Tenex	1–3/ 1, 2	1	
propranolol	Inderal	10–600/ 10, 20, 40, 60, 80	2–3	

TYPE 3 (OVERFOCUSED) ADD

Type 3 (Overfocused) ADD is most likely due to a deficiency of both serotonin and dopamine. Medication interventions need to be targeted at enhancing both of these neurotransmitters. If one neurotransmitter is enhanced by itself, it can make this type worse. For example, when stimulant medications are given to people with Type 3 (Overfocused) ADD, they often become overstimulated, stuck on certain issues, and anxious. Used by themselves, stimulant medications further overheat the cingulate gyrus. Likewise, serotonin medications (such as Prozac or Paxil) by themselves tend to help the overfocus but cause additional problems with focus and motivation. A balance is needed.

Effexor (venlafaxine) is my first choice for Type 3 (Overfocused) ADD. Effexor increases both serotonin (helping to cool the anterior cingulate gyrus and shift attention) and norepinephrine and dopamine (stimulating the brain). Often Effexor can be used alone, without the need for a stimulant medication. When Effexor is ineffective or not well tolerated, I often prescribe a SSRI (selective serotonin reuptake inhibitor) medication with a stimulant. These medications only increase serotonin availability in the brain. Adding a stimulant medication like Adderall helps to treat fully this type of ADD. Here is a table of Type 3 (Overfocused) ADD medications:

SSRIs are generally very safe medications. In our experience, however, people who have temporal lobe problems may experience

Generic name	Brand name	Milligrams a day/ available strengths	Times a day	Notes
venlafaxine	Effexor	37.5–375/ 18.75, 25, 37.5, 50, 75, 100	2–3	Drug of choice for this type.
venlafaxine slow release	Effexor XR	75–375/ 37.5, 75, 150	1–2	The slow-release form is usually tolerated better.
fluoxetine SSRI	Prozac	10–80/ 10, 20	1	Long acting; do not use if temporal lobe symptoms present.
clomipramine TCA* and SSRI	Anafranil	10–200 in children; 10–300 in adults/ 25, 50, 75	1–2	Tends to have more side effects than the rest. Do not use as a first-line drug.
sertraline SSRI	Zoloft	25–200/ 50, 100	1	My first choice among the SSRIs.
paroxetine SSRI	Paxil	10–60/ 12, 20	1	Watch for withdrawal symptoms when meds are forgotten.
fluvoxamine SSRI	Luvox	25–200/ 50, 100	1	
citalopram SSRI	Celexa	20–60/ 20–40	1–2	
nefazodone SSRI	Serzone	100–600/ 50, 100, 150, 200, 250	1–2	Good if sexual dysfunction is present.
mirtazapine	Remeron	15–60/ 15, 30	1	Smaller doses cause drowsiness.

*tricyclic antidepressant

a higher intensity of angry and aggressive feelings on Prozac or other serotonin enhancing medications. Therefore, we are careful to screen for these before placing someone on these medications. If there are side effects on any medication, it is important to contact your doctor and discuss them. In contrast to the stimulants, these may take several weeks to a month in order to be effective and even three to four months to see the best benefit.

TYPE 4 (TEMPORAL LOBE) ADD

The medications used to treat Type 4 (Temporal Lobe) ADD are classified as anticonvulsant medications. They stabilize temporal lobe activity and help symptoms of aggression, mood instability, headaches, and in some cases learning problems. Treating Type 4 ADD often involves combining them with a stimulant medication. Even though these medications are classified as anticonvulsant or antiseizure medications, I am not saying that Type 4 patients have a seizure disorder. Rather, they have dysfunction in a part of the brain that is also associated with seizures. In treating ADD, we often use much lower doses than are used to combat seizures. Sometimes very small doses are all that is necessary. Anticonvulsants are thought to enhance the availability of the neurotransmitter GABA, which has a calming or inhibitory effect on nerve cells. In the last twenty years, psychiatry has come around to using these medications for many different conditions. Anticonvulsants, such as carbamazepine or divalproate, have been used for manic-depressive illness, pain syndromes, aggression, and resistant depression.

Here is a list of common anticonvulsant medications used for this type of ADD:

Generic name	Brand name	Milligrams a day/ available strengths	Times a day	Notes
carbamazepine	Carbatrol (slow release only), Tegretol (regular and slow release)	100–1200/ Carbatrol 200/400 Tegretol 100, 200	2–3	Most effective in my experience, but it is essential to monitor white blood cell counts and blood levels.
valproic acid	Depakene	125–3,000/ 250	2–3	Very effective, but need to monitor liver function and blood levels.
Divalproex Sodium	Depakote	125–3,000/ 125, 250, 500	1–2	Very effective, but need to monitor liver function and blood levels.
gabapentin	Neurontin	100–4,000/ 100, 300, 400	2–3	Usually our drug of choice to start.

topiramate	Topamax	50–400/ 25, 100, 200	2	Has been shown to help decrease weight. In doses over 300 mg, may cause memory problems.
lamotrigine	Lamictal	25–500/ 25, 100, 150, 200	1–2	Watch for rash.
phenytoin	Dilantin	30–300/ 30, 100		Monitor blood levels.

In addition to anticonvulsants, I often use memory-enhancing medication for people with temporal lobe problems. Memory problems are very common in this ADD type. Donepezil (Aricept) is a medication indicated for Alzheimer's disease that works by increasing the amounts of acetylcholine in the brain. Acetylcholine is a neurotransmitter involved in the laying down of new memories. One woman wrote me that after she took Aricept, it was like going from 4 megabytes of RAM in her head to 128 megabytes. In addition, Piracetam, a medication that is difficult to obtain in the U.S. but not in Europe or Canada, has been shown in a number of studies to help memory. A number of my patients through the years have written away for it and found it beneficial and without side effects. Mark, a 17-year-old patient with learning disabilities stemming from memory problems, was placed on Piracetam. In three weeks he noticed that he felt that he was clearer and that his memory was better. Piracetam has become available recently through a compounding pharmacy in Virginia (800-723-7455). Your doctor can write you a prescription for it, and you can send it to the pharmacy. In the supplement chapter, I will also discuss a number of natural or herbal memory remedies.

TYPE 5 (LIMBIC) ADD

Type 5 (Limbic) ADD is often best treated with a stimulating antidepressant medication, such as desipramine, imipramine, buprion, and venlafaxine (if there are anterior cingulate issues as well). These medi-

Generic name	Brand name	Milligrams a day/ available strengths	Times a day	Notes
desipramine TCA	Norpramin	10–300/ 10, 25, 50, 75, 100, 150	1–2	Stimulating; often helps ADD in adults; not currently used in kids.
imipramine TCA	Tofranil	10–300/ 10, 25, 50, 75, 100, 125, 150	1–2	Also used for anxiety, panic disorder, bedwetting.
bupropion	Wellbutrin	50–450/ 75, 100	1–3	Never give more than 150 mg a dose. Do not use if the person is prone to seizures.
bupropion sustained release	Wellbutrin SR	150–450/ 100, 150	1–3	Never give more than 300 mg a dose. Do not use if the person is prone to seizures.
amitriptyline TCA	Elavil	10–300/ 10, 25, 50, 75, 100, 150	1–2	Very low doses are often used to help with sleep problems, fibromyalgia, and pain syndromes. Higher doses tend to have many side effects.
nortryptiline TCA	Pamelor	10–150/ 10, 25, 50, 75	1–2	Similar to Elavil, but generally it is better tolerated.
doxepin TCA	Sinequan	10–300/ 10, 25, 50, 75, 100, 150		Often used to help with sleep problems.

TCA=tricyclic antidepressant

cations increase the neurotransmitters norepinephrine and/or dopamine. They tend to be more stimulating than other antidepressants.

These medications need to be monitored more closely than stimulants, especially for their effect on heart function. Many adults respond to very low doses of these medications for ADD symptoms. Low doses often produce far fewer side effects than the higher "antidepressant" doses. Unlike the brain stimulants, these medications may take several weeks to a month to become effective. When Wellbutrin was first released in the United States, a number of people developed seizures while on it, resulting in it being pulled from the market in the early 1980s. The manufacturer figured out the dosage pattern was wrong and the FDA allowed them to rerelease it with a different dosage regimen. Do not take more than 150 milligrams at a time of the regular-release preparation or 300 milligrams of the slow-release preparation. I also use these medications to treat depression, anxiety disorders, bedwetting (imipramine), and smoking addiction (Wellbutrin), often in conjunction with one of the stimulants.

TYPE 6 ("RING OF FIRE") ADD

This type of ADD seems to respond best to the anticonvulsants listed under Type 4 ADD, often with the addition of a stimulant medication. Stimulants by themselves often make this type worse. Serotonergic medications, by themselves, seem to make it worse as well, although they may be needed for overfocused symptoms. If the anticonvulsants do not work, I use the new, novel antipsychotic medications, such as Risperdal or Zyprexa. I often use dosages of the anticonvulsants or antipsychotic medications that are much smaller than those needed for seizure disorders or psychotic illnesses.

The antipsychotic medications can be very effective. Many of my teenage patients have avoided the hospital or residential treatment centers due to these medications. These drugs can produce significant weight gain. I have a number of patients who have gained twenty to thirty-five pounds in less than a year. If it had not been for the amazing response, I would not have persisted with the medication. The anticonvulsant Topamax is known to promote weight loss in some patients, and I have used it successfully in some of my "Ring of Fire" patients. Despite the great results with antipsychotics, I still prefer the anticonvulsants because of the fewer side effects.

COMBINATIONS

Sometimes a combination of medications is needed to obtain the full therapeutic effect. I particularly like the combination of stimulants and antiobsessive medications for children of alcoholics. Sometimes a person may have three or four different subtypes of ADD operating at once and may be on three or even four medications. Brain studies have taught us that some people have multiple brain systems involved in their symptoms and need sophisticated combinations of medications. I recommend that you be evaluated and treated by a specialist in the field.

REMEMBER:

The goal is to function as well as possible,
not to be off medication!

Many people have the misguided belief that it's better if they only take a "little bit" of the medication. Often this attitude causes the medication to be ineffective. I give patients the following metaphor:

When a person goes to the eye doctor because he or she is having trouble seeing, they want a prescription for the glasses that will help them see the best. They don't ask for "just a little bit of a lens." They want to see clearly!

So it is with ADD: Everyone is different in the quantity of medication they require to function at their best. For some people it is 5 milligrams of Adderall one to two times a day. For others it is 20 milligrams of Adderall three times a day. Everyone is different.

The side effects of having untreated ADD are immeasurably worse than any caused by the medication!

CHAPTER 19

Supplement Strategies for ADD Types

Through the years many people have asked me about natural treatments for ADD. At least once a month a parent tells me about an amazing new treatment for ADD. Vitamins, herbs, fish oil, amino acids, grape-seed extract, and magnets, to name a few. With three ADD children of my own, I've kept an open mind. I want to know about everything that works. Through the years I have tracked each of these treatments, kept up on what little scientific literature exists, and constantly stayed on the lookout to see what works. Wading through the claims, parental excitement, and failures is sometimes discouraging. The good news, however, is that many of these supplemental treatments are helpful, especially if you target the interventions to specific ADD types.

A word of caution: Ignoring the ADD type can cause some of these interventions to backfire. Just because something is natural does not mean it's innocuous. Here's an example:

Seven-year-old Justin was brought to see me by his mother. He had symptoms of Type 4 ADD with severe temper problems. A month before I met Justin, his mother had read a magazine article about St. John's wort: The article said that it helped with mood and temper problems. She gave St. John's wort to her son. Justin's behavior got much worse. He was more hyperactive and angrier, and he started to have dreams of decomposing bodies. When she stopped the St. John's wort, his symptoms lessened. During Justin's evaluation at my clinic, I did a SPECT scan. It showed decreased activity in his left temporal lobe. I have often seen that serotonergic interventions like Prozac or St. John's wort make temporal problems worse. It was clear to me that Justin needed an anticonvulsant medication and a stimulant. He had a very positive response to Depakote and Adderall.

Always check with your doctor before adding supplements to medication. Some supplements will interact with medication, so caution is needed.

In this chapter I will go through each ADD type and tell you what supplements that I have seen to have clinical benefit. I'll give you the rationale and dosage protocols that I suggest to my patients. If you decide to use these supplements *instead* of medication, as many people do, make sure you keep tabs on their effectiveness. I want my patients to take only something that is clearly beneficial. If the supplements are not fully effective, I urge you to add medication. Many patients say that they want to try the natural supplements before they try medication. I'm not opposed to that, but I worry that if the supplements are not fully effective, patients will not pursue more effective treatments. Follow through to find what works for yourself or your child. Be open to new ideas and persist until you get the best brain and life functioning.

NO MATTER WHAT TYPE: 100-PERCENT MULTIVITAMIN AND MINERAL SUPPLEMENT

No matter what type of ADD you or your child has, take a vitamin and mineral supplement a day. When I was in medical school, the professor who taught our course in nutrition said that if people eat a balanced diet, they do not need vitamin or mineral supplements. I have seen that balanced diets are a thing of the past for many of our "fast-food families." In my experience, ADD families in particular have problems with planning and tend to eat out much more frequently than non-ADD families. Protect yourself and your child by taking a vitamin and mineral supplement that provides 100 percent of your daily allowances. In a 1988 study published in the British journal *Lancet,* ninety children between the ages of 12 and 13 were divided into three groups. One group took no tablet, one group took a typical multiple vitamin and mineral tablet, and the last group took a placebo. The group that took the vitamin and mineral tablet had a significant increase in nonverbal intelligence, while the other two groups showed no difference at all. Their subclinical vitamin and mineral deficiencies may have been contributing to these students' performing below their abilities.

TYPE 1 (CLASSIC) ADD AND TYPE 2 (INATTENTIVE) ADD

As already mentioned, these types seem to have deficiencies of the neurotransmitter dopamine. I frequently prescribe the amino acid L-tyrosine in doses of 500 to 1,500 milligrams two to three times a day for adults, and 100 to 500 milligrams two to three times a day for children under 10. L-tyrosine is the amino acid building block for dopamine. It is reported to increase the brain level of phenylethylamine (PEA), a mild stimulant also found in high concentrations in chocolate. Many of my patients have reported that it helped them. It is softer in its effect than the prescription stimulants. Because of absorption patterns, I recommend that they take it on an empty stomach (a half hour before meals or an hour after meals). I have not seen any side effects with L-tyrosine, except for mild weight loss. L-tyrosine does not work well by itself in treating Type 3 (Overfocused) ADD because it tends to increase the intensity of overfocused symptoms. Symptoms of dopamine deficiency include hypothyroidism, low blood pressure, low body temperature (cold hands and feet), and restless leg syndrome.

Phil had been treated for Type 1 ADD for several years. He was taking Ritalin, which would work for a while and then seem to wear off. The up-and-down effectiveness of the medication frustrated him. He tried Adderall, but it seemed to have the same effect. I stopped the stimulant medications and put him on 1,000 milligrams of L-tyrosine three times a day. In addition, I urged Phil to be vigilant about his dietary guidelines, and encouraged him to walk fast for an hour five times a week. Within a week he said he felt better. He has maintained the regimen for four years now.

Grape-seed extract and Pycnogenol (a patented French pine bark extract) have also shown some mild benefit for Type 1 and Type 2 ADD. Grape-seed extract and Pycnogenol contain proanthocyanidin compounds. These compounds have been found to increase blood flow and act as superantioxidants, twenty to fifty times as powerful as vitamin E. There are no published studies on the use of these supplements in treating ADD, but there are a number of published case reports.

TYPE 3 (OVERFOCUSED) ADD

This type of ADD seems likely due to a relative deficiency of both serotonin and dopamine. I have seen that a combination of St. John's wort and L-tyrosine is often very helpful. St. John's wort comes from the flowers of the St. John's wort plant ("wort" is Old English for "plant"). It got its name either from the fact that it blooms around June 24, the feast day of St. John the Baptist, or the red ring round the flowers that, when crushed, looks like blood—the blood of the beheaded John the Baptist. Much like SSRIs, St. John's wort seems to work by increasing serotonin availability in the brain. The starting dosage of St. John's wort is 300 milligrams a day for children, 300 milligrams twice a day for teens, and 600 milligrams in the morning and 300 milligrams at night for adults. Sometimes I'll go as high as a total of 1,800 milligrams per day in adults. Look for brands that contain 0.3% hypericin, which is believed to be the active ingredient of St. John's wort. I have done a number of before and after SPECT studies with St. John's wort, and I have no doubt that it decreases anterior cingulate gyrus hyperactivity for many patients. It also helps with moodiness and trouble shifting attention. Unfortunately, I have also seen it decrease prefrontal cortex activity. One of the women in my study said, "I'm happier, but I'm dingier." When anterior cingulate symptoms are present with ADD symptoms, it's important to use St. John's wort with a stimulating substance like L-tyrosine or a stimulant such as Adderall. St. John's wort may increase sun sensitivity. Also don't use it if temporal lobe symptoms are present without first stabilizing the temporal lobes.

Elaine, 16, had always been a worrier. She also had problems with anger at home. If things did not go her way, she would explode at her parents or at her younger sister. As a student she was a perfectionist, which caused her to spend excessive time on assignments. Her mother, a school principal, brought her to my clinic after she heard me lecture. She told me that she was sure Elaine had Overfocused ADD. Her SPECT study showed marked increased activity in her anterior cingulate gyrus. She also had mild decreased activity in her prefrontal cortex. I placed her on 600 milligrams of St. John's wort, in the morning and 300 milligrams at night. I also had her take 500 milligrams of L-tyrosine two to three times a day. Within a month Elaine was much better. She was more relaxed and less reactive, and did much better in her classes. She said that studying was easy because she no longer felt the need to have everything just so. She still wanted to excel but didn't have to copy pages over three and four times until things were perfect.

L-tryptophan (the amino acid building block for serotonin) and 5-HTP (also a serotonin building block) are other ways of increasing cerebral serotonin. L-tryptophan was taken off the market a number of years ago because one contaminated batch, from one manufacturer, caused a rare blood disease and a number of deaths. The L-tryptophan actually had nothing to do with the deaths. L-tryptophan is a naturally occurring amino acid found in milk, meat, and eggs. I have found it helps patients improve sleep, decrease aggressiveness, and improve mood control. In addition, it does not have side effects—a real advantage over antidepressants.

L-tryptophan was recently reapproved by the Food and Drug Administration and is now available by prescription. One of the problems with dietary L-tryptophan is that a significant portion of it does not enter the brain. The body uses it up to make proteins and vitamin B_3. This necessitates taking large amounts of tryptophan. I recommend L-tryptophan in doses of 1,000 to 3,000 milligrams taken at bedtime.

5-HTP is a step closer in the serotonin production pathway (see below). It is also more widely available than L-tryptophan and is more easily taken up in the brain. Seventy percent is taken up into the brain, as opposed to only 3 percent of L-tryptophan. A number of double blind studies have shown 5-HTP to be as effective as antidepressant medication in treating depression. 5-HTP boosts serotonin levels in the brain and helps to calm anterior cingulate gyrus hyperactivity ("greasing" the anterior cingulate, if you will, to help it shift attention). The dose of 5-HTP for adults is 50 to 300 milligrams a day. Children should start at half dose. Take 5-HTP and L-tryptophan on an empty stomach for better absorption. The most common side effect of 5-HTP is an upset stomach. It is usually very

SEROTONIN PATHWAY

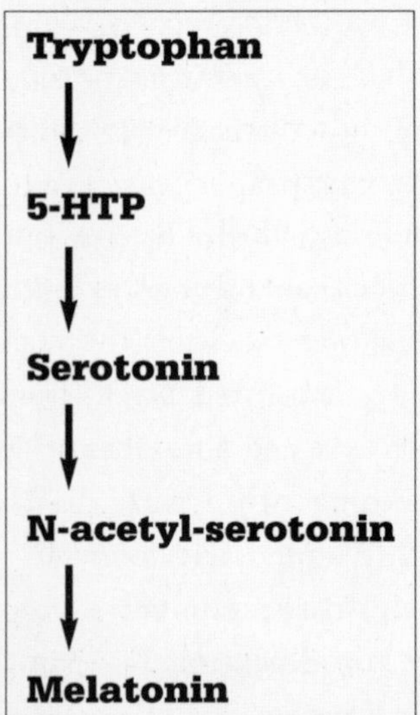

mild. To eliminate it, start with a small dose and work your way up slowly.

There have also been some recent studies with Inositol, a vitamin from the B vitamin family, which is available from health food stores. In doses of 12 to 20 milligrams a day, it has been shown to decrease moodiness, depression, and overfocus issues.

Do not take St. John's wort, L-tryptophan, or 5-HTP with prescribed antidepressants without the knowledge and close supervision of your physician.

TYPE 4 (TEMPORAL LOBE) ADD

Temporal Lobe ADD is a combination of temporal lobe dysfunction and poor prefrontal cortex activity. Strategies geared toward temporal lobe stabilization and enhancement have proven valuable for this ADD type. We suspect that the medications that work for Type 4 enhance the availability of the amino acid gama-aminobutyric acid (GABA), an essential neurotransmitter in the brain. Formed in the body from glutamic acid, GABA calms neuronal activity and inhibits nerve cells from overfiring or firing erratically. GABA can be taken as a supplement. It acts like an anticonvulsant and also as an antianxiety agent. In the herbal literature it is reported to work in much the same way as diazepam (Valium), chlordiazepoxide (Librium), and other tranquilizers, but without the fear of addiction. I have seen it have a nice calming effect on people who struggle with temper, irritability, and anxiety—all which may be temporal lobe symptoms. The doses of GABA range from 100 to 500 milligrams a day for adults, half that for children.

Many people with temporal lobe problems suffer from memory problems. I have found a number of natural substances helpful to enhance memory. These include:

- **Phosphatidyl serine (PS)** plays a major role in determining the integrity and fluidity of brain cell membranes. Normally the brain can manufacture sufficient levels of PS, but if there is a deficiency of folic acid, vitamin B_{12}, or essential fatty acids, the brain may not be able to make enough. Low levels of PS are also associated with memory problems and depression in the elderly. I often recommend PS as a supplement for memory problems. There are eighteen double-blind studies that report how effective PS can be for memory issues. In the largest study, 494 elderly patients (ages 65 to 93) with moderate to severe senility were given PS (100 milligrams three times a day) or a placebo for six months. The patients were assessed for cognitive function, behavior, and mood at the beginning and end of the study. Statistically significant improvements in all three areas were noted in the PS group. I recommend that my patients take 100 milligrams twice a day for two weeks then, if needed, 100 milligrams three times a day for memory.

- ***Ginkgo biloba,*** from ginkgo trees, is a powerful antioxidant that is best known for its ability to enhance circulation. In a number of studies at major universities, ginkgo biloba has been shown to improve energy, concentration, focus, and memory. *Ginkgo biloba* has been reported to enhance cerebral blood flow and reduce or slow the symptoms of Alzheimer's disease. There are many different forms of ginkgo, making dosing confusing. Ginkoba and Ginkgold (Nature's Way) are brands that have been compounded to reflect those done in the major studies on ginkgo biloba. I recommend doses of 60 to 120 milligrams twice a day.
- **Vitamin E** is an antioxidant that has been shown to be helpful for many things, including memory problems and muscle movement disorders. Doses of 400 to 600 IU twice a day are often recommended for enhancing memory. Choose the "natural" form of vitamin E.
- **Ibuprofen,** an antiinflammatory pain medication, has been shown in several studies to enhance memory and decrease the progression of Alzheimer's disease. It probably works by decreasing inflammation in the brain, allowing for better circulation. Doses of 200 milligrams twice a day are usually recommended. Do not take ibuprofen if you suffer from ulcers or other gastrointestinal problems.

TYPE 5 (LIMBIC) ADD

Limbic ADD has many symptoms of mild depression, including negativity, sadness, feelings of hopelessness, and an overabundance of ANTs (automatic negative thoughts). The supplements that seem to help this type of ADD best are DL-phenylalanine (DLPA), L-tyrosine, and S-Adenosyl-Methionine (SAMe).

DLPA is the amino acid precursor for norepinephrine. In a number of studies norepinephrine and epinephrine (adrenaline) have been shown to be low in people with ADD and/or depression. The antidepressants imipramine and desipramine work by increasing norepinephrine in the brain. DLPA, by boosting norepinephrine's precursor, can have a positive impact on mood and focus. In a number of studies DLPA has been found to be helpful for depression, energy, and pain control. I have used it for fifteen years as a mild antidepressant in children, teens, and adults. It is more mild in its effect than prescribed antidepressants, but it also has significantly fewer side effects. People who have PKU (phenylketonuria) should not take DLPA, as they do not have the enzyme that metabolizes it. I recommend doses of 400 milligrams three times a day on an empty stomach, half that dose for children.

Another effective supplemental treatment for Type 5 (Limbic) ADD is SAMe. Involved in the production of many important brain compounds, such as neurotransmitters, SAMe's unique chemical action (it's called a methyl donor, a rare property) helps the brain to function properly. Normally the body manufactures all the SAMe it needs from the amino acid methionine. In depressed people, however, this synthesis can be impaired. Supplementing the diet with SAMe increases the neurotransmitters involved with depression and improves cell membrane fluidity. SAMe is one of the best natural antidepressants available, and a number of recent studies have shown that it is as effective as antidepressant medication. SAMe has also been found helpful for people who suffer from fibromyalgia, a chronic muscle pain disorder. Fibromyalgia and ADD commonly coexist. I think the chronic stress associated with ADD is in part responsible for the muscle pain. *People who have bipolar disorder or manic-depressive illness or Type 6 ("Ring of Fire") ADD should not take SAMe.* There have been reports of a number cases where SAMe induced manic or hypomanic episodes (excessively up or happy moods, extreme impulsivity in sexuality or spending money, pressured speech, or decreased need for sleep). I think these reports highlight that SAMe is an effective antidepressant, considering that all the prescription antidepressants have that capability as well. The dosage of SAMe is between 200 and 400 milligrams two to four times a day, and half that for children.

TYPE 6 ("RING OF FIRE") ADD

Type 6 ("Ring of Fire") ADD is often associated with fierce ADD symptoms, such as intense hyperactivity and distractibility, severe impulsiveness, hypersensitivity to the environment, pressured speech, and cyclic mood changes. As already discussed, this type of ADD may be related to bipolar disorder. Stimulants tend to make it worse. However, GABA and fish oil often have a positive effect on Type 6 ("Ring of Fire") ADD. GABA, which was discussed under Type 4 (Temporal Lobe) ADD, has a calming effect on nerve cells. In "Ring of Fire" ADD there is diffuse hyperactivity throughout the brain, and GABA has been helpful for a number of my patients.

Supplementation with fish oils containing high levels of omega-3 fatty acids also helps. An insufficiency of omega-3 fatty acids has been linked to both ADD and depression. This may be related to how fatty acids make up nerve cell membranes. Without high levels of omega-3 fatty acids, the nerve cell membranes are less fluid, possibly causing nerve cells to react sluggishly or misfire. Population based studies in various countries (including the U.S.) have indicated that decreased consumption of omega-3 fatty acids correlates with increased rates of depression. Well-intentioned dietary advice to lower cholesterol levels tends to harm the balance of fatty acids (especially the essential omega-3, DHA) in the body. Recent studies have suggested that lowering levels of plasma cholesterol too much increases the risk of suicide, homicide, and depression. Clearly, omega-3 fatty acids are essential to good brain health. A study done at Harvard and reported in the Archives of General Psychiatry demonstrated that supplementation with high-dose administration of purified fish oils provided a statistically significant improvement in bipolar depression. Here are three ways to boost the level of omega-3 fatty acids in the body:

- eliminate transfatty acids by avoiding margarine, shortening, and most processed foods (to improve the ration of good fatty acids to bad fatty acids)
- increase the consumption of tuna and other cold water fish, such as salmon, mackerel, herring, and halibut
- take 1 tablespoon a day of flaxseed oil.

Here's an example of how the right supplements can literally change someone's life. Stuart was 11 years old when he first came to see us. His grandmother had heard me speak at a conference and she

Stuart's Concentration SPECT Study Before Treatment

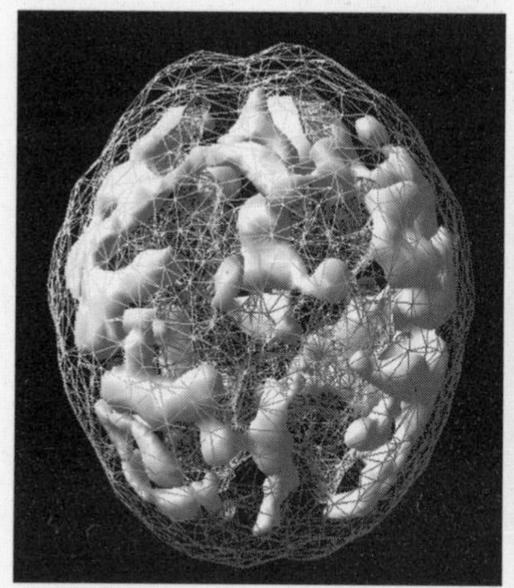

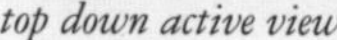

top down active view

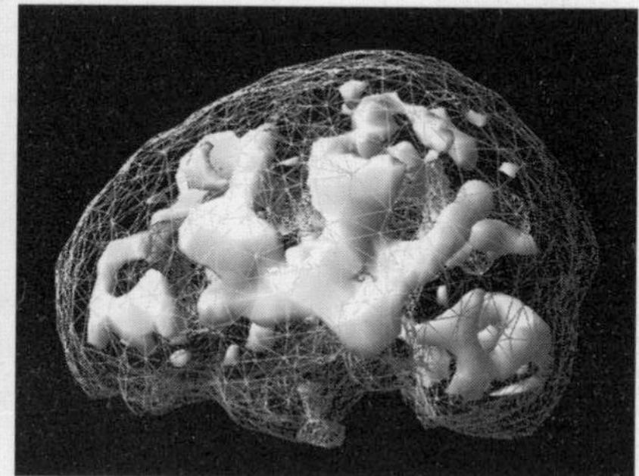

left side active view

Stuart's Concentration SPECT Study with Supplement Treatment

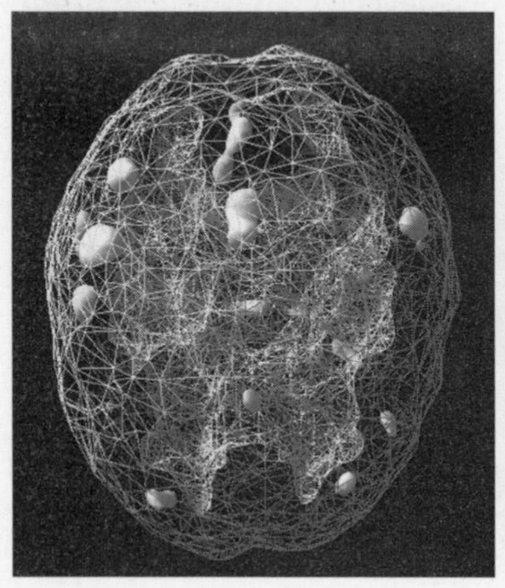

top-down active view

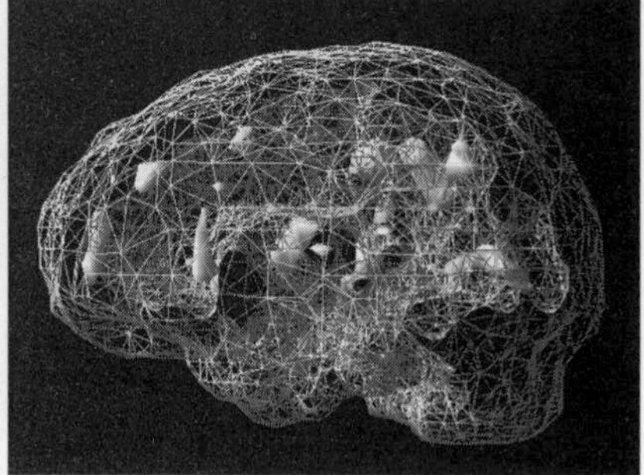

left-side active view

knew from my description that he had the "Ring of Fire" type. He was argumentative, angry, moody, inattentive, hyperactive, easily distracted, and very sensitive to noise in the environment. He had been tried on a number of traditional treatments without success. His SPECT study showed a severe "Ring of Fire" pattern with hyperactivity throughout his whole cortex. We put him on a combination of GABA, omega-3 fatty acids, and St. John's wort. Within two months he was dramatically different. When we repeated his SPECT study, we were delighted by his progress.

CHAPTER 20

Neurofeedback Strategies for ADD Types

Over the past twenty years, Joel Lubar, Ph.D., of the University of Tennessee; Sigfried Othmer of EEG Spectrum in Los Angeles; Michael Linden, Ph.D., of San Clemente, California; and other clinicians have reported the effectiveness of brainwave biofeedback, also known as neurofeedback, in the treatment of ADD children and teenagers. Biofeedback, in general, is a treatment technique that utilizes instruments to measure physiological responses in a person's body (such as hand temperature, sweat gland activity, breathing rates, heart rates, blood pressure, and brainwave patterns). It's the same technique I explored when I was an army psychiatrist. The instruments then feed the information on these body systems back to the patient, who can then learn how to change them. In neurofeedback, electrodes are placed on the scalp, measuring the number and type of brainwave patterns.

There are five types of brainwave patterns:

- **delta waves** (1 to 4 cycles per second), very slow brainwaves, seen mostly during sleep
- **theta waves** (5–7 cycles per second), slow brainwaves, seen during daydreaming and twilight states

- **alpha waves** (8 to 12 cycles per second), brainwaves seen during relaxed states
- **SMR (sensorimotor rhythm) waves** (12–15 cycles per second), brainwaves seen during states of focused relaxation
- **beta waves** (13 to 24 cycles per second), fast brainwaves seen during concentration or mental work states.

In evaluating over 1,200 children with ADD, Dr. Lubar has found that the basic issue for these children is their inability to maintain beta concentration states for sustained periods of time. He also found that these children have excessive theta daydreaming brainwave activity. Dr. Lubar found that through the use of neurofeedback, children can be taught to increase the amount of beta brainwaves and decrease the amount of theta or daydreaming brainwaves. They can train their brains to be more active.

The basic neurofeedback technique asks the patient—child, teen, or adult—literally to play mind games. The patient's brain is hooked up to the computer equipment through electrodes placed on the head. (Don't worry, no brain surgery here!) The computer feeds back to the patient the type of brainwave activity it's monitoring. The patient is rewarded for producing concentration or beta waves, and the more beta states he or she produces, the more rewards accrued. On the neurofeedback equipment, for example, a child sits in front of a computer monitor and watches a game screen that reflects the composition of his or her brainwaves. If the child increases beta activity or decreases theta activity, the game continues. The game stops, however, when the patient cannot maintain the desired brainwave states. Children find the screen fun and many are able to gradually shape their brainwave patterns to more normal ones. This treatment technique is not an overnight cure. Children often have to do neurofeedback for one to two years to produce significant improvement.

In my experience with neurofeedback and ADD, many people are able to improve their reading skills and decrease their need for medication. Also, neurofeedback has helped to decrease impulsivity and aggressiveness. It is a powerful tool, in part because we are making the patients part of the treatment process and giving them more control over their own physiological processes.

The use of neurofeedback is considered controversial by many clinicians and researchers. More published research needs to be done in order to demonstrate its long-term effectiveness. Some of the controversy stems from exaggerated claims for neurofeedback. Some clinics have advertised that they can cure ADD with neurofeedback alone. That is not my experience. Overselling neurofeedback has hurt its credibility, but in my clinical experience it is a powerful and exciting treatment and we are yet to see its full development.

SPECT HELPS TO FOCUS NEUROFEEDBACK

Through SPECT we have seen that ADD is a complex condition. Therefore successfully treating it requires more than one neurofeedback treatment. The figure below shows standard electrode placements. For people interested in neurofeedback, here is a list of training sites that we use in our office for the different ADD Types. Share them with the neurofeedback professional in your area.

TYPE 1 (CLASSIC) ADD AND TYPE 2 (INATTENTIVE) ADD

Classic and Inattentive ADD shows decreased activity (excessive theta activity and poor beta activity) in the prefrontal cortex. It is helpful to do the neurofeedback training as close to the prefrontal poles as possible. The training consists of enhancing prefrontal beta activity and decreasing prefrontal theta activity.

Joey, age 7, was brought to our clinic by his mother for hyperactivity, restlessness, impulse control problems, inattention, and distractibility. She heard about our work with neurofeedback and wanted an alternative to medication. Joey did neurofeedback twice a week for two years. After six months we began seeing significant

Standard Electrode Placement Areas (Top-Down and Left-Side Views)

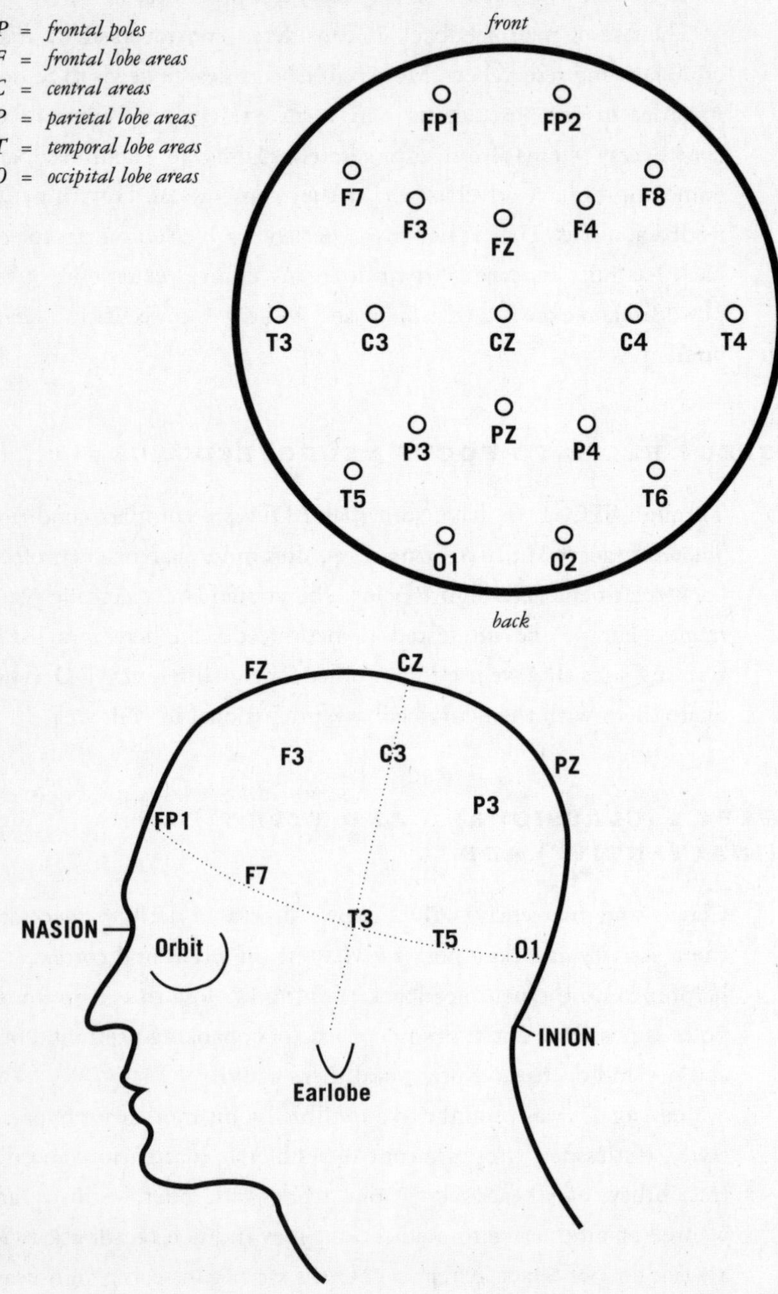

Type 1 & 2 Training Site

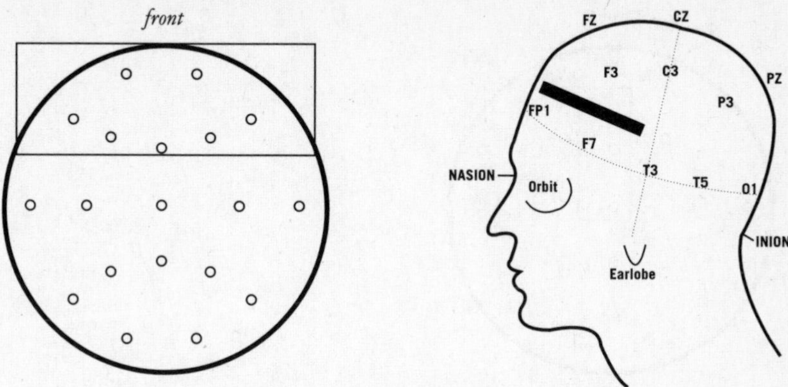

changes, including less hyperactivity and longer ability to focus. In addition, his interest in reading significantly increased. After he stopped the neurofeedback, he continued to do well in school and at home. He maintained an exercise program and a higher-protein, lower-carbohydrate diet.

TYPE 3 (OVERFOCUSED) ADD

In Overfocused ADD there is excessive activity in the anterior cingulate gyrus. It is helpful to do the neurofeedback training over the front central part of the brain between FZ and CZ. This training helps people shift attention and feel more settled, less worried, and more easygoing. It also enhances attention span. The training focuses on enhancing high alpha activity (relaxed but focused).

Monica, age 17, came to the clinic for problems with anxiety, worrying, temper outbursts, poor school performance, and oppositional behavior. Her symptoms were much worse right before the onset of her menstrual period. She was in psychotherapy for two years, which seemed to help her temper problems but not her oppositional behavior or school performance. She had tried Prozac and Paxil with her family doctor, but she did not like the side effects. Monica's SPECT study showed marked increased activity in the an-

Type 3 Training Site

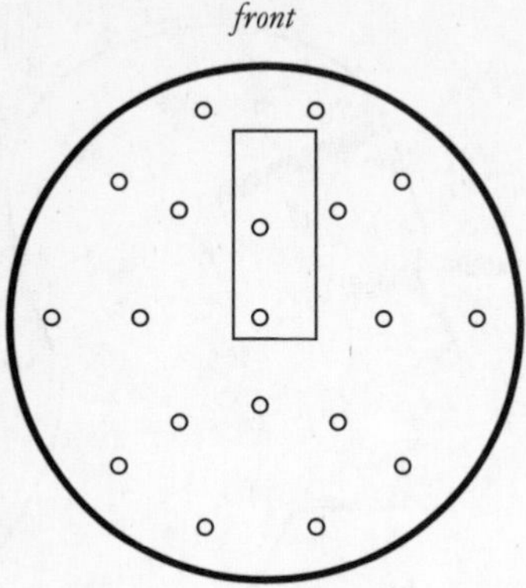

terior cingulate gyrus on both the rest and concentration studies. When she learned about neurofeedback, she liked the idea of learning how to control her own brain (sort of a "anterior cingulate control thing"). We did neurofeedback over her anterior cingulate gyrus twice a week for six months. In the first month she noticed less worrying. By the end of six months she felt more focused, less anxious, and more cooperative, an assessment her family validated. Nevertheless, she still had a hard time right before her period. I placed her on a small dose of St. John's wort (300 milligrams twice day), which seemed to smooth out her menstrual mood swings.

TYPE 4 (TEMPORAL LOBE) ADD

Temporal Lobe ADD has decreased activity (excessive theta activity) over the temporal lobes on one or both sides. Neurofeedback training over the affected temporal lobe seems to do the most good. We have seen this training improve mood stability, reading ability, and memory. The training consists of enhancing SMR activity and suppressing theta activity over the affected temporal lobe.

Marty, age 14, came to see us for temper outbursts, memory problems, poor reading skills, inattention, disorganization, and language problems (he had problems finding the right words and he often misunderstood people). His SPECT study showed signifi-

Type 4 Training Site

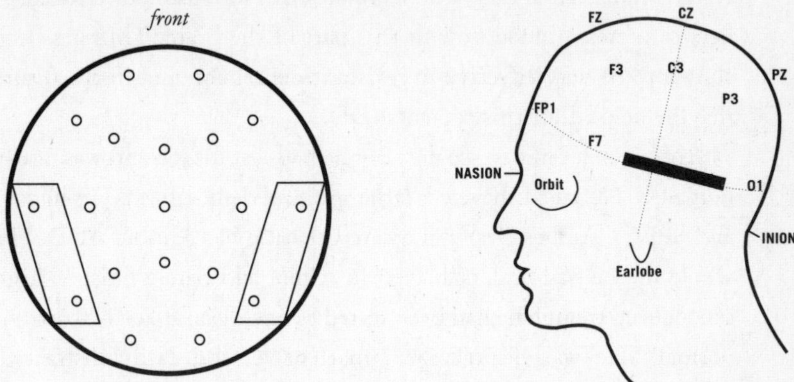

cantly decreased activity in his left temporal lobe at rest. When he concentrated, the temporal lobe activity decreased even further along with his prefrontal cortex. He had had a poor response to Ritalin and his parents were hesitant to try an anticonvulsant medication. They wanted to try nonmedication options first, and they liked the idea of neurofeedback. We started neurofeedback training over Marty's left temporal lobe. Within two months we noticed that his reading was starting to improve and his temper was better. After six months Marty's moods began to show stability. Once that happened, we started training his prefrontal cortex to be more active. He learned quickly. After eighteen months of training, Marty felt more in control of himself and much improved. In addition to training, he also exercised regularly and ate a consistent simple carbohydrate-free diet.

TYPE 5 (LIMBIC) ADD

In Limbic ADD there is decreased activity in the left prefrontal cortex and increased activity in the deep limbic areas. Since the limbic areas are too deep in the brain to do neurofeedback training, we have found that teaching the patient to increase beta activity over the left prefrontal cortex has the most beneficial effect. This training helps improve focus and mood while decreasing negativity and negative thoughts. Of interest, a new treatment for depression termed transcranial magnetic stimulation (TMS) uses powerful magnets to increase blood flow in this part of the brain. TMS has been shown to be very effective in resistant depression and in the future may be helpful for this type of ADD.

Robbie, 42, came to see me after he had lost his job and was nearly homeless. He was disheveled, lethargic, and demoralized. His history and SPECT studies clearly indicated that he had Limbic ADD. His whole life he had underachieved in school and barely finished high school even though he had been tested as having an IQ of 120 (bright normal). He was disorganized, inattentive, and easily distracted. Teachers used to say that he did not live up to his potential and that he would do better if he tried harder. There were also teacher comments on his report cards that he should try to be more cheerful and positive. He wanted to do neurofeedback instead of medication. Robbie trained his left prefrontal cortex to be more active. At first the training was very slow. It took him six months to be able to tune in to his own brainwave patterns. But once he caught on to how to do the neurofeedback, the training went much faster. Within a year he felt better energy and he was more positive. He went to junior college and enrolled in an airline mechanics course. He got straight A's in the course and was very proud of his abilities. He surprised himself by discovering a hidden artistic side, and he started bringing us sculp-

Type 5 Training Site

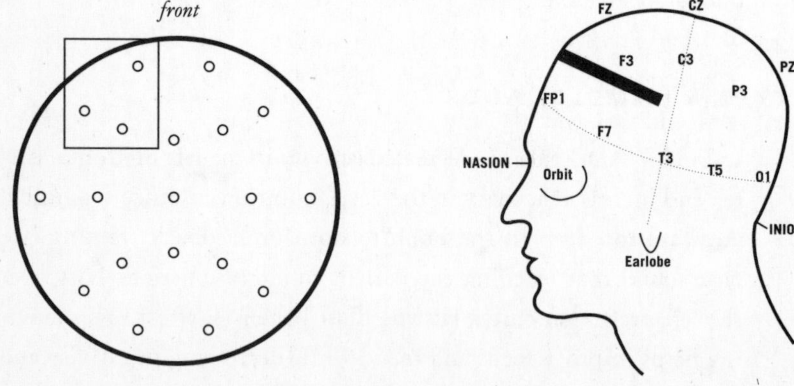

tures and drawings. At the end of three years of neurofeedback training, he was significantly better. Five years later he remains so.

TYPE 6 ("RING OF FIRE") ADD

The neurofeedback protocol for this type of ADD is unknown at this time. Due to the diffuse nature of the cerebral hyperactivity, we doubt that one training site will work. It's possible that multiple training sites will be helpful, such as SMR training over the parietal and lateral prefrontal areas and high alpha training over the anterior cingulate area, but it is yet to be determined.

AUDIO-VISUAL STIMULATION

A similar treatment to neurofeedback is something called audio-visual stimulation. This technique was developed by Harold Russell, Ph.D., and John Carter, Ph.D., psychologists at the University of Texas, Galveston. Both Drs. Russell and Carter were involved in the treatment of ADD children with neurofeedback, but they wanted to develop a treatment technique that could be available to more children. They based their technique on a concept termed "entrainment," in which brainwaves pick up the rhythm of the environment around them. Drs. Russell and Carter developed special glasses and headphones that flash lights and sounds at specific frequencies that help the brain "tune in" to a more focused state. Patients wear these glasses for thirty to forty-five minutes a day.

I have tried this treatment on a number of patients, with some encouraging results. One patient, who developed tics on both Ritalin and Dexedrine, tried the glasses for a month. His ADD symptoms significantly improved. When he went off the audio-visual stimulator, his symptoms returned. The symptoms again subsided when he retried the treatment.

I believe that both neurofeedback and audio-visual stimulation techniques show promise for the future. More research is needed in these promising areas.

BIOLOGICAL TREATMENT SUMMARY

Here is a summary of the biological treatments for each type:

ADD Type	Type 1 (Classic) ADD	Type 2 (Inattentive) ADD	Type 3 (Overfocused) ADD
Diet	higher protein, lower carbohydrate	higher protein, lower carbohydrate	lower protein, higher carbohydrate
Exercise	intense aerobic	intense aerobic	intense aerobic
Herbs, supplements	L-tyrosine	L-tyrosine	St. John's wort, 5-HTP, L-tryptophan, Inositol with L-tryrosine
Medications	stimulants such as Adderall, Ritalin, Dexedrine, and Cylert	stimulants such as Adderall, Ritalin, Dexedrine, and Cylert	serotonin-enhancing meds such as Effexor, Zoloft, Paxil, Prozac, or Luxox; may also need a stimulant
EEG biofeedback	enhance beta and suppress theta over the prefrontal area	enhance beta and suppress theta over the prefrontal area	enhance alpha over the anterior cingulate gyrus

ADD Type	Type 4 (Temporal) Lobe ADD	Type 5 (Limbic) ADD	Type 6 ("Ring of Fire") ADD
Diet	higher protein, lower carbohydrate	higher protein, lower carbohydrate	higher protein, lower carbohydrate
Exercise	Intense aerobic	intense aerobic	intense aerobic
Herbs, supplements	GABA, *ginkgo biloba,* phosphatidyl serine, vitamin E, Piracetam	DL-phenylalanine, L-tyrosine, SAMe	GABA, omega-3 fatty acids
Medications	anticonvulsants such as Depakote, Carbatrol, Neurontin, Topamax, Lamictal, Gabatril, Dilantin	stimulating antidepressants (Norpramin, Wellbutrin)	either anticonvulsants as listed for Type 4 or the new antipsychotic medications such as Risperdal or Zyprexa
EEG biofeedback	enhance SMR and suppress theta over the affected temporal lobe	enhance beta and suppress theta over the left prefrontal area	unknown at this time; possibilities are to enhance SMR activity over the parietal and lateral prefrontal areas and high alpha over the anterior cingulate gyrus

PART 4

Optimizing the ADD Life

CHAPTER 21

Parenting and Family Strategies

Even those with the best parenting skills deteriorate when they're up against the day-to-day stress of ADD kids, and intervention with the parents and family is crucial to a healthy outcome for these children. Having an ADD child or teenager is often extremely stressful on a family system. Siblings are often embarrassed by the child's behavior, and parents often feel guilty for struggling so much with these children. One of the most helpful things I have done for these families is to lead a weekly parent education and support group. When parents become more effective with these children, the entire household does better.

Before undertaking parent training, it is important to screen parents and other siblings for ADD. Untreated ADD in parents or siblings sabotages treatment. Untreated ADD parents are often unable to follow through on their homework. Untreated siblings can disrupt the progress of the child or teen in treatment.

Here is a summary of the important points from the parenting course:

- **Be focused.** Set clear goals for yourself as a parent and for your child. Then make sure that you act in a manner consistent with your goals.

- **Relationship is key.** With a good parent-child relationship, almost any form of discipline will work. With a poor parent-child relationship, any form of discipline will probably fail. Relationships require two things: time and a willingness to listen.
- **Spend some "special time" with your child each day, even if it's only ten to fifteen minutes.** Being available to the child will help him or her feel important and enhance self-esteem.
- **Be a good listener.** Find out what the child thinks before you tell him or her what you think.
- **Be clear about what you expect.** It is effective for families to have posted rules, spelling out the "laws" and values of the family. For example: "We treat each other with respect, which means no yelling, no hitting, no name calling or putdowns. We look for ways to make each other's lives easier."
- **When a child lives up to the rules and expectations, be sure to notice him or her.** If you never reinforce good behavior, you're unlikely to get much of it.
- **Notice the behaviors you like in your child ten times more than the behaviors you don't like.** This teaches them to notice what they like about themselves, rather than to grow up with a negative self-image.
- **Mean what you say.** Don't allow guilt to cause you to back down on what you know is right.
- **Don't tell a child ten times to do something.** Expect a child to comply the first time! Be ready to back up your words.
- **Never discipline a child when you're out of control.** Take time out before you lose your cool.
- **Use discipline to teach a child rather than to punish or get even for bad behavior.**
- **See misbehavior as a problem you're going to solve rather than that "the child is just trying to make you mad."**
- **It's important to have swift, clear consequences for broken rules, enforced in a matter-of-fact and unemotional way.** Nagging and yelling are extremely destructive as well as ineffective, and tend to be addictive to the ADD child.

- **Give a child choices between alternatives, rather than dictating what they'll do, eat, or wear.** If you make all the decisions for your child, he or she will be unable to make decisions independently later on.
- **Parents need to be together and support each other.** When children are allowed to split parental authority, they have far more power than is good for them.
- **Keep promises to children.**
- **Children learn about relationships from watching how their parents relate to each other.** Are you setting a good example?
- **Be careful of the nicknames and phrases you use to describe your children.** Children live up to the labels we give them.
- **Parents need time for themselves.** Parents who are drained do not have much left that is good for their children.
- **Teach your children from your own real-life experiences.**
- **In parenting, always remember the words "firm but kind."** One parent used the phrase "tough as nails and kind as a lamb." Try to balance them at the same time.
- **Do not yell at, hit or berate an ADD child.** The more emotionally intense you get, the more they will bring out the animal in you.

GET RID OF GUILT

Perhaps the biggest roadblock to effective discipline of ADD children and teens is *guilt.* Too often parents allow guilt to get in their way and render them totally ineffective in dealing with the difficult child.

Here is the *guilt cycle* that often perpetuates bad behavior.

1. **Parent explodes** because he or she can't take the bad behavior anymore.
2. **Parent feels guilt** because he or she overreacted or was excessively harsh.

3. **Parent allows the child to get away with misbehavior** because of his or her guilt over the explosion toward the child.
4. **Parent feels tension building up** because he or she is not effectively dealing with the misbehavior.
5. **Parent explodes** and the cycle starts all over again.

It's very important when dealing with the ADD child to break the guilt cycle. Do this is by dealing with difficult behavior whenever it occurs. Do not allow the tension to build up in you to the point where you explode.

STEPS TO SHAPING POSITIVE BEHAVIOR

Retraining difficult behavior patterns is an essential part of the treatment for ADD. As I've mentioned, having this disorder causes faulty learning in many areas of life. For example, many children with ADD are repeatedly given the message that they're stupid (i.e., by parent or teacher complaints and/or by being teased by other children). Too often, they begin to believe they really are stupid. As such, they stop doing their work, believing it is too hard for them.

Behaviorally, many children, teens, and adults learn to get other people upset with their difficult behavior. They learn, on a purely unconscious and biological level, that when there is turmoil between people, it stimulates their brain, making them feel more alert and awake. They do not know this on a conscious level and would, in fact, deny that they ever do it. But when you watch these people with their parents or in social situations, their behavior seems goal-directed toward turmoil. After listening to hundreds of mothers, I'm convinced that this is a technique to treat underlying brain deactivation with turmoil, as an alcoholic may treat underlying restlessness or anxiety with alcohol.

Retraining behavior patterns or behavior modification involves several clear steps:

Step One: Define the desired and undesirable behaviors specifically.
Step Two: Establish a baseline period.
Step Three: Communicate the rules and expectations clearly.
Step Four: Reward desired behavior.
Step Five: Give clear, unemotional consequences for the negative behavior.

Step One

Define the desired and undesirable behaviors specifically. Before you can shape behavior, it is critical to clearly know exactly what behaviors you want and what behaviors you don't want.

Step Two

Establish a baseline period of how often either negative or positive behavior occurs. Take some time (a week to a month) to keep a log on how many times a behavior occurs. For example, if the desired behavior is getting homework done before a child or teen goes out of the house, keep a log on how many times that occurs during the baseline period. Doing this will allow you to know whether or not your interventions are effective.

Step Three

Communicate rules and expectations clearly. Establishing clear, written rules and expectations is the next step in effective behavior modification. These rules need to give direction for the child's behavior. When the child knows what is expected, he or she is much more likely to be able to give it. Too often, parents believe that children should know how to act without the rules being clearly communicated to them.

Children respond to symbols of rules in the environment (traffic signals, posted rules at the pool, etc.). My nephew Andrew went through a time when he was three years old during which he was afraid of monsters in his room at night. Week after week Andrew's parents searched the room with Andrew, trying to prove to him that there were no monsters in his room. They looked under the bed, in the closet, behind the door, and under the covers. Finally they realized that they were only making the fear worse by exploring the room for the monsters. Andrew's mother decided that they would make a sign saying that monsters were not allowed in Andrew's room. She and Andrew drew a picture of a monster and then drew a red circle around it with a slash across the monster. Underneath the picture they wrote NO MONSTERS ALLOWED. Amazingly, Andrew's fear of monsters in his room vanished because he knew the sign kept them away.

Written rules have power! They let children know what is expected of them in a clear way. They keep the standards of good behavior unambiguous and serve as a touch point for clear, unemotional consequences.

Here is a set of rules that I've found helpful, both for my own household and for my patients'. Post them up where the family can see them every day.

FAMILY RULES

TELL THE TRUTH

TREAT EACH OTHER WITH RESPECT
(which means no yelling, no hitting, no kicking, no name calling, and no putting down).

NO ARGUING WITH PARENTS.
(As parents, we want and value your input and ideas,
but arguing means you have made your point more than twice.)

RESPECT EACH OTHER'S PROPERTY
(which means we ask permission to use something that does not belong to us).

DO WHAT MOM AND DAD SAY THE FIRST TIME
(without complaining or throwing a fit).

ASK PERMISSION BEFORE YOU GO SOMEWHERE.

PUT THINGS AWAY THAT YOU TAKE OUT.

LOOK FOR WAYS TO BE KIND AND HELPFUL TO EACH OTHER.

These rules set the tone and "values" for the family. They clearly state that there is a line of authority at home, and that it is expected that children will follow the rules and respect their parents, their siblings, and the family's property. These are good social expectations and teachings. When you tell someone what you expect, you're much more likely to get it.

In establishing expectations at home, it's often important to use visual clues, such as pictures or short printed directions. Try to minimize verbal directions, since people with ADD may have trouble processing verbal input, especially in a noisy environment. Writing expectations down also has the advantage of being able to refer to it later when the ADD person denies that you ever told him or her about it.

Step Four

Reward desired behavior. After clear expectations are given, it is essential to praise and reward the behavior that meets those expectations. When positive behavior goes unnoticed, it often ceases to exist. Most children, teens, and even adults enjoy being noticed by others. Rewards or reinforcements may take many forms. As adults, we often work for monetary gain. The more financial benefit, the harder we'll work. But we also work for praise from our boss or spouse. Our personalities also determine the rewards we're interested in working toward. Children are the same way: Some children will work hard to comply for the verbal praise of their parents, while others need different types of rewards.

Social rewards: verbal praise ("I really like it when you . . ."); physical affection, such as hugs or looks.

Material rewards: toys, food, "Clean your room before your snack," little presents or surprises.

Activity rewards: sports, trips to library, park, arcade.

Token rewards: star or point systems, money.

Here are some simple principles in rewarding good behavior:

- Use more rewards than consequences.
- Reward as soon as possible after a child fulfills your expectations.
- Focus your energy on catching them being good.
- Look for ways to reinforce them.
- Reward the child in a way he or she likes. (All children are different; use what works!)
- Be consistent.
- Make it to the child's benefit to behave.

Many parents object to the use of reward systems when it comes to reinforcing good behavior. They say, "I'm not going to bribe my child to behave. They should do it anyway." I respond that the definition of a bribe is to give someone something of value to encourage them to do something illegal. Behaving is not illegal! Generally, adults would not go to work if there were not some sort of payoff. It is important to think that children also work for goals and payoffs that turn them on. For difficult kids, it is often necessary to set up a token system or a point system to help keep them on track.

Here is a simple five-step "point" or "chip" system that has worked well for hundreds of parents.

1. **Choose**
   - three chores (such as doing the dishes, cleaning his or her room, vacuuming, feeding the animals, etc.)
   - three behaviors (such as treating his or her sister well, getting ready for school on time, doing what Mom and Dad say the first time, etc.).

2. **Assign a point (or poker chip) value to each chore and behavior,** depending on how difficult each is for the child to ac-

complish. If the child has a lot of trouble doing something, make it worth more points or chips than something he or she does readily. Add up the possible points or chips the child can get each day if he or she has a perfect day. Also, let the child know that he or she can earn bonus points or chips for especially cooperative and pleasant behavior. Tell the child that points or chips will be given only for chores and behaviors done on the first request. If you have to repeat yourself, the child will not get any points or chips, and he will still have to do it!

3. **Establish two lists of rewards:**
   - one for future incentives the child wishes to work for (a toy, having a friend spend the night, a special trip to a restaurant or arcade, renting a video, etc.)
   - another list for everyday rewards (watching TV, playing with friends, playing video games, staying up an extra half hour, etc.).

4. **Determine the point value necessary to redeem each reward.** About half should be spent on everyday rewards. This allows a child, if he or she has a really good day, to save about half of the accumulated points or chips for special rewards down the line.

5. **Add up the points every day.** Allow the child to use his or her rewards to buy everyday privileges and keep a "savings account" for points or chips to be used later on. This works to teach them the value and need for saving.

Note:

- Initially, make the system very reinforcing so that children will want to participate. Then slowly tighten the reins on it as their behavior improves.
- You can use the rewards for almost any behavior you like.
- Reward as quickly as possible.
- Do not give chips or points away before the actual behavior or chore is done. In this system there is no credit!

FAT FREDDY AND CHANGING BEHAVIOR

Anyone who has been to my clinic in Fairfield knows that I collect penguins. I now have over a thousand penguins in my office. They remind me of the need to shape behavior in a positive way. I used to live in Hawaii. On the island of Oahu there is a place by the name of Sea Life Park. At Sea Life Park they had a penguin show, and the star penguin's name was Fat Freddy. Freddy could do amazing things. He could jump off a twenty-foot board, he could bowl with his nose, he could count—he even jumped through a hoop of fire. I remember watching Freddy's show with my son, Antony, who was seven at the time.

Toward the end of the show, the trainer asked Freddy to go get something. Freddy went and got it and brought it right back. I was taken aback when I saw that. I thought to myself, "I ask this kid to get me something and he wants to have a discussion with me for twenty minutes and then he doesn't want to do it. What's the difference? I know my son is smarter than this penguin." Anyway, we went up to the trainer after the show and I asked her how she got Freddy to do all of those really neat things. The trainer looked at my son and then she looked at me and she said, "Unlike parents, whenever Freddy does anything like what I want him to do, I notice him. I give him a hug and then I give him a fish."

Even though my son didn't like fish, the light really turned on in my head: Whenever he did things that I liked, I paid no attention to him at all because I'm a busy guy. But whenever he did something I didn't like, I gave him a ton of attention because I don't want to raise bad kids. Well, guess what I was doing: *I was encouraging him to be a pain in the neck.* By misbehaving he got noticed more and more by me!

So I collect penguins as a way to remind myself to notice the good things about the people in my life a lot more than the bad things about them. This is the essence of shaping behavior.

Step Five

Administer clear, unemotional consequences for negative behavior. In order for consequences to be effective, they must be used with the other steps in shaping behavior, i.e., clear expectations and positive reinforcement. Consequences by themselves change nothing, but when used in conjunction with the other steps of the program, they can be very powerful in helping to parent the difficult child.

I once saw an interaction between a mother and her 4-year-old son in a grocery store that turned my stomach. After the child ran off for the third time, the mother jerked him by the arm, picked him off the ground, and whacked him so hard his little body flew into the air. She then slammed him down into the cart and said, "You little brat, do what I say!" With a panicked look, he held his little arms up to hug her, at which point she turned and looked away from him. He then started to cry.

Too often parents punish children as a reaction to the anger they feel inside and when they're out of control of themselves. This type of punishment causes the child to feel frightened and angry and the parent to feel guilty and frustrated.

It's important to distinguish between punishment and discipline. Punishment means to inflict a penalty for wrongdoing. Discipline, from the root word "disciple," means to teach or train. It's critical that we use discipline to teach children how to be good, rather than inflict punishment when they're not.

As I mentioned above, reinforcing good behavior is a much more effective change agent than giving consequences to bad behavior. Yet, there still are times when consequences are needed.

Here are eight components of effective discipline:

1. **A good relationship with a child is a prerequisite to effective discipline.** When parents have a good relationship with a child, almost any form of discipline is effective. When the relationship is poor, however, almost no form of discipline works

well. Never discipline children in a way that damages your relationship with them.

2. **You must be in control of yourself.** If you feel like you're going to explode, take a timeout: Take several deep breaths, count to fifty, hit a pillow, take a walk, call a friend—do anything to avoid exploding at the child. It's impossible to discipline effectively when you're out of control, and it does more harm than good.

3. ***Don't yell, nag, or belittle!*** What happens inside you when someone yells, nags, or belittles you? If you're like me, you immediately turn them off. These are ineffective techniques, and they harm the relationship more than they help the situation. Also remember: When you feel like yelling, talk softly. (The difference in your behavior will get their attention.)

4. **Have a goal in mind for the behavior you're trying to change.** For the mother in the grocery store, the goal was to get the child to stay near her. She would be more effective if she gave him a lot of positive attention for the time he stays near her, rather than giving him a lot of negative attention when he goes away. By viewing the process to change the behaviors you don't like in a positive light, you're more likely to be helpful to your child.

5. **Develop a plan for discipline before you're actually in the situation.** This also prevents you from overreacting. Discipline should be as immediate as possible and should be a reminder to the child on how to change his or her behavior. It should not be an assault. I often recommend a short timeout method for younger children and a slightly longer one for older children. Parents can also have their children write lines or essays on how they'll change their behavior.

6. **Whenever possible, use *natural* and *logical* consequences.** Ask yourself, *What's the natural or logical consequence to the misbehavior?* If the child refuses to do his or her homework, then he or she goes to school without it. If the child is acting up at dinner, then he or she doesn't get to finish dinner if everyone else is done. If the child refuses to put away his or her toys, then it is logical that the toys will be taken away for several days. Using these natural or logical consequences help children learn cause and effect and teaches them that they are responsible for their behavior.

7. **Attitude is everything.** Many parents ask my opinion on spanking. I generally tell them that whether or not you spank a child has nothing to do with effective discipline. How you discipline, not the method, is what's important. When you mildly spank a child on the buttocks when you're in control of yourself, for a specific reason, and afterward give the child a hug, then spanking can be very effective. However, most parents don't use it that way. They spank a child when they're angry and on the verge of being out of control themselves. Use discipline for teaching. You and your child will both feel better.

8. **Never withhold love, affection, or time from a child who has misbehaved.** When children are in trouble, they need you the most. Let them know it's their behavior you're disciplining, but you still love them very much.

A TIMEOUT METHOD THAT WORKS

When used properly, Timeout is an extremely effective discipline technique for children 2 to 12 years of age. Use following guidelines:

- **Give clear commands.** For example, "Antony, take out the trash now." And then count to five or ten seconds to yourself. If you count out loud, you teach the child to cue off your voice.

- **Expect immediate compliance.** We teach our kids when to respond to us. When we repeat ourselves ten times and then get serious with a child, we're teaching them not to listen to us until the tenth time we say something. Expect your child to obey you the first time you say something. When they do comply, notice and appreciate them. (In our example, "Thanks Antony, I really like it when you do what I say the first time.")

- **When the child doesn't comply, warn them only once and give them the choice to comply or not.** In our case, "Antony, I told you to take out the trash now [spoken in a firm but not hostile tone]. You have a choice: You can take it out now or you can spend ten minutes in Timeout and then you can do it. It's up to you."

- **If the child still doesn't comply *immediately,* put him or her in Timeout!**

- **Timeouts are best served in a neutral, boring corner of the house.** Don't use the child's bedroom because you have probably gone to great lengths and expense to make his or her bedroom a nice place to be. Use a Timeout chair, because there may be times when the child has to be in it for a while. Also, with a chair you can set the rule that in order for the child to be in Timeout, both buttocks need to be on the seat of the chair.

- **The time in Timeout should be the child's age in minutes or twice his or her age in minutes for more severe offenses.** For example, if the child is 5 years old, the Timeout should be five minutes long (or ten minutes if it was a particularly bad offense). It's often good to get a timer to clearly set the time.

- **A child's time starts when he or she is quiet.** Children should not be allowed to badger parents when they are in Timeout. It is a time for them to think about their behavior, and they can't think about it when their mouths are going! If your child starts to cry, whine, or nag you, simply reset the timer. Say very little: Difficult kids may try to engage you in a fight, but don't take the bait.

- **Don't give in to protests about being in Timeout.** The first few times you use this method, your child may become extremely upset. Expect it. But *know* you're going to follow through! In unusual situations, a child may cry, fight, or whine for several hours. The child believes if he or she irritates you enough, then you'll give in to the tantrum. Whatever you do, do your best to hang in there. Simply repeat: "Your time starts when you are quiet," and nothing else. If you go for two hours the first time and hold firm, it's likely the next time will be only an hour, then a half hour, then pretty soon the child will go to Timeout without a fuss. The first time you use Timeout, don't do it when you're in a hurry to go somewhere. Be sure to leave yourself enough time to be able to do it right.

- If the child refuses to stay in Timeout, you have several choices.

(1) You can tell the child that he or she will get two spankings on the buttocks for leaving Timeout. (Make sure you're in control of yourself before you use this method.)
(2) You can take away points or chips if you are on a token system.
(3) You can ground them from activities he or she enjoys.

- In order for the child to get out of Timeout, he or she must promise to do the thing that was originally asked and apologize for not doing it the first time he or she was asked. If he or she refuses to do it, the child remains in Timeout until the request is carried out. It's very important to give the child the message that *you're serious* and that *you mean what you say*! If the child can't do what was asked or he or she broke a rule such as "No hitting," the child must promise not to do it again. The apology your child gives you must be sincere. It's important that we teach our children the value of "conscience" and regret for doing things that are wrong.

- If the child is bothered or teased by siblings while he or she is in Timeout, have the sibling take the child's place in Timeout. This is a very effective technique to keep the others kids from further inflaming the situation.

For teenagers, it is more effective and less humiliating to use "response cost" methods. When they break a rule or fail to comply with a request, the negative response costs them something important to them, such as privileges, money, phone time, going out on the weekends, etc. Make sure the consequence fits the crime. I've treated some teenagers who were grounded for the summer. By July they became depressed.

Make discipline a time for teaching and reshaping behavior.

FAMILY EFFECTIVENESS STRATEGIES

Families often fall victim to undiagnosed or untreated ADD. Involving the whole family in treatment is often essential for a healthy outcome. Here are some important family treatment issues to consider.

Screen Other Family Members for ADD

ADD usually has genetic underpinnings. When one member has ADD, it is likely that another person may have it as well. Trying effectively to treat one family member when others in the family have untreated ADD invites frustration and failure. Screen every member of the immediate family. I have found that when parents have untreated ADD, they have trouble following through on medication schedules for their children or the parent training suggestions given as part of therapy. When a sibling goes undiagnosed, he or she sabotages the process by his or her own conflict-seeking behavior.

Communication Issues

Families with one or more persons with ADD often have serious communication issues. These families tend to misinterpret information, react prematurely, or have emotional outbursts over real or imagined slights. It is essential to teach families how to listen, clarify misunderstandings, and avoid mind reading. (Believe me, when it comes to mind reading, everyone's illiterate.) It is also essential to teach families with one or more ADD members to communicate in a clear, unemotional manner. Emotionality decreases effectiveness in communication.

Calm the Drive Toward Turmoil

As I've mentioned many times now, ADD children, teenagers, and adults are experts at getting others to yell at them. It is essential, therefore, to teach families how to calm volatile situations. Teaching simple breathing techniques to all family members can be valuable in calming disagreements. Also, the use of family timeouts helps when a situation starts to escalate. In family timeouts, everyone in the family goes to a quiet part of the house for a designated period of time (ten to fifteen minutes) whenever voices are raised or someone is losing control. Of course, family timeouts need to be set up ahead of time if they are going to work in calming difficult situations.

Get Rid of Guilt

Guilt is an issue for many in an ADD family. Resentment, bad feelings, and anger are common in family members. However, parents, spouses, or siblings feel that they are not "supposed" to have bad feelings toward people they love. They end up burdened by feelings of guilt. These resentments are normal, given the difficulties in the family. Explaining the biological nature of ADD to family members often helps them understand the turmoil and have more compassion toward the person with ADD, while alleviating any guilt they may feel.

Dealing with Embarrassment

Embarrassment is a common feeling among ADD family members. The outrageous behavior and public displays of turmoil often lead family members to want to hide from the outside world. Siblings complain that their friends tease them at school because of a brother's or sister's behavior; parents are frequently subjected to disapproving looks from store clerks or other parents who have "perfect" kids. Understanding ADD helps families deal with the embarrassment.

Good Guy versus Bad Guy

In families with ADD, people often get a "good guy" versus "bad guy" label. Children with the disorder often find that their behavior causes them to be outcasts or "black sheep." Whenever there is trouble, parents, unconsciously, look to them first. This "good guy" versus "bad guy" perception also applies to parents. A parent who has ADD often gets labeled by the other parent as emotional, irrational, or troubled. By doing this, the ADD parent may be stripped of his or her authority, causing resentment and turmoil. Treating the disorder in all family members who have it, along with teaching the family to share power, is essential to treating this "good guy" versus "bad guy" phenomenon.

Split Families

Divorce is more common in ADD families. This may be due to many factors, such as the increased turmoil caused by ADD children or the interpersonal problems of the ADD adults. Thus, the issues of divorce, custody, and stepfamilies often need to be addressed in treatment.

Without question, I've seen a higher percentage of families with ADD children break up through divorce. This is due, in large part, to the turmoil caused by these children. Parents often blame each other for the problems and begin to pull apart. Who wants to work all day and then come home to a house filled with tension? Who wants to be in a battle zone all day and then have a spouse come home who doesn't want to hear about all of the problems of the day? After a while, people get burned out and they may look elsewhere for some satisfaction in their lives. This dynamic may make them more vulnerable to becoming workaholics or having extramarital affairs.

Because of the higher divorce rate, child custody often becomes an issue. I have done many child custody evaluations in my practice. I look for the parent who is best suited to help the child have a good relationship with both parents, rather than a parent who vilifies the other one.

Stepfamily issues are also very important for many of these families. All members of the families need to be educated about ADD, its effects on families, and its treatment. Positive attitudes are especially important here. Considering the ADD person's drive toward turmoil, the child or adult may unconsciously seek conflict, and stepfamilies are often more vulnerable to misunderstandings and tension.

What to Do About Dad

Unfortunately, men are often the last people to admit that there are emotional or family problems. They often delay treatment, for their children or themselves, until there has been a negative effect on self-esteem or functioning. I have heard many a father tell me that there is nothing wrong with his son, even though the child may have been expelled from school on numerous occasions three years in a row. A typical comment I hear is "He is just like I was when I was young, and I turned out okay."

Why men are less likely to see emotional or family problems is the subject of many debates. Here are some possibilities:

- many men have trouble verbalizing their feelings
- many men have difficulty getting outside of themselves to see the needs of others

- men tend to be more action oriented than women, and they want to solve the problems themselves
- societal expectations teach men that they can handle problems on their own and that they are weak if they seek help
- men aren't allowed to cry or express any negative feelings, and they often do not learn to seek help or talk through their problems.

Whatever the reason, men in ADD families need education about the disorder, and they need to be part of the treatment process if it is to have the best chance of being successful. To this end, it is important for wives, mothers, and the therapist to engage the father in a positive way, encouraging him to see his valuable role in helping the whole family heal. ADD is a family problem and needs the support of everyone to be successful.

It is ineffective (and may turn into a disaster) to blame the man or set him up as the cause of all the problems. Approach him in a positive way and there is likely to be cooperation. Approach him in a negative way and there is likely to be resistance. In general, men are more competitive than women are and they need encouragement, as opposed to badgering, to be helpful. In my experience, once a resistant father becomes part of the treatment, he often takes much more responsibility for healing in the family.

Living with a Partner with ADD

When one or both partners in a marriage (or other living situation) has ADD, it is important to understand the couple dynamics and the treatment process. Here are important issues to consider:

- Have empathy for the ADD person and try to see the world through his or her eyes of frustration and failure.
- Go to at least some appointments with the doctor together. When I treat adults with ADD, I prefer to see both partners together, at least some of the time, to gather another perspective on

the treatment progress. I'm often amazed at the different perspective I get from a person's partner.

- Both partners need clear education on ADD, its genetic roots, how it impacts couples, and its treatment.
- After the initial diagnosis, take a step back from the chronic turmoil that may have been present in the relationship. Look at your relationship from a new perspective and, if need be, try to start over.
- Set up regular times for talking and checking in.
- Keep lists to avoid resentments for chores and tasks not done.
- Assume the best about the other person.
- Set clear goals for each area of your life together and review them on a regular basis. Evaluate whether your behavior is getting you what you want. When you know what you want, you are much more able to make it happen.
- Set clear individual goals and share them with each other. Then look for ways to help the other person reach his or her own personal goals.
- Avoid stereotyped roles of "caretaker" and "sick one."
- Talk out issues concerning sex, in a kind and caring manner.
- Frequently check in with each other during social gatherings to determine the comfort level of each partner.
- Get away alone together on a regular basis. This is especially important when there are ADD kids in the family.
- Work together in parenting children. Children with ADD put a tremendous strain on relationships. This is magnified even further when one of the parents has ADD. See yourselves as partners, not adversaries.
- Praise each other ten times more than you criticize!
- Get rid of the smelly bucket of fish (hurts from the past) that you carry around. Many couples hold on to old hurts and use them to torture each other months to years later. These "smelly fish" are destructive and stink up a relationship. Clean them out of your life.

- If the ADD person refuses to get help, even after repeated encouragement to do so, the partner must consider whether or not to stay in the relationship. Many people with ADD have such a wounded sense of themselves that they refuse to acknowledge any problems and refuse to accept any help or treatment. At this point, the spouse or lover should not protect or cover for the ADD person, since this only makes them more dependent and less likely to seek help. In fact, I have seen many occasions where the spouse's leaving the relationship led the ADD person to seek treatment. "Codependency" is not just a term for spouses of alcoholics: It applies to those who protect and help adults with ADD, thus preventing them from having to grow up on their own.

CHAPTER 22

School Strategies

Finding the best classroom and homework strategies are critical to school success for people with ADD. Here are lists of the strategies I give my patients:

THE TEACHER

The teacher is a major determining factor on how well the child or teen will do in school. Choose carefully! Look for a teacher who:

- understands ADD or is at least willing to learn about it
- will keep in regular contact with you about your child's progress
- protects the child or teen's self-esteem and will not put him down in front of other children or allow other children to make fun of him (Singling out a child sets him or her up to be to be teased by peers!)
- has clear and consistent rules, so that the child or teen knows what to expect
- cannot be manipulated easily and who is firm yet kind
- will motivate and encourage
- realizes the tremendous effort these children and teenagers need to put out in order to be average

- has an exciting and stimulating presentation style, using multisensory teaching methods (visual, auditory, and kinesthetic)
- gives directions slowly and clearly, and is willing to repeat them if necessary and check to see if the ADD child or teen is following them correctly
- will make adaptations as necessary, such as decrease the size of an assignment, allow more time for tasks, allow for the use of calculators, etc.
- will not undermine the treatment you have with your doctor (I've known some uninformed teachers who had the nerve to tell parents, "I'm really opposed to medication.")

I realize that it's unlikely you'll find a teacher who possesses all of these traits, but look for teachers who have an open mind and know or are willing to learn about ADD. Having a helpful, positive teacher is often the difference between success and failure for your child.

THE LEARNING ENVIRONMENT

Here are some tips I frequently give to parents and especially teachers to make the environment, pacing, and total school experience more conducive to learning. Parents, I suggest you show this section of the book to your child's teacher. Oftentimes the secret to a successful learning experience for an ADD child is a well-prepared teacher.

- Keep the walls simple: Do not cover every wall with artwork, posters, and pictures. (Visually stimulating material may distract ADD students.)
- Usually it is best to seat the ADD child up front, near the teacher, with his or her back to the rest of the students, away from the door; this decreases distractions.
- Reduce or minimize distractions (both audio and visual): Do not place an ADD student near the air conditioner, heater, high traffic areas, doors or windows.

- Make earphones available to allow children to decrease auditory distractions.
- Allow for cooling off periods when the student (or teacher) becomes upset.
- Use written, displayed rules in the classroom.
- Surround ADD students with "good role models."
- Encourage cooperative and collaborative learning, and give the non-ADD students praise and reinforcement for helping out.
- Help the ADD student feel comfortable seeking help. Many of these students won't ask questions for fear of appearing stupid to their peers, and they need to be "brought out" and encouraged.
- Most fights and "acting out" behavior at school occur in the cafeteria because of the noise and confusion. Providing a quiet place for lunch may decrease the number of lunchtime problems for these children.
- ADD children often come in from recess or lunch "wound up." Have the entire class walk around the room, then pretend to be palm trees swaying in the breeze. "How slowly can you sway?" is a calming-down exercise that will help start the late-morning or -afternoon session off right.
- If lines are a problem for the child, place him or her at the end of the line, where people will not be brushing up against his or her body: Many of these kids are sensitive to touch.

Pacing

- Adjust time for completion of projects.
- Allow frequent breaks and vary activities often.
- Omit assignments requiring copying in a timed situation.
- Give only one assignment at a time.

Increasing Attentiveness

- Pause after a question and look at different students before calling on anyone to answer.
- Alert students that you are going to ask a question (e.g., "I am going to call on someone soon—I don't know who yet.").

- Encourage students to look at the student who is answering.
- Create a level of uncertainty that requires more than passive receptivity (e.g., "What do you think will happen next?").
- If a teacher sees a student's attention wandering, call his name and ask a simple question he can answer.
- Use "attention recording sheets" for self-monitoring: The student marks a plus each time he realizes he has been paying attention and a minus each time he realizes his mind has wandered.
- Have students record time taken to complete tasks (e.g., note starting time at the top of the page and ending time at the bottom; actual time is not important, but the process of self-monitoring is crucial). A watch with a stopwatch and an alarm can help.
- Have students grade their own papers and tests. This instills a habit of reviewing their own work.
- Use nonverbal or secret cues to keep the child on track.

Presentation of Subject Matter

- Emphasize the teaching approach according to learning style of student (audio/visual/tactile/multisensory).
- Increase class participation in lectures.
- Make the material highly interactive, interesting, novel, and stimulating.
- Foster individual or small group discussions.
- Provide taped lectures for replay.
- Use demonstrations to illustrate points.
- Utilize "hands-on" activities.
- Emphasize critical information: teach "The Big Picture."
- Preview new concepts and vocabulary at the beginning of the lesson and highlight them again at the end of the lesson to reinforce learning.
- Use advanced organizers.
- Provide visual clues.
- Maintain good eye contact.
- Present more difficult lessons early in the day: Children and teens with ADD become fatigued more easily than others; also,

their medication often wears off in the late morning (if they are taking the regular form of Ritalin or Dexedrine).

- Make auxiliary materials/services available, such as:

1. taped texts
2. highlighted texts/study guides
3. supplementary materials as needed
4. note-taking assistance; copies of notes from excellent students
5. typed notes from the teacher
6. calculators or word processors
7. adapted or simplified texts
8. graph paper for math problems, handwriting, etc.

Assignments

- Give directions in small, distinct steps.
- Allow copying from paper or book.
- Use written backup for oral instructions.
- Lower reading level of assignment if necessary.
- Adjust length of assignment.
- Change format of assignments to best fit needs of child.
- Give assignments in chunks, or a series of smaller assignments; this is especially helpful for longer projects.
- Reduce pencil and paper tasks.
- Read directions/worksheets to students.
- Give oral/visual clues or prompting.
- Allow assignments to be typed or dictated.
- Adapt worksheets/packets.
- Maintain an assignment notebook.
- Avoid penalizing for spelling errors. (Andrew Jackson said it is the dull man who can only spell words one way.)
- Encourage the use of dictation or word processing for those with writing difficulties. You may have people with visual processing problems read their material into a tape recorder and then listen to the material over and over.

Reinforcement and Follow-Through

- Use reward systems for positive behavior.
- Use concrete rewards.
- Check often for understanding and review.
- Request parental reinforcement if it is a positive experience for the student and parent.
- Have the student repeat the instructions.
- Make/use vocabulary files.
- Teach study skills.
- Teach organizational skills, and supervise their implementation on a regular basis.
- Use study sheets to organize material.
- Reinforce long-term assignment timeliness (cut into short chunks).
- Use behavioral contracts/daily or weekly report cards.
- Arrange for tutoring.
- Have regular conferences with student and parents, emphasizing the positive as well as giving feedback on the negative.

Testing Adaptations

- Give some tests orally (some students need most tests orally due to other learning disabilities).
- Have someone read the test to the student if there are reading problems.
- Reduce the reading level of the test if necessary.
- Adjust the time for test completion.
- Short-answer/multiple-choice questions are best for many ADD students.
- Shorten the length of the test.
- Test for knowledge, not attention span.

Grading

- Modify weights of examinations.
- Give extra credit for projects.

- Give credit for appropriate class participation.
- Increase or eliminate time limits.
- Shorten the lengths of exams.

Encourage Questions

- Take time to encourage the child or teen to ask questions when he or she feels confused or lost.
- Establish a positive feeling about asking questions. Most students do not ask questions for fear of appearing stupid. If they can overcome this barrier, it will serve them well for the rest of their academic careers.
- Praise the child for asking appropriate questions.

Discipline

- "Firm and kind" are the words to remember.
- When you say something, mean it; be willing to back it up, but in a kind, caring tone.
- Be very careful not to discipline a child when his misbehavior is the result of confusion or misunderstanding instructions.
- Use discipline for teaching, not punishment.
- Never discipline a child when you feel you're out of control.
- Show disapproval of the behavior, not the child.
- Stay calm and unemotional. (Remember, ADD children are often trying to get a rise out of you!)
- Have well-thought-out consequences to certain behaviors ahead of time. (Anticipation is the key to success.)
- Focus 90 percent of your efforts with the child on noticing behavior you like, to set a positive tone.
- Have frequent contact with the parents. (They need to be allied with you if discipline is going to be effective.)

Finger Agnosia

"Finger agnosia" is a term for students who struggle with the mechanics of writing. When they try to write, their minds go blank. This is common in people with ADD and occurs in part because the person has to concentrate so hard on the actual physical act of writing that they forget or are unable to formulate what they want to write.

Common symptoms of finger agnosia include:

- messy handwriting
- trouble getting thoughts from the brain to the paper
- staring at writing assignments for long periods of time
- writing sentences that don't make sense
- frequent spelling and grammatical errors
- many erasures and corrections
- difficulty with timed writing assignments
- printing rather than writing in cursive.

Here are some helpful suggestions for dealing with finger agnosia:

- Allow the student to print as often as possible. (For many students it's easier and requires less effort.)
- Encourage early use of typing and word processing programs. (Mavis Beacon Teaches Typing is an excellent computer typing program for children and teens.)
- Try out different types of pens and pencils to see which ones work best. Some are easier to use than others.
- Break down assignments and long reports into pieces, and work on them over time, rather than all at once (such as on the night before they are due).
- Before an actual writing project is done, encourage students to write an outline of the assignment to help keep them on track.
- Encourage students to write down their ideas before worrying about spelling/grammar.
- If it helps, have students dictate their answers or reports first. This often helps them add ideas and substance to the article that would not have been present through writing alone.

- Use a binder/organizer to keep written assignments together.
- Modify writing workloads at work and school as needed.
- Avoid timed situations; give tests orally if necessary.
- Avoid having other students grade the work, as this may set up embarrassment and teasing.

Homework

Here are suggestions for taking the nightmare out of homework:

- Provide a "special" quiet spot without distractions in which to do homework.
- Break assignments into short segments of about fifteen to twenty minutes; set a timer to structure work periods.
- Intersperse physical activity between segments.
- Check assignment sheets and notebooks on a regular basis.
- Continually work on good communication between home and school.
- Reward positive homework behavior.
- If problems continue, use a daily report system to ensure compliance.

Useless and/or Harmful Strategies

- Tell the child or teen to try harder. (The harder they try, the worse it gets.)
- Lecture the student about showing his "true" ability.
- Notice only the negative.
- Compare the student to other students.

DAILY PROGRESS NOTE (DPN)

Supervision is the key to helping students with ADD or other students who are having difficulty adapting to the rigors of school. They often have not developed the internal discipline to be successful day-to-day at school and with their homework. I use this system for both children and teenagers. Even though teenagers may balk at this system, many teens in my practice have used it successfully. I'm convinced that many students have graduated from high school because we kept them on track with this system! ADD students tend to do much better if they know someone is watching.

Directions

Every school day the child or teen is to bring the Daily Progress Note to school for the teacher or teachers to fill out (at the end of the day if there is only one teacher, at the end of each class for those who have multiple teachers). The teacher (or teachers) rates the student on a scale of 1 to 5 (1 = best, 5 = worst) in four different areas: homework, class participation, classwork, and peer interactions. After rating the child in each area, the teacher then puts his or her initials at the bottom of the form. (It is important to emphasize to the teacher the importance of giving an accurate assessment. Some teachers give out "good" marks just to be nice and then put the real grades down on the report card, shocking the student and parents.)

At the end of the day, the child or teen brings the DPN home. This note provides the student, parents, and teacher with immediate feedback on performance and helps everyone track progress throughout the year. Good performance is noticed and reinforced. Mediocre or poor performance is observed and necessary corrective measures can be put into place. When the child or teen brings the DPN home, it is helpful if parents first look for something they like. (Too many parents only notice the negative.) If the child or teen's marks are particularly poor, the parents need to question the reasons behind the difficulties of the day.

After the discussion, the parent assigns points for the day. Here is a sample point system:

1 = 5 points
2 = 2 points
3 = 1 point
4 and 5 = 0 points

In the system listed above (for students with one teacher a day), there is a total of 20 possible points that the child can earn (a score of 1 [5 points] multiplied by 4 areas = 20 points).

The points are then spent in two different ways: one, on daily wants and needs, the other for future privileges. Earning points for daily wants and needs is significant, as these reinforce and discipline behavior on a more immediate basis. To do this, the parent and child make up a list of the things he or she likes to do on a daily basis, such as watching television, playing outside, having a friend over, playing a video game, talking on the telephone, etc. Half of the possible points (10 in the example above) should be spent on daily privileges. This lets the child know that he or she can't just blow a day at school and expect everything to be okay at home. For example, points needed for daily wants may be as follows:

2 = ½ hour of television
2 = 1 hour of playing outside
3 = having a friend over for an hour
2 = playing a video game
3 = ½ hour of telephone privilege.

The other half of their points can be saved for special treats and privileges as the child earns enough points (such as a special toy, a trip to his or her favorite restaurant, having a friend spend the night, or being able to stay up past his or her bedtime). It is important to make up a wish list of the things the child or teen is willing to work for. The child or teen needs to develop this list in order to more fully buy into this program.

In some cases, children will intentionally lose their DPN or forget to have their teacher sign it if their performance that day was poor. In the case where the child claims to have lost the DPN or says that the teacher didn't fill it out, the child loses all of his or her points for the day (or a portion of the points if multiple teachers are involved). The child or teen must take responsibility! On a day when the child earns little or no points for various privileges, he or she is to be encouraged to do better the next day. In lieu of normal privileges, encourage the child to read books or play in his or her room.

Almost all children find this system to be very rewarding after they have used it for several days. Some children refuse to participate initially, but if the parents persist, the child will adapt. One of the advantages of this system is that some children become "miserly" with their points and will often give up watching television and playing video games to save points for other things they are interested in. In addition, many begin to develop a more positive attitude toward school because of their ability to earn extra privileges for performing well in school.

Some parents have asked me if the DPN does not single out the child for teasing from peers. I have rarely found this to be the case. In fact, this helps ADD children to modify their behavior in school, which in turns helps their interactions with peers.

Daily Progress Note

Name: ______________________________ **Date:** ________________

Please rate this child/teen in each of the areas listed below according to how he/she performed in school today, using ratings of 1 to 5. (1 = excellent; 2 = good; 3 = fair; 4 = poor; 5 = terrible or did not do the work.)

	Class Periods						
Subjects	1	2	3	4	5	6	7
Homework	☐	☐	☐	☐	☐	☐	☐
Class Participation	☐	☐	☐	☐	☐	☐	☐
Class Work	☐	☐	☐	☐	☐	☐	☐
Peer Interactions	☐	☐	☐	☐	☐	☐	☐
Teacher's Initials	☐	☐	☐	☐	☐	☐	☐

GET SCHOOL RESOURCES INVOLVED EARLY

Under federal law (PL 94-142), all students are entitled to an educational setting in which they can learn. If they are handicapped, the school system must make proper modifications so that they can receive an education. As you have seen, ADD often handicaps a child or teen from taking advantage of education. Due to a lack of funding and personnel, however, many schools overlook children with ADD and learning problems unless they are forced to take action. Parents need to be the prime force that gets the child appropriate help.

Parents need to *advocate* for their children and not just rely on the overworked principal, counselor, or school psychologist. To that end, parents must be educated on ADD and know the proper school interventions. I often tell my parents that they are the ones who need to intervene when things are not going well at school. The squeaky wheel gets the grease! Don't give in to a school administrator who tries to intimidate or condescend to you!

If you are not "the assertive type," consider obtaining a school advocate for your child. A school advocate is someone who has experience in dealing with the school system to ensure the child gets all the help he or she needs. To get the name of an advocate in your area, contact the local chapter of CHADD (a national support group for parents of children with ADD, with local chapters) or the Disability Rights Education and Defense Fund in Berkeley, California, at (510) 644-2555.

Most school systems are willing to test preschool children if there is a suspected learning or speech problem. Contact your local school counselor or principal for more information on special testing. The earlier you address problems, the more hope there is for successful interventions.

CHAPTER 23

Sleep Strategies for Getting Up and Going to Bed

Getting up in the morning and going to sleep at night are frequently significant problems for people with ADD. Sleep-cycle problems can interfere with relationships, work, school, and overall energy level. Chronic sleep deprivation makes ADD worse.

GETTING UP

Mornings are difficult for many people with ADD. Here are some common statements people with ADD say as they're trying to get out of bed:

"Later . . ."
"Just a few more minutes."
"I'll get up in a little bit."
"Leave me alone."
"My alarm is set" (even though it already went off).
"I'm too tired to get up."
"OK, I'm up" (only to lay back down for several hours).

Many people with ADD feel very groggy or fuzzy-headed in the morning. The harder they try to get out of bed, the worse it gets.

One teenager I know had such a hard time getting out of bed that she almost got fired from her summer job. Her boss told her if she was late one more time, she was gone. She had three alarm clocks and she had two of her friends call her in the morning. Many high school students are frequently late for school because of the trouble getting up. Adults with ADD also have this problem. Have you ever heard of adults who say that they have to have a couple of cups of coffee in the morning to get going? Coffee contains the stimulant caffeine. (Stimulants are a common treatment for ADD.)

Parents complain that they have to wake up ADD children and teenagers three, four, five, six, even ten times before they get out of bed. This can cause a lot of family turmoil in the morning. When parents have to tell a child over and over to get out of bed, they can get pretty irritable. They may start yelling, threatening, or using force to get the child moving. Some parents we know use water or ice to help the child or teen get up. The morning grogginess causes many people with ADD to be chronically late, which stresses out everyone in the morning, especially if the parent has to get to work or has other children to get to school.

The child or teen who wakes up to parental hostility starts the day off in a bad mood. It's hard to concentrate in class when you have just been yelled at, threatened, or grounded because you couldn't get out of bed on time. This leads to other problems. For example, if you can't get up on time, you may miss the bus, get a speeding ticket, end up in the tardy tank, or just cut class so that you're not late again. Starting the day off on the wrong foot can affect your mood and attitude for the whole day.

Many ADD people say that when they get up on their own, they tend to do better than if someone is screaming at them to get out of bed. It often becomes a battle of wills. Both people end up feeling terrible.

Without parents hassling kids, some children and teenagers won't get out of bed until noon, 1, 2 or even 3 P.M. This can cause serious problems. When kids get up late, they will have trouble going to sleep at night. Getting up late causes a large part of the day to go by without participating in it. Many parents complain that their kids are wasting the day.

HELPFUL HINTS FOR GETTING GOING IN THE A.M.

1. Go to bed at a reasonable time. (See bedtime suggestions below.)
2. Set the alarm clock to play the kind of music that gets the person going. (Some people like fast rock music to wake them up, others like rap, some like country music.)
3. Keep the alarm clock (or clocks) across the room so that the person has to get out of bed to turn it off. Don't have the kind of alarm that turns itself off after thirty seconds. Have one that keeps going, and going, and going.
4. Take your medicine a half hour before you're supposed to get out of bed. Keep it by the bed with a glass of water. Set two alarms: One to take your medicine and one to get up.
5. Have something for the ADD person to do that motivates him or her in the morning. Sometimes having a girlfriend or boyfriend call you can be great motivation. Some people enjoy working out with weights in the morning as a way to get their bodies (and brains) feeling alive.
6. Stay away from early classes and early-morning jobs if possible. In college, many of my patients don't start class until after 10:00 A.M. Being late irritates teachers and bosses, which is the last thing someone wants to do if he or she wants to do well in school or in a job!
7. Watch the body's own cycle. Some people are good in the morning and some later on. Fit your schedule to your body's rhythms.

GOING TO BED

Many people with ADD have sleep problems. Some "go and go" all day until they drop from exhaustion. Others have difficulty getting to sleep, or they wake up frequently throughout the night. Some are even hyper in their sleep and constantly on the move. Getting a restful night's sleep helps you feel calmer in the morning. After a poor night's sleep, the ADD person has even more trouble awakening. Here are some of the things people with ADD have said about their sleep problems:

"I have to count sheep to get to sleep, but the stupid sheep are always talking to me."

"When I try to get to sleep, all kinds of different thoughts come into my mind. It feels like my mind spins when I try to calm it down."

"I feel so restless at night. It's hard to settle down, even though I'm tired."

"The worries from the day go over and over in my head. I just can't shut my brain down."

"I have to sleep with a fan to drown out my thoughts. I need noise to calm down."

Sleep disturbances can cause many other problems, in addition to the obvious problems of difficulty waking up and morning grogginess. If it is hard to settle down at night, it may make parents mad, because they know too well about the morning problems. Not getting enough sleep continues the cycle of feeling tired and wanting to sleep during the day.

One teenager I know had such trouble sleeping that he could never go to bed before three o'clock in the morning. This caused terrible problems: He couldn't get up in the morning and had to drop out of school. He even went to the Stanford University Sleep Center for help with his problem. In the end, medication was needed to help his sleep cycle.

Doctors aren't sure why people with ADD have more sleep problems. Some doctors think it has to do with serotonin, the neurotransmitter most closely tied to types 3 and 6 ADD. However, we all depend on serotonin to fall asleep, and when there is not enough of it, getting to sleep can be an awful chore.

THIRTEEN WAYS TO GET TO SLEEP

Here are thirteen ways to make it easier to go to sleep. No one suggestion will work for everyone, but keep trying new tactics until you find what works for your situation:

1. Don't watch television one to two hours before bedtime, especially any program that may be overstimulating (i.e., the shows you most like). This includes news programs, as people with ADD tend to ruminate on the bad things that happened that day in their own world and the world at large.
2. Stimulating, active play such as wrestling, tickling, teasing, etc., should be eliminated for one to two hours before bedtime. Quiet activities such as reading, drawing, or writing are more helpful in the hours before bedtime.
3. Some people try to read themselves to sleep. This can be helpful. But read boring books. If you read action-packed thrillers or horror stories, it's not likely that you'll smoothly drift off into peaceful never-never land.
4. Try a warm, quiet bath.
5. A bedtime back rub in bed may be soothing. Starting from the neck and working down in slow, rhythmic strokes can be very relaxing. Some children and teens say that a foot massage is particularly helpful (although it may be hard to find someone to give a teen a foot massage if they haven't showered or taken a bath before bed).
6. Soft, slow music often helps people drift off to sleep. Instrumental music, as opposed to vocal, seems to be the most helpful. Some people with ADD say that they need fast music in order to block out their thoughts. Use what works.
7. Nature-sounds tapes (rain, thunder, ocean, rivers) can be very helpful. Others like the sound of fans.
8. Some people with ADD say that restrictive bedding is helpful, such as a sleeping bag or being wrapped tightly in blankets.

9. A mixture of warm milk, a teaspoon of vanilla (not imitation vanilla, the real stuff), and a teaspoon of sugar can be very helpful. This increases serotonin in your brain and helps you sleep.
10. I make a sleep tape in my office with a special sound machine that produces sound waves at the same frequency as a sleeping brain. The tape is played at bedtime and helps the brain "tune in" to a brainwave sleep state, encouraging a peaceful sleep. The tape is called "Brain Train" and can be obtained at www.mindworkspress.com.
11. Learn self-hypnosis. Self-hypnosis can be a powerful tool for many different reasons, including sleep. Here's a quick self-hypnosis course:
    - Focus your eyes on a spot and count slowly to twenty. . . . Let your eyes feel heavy as you count, and close them as you get to twenty.
    - Take three or four very slow, deep breaths.
    - Tighten the muscles in your arms and legs and then let them relax.
    - Imagine yourself walking down a staircase while you count backward from ten. (This will give you the feeling of "going down" or becoming sleepy.)
    - With all of your senses (sight, touch, hearing, taste, smell), imagine a very sleepy scene, such as by a fire in a mountain cabin or in a sleeping bag at the beach.
12. Seek sleep control therapy. Here are the tips many sleep experts give to chronic insomniacs to help them get to sleep on a regular basis:
    - Go to bed only when sleepy.
    - Use the bed and bedroom only for sleep.
    - Get out of bed and go into another room when you are unable to fall asleep or return to sleep easily, and return to bed only when sleepy.
    - Maintain a regular rise time in the morning regardless of sleep duration the previous night.
    - Avoid daytime naps.

13. Sometimes medications are needed if getting to sleep is a chronic problem. There are pros and cons to using medications as sleep aids. On the positive side, medications tend to work quickly and can help normalize a disturbed sleep pattern. On the negative side, medications can have side effects (such as grogginess in the morning), and you can become dependent on them if you take them for too long. It is best to think of medications for sleeping problems as a short-term solution. Use the other ideas first.

    The different medications doctors prescribe to help promote sleep include:

    - Over-the-counter medications: Benadryl, Unisom, Sominex, Exedrin PM, Nyquil, etc.
    - Some antidepressants: imipramine (Tofranil), amitriptyline (Elavil), or trazodone (Desyrel). (Trazodone is used only in females; in men it may cause painful erections that won't go away.) Often these are used in very low doses to help promote sleep. They are helpful in people who have a tendency toward depression.
    - Certain blood pressure medications: clonidine (Catapres), for example. Clonidine is often used to calm down the restlessness or hyperactivity that often goes along with ADD.
    - Sleeping medications: temazepam (Restoril), triazolam (Halcion), zolpidem (Ambien), flurazepam (Dalmane), estazolam (ProSom). These medications tend to lose their effectiveness after a few weeks. They should be used on a short-term basis only.

Getting up and going to sleep can hinder the success of a person with ADD. Use the techniques in this chapter to help. Be persistent. If one technique doesn't work for you, don't give up: Try others.

CHAPTER 24

Killing ADD ANTs

Thinking Skills for Overcoming Past Trauma, Fear, and Failure

Children, teens, and adults with ADD often develop erroneous thought patterns, based on the failures they have experienced in their lives. It often helps to investigate the way an ADD person thinks and then teach him or her to correct any erroneous thought patterns.

Here are some examples of common negative thoughts:

"I'm a terrible student."
"I'm always messing things up."
"No one ever wants to be with me."
"Anybody could have done that. I'm not so special."
"The teacher (or boss) doesn't like me."
"I will fail at this."
"I feel you don't love me."
"I should do better."
"I'm so stupid."

These thoughts severely limit a person's ability to enjoy his or her life. How people think "moment by moment" has a huge impact on how they feel and how they behave. Negative thoughts often drive difficult behaviors and cause people to have problems with their self-esteem. Hopeful thoughts, on the other hand, influence positive behaviors and lead people to feel good about themselves and be more effective in their day-to-day lives.

Most ADD children, teens and adults have lots of negative thoughts. These thoughts come from many sources. Some of the negative thoughts come from what other people have told them about themselves (i.e., "You're no good! Why can't you ever listen? What's the matter with you? You make me crazy!"). Other negative thoughts originate from experiences where the person is continually frustrated, either at home, school, or work. They begin to think thoughts such as, "I'm stupid. I can't ever do anything right. It will never work out for me."

In many ways our brain works like a computer. When a person receives negative INPUT about themselves, they STORE it in their subconscious mind, and the input becomes EXPRESSED as negative thoughts, feelings, or behaviors. Unless people are taught how to talk back to these harmful thoughts and messages, they believe them unconditionally. This is a critical point. Most people never challenge the thoughts that go through their heads. They never even think about their own thoughts. They just believe what they think, even though the thoughts may be very irrational. Their behavior is therefore based on false assumptions or false ideas.

Unfortunately, many ADD children carry these negative thought patterns into adulthood, causing them to have problems with their moods and behavior. These negative thoughts affect their moods and in many children become the seeds of anxiety or depression later on in life. It's critical to teach people about their thoughts and to teach them to challenge what they think, rather than just accept blindly the thoughts that go through their heads. But when you're a child, no one teaches you to think much about your thoughts or to challenge the notions that go through your head, even though your thoughts are always with you. Why do we spend so much time teaching kids about diagramming sentences and so little time teaching them how to think clearly? Most people do not understand how important thoughts are and leave the development of thought patterns to random chance. Did you know that thoughts have actual weight and mass? They are real! They have significant influence on every cell in your body (more detail on this in a little bit). When a person's mind is burdened with many negative thoughts, it affects that person's ability to learn, his or her ability to relate to other people, and his or her physical health. Teaching people with ADD how to control and direct their thoughts in a positive way can be helpful in all areas of their lives.

Here are the step-by-step "positive thinking" principles that I use in my psychotherapy practice with children, teens, and adults. When people truly learn these principles, they gain more control over their feelings and their behavior.

Did you know . . . ?:

Step #1: Every time you have a thought, your brain releases chemicals. That's how our brain works:

- You have a thought
- your brain releases chemicals
- an electrical transmission goes across your brain, and
- you become aware of what you're thinking.

Thoughts are real and they have a real impact on how you feel and how you behave.

Step #2: Every time you have a mad thought, an unkind thought, a sad thought, or a cranky thought, your brain releases negative chemicals that make your body feel bad. Whenever you're upset, imagine that your brain releases bubbles with sad or angry faces, looking to cause problems. Think about the last time you were mad. What did you feel inside your body? When most people are mad, their muscles get tense, their hearts beat faster, their hands start to sweat, and they may even begin to feel a little dizzy. Your body reacts to every negative thought you have.

Step #3: Every time you have a good thought, a happy thought, a hopeful thought, or a kind thought, your brain releases chemicals that make your body feel good. Whenever you're happy, imagine that your brain releases bubbles with glad or smiling faces, making you feel good. Think about the last time you had a really happy thought (such as when you got a good grade on a test or cuddled a child). What did you feel inside your body? When most people are happy, their muscles relax, their hearts beat slower, their hands become dry, and they breathe slower. Your body also reacts to your good thoughts.

Step #4: Your body reacts to every thought you have! We know this from polygraphs, or lie detector tests. During a lie detector test, you are hooked up to equipment that measures:

- hand temperature
- heart rate
- blood pressure
- breathing rate
- muscle tension, and
- how much the hands sweat.

The tester then asks questions, such as, "Did you do that thing?" If you did the bad thing, your body is likely to have a "stress" response and it is likely to react in the following ways:

- Your hands will get colder
- your heart will go faster
- your blood pressure will go up
- your breathing gets faster
- your muscles will get tight, and
- your hands will sweat more.

Almost immediately, the body reacts to what you think, whether you say anything or not.

Now the opposite is also true. If you did not do what they are asking you about, it is likely that your body will experience a "relaxation" response and will react in the following ways:

- Your hands will become warmer
- your heart rate will slow
- your blood pressure will go down
- your breathing will become slower and deeper
- your muscles will become more relaxed, and
- your hands will become drier.

Again, almost immediately, your body reacts to what you think. This not only happens when you're asked about telling the truth, your body reacts to every thought you have, whether it is about school, friends, family, or anything else.

Step #5: Thoughts are very powerful! They can make your mind and your body feel good and they can make you feel bad! Every cell in your body is affected by every thought you have. When people get emotionally upset, they develop physical symptoms, such as headaches or stomachaches. If you can think about good things, you will feel better. It worked for Abraham Lincoln. He had periods of serious depression when he was a child and adult. Some days he didn't even get out of bed. In his later life, however, he learned to treat his bad feelings with laughter. He learned that when he laughed, he felt better.

STEP #6: Unless you think about your thoughts, they are "automatic" or "they just happen." Since they just happen, they are not always correct. Your thoughts do not always tell you the truth. Sometimes they even lie to you. I once knew a boy who thought he was stupid because he didn't do well on tests. When we tested his IQ (intelligence level), however, we discovered that he was close to a genius! You don't have to believe every thought that goes through your head. It's important to think about your thoughts to see if they help you or they hurt you. Unfortunately, if you never challenge your thoughts, you just believe them as if they were true.

Step #7: You can train your thoughts to be positive and hopeful or you can just allow them to be negative and upset you. Once you learn about your thoughts, you can choose to think good thoughts and feel good, or you can choose to think bad thoughts and feel lousy. It's up to you. You can learn how to change your thoughts, and you can learn to change the way you feel.

One way to learn how to change your thoughts is to notice them when they are negative and talk back to them. If you can correct negative thoughts, you take away their power over you. When you just think a negative thought without challenging it, your mind believes it and your body reacts to it.

Step #8: As I mentioned above, negative thoughts are mostly automatic: They "just happen." I call these thoughts Automatic Negative Thoughts. If you take the first letter from each of these words, it spells the word "ANT." Think of these negative thoughts that invade your mind like ants that bother people at a picnic. One negative thought, like one ant at a picnic, is not a big problem. Two or three negative thoughts, like two or three ants at a picnic, and it's more irritating. Ten or twenty negative thoughts, like ten or twenty ants at a picnic, can cause real problems.

Whenever you notice these automatic negative thoughts (ANTs), you need to crush them, or they'll begin to ruin your whole day. One way to crush these ANTs is to write down the negative thought and talk back to it. For example, if you think, *Other kids will laugh at me when I give my speech,* write it down and then write down a positive response—something like *The other kids will like my speech and find it interesting.* When you write down negative thoughts and talk back to them, you take away their power and help yourself feel better.

Some kids tell me they have trouble talking back to these negative thoughts because they feel that they are lying to themselves. Initially they believe that the thoughts that go through their mind are the truth. Remember, thoughts sometimes lie to you: It's important to check them out before you just believe them!

Here are nine different ways that our thoughts lie to us to make situations out to be worse than they really are. Think of these nine ways as different species or types of ANTs (automatic negative thoughts). When you can identify the type of ANT, you begin to take away the power it has over you. I have labeled some of these ANTs as red, because these ANTs are particularly harmful to you. Notice and exterminate ANTs whenever possible.

ANT #1: "All or nothing" thinking. These thoughts happen when you make something out to be all good or all bad. There's nothing in between. You see everything in black or white terms. For children, the thought that "There's nothing to do" is an example of this. When children say, "There's nothing to do," they feel down and upset, bored, and unmotivated to change the situation. But is *There's nothing to do* a rational thought? Of course not: It's just a thought. Even on a day when it's raining outside and children have to stay in, they can probably list twenty things to do if they put their minds to it. But if they never challenge the thought *There's nothing to do,* they just believe it and spend the rest of the day feeling crummy. Other examples of "all or nothing" thinking include thoughts such as *I'm the worst ballplayer in the city* and *If I get an* A *on this test, I'm a great student, but if I do poorly, then I'm no good at all.*

ANT #2: "Always" thinking. This happens when you think something that happened will "always" repeat itself. For example, if your wife is irritable and she gets upset, you may think to yourself, *She's always yelling at me,* even though she yells only once in a while. But just the thought *She's always yelling at me* is so negative that it makes you feel sad and upset. Whenever you think in words like "always," "never," "no one," "everyone," "every time," and "everything," those are examples of "always" thinking. There are many examples of "always" thinking: *No one ever plays with me. Everyone is always picking on me. You never listen to me. You always give her what she wants.* This type of ANT is very common. Watch out for it.

ANT #3 (red ANT): Focusing on the negative. This occurs when your thoughts only see the bad in a situation and ignore any of the good that might happen. For example, if you have to move and you're sad to leave your friends, you don't think of the new places you'll see and the new friends you'll make. It's important, if you want to keep your mind healthy, to focus on the good parts of your life a lot more than the bad parts. I once helped a child who was depressed. In the beginning he could only think about the bad things that happened to him. He had recently moved and told me that he would never make new friends (even though he already had several). He thought he would do poorly in his new school (even though he got mostly good grades), and that he would never have any fun (even though he lived near a bay and an amusement park). By focusing on the negative in his new situation, he was making it very hard on himself to adjust to his new home. He would have been much better off if he looked at all the positives in the situation rather than the negatives.

ANT #4 (red ANT): Fortune-telling. This is where you predict the worst possible outcome to a situation. For example, before you have to give a speech in front of a class or work meeting, you may say to yourself, *Other people will laugh at me or think I'm stupid.* Just having this thought will make you feel nervous and upset. This is a red ANT because it can do real damage to your chances of feeling good.

I once treated a 10-year-old boy named Kevin who stuttered in class whenever he read out loud. In private he was a wonderful reader, but whenever he started to read in class he thought to himself, *I'm a lousy reader; the other kids will laugh at me.* Because he had these thoughts, he stopped raising his hand to volunteer to read. In fact, this thought made him so upset that he started getting sick before school and stayed home nearly a month before his mother brought him to see me. He also stopped answering the telephone at home for fear that he would stutter whenever he said hello. When he told me about his thoughts in class and at home, I understood the problem. When you predict that bad things will happen, your mind then often makes them happen: the classic self-fulfilling prophecy. The treatment for Kevin was to get him to replace the negative thoughts and pictures in his head with the image of him being a wonderful reader in class. Learning breathing techniques (we'll cover this later) and being the designated person to answer the telephone at home also helped his confidence. Whenever you're afraid of unreasonable things, such as answering the telephone or reading in class, it is important to face your fears. Otherwise, fears develop power over you. Over the next couple of weeks he was able to go back to school, and he even volunteered to read. At home his mother told me that he ran to answer the telephone whenever it rang. If you are going to predict anything at all, it is best to predict the best. It will help you feel good and it will help your mind make it happen.

ANT #5 (red ANT): Mind reading. This happens when you believe that you know what another person is thinking when they haven't even told you. Many people do mind reading, and more often than not it gets them into trouble. It is the major reason why people have trouble in relationships. I tell people, "Please don't read my mind: I have enough trouble reading it myself!" Mind reading isn't just thinking about the same thing as someone else. The dangerous sort of mind reading I'm talking about is when you have thoughts such as *Those people are mad at me. They don't like me. They were talking about me.*

ANT #6: Thinking with your feelings. This occurs when you believe your negative feelings without ever questioning them. Feelings are complex, and, as I mentioned above, sometimes they lie to you. But many people believe their feelings even though they have no evidence for them. "Thinking with your feelings" thoughts usually start with the words "I feel . . ." For example, "I feel like you don't love me," "I feel stupid," "I feel like a failure," "I feel nobody will ever trust me." Whenever you have a strong negative feeling, check it out. Look for the evidence behind the feeling. Do you have real reasons to feel that way? Or are your feelings based on events or things from the past?

ANT #7: Guilt beatings. Guilt is not a helpful emotion. In fact, guilt often causes you to do those things that you don't want to do. Guilt beatings happen when you think with words like "should," "must," "ought to," or "have to." Here are some examples: *I should be nice to my younger brother. I must never lie. I ought to call my grandmother. I have to do my homework.* Because of human nature, whenever we think that we "must" do something, no matter what it is, we don't want to do it. Remember the story of Adam and Eve: The only restriction that God put on them when he gave them the Garden of Eden was that they shouldn't eat from the Tree of Knowledge. Almost immediately after God told them what they "shouldn't" do, they started to wonder why they shouldn't do it. Well, you know the rest of the story. It is better to replace "guilt beatings" with phrases like *I want to do this. . . . It fits my goals to do that. . . . It would be helpful to do this. . . .* So in our examples above, it would be helpful to change those phrases to *I want be nice to my younger brother. It's helpful for me not to lie, because people will trust me. I want to call my grandmother. It's in my best interest to do my homework.*

ANT #8: Labeling. Whenever you attach a negative label to yourself or to someone else, you sabotage your ability to take a clear look at the situation. Some examples of negative labels are "nerd," "jerk," "idiot," "spoiled brat," and "clown." Negative labels are very harmful. Whenever you call yourself or someone else a spoiled brat or an idiot, you lump that person in your mind with all of the "spoiled brats" or "idiots" that you've ever known and you become unable to deal with them in a reasonable way. You begin to expect the worst of them (or yourself). Stay away from negative labels. It's too easy to make them come true.

ANT #9 (the most poisonous red ANT): Blame. People who ruin their own lives have a strong tendency to blame other people when things go wrong. They take little responsibility for their problems. When something goes wrong at home, school, or work, they try to find someone to blame. They rarely admit their own problems. Typically you'll hear statements from them like "It wasn't my fault that . . ." "That wouldn't have happened if you had . . ." "How was I supposed to know . . . ?" "It's your fault that . . ." and so on. The bottom-line statement goes something like this: "If only you had done something differently, then I wouldn't be in the predicament I'm in. It's your fault, and I'm not responsible."

Blaming others starts early. I have three children. When my youngest, Katie, was 18 months old she would blame her brother, who was 11, for any trouble she might be in. Her nickname for him was DiDi, and "Didi did it," even if he wasn't home. One day she spilled a drink at the table while her mother's back was turned. When her mother turned around and saw the mess and asked what had happened, Katie told her that "Didi spilled my drink." When her mother told her that her brother was at a friend's house, Katie persisted in saying that "Didi did it."

Whenever you blame someone else for the problems in your life, you become powerless to change anything. Many kids play the "Blame Game," but it rarely helps them. Stay away from blaming thoughts and take personal responsibility for your life.

Whenever you notice an ANT entering your mind, train yourself to recognize it and write it down. When you write down automatic negative thoughts (ANTs) and talk back to them, you begin to take away their power and gain control over your moods. When you write them down, you realize that they're just little tiny ANTs, and you can squash them.

Here are some examples of ways to kill these ANTs:

ANT	Species of ANT	Thoughts to kill the ANT
There's nothing to do.	"all or nothing"	There are probably lots of things to do if I think about it for a little while.
No one ever plays with me.	"always" thinking	That's silly. I have played with lots of kids in my life.
The boss doesn't like me.	mind reading	I don't know that. Maybe she's just having a bad day. Bosses are people too.
The whole class will laugh at me.	fortune telling	I don't know that. Maybe they'll really like my speech.
I'm stupid.	labeling	Sometimes I do things that aren't too smart, but I'm not stupid.
It's my wife's fault.	blame	I need to look at my part of the problem and look for ways I can make the situation better.

Your thoughts and the thoughts of your children matter. Teach them to be positive and it will benefit their minds and their bodies. Take time to teach yourself and your kids how to think positive and feel good.

CHAPTER 25

Focused Breathing

The Immediate ADD Salve

Temper problems, anxiety, impulsivity, restlessness, insomnia, and lack of focus are common problems in people with ADD. I have found that a very simple biofeedback breathing technique helps to combat these problems. It is so simple, in fact, that many of you will be skeptical about how helpful it can be and not use it. Big mistake. Let me tell you why.

Like brain activity, breathing is also involved in everything you do. Breathing is essential to life. The purpose of breathing is to get oxygen from the air into your body and to blow off waste products such as carbon dioxide. Every cell in your body needs oxygen in order to function properly. Brain cells are particularly sensitive to oxygen, as they start to die within four minutes when they are deprived of it. Slight changes in oxygen content in the brain can alter the way a person feels and behaves. When a person gets angry, his or her breathing pattern changes almost immediately. Breathing becomes more shallow and the rate increases significantly (see diagram below). This breathing pattern is inefficient and the oxygen content in the angry person's blood is lowered. Subsequently there is less oxygen available to a person's brain and he or she may become more irritable, impulsive, and confused, causing him or her to make bad decisions, such as to yell, threaten, or hit another person.

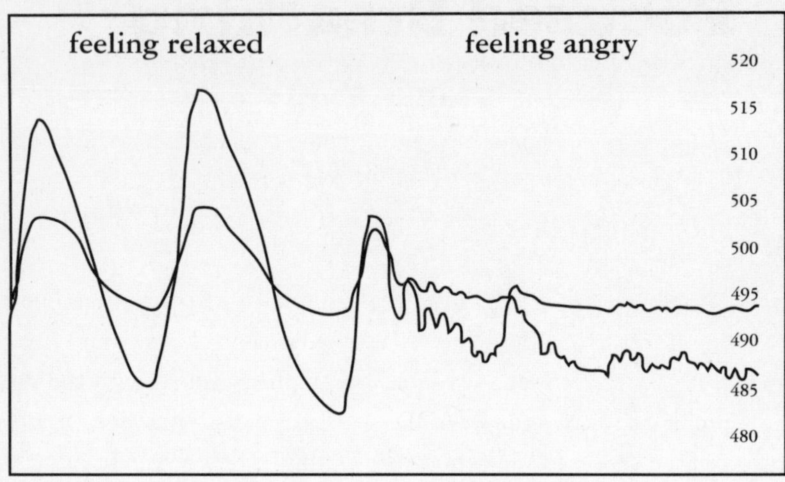

Breathing diagram: The large waveform is a measurement by a gauge attached around the belly during abdominal or belly breathing; the smaller waveform is a measurement by a gauge attached around the upper chest during chest breathing. At rest, this person breathes mostly with his belly (a good pattern), but when he thinks about an angry situation, his breathing pattern deteriorates, markedly decreasing the oxygen to his brain (common to anger outbursts). No wonder people who have anger outbursts often seem irrational!

To correct this negative breathing pattern, I teach my patients to become experts at breathing slowly and deeply, mostly with their bellies. In my office I have some very sophisticated biofeedback equipment that uses strain gauges to measure breathing activity. I place one gauge around a person's chest and a second one around his or her belly. The biofeedback equipment then measures the movement of the chest and belly as the person breathes in and out. Many people, especially men, breathe exclusively with their chests, which is an inefficient way to breathe. If you watch a baby or a puppy breathe, you notice that they breathe almost solely with their bellies. That is much more efficient. If you expand your belly when you breathe in, it allows room for your lungs to inflate downward, increasing the amount of air available to your body. I teach patients to breathe with their bellies by watching their pattern on the computer screen. In twenty to thirty minutes, most people can learn how to change their breathing patterns, which relaxes them and gives them better control over how they feel and behave.

To do this at home, lie on your back and place a small book on your belly. When you breathe in, make the book go up, and when you breathe out, make the book go down. Shifting the energy of breathing lower in your body will help you feel more relaxed and in better control of yourself.

You can use this breathing technique to help you be more focused and less anxious and to have better control over your temper. It is easy to learn and it can also be applied to help with the sleep problems so common in ADD.

Here's an example of how helpful this technique can be. Twenty-two-year-old Bart came to see me for ADD symptoms and problems with anxiety and temper. During my first session with him, I noticed that he talked fast and breathed in a shallow, quick manner. One of my recommendations was for Bart to do three sessions of breathing biofeedback. He was amazed at how easy this form of breathing was and how relaxed he could make himself in a short period of time. He noted that his level of anxiety improved and that he had better control of his temper.

Ever since I learned this technique fifteen years ago, I have used it personally. I use it when I feel anxious, angry, or stressed. It sounds so simple, but breathing is essential to life, and when we slow down and become more efficient at it, most things seem better.

CHAPTER 26

ADD Coaching

with Master ADD Coach Jane Massengill

A new, powerful treatment for many people with ADD is something called "coaching." ADD coaching is a specific set of interventions that help people set and reach their goals in life. It helps develop structure and skills that can reduce problems with focus and procrastination. In this chapter I have asked my good friend, colleague, and ADD coach Jane Massengill to help me write a synopsis of ADD coaching. Jane is a licensed clinical social worker and a certified professional coactive coach. Together we will address how a coaching relationship works. We will delineate the responsibilities of both the coach and the client, as well as how someone with ADD can expect to benefit by having an ADD coach.

Although there is a tremendous amount of variety in how people do ADD coaching, at our clinic the general format looks like this. An initial meeting is scheduled for two to three hours, in person if possible. It can be done over the phone if distance is a factor. Clients are given a workbook with numerous tools. This is the beginning: a place to record how they want to create change in their life. Some of the key topics in the workbook include the following: Action List, Balance Wheel, Habits, Commitments, Time Management, Organization, Goals, Vision, Values, Skills, and Money Management.

During the initial meeting, clients identify several areas that they want to keep as the focus of the work with the coach. They overview where they are in life and begin to identify goals and habits that will move them toward where they want to be. This is also a place where the coaching relationship will be designed. Clients identify how they are best motivated and how they have been most successful in the past.

Here's what we ask:

1. **Be honest.** Honesty is the best policy in coaching—in fact, the only policy! You must be honest with your coach about whether you completed an assignment or tried something you were challenged to. If you don't, you are sabotaging your chances for making the relationship work. In coaching, everything is celebrated, including successes and failures! If you aren't willing to fail, you aren't willing to succeed! Your coach creates a very safe environment where you can be honest about even your most difficult areas.

2. **Give your coach permission to be honest with you.** Sometimes it's hard to hear things about ourselves that other people notice. And yet, that's part of the power of coaching. Your coach must have your full permission to tell you when he or she notices you are moving away from rather than toward your goals. This is done without judgment and solely for the sake of your learning.

3. **Be willing to work at change.** You have to have a desire to change yourself when you enter a relationship with a coach. You are the one who will be taking action and creating new habits. Therefore, it has to be something that's important for you, not your spouse, your parent, or your employer.

The coaching sessions after the initial meeting generally take place over the phone for thirty minutes a week. Some clients prefer meeting in the office for an hour once a week, or twice a week for fifteen or thirty minutes. Some coaches include a daily check-in period via phone, e-mail or fax to help with accountability.

To illustrate just how powerful coaching can be, we'll take you through someone's real-life coaching experience. . . .

Thomas wanted to work with an ADD coach for help with being more disciplined. He had been diagnosed with ADD three years before and was not feeling he was doing all that he could to control his symptoms. He owned his own business and was financially successful, but he felt he was poor at keeping commitments and being organized, both personally and professionally. He was very critical of himself, despite his professional achievements. Thomas attributed his financial success to good fortune rather than to any intentional effort. He was not convinced that he could recreate this same success anywhere else in his life.

BALANCE

The first thing we looked at was the overall "balance" in Thomas's life. Balance is the way we choose to divide ourselves among the different areas of our life: home, family, work, etc. Although we think of "being in balance" as an equal division among these areas, the truth is that balance is never completely equal. It is always in motion. Stand on one foot and try to balance yourself and you will see that even though you are balanced, you are never completely still. Although clients come to coaching for specific issues, a coach helps them develop the skills to look at their whole lives and be able to see how they divide their time. We call this "seeing The Big Picture." The coach's role is always to be watching for whether her client is moving toward or away from balance in their life.

Using a pie-shaped diagram with each "slice" representing a different area of life, the client scores him- or herself on the current level of satisfaction he or she is experiencing. The scale is from 1 to 10, with 10 being the greatest degree of satisfaction and 1 being the lowest. Thomas's life looked like this:

career: 5
money management: 3

physical health: 3
family and friends: 5
significant other/romance: 5
personal growth: 6
fun and recreation: 6
physical environment: 5

By having a visual tool to help Thomas see The Big Picture, he was able to recognize which areas of his life needed the most attention. He also could see which area, if brought to a 10 first, would have the most impact on the other areas. Physical health was the area that Thomas saw as having the greatest effect on the other areas of his life. When he gets regular exercise, he feels clearer and more connected to the rest of the world. Ultimately he will have better relationships with friends and family and more energy to pursue his other goals.

PRIMARY FOCUS

During the initial session, clients are asked to list those things that they want to have as their focus while they are in this coaching relationship. This gives both the coach and the client some clarity about what is expected.

Thomas chose several areas to have as his primary focus of coaching:

1. to create and follow a regular schedule for routines, both personally and professionally
2. to be more in control of rigid thought patterns
3. to better follow through on commitments
4. to create and follow a consistent exercise program.

The coach's role is to hold the focus for the clients in creating a way to get what the clients want. Often clients with ADD will forget why they came to coaching in the first place or why they even wanted to make changes in their lives. Coaches help to keep clients pointed toward their goals and remind them, especially when the going gets tough, of what they are trying to create for themselves. When a client brings up issues that seem unrelated to his or her primary focus, the coach helps by asking questions that explore how the current issue may or may not relate to what the client wants.

VALUES

Our values are a thumbprint of who we are. They are those things in life that we hold sacred. Love, family, humor, joy, honesty and spirituality are examples of values. When we allow values to be honored in our lives, our true selves show up: not who we would like to be, but our unique selves, the selves that appear when we are being authentic in expressing and relating to ourselves and others. Our values are like an arrow, pointing us in the direction of being true to ourselves. They can be turned to when making decisions, when trying to understand interpersonal relationships, and when problems with procrastination occur.

Discovering one's values is a starting point in coaching that gives the client a sense of direction and ownership. During our first meeting, we helped Thomas identify his nine most important values. We did this by exploring peak moments in his life and looking for times when he felt completely fulfilled and totally alive. We also looked at his biggest arguments and what values were getting squished. The list took shape like this:

1. family
2. freedom
3. integrity/honesty
4. joy
5. spirituality
6. emotional and physical health
7. humor
8. sensuality
9. service/contribution

Once we identified the values that were important to him, we looked at how much he was honoring these values by the actions in his life. Thomas was pleased to see that the majority of his key values were indeed being given attention. What he needed to focus on more was finding more ways to honor his values of family, spirituality, physical health, and integrity. These were used as a springboard for action in the coaching relationship. By the end of the first session, Thomas agreed to take on a daily habit of spending fifteen minutes every evening planning for the next day. He also committed himself to find a place to keep his wallet, which he frequently lost at home. For the longer term, he agreed to begin the process of developing a social schedule with several of his friends. He asked to be held accountable to all these things, to be reviewed on the first call.

GREMLINS

For the first several weeks Thomas was on a roll, accomplishing most things to which he set out to be held accountable. Then the real change began. Thomas was beginning to hit roadblocks for the bigger areas that he wanted to work on, such as organizing his desk, sticking to a routine, and exercising. He was stuck in a cycle of belief that he was incapable of being able to do these things because of his past performance, his ADD, and his procrastination in making a commitment. It was time to go "gremlin hunting"! The "gremlin" is a concept used in coaching to identify the voice within us that holds us back from being who we want to be. It sabotages our growth and keeps us from taking action. Richard Carson, in his book *Taming Your Gremlin,* provides a format to help you become aware of the gremlin and how to control it. The concept of the gremlin is one of the most powerful tools someone takes away from coaching.

Thomas agreed to "polish his gremlin radar" for the week, simply noticing when it was present. He would notice where in his body his gremlin liked to live, in what situations he was most likely to show up, and what his favorite sayings of sabotage were. Best of all, he could begin to fantasize about how he would like to get rid of him! For someone who values humor, this can be fun!

The following week, Thomas was in amazement about how his gremlin was controlling him! He realized that the tightness in his neck and shoulders was part of his gremlin, telling him to work harder because nobody believed he could keep up. He also began to see that his belief system was being controlled by his gremlin. He heard messages such as *You can't be organized, You are too old to exercise consistently,* and *Why try to follow a routine? You never stick to anything anyway!*

Thomas developed an imaginary jail to send his gremlin to when he noticed he was acting up as a way of learning to control him. Once the gremlin was aside, Thomas was instructed to ask himself this question: *I've noticed my gremlin has a judgment or an opinion here. What are my choices in this situation?* This gave the control back to Thomas to make his own decisions and not let his gremlin decide for him. We tied his values into his decision-making process, choosing actions that included integrity, spirituality, and family. Thomas's self-esteem started to take off at this point!

VISION

Having an idea of what you want your future to look like is an important part of coaching. Before you can set goals and work toward them, it helps to have a mental picture of what you want to create. The most commonly asked question in coaching is "What do you want?" Lots of time is spent developing the skill of "metaview," meaning seeing things in The Big Picture. This is an area that tends to be weak for people with ADD, especially the overfocused subtype. We use metaphors like gardening to help clients get an image of what they want the "landscape" to look like, what type of flowers they want to plant, and what sort of care the garden is going to require. Clients often find that they are spending too much time nurturing a flower they don't even like or studying one part of the garden while not seeing that another section is dying.

For Thomas, this vision started with an assignment to write out his idea of a perfect day, from start to finish. He had full permission to be as creative as he wanted, as long as he completed the task. He faxed it before the next session. We compared his vision of a perfect day to his list of values and to his balance wheel. When exercise was missing, we looked for what there might be to learn from that. For Thomas, there was a gremlin lurking with his message about not being able to get his body in shape at this age. Once he realized that, Thomas was able to look at his choices and make a commitment to include exercise in his perfect day because of the benefits he knew it would give him both physically and mentally.

Thomas also created a two-year vision for the areas of his life that matched his balance wheel. He became very specific about what he wanted his life to look like, including how much he wanted to weigh, what he wanted his office to look like, how often he will take trips with friends and family, and what he wanted his net worth to be. From this we created a list of goals and prioritized which one would have the biggest impact on his life once completed. We also worked on raising his awareness about The Big Picture of his life. We did this by imagining jumping into a helicopter together and spying on his life to see what we could see from a distance. Thomas's coach gave him the question "What am I choosing right now?" to ponder for the week and see what he could learn from it.

GOALS

Reaching a goal that you never imagined you could reach is one of the best feelings in the world! Ask anyone who had been told they will never walk again and what they felt like when they took their first step. Wow! Most people come to coaching with fear that they will not be able to be organized or to be successful in a job due to their ADD. They believe that because of their programming, change is impossible. One of the most significant moments for most people in ADD coaching is when they are asked the following question: "Okay, you have ADD. How do you want to *be* with it? How do you want to show up in life, given that you have this? You have some choices here. What do you want?" Once a client sees that they do indeed have some choices about their attitude and the language they use in dealing with their ADD, goals begin to flow naturally.

Breaking things down into baby steps is very helpful in reaching goals. People with ADD tend to have trouble looking at the big picture and seeing a path to the goals. There is a feeling of being overwhelmed, sensory overload, and then defeat. In coaching, we teach people how to approach goal setting and then keep them accountable about doing what they say they are going to do. Clients learn to take on a 360-degree view of what it will take to accomplish their goals. They look at the following questions:

What will I have when the goal is accomplished?
What am I saying yes to by working toward my goal?
What do I need to say no to by working toward my goal?
What resources do I need to obtain or develop?
What habits do I need to have in place?
In the past, what has gotten in the way of obtaining my goal?
What are three things I can do differently from what I have tried in the past?
What is the action I will take on a daily basis that will move me closer to my goal?
By what date do I wish to accomplish my goal?

For Thomas, we mapped out all the steps that needed to be done to accomplish one particular goal. At the end of his road map, he would have a clean desk at home and at work. He began by looking at what got in his way in the past. Distractions seemed to be the number one problem in both places. He broke the steps of this goal down like this:

1. Review material on organizing for executives.
2. Decide which organizational system I want to choose.
3. Purchase baskets and files needed for desk organizing system.

4. Spend ten minutes a day at my desk to organize materials, standing up! (Keep my attention focused! I will use a timer as an auditory reminder of when my time is finished.)
5. Ask my daughter if she wants to spend one hour a week to file materials. I will pay her for this.

Simply having a system in place seemed to reduce procrastination. Thomas also liked the idea of standing as it was something physical he could do to be more in charge of his distractions.

LIFE PURPOSE

A life purpose statement, often referred to as a mission statement, is a way to describe one's intention in life. It is a statement about how you will make a difference on the planet, both in your life and in the lives of others. When clients are living their lives with the knowledge of their life purposes, they are living intentionally, not by accident. They are focused on paths with direction.

In coaching, we ask clients this key question: "What needs to change on the inside to create change on the outside?" It isn't just about setting up good systems or structures. Lasting change comes from the understanding of what our life purposes are, who we are, and how we uniquely impact the people around us. Knowing one's purpose is like the battery that drives the motor. Over and over, it drives clients in coaching to look at whether the choices they are making are consistent with The Big Picture of their lives.

Defining Thomas's life purpose was quite meaningful for him. We spent several weeks working on the idea of who he is and how he impacts the world. He was very clear on this in his role as a father and husband, but not so with the rest of his life. Once he took the time to explore it, he began to acknowledge himself for his gifts and talents, while at the same time following the vision of the life he was creating for himself. He began to realize that he wasn't just lucky in how his life was turning out. It was because of who he is in the world, his attitude, his drive, his caring about others. We tapped into the things in life that give him passion, such as community outreach, spending quality time with his kids, and stopping to say hello to a stranger. He started to see how he could make choices that would give him more of a sense of fulfillment and balance in his life.

SKILLS

Skill building is an art. The two most important parts of developing a skill are practice and commitment. During this awkward stage of development, there is usually a period of ups and downs, being excited, testing the waters, retreating because of failure, moving forward with fear, and finally making a commitment to succeed. Most people find relief in knowing that a coaching relationship is a safe place to practice these skills without worry of being judged or measured. This gives them permission to practice the skills in ways that are unfamiliar to them. For people with ADD, this is refreshing, exciting, and stimulating.

Here are several skills used in ADD coaching:

Awareness

One of the biggest aspects of building any skill is the awareness of when and where to use the skill. Awareness is a common issue for most people with ADD. "Feeling fuzzy" is the way one client describes what gets in the way of making decisions and following routines. Another client calls it his "deer in the headlights" feeling. For him, this is when he is immobile, even with the knowledge of impending disaster. A third person refers to it as "the twirls." "I go from room to room, not even sure why I went there in the first place." In ADD coaching, building one's awareness is imperative to success. The client develops an internal awareness monitor through the coach's use of questions. Questions like "How do I know when I am fully present?" "What am I choosing right now?" and "Where is my awareness?" are ways for clients to be reminded of when they are on or off track. We set up systems to help them ask these questions, such as visual or auditory reminders on watches, clocks, computers, etc.

Thomas chose several ways to develop his awareness. First of all, he implemented a system of using timers to keep him on track. He put a timer on his desk at work, on his watch, and in his home office. He used the timer to get him started on a job he didn't feel very motivated to do, like clean his briefcase or pay the bills. Once the timer ran for fifteen minutes, he had the choice to continue or quit. Usually he chose to continue. Getting started was the hardest part for him. Secondly, he used the timers to stay on task and not get too far distracted. For example, when he wanted to surf the Internet at night, he would set the timer for one hour to set boundaries for himself to go to bed. He also developed a system of stickers as a reminder to be mentally present and look at his choices of the moment. He placed the stickers in places where he found himself most often distracted, such as on the phone, in his car, on his computer screen, and on his daytimer. Thomas had to change the stickers about once a month, otherwise he got used to them and would not see them. He found them helpful in bringing him back to reality when he was daydreaming and reminding him to focus on what was important just then.

Habits

The definition of a habit, according to the *Random House Dictionary* is this: "an acquired behavior pattern regularly followed until it has become almost involuntary." We have come to believe that our habits are a part of our personality and therefore impossible, or at least gruelingly difficult, to change. And yet, most people come to coaching with a genuine desire to change and get rid of the struggles they experience. A coach—being with you in the journey, and there to pick you up when you fall and cheer you at the finish line—believes that you can change your habits. Although there is an acknowledgment that the symptoms of ADD are difficult, a coach understands that with practice and commitment, change is possible. Coaching is most powerful when the client is committed to the belief that habits can be changed, and that means getting the gremlin out of the way. There are several techniques we use to strengthen this commitment. One is "stepping over the line." The client literally steps over a threshold to symbolize that leaving behind what he or she does not want and "stepping into" a new place where the client will take action to get what he or she does want. We also use a technique called a "yes/no" board. This is a poster with YES on the left and NO on the right. Clients write out the things in their lives that they are saying yes to as well as the things to which they are saying no in order to achieve their goals. For example, saying yes to taking a continuing education class may mean saying no to a regular night out with friends. This tool helps in visualizing what they must give up in order to gain something else. We find that these types of tools aide in memory as well as offer an opportunity to acknowledge consistency or to look at what got in the way of success.

Thomas had daily and weekly habits that he recorded. For most people, habits change throughout the course of coaching. After they achieve the first few, others are added. At the beginning of coaching, Thomas's list included these items:

1. Take fifteen minutes before bed to plan for the next day.
2. Spend ten minutes in some type of spiritual reflection daily.
3. Exercise three times a week.
4. Do something nice for my wife weekly.

As Thomas developed these items to his satisfaction, he would add new things to be tracked. After a year in coaching, his list looked like this:

1. On Sunday night, spend fifteen minutes planning for the week.
2. Exercise daily.
3. Listen to thirty minutes of spiritual music or tapes while commuting, three times a week.
4. Spend one hour of quality time with wife and/or kids daily.

By developing the skills he wished to incorporate into his life, Thomas was able to rearrange his thinking about how he could run his business. Eventually he made choices that allowed him more time for the things in his life that were the most important to him.

The biggest change in coaching for Thomas was when he honestly believed that he could change his habits. Despite having ADD, he did have some control in his life over his ability to be organized and focused. This was truly a time to be celebrated! It was from this point forward that his energy and momentum took off!

Perspective and Choice

When ADD clients seek out a coach, they are desperate to be relieved of their pain. They feel out of balance and stuck, unsure which way to turn and unsure of their abilities to be able to succeed. One thing that makes coaching so powerful is the questions asked by the coach to help clients look at their lives from different perspectives or angles. We often choose the perspective we have for a good reason. We get stuck in believing that there is only one way, based on the experiences we've had or the knowledge we currently hold. For example, one client saw no hope for herself in passing a medical board exam. She had failed on several occasions. From her perspective, that meant she was incapable of ever passing it. After several sessions of exploring her current perspective, the client realized that by not passing the exam, she was validating her feelings about herself as a loser. She recognized that past attempts at test taking did not include all that she could do to pass, such as having a study partner and creating a review schedule. Once she saw that her gremlin was the one who actually held her in this perspective, she was able to move forward with zest in her belief that she was indeed a winner and fully capable of taking and passing this exam! Even if she never passed, she gained a perspective about herself that was liberating and gave her a choice to be whoever she wanted to be. The transformation was breathtaking!

In coaching, we are always looking for other perspectives that the clients can choose. "Choice" is an important word here. What makes coaching work is the clients' ability to choose what will work for them. Being able to choose gives you a sense of power and fulfillment like nothing else! It takes you out of a role of being a victim and places you in the role of being an "owner," as described by Steve Chandler in his book *Reinventing Yourself:* "Owners create and victims react. Taking ownership is the highest form of focus." When you are intentional in your choices, you are living a life that has clarity and fullness. You are living on purpose, not by accident.

Throughout his period of being coached, Thomas had many opportunities to look at what perspective he was holding and see what other ones he could choose. This is one habit that develops for most clients in coaching. An inner voice pipes in to encourage them to see things from different perspectives—just for the fun of it, if nothing else. A coach might ask how Elmer Fudd would look at this situation or what a blind man might say about it. From this comes a lightness about choice instead of the well-known heaviness that is often experienced. There is also an acknowledgment about the fear that gets in the way of making choices. For Thomas, when this fear got in the way, he was challenged to wear a sticker that said, "I can handle it." In this way, he was creating a mantra for himself that gave him freedom to take risks and make mistakes, all with the greater goal in mind of getting what he wants for himself in life.

THE PROCESS OF THE PATH

As for most people in coaching, there are roadblocks that get hit while they are in the process of change. Many don't even see these blocks because they have become so ingrained in who they are. Our gremlins want us to believe that these blocks are absolutely impossible to move. In coaching, we get right in the face of the roadblocks and try to look at them from as many different perspectives as we can to see what we can learn about them. We even try to experience the feelings that arise when we imagine the worst thing that could happen. Some of the most common roadblocks include fear of failure, fear of success and responsibility, loneliness, rejection, sadness, emptiness, and commitment. We look at the associations clients have with these ideas and how they hold certain beliefs as the absolute truth about them. By actually experiencing these emotions in coaching sessions, clients begin to see the absurdity of their beliefs and how maintaining the beliefs only hold them back in life. In this way they face their fears. The power the roadblocks had over them is dissipated.

Coaching invites people to be challenged in a way that holds them in a soft, friendly light. The coach creates an environment where exploration is safe and where curiosity wins out over judgment. No one loses. Risk taking is celebrated, no matter what the outcome is. It demonstrates that the client is taking action and moving in the direction of their path. This is a tremendous relief for people with ADD who have had what feels like a long list of failures. By breaking through a roadblock that they thought was impossible to move, they develop a greater sense of confidence in their abilities. This in turn gives them momentum to move forward with their goals. Because of the drive for stimulation, once they find a goal that has meaning, they are difficult to stop!

One area in which Thomas got stuck was in his belief that he could not be organized due to his biology of having ADD. Whenever he sat down at his desk, he was overwhelmed by the quantity of papers and the tasks that lay ahead. He would turn off and do something that would distract him from his desk. Often this was getting on the Internet or calling business associates to discuss ideas. But this wasn't getting him what he wanted: a clean desk! So we explored what feelings come up for Thomas when he sits down at his desk and wants to dive into his work but instead flounders. All he saw was a big black hole. We "got curious" about this hole, visualized jumping in, and enveloped ourselves in what it was like. After several minutes "in the hole," Thomas realized that he had a negative association with perfectionism. In his mind, perfectionism was equal to exposure. If he tried to be organized and orderly, people would discover that he was not as smart as he appeared. They would see that he wasn't a great speller and didn't graduate from the best college. This would negate him in their eyes, and consequently he would lose his business and end up poor and rejected. With the coach's acknowledgment of Thomas's strengths, accomplishments, and values, Thomas was able to see the absurdity of his association with perfectionism and how it impacted his energy to be organized. He became more committed to himself at this point and started to tackle his daily habits with enthusiasm and a belief that he could succeed!

ENDINGS

The length of coaching varies. Clients are asked to make a three-month commitment to the process, primarily to acknowledge that long-term change takes time. For most clients, six months seems to be a minimum. At this writing Thomas has been in coaching for one year and has recently lengthened the time between sessions to once a month to test his abilities to maintain his new habits. Many clients choose to stay in a coaching relationship over time, perhaps talking once or twice a year. Because coaching is primarily done over the phone, distance is not an issue. When someone moves, the relationship does not have to be terminated. It's calming to know that there is always a place to go where you will be accepted for whoever you are, where your failures will be celebrated just as much as your achievements, and where you can be reminded of the big picture of your life. Here are some of the comments clients have made about ADD coaching:

"I feel like I lost weight in a whole different way!"
"I am living a life of intention."
"This is more powerful than any therapy I've ever done."
"When someone else believes in you, you start to believe in yourself."

"I feel so much more focused and aware of the choices I make."
"The myths I had about myself being disorganized have disappeared!"
"You aren't just an ADD coach, you are a life coach."

Coaching is about action and learning. Both pieces must be present if coaching is to take place. The best learning occurs when the coach gets out of the way and asks questions that will generate the client's own deductions and intuitions. The client learns not to look to the coach for the answers but rather looks inside him- or herself. Clients will often say to their coach, "I know what to do. I just don't do it!" This is the basis on which coactive ADD coaching is built. When clients come up with their own answers, they develop a genuine awareness of themselves and their abilities that allows them to acknowledge who they are and the gifts they have. Yes, there is still some frustration with piles and lists, even when the coaching relationship winds down. But what is in its place is an ability to be focused on the things in life that are truly important. The piles may take on less meaning or may be completely under control, depending on what the clients value. The important part is that the clients leave the coaching relationship realizing that they have a choice about the piles and how they want to see them. They may have begun to dream of even bigger "piles" to tackle, such as starting businesses or going after careers they were always afraid to pursue. This is the exhilarating part of coaching: watching people go headfirst in life, with confidence, enthusiasm, passion, and intention.

RECOMMENDED READING

Daniel G. Amen, *Coaching Yourself to Success,* Mindworks Press, 1995.

Richard D. Carson, *Taming Your Gremlin: A Guide to Enjoying Yourself,* Harper Perennial Publishers, 1990.

Steve Chandler, *Reinventing Yourself,* Career Press, 1998.

Steven Covey, *First Things First,* Simon & Schuster, 1994.

Susan Jeffers, Ph.D., *Feel the Fear and Do It Anyway,* Fawcett Columbine Publishers, 1987.

Laura Whitworth, Henry Kimsey-House, and Phil Sandahl, *Co-Active Coaching: New Skills for Coaching People Toward Success in Work and Life,* Davies-Black Publishing, 1998.

CHAPTER 27

Self-Hypnotic Reprogramming for Success

with Emmett Miller, M.D., author of *Deep Healing: The Essence of Mind/Body Medicine*

Dr. Miller is a world renowned expert in the field of hypnosis, cognitive reprogramming, and achievement. He has a private practice in Nevada City, and he is also on staff at the Amen Clinic.

PROGRAMMING AND THE HUMAN BRAIN

To some people the idea of "programming" or "reprogramming" sometimes sounds somehow cold and calculating. Science fiction books and movies often portray evil mind-control tyrants as using "programming" to turn susceptible people into robotlike subjects. The truth is that the human brain acquires information and makes decisions based upon the instructions it has been given, just like a computer. Many of the instructions for how to interpret the world and how to react to it were trained into us when we were children, and we had no say over what programs were being implanted. These programs persist as our beliefs. Often, especially for people with ADD, these beliefs, especially about themselves, can be very harmful.

What we see and feel as we confront the challenges of everyday life is dramatically affected by what we believe. A little trick one of our college roommates used to do was to wet his hands, then, while walking behind another student, let out a huge sneeze, flicking the water over the back of the neck and head of his unsuspecting mark. The reaction of the student to what he felt was often dramatic and hilarious. The reaction would have been much different had he realized that someone was just flicking some clean, cold water on the back of his head and neck.

The programming each of us has received has served to convince us that certain of our beliefs about the world are "true," even though they may become completely arbitrary. For example, if a talented, attractive student tries out for the school play, but he believes that he is not very attractive or talented, he has little chance of getting the part. Many of our convictions about ourselves—whether we feel like a success or failure, whether we feel lucky or unlucky, whether the glass is half empty or half full—are just beliefs and can all be changed. If they are not changed, they become self-fulfilling prophecies. Many people with ADD have been programmed into believing they can't change the things that are holding them back from being successful in their lives. This negative belief system is one of the first things that must change. A person with ADD often finds himself experiencing failure: failure to perform to his highest potential, failure to be able to sit still, failure to concentrate well, failure to organize well, failure to avoid distraction and addictive tendencies. This can lead to intense feelings of shame, guilt, fear, anxiety, and anger. Your attitudes about yourself or the things that people said to you in the past created an internal set of beliefs that hold you back. If you can recognize that these thoughts are just beliefs that belong to you, you can change them and convert them into positive beliefs that support you.

Common negative beliefs developed by people with ADD are:

"People are mad at me."
"I am an annoying person."
"I mess things up."
"For some reason, no one can ever understand me."
"I'm not worth very much."
"The world is very overwhelming to me."

"No matter how hard I try, I just can't get organized [be on time, focus for a long period of time, avoid distractions, etc.]."

The process you learn in this chapter will enable you to recognize both that you have these beliefs and that you can change them. You will learn how, through self-hypnosis, you can replace the faulty beliefs with positive, helpful ones.

CHANGING YOUR BELIEFS WITH SELF-HYPNOSIS

The good news is that your brain and your mind belong to you. You have the right and the power to look at the beliefs, feelings, and behaviors that run your life, and to decide which you want to keep and which you want to change. One of the most powerful tools for doing this is the tool known as *self-hypnosis.* The techniques of self-hypnosis are widely used by psychologists and psychiatrists in clinical settings, and by peak performers such as athletes, musicians, actors, and public speakers, whose success depends upon their using their minds at peak efficiency. Self-hypnosis is simply a tool—a powerful tool—that can be used to dramatically change your beliefs and your life.

The fundamental steps of self-hypnosis are:

1. entering a state of deep relaxation
2. positive affirmations
3. visualizing success, and
4. leaving the state of deep relaxation and returning to a more usual, wakeful state of consciousness.

STEP ONE: ENTERING THE DEEPLY RELAXED (SELF-HYPNOTIC) STATE

To enter the state of deep relaxation, you will first learn how to use autosuggestion to separate yourself from all the fears, tensions, stresses, and confusions of the outside world for a few minutes. This is done by letting go of mental and physical tension, by focusing on the present moment, and by allowing yourself to experience inner silence, stillness, and mental and physical relaxation. The technique we will use is counting to twenty, allowing the eyes to close, sending waves of relaxation throughout your body, then going to your own special place, your "haven." The first few times you do this, you may not find yourself relaxing as deeply as the words seem to suggest. This is merely because you need practice. The world has trained most of us to be tense. After you have done this a number of times, you will find it easier to enter a deep state of relaxation quickly.

STEP TWO: POSITIVE AFFIRMATIONS

The second step is to hear positive self-talk. Most of us talk to ourselves each day, but much of what we say is negative, e.g., "I'm such a dolt," "I'll never be successful," and "Everybody else is doing better than I am." The statements you will read to yourself on the tape will replace these negative statements with positive ones. These will then begin to create positive beliefs about yourself to replace the negative, harmful ones. Our goal is to create confidence where there was shyness; focus where there was disorganization; self-confidence where there was self-doubt; self-awareness where there was denial; self-acceptance where there was self-criticism; self-control and empowerment where there was helplessness.

STEP THREE: VISUALIZING SUCCESS

One of the most powerful learning tools is the human imagination. When children are playing house or building a fort in the backyard, they are actually learning very important skills. They are willfully suspending their disbelief and allowing themselves to pretend, to temporarily believe that they are actually parents or soldiers. Wise teachers know how to use imagination and pretend to teach valuable lessons. We will use imagination in a very similar way. If we asked you to close your eyes and imagine sitting in your living room, you would be able to point to the window and to the front door, and to reach over and pretend to flip on the light. In order to do this, you would be holding in your mind an image, a kind of mental model, then referring to it to give your responses to the questions. This is an example of mental imagery, or visualization. Even though we may use the word "visualization," do not think it is absolutely necessary to "see" a clear "picture" in your mind. Fifty percent of adults, and most children, can "see" mental images in this way. It is helpful but not necessary for our purposes here. In the same way that you can make this mental model of your living room, you can make a mental model of your workplace (where your desk is, where your boss's office is, where the phone is, etc.), or your child can make a mental model of his/her classroom. Your goals will be to:

1. mentally picture a challenging situation that may occur in the future—one in which you might have used inappropriate behavior (anger, distraction, fear, avoidance, etc.) in the past, and
2. visualize the kind of behavior you would use if you truly believed the positive affirmations you have just given yourself.

As you go through this scene, you will imagine yourself actually being there and carrying out the most successful behavior you can imagine. This will serve to be a kind of "post-hypnotic suggestion" to your deeper mind.

STEP 4: DEHYPNOTIZING YOURSELF

No matter how deeply you relax, you will always have the ability to wake yourself up if there is an emergency or some other situation you need to respond to. You are not "under a spell," and can wake up even faster than if you had been sleeping! The deeply relaxed state is a very sensitive one. Your vulnerable inner mind is exposed, much as it was when you were a young child. Most of the time you keep this part of you protected by your "ego," allowing it to be openly available only when you know you are in a safe, secure situation. In the deeply relaxed state, you have dropped your guard, so to speak, and when you return to your normal waking state, it is best to do it gradually. In this way you will be able to reestablish the ego protections you need to be able to function smoothly as you go about your next activities. If you rouse yourself too quickly, you may feel a bit groggy, half asleep, or even a little anxious. If this should happen, simply sit or lie down and relax briefly, then bring yourself back into full activity more slowly.

A MOST REMARKABLE TOOL

Technically, once you have learned how, you can enter the hypnotic state just by speaking silently to yourself with your eyes closed. In the beginning, however, it is too difficult to remember all the steps in the right order while still remaining relaxed. The act of trying to remember creates tension, which directly contradicts what you are trying to do. So what you need is a way to be guided through this experience. One way is to have someone read the instructions to you. If you are working with your child, you may choose to read these instructions out loud some of the time, and if you are the subject, it is a virtual necessity. What you need is a way to have the words spoken to you easily whenever you want. The most remarkable tool for accomplishing this lies right at your fingertips: the tape recorder! By following through with the very simple steps in this chapter, you will create a most powerful and effective tool for gaining control of your physiology, your mind, your behaviors, your brain, and your life.

PREPARING YOUR SCRIPT

Get a pad and pencil and settle back in your easy chair. Open a page and entitle it "Wise Messages to Myself." As you read the rest of this chapter, make notes on the things that come to you as you read each of the steps below. Then, using this chapter together with your notes, you will create a custom-designed self-programming audiocassette.

Create a statement of purpose, a single sentence that describes why you will be listening to this tape. For example: "The purpose of this deep relaxation and imagery experience is to help my conscious and subconscious mind function better, to improve my organization, to improve focus, to stabilize my emotions, and to create patience. Its goal is to self-program at every level the wisest thoughts, feelings, and behaviors that will lead to ever higher degrees of success."

Read the section below entitled "Script" and familiarize yourself with the instructions. When you reach the section entitled "Positive Affirmations," if there are any that you do not want to become true for you, draw a line through them and don't read them into the tape. Likewise, if there are certain affirmations that are especially appropriate for you (or your child), you may add them. Feel free to consult with your therapist, teacher or other *trusted* advisor about which statements they think it would be most valuable to include. But only include those that you feel very certain that you would like to believe. Do not use suggestions that hurt other people. Stay positive.

Make any changes to the script that you are sure will make it more effective for you. Most people will find the wording we have given here perfect just as it is, but don't feel constrained if you have strong feelings in any way. (Sometimes folks with strong religious or spiritual convictions will want to put in certain statements of gratitude to a higher power. This tape is you talking very intimately and personally to yourself or to your child.)

When you reach the imagery about "Your Special Haven," make notes or write out in detail (whichever you like) a description of a place you associate with relaxation. This may be a place you have been on vacation, a place you would like to visit someday, or even a completely imaginary place. If you find the imagery of the beach satisfactory, you may use the words written there.

Many people find the tape to be more enjoyable and effective if music plays in the background. If you want music, set up a separate tape deck or CD player nearby, so you can control the volume from your chair. Locate a long piece of relatively slow music that you find relaxing. (Many people find that a tempo of about sixty beats per minute, the speed of the resting heart, is about right.) During the relaxation phase, play very slow music such as Bach's "Air for the G String," Pachelbel's "Canon," or slow "New Age" music. The only requirement is that the music be slow, gentle, relaxing, and appealing to you. You may play this throughout the *entire* tape, or, if you wish, you may substitute a more upbeat piece near the end, as you are visualizing success in the future, as you are awakening. Most of the time it is best to use only instrumental music, so the words of the songs won't compete in any way with the positive words you are reading to yourself.

Place a tape recorder next to a comfortable chair. *Use a tape recorder that will clearly record your voice. Use your voice on the tape.* It is better to use a separate microphone rather than to use the one physically built into your recorder. Place the microphone in a holder about one to two feet in front of your mouth.

INSTRUCTIONS FOR READING THE SCRIPT YOU PREPARE

It is probably best to think of your first attempt to record as a practice session. This way you can listen to what you have done, closing your eyes and following the instructions to see if the speed, the volume of the music, and other aspects of your recording are just right. Play it back and make a note of changes you want to make in it.

Speak the words clearly, directly toward the microphone. Speak *slowly* and clearly, enunciating each word carefully but not so stiffly as to sound rigid. Try for a gentle, flowing sound, one that is soothing yet filled with confidence and enthusiasm. During step one, deep relaxation, your tone should be similar to one you would use to lull a child to sleep. Then, for the affirmations and imagery, you may want to shift your tone slightly to one that is a little more upbeat, the kind a coach or support person might use.

Most of the time it is a very good idea to personalize the tape by speaking the name of the person for whom you are making the tape several times throughout the tape. So you might begin with "Let yourself sit comfortably back in your chair, Johnny, and listen carefully. . . ." or "Now, Mary, picture yourself walking into your class feeling confident, and as you see your teacher, Mr. Wilson, you feel even better. . . ." Later you might say, "Each time you listen to this tape, Tommy, you will feel more and more confident in yourself."

If you are making this tape for a child, it is almost always a good idea to include the child's name a number of times. If you are making a tape for yourself, you need to decide whether or not you will feel comfortable hearing your own voice say your name on several occasions.

Turn on your tape recorder, wait about five seconds for the leader tape to pass, then immediately start the background music you're going to play. Let about ten or fifteen seconds of music play on the tape before you begin to speak. As you begin to speak, try to get your voice to flow along with the music, even fitting into the tempo of the music if possible. The music should be played at a low volume so that it is just gently audible behind your speaking voice, which should be recorded quite a bit louder on the tape than the music. The music is there to help mask background sounds and create relaxation only, and should never be allowed to interfere with the intelligibility of the words you speak.

If you make a mistake, stop the tape recorder and the music. Rewind the tape recorder to the place where the error was made. (If you make sure to leave pauses every couple of sentences, there will always be an easy point for you to go back and edit.) Next, rewind the music approximately the same amount of time. It is not essential to start the music at the exact same passage you were in. The music will be very soft in the background, and the change will barely be noticed, if at all. Start the music, then start the tape recorder and continue reading from where you left off. If you need to pause at any point to read the instructions, you can do so: This is a lot to get through at a single reading. You may pause and, just as you would do if you made a mistake, follow this procedure.

After completing the recording, take a short break, have a glass of water, or take a little walk. When you come back, sit back and listen to what you have done, following the instructions. Have a pad and pencil in your hand so you can make notes on changes you want to make in your final recording. Do not be surprised or critical when you hear your voice sounding different over your small tape recorder. It sounds very different from what you hear inside. It's important to remember that when you listen to your speaking voice, you have a stereophonic, high-fidelity connection augmented by the bass reflex subwoofer of your chest and the echo chamber of your sinuses. It's never going to sound that good coming out of that little speaker. Everyone tends to react with disappointment when they hear the sound of their recorded voice. Just ignore any tendency toward self-criticism. When you listen to the tape, you will become so relaxed, you will forget the sound of the voice and focus on the sound of the words. *Change is going to occur within you; get used to listening to your own voice. (A parent's voice is often soothing and acceptable to a child. If you are doing this for your child, modify the instructions as appropriate.)*

You may end up making three or more versions before doing one you feel comfortable with. Don't be a perfectionist. You are making a tape for yourself, not something you are entering into a contest. Even a sloppy tape will work fine. Be reasonable.

SCRIPT: SELF-HYPNOTIC REPROGRAMMING FOR SUCCESS

Turn off the phone, put a DO NOT DISTURB sign on the door, and turn off all the noise possible, especially extraneous alarms like washers, timers, cell phones, beepers, etc. Find a comfortable chair; many people prefer a reclining or lounge chair so their head is supported; some people prefer to lie flat, perhaps with something supporting the knees and under the head. If you find that you tend to go to sleep while listening to the tape, then it is probably better to sit up—and if you still fall asleep, sit in a straight-backed chair. The actual script to read into the tape recorder is in boldface type.

STEP ONE: ENTERING THE DEEPLY RELAXED, SELF-HYPNOTIC STATE

Hello, [put in your name]. . . . **We are here to clear your mind, relax your soul, break through old barriers, and program success. Pick a spot on the wall a little above your eye level and stare at it.** [You may find it helpful to put a little thumbtack there to look at.] **As you focus on this spot, become aware of the fact that there's no other place that you need to go at this moment, nothing else that you need to do, and no problem that you need to solve right now. Therefore, you can give yourself permission to relax. Continue to look at that point, and as you do, I am going to begin to count, slowly, from one to twenty.**

As I count, say the number to yourself, silently, in your mind. You may find it helpful to picture each number as you count it.

[Leave a couple of seconds between each number.]

One . . . two . . . three . . . four . . . five . . . six . . .

Notice your eyelids beginning to feel heavier and heavier. . . .

Seven . . . eight . . . nine . . . ten . . . eleven . . . twelve . . .

Notice how that spot in the distance is fading out of focus and your eyelids are feeling still heavier and heavier. . . .

13 . . . 14 . . . 15 . . . 16 . . . 17 . . . 18 . . .

Your eyelids are feeling so heavy, they feel as though they really want to close.

19 . . . 20 . . .

Take a deep breath in . . . and as you let that breath out, let your eyelids slowly close.

[Some people may actually find that they relax more if they leave their eyes open through the entire experience. If you choose to do this, simply keep them focused on that spot and don't be concerned that your eyes stay open in spite of your voice saying they are growing heavier. After a while, you may find that your eyelids *will* prefer to close.]

In a moment, I'm going to ask you to take three deep breaths, and with each breath in, feel relaxation flowing in like pure, white light. And with each breathing out, let yourself feel the feeling of letting go. With each breath in, say, silently, to yourself, "With each breath in, I breathe in relaxation," and with each breath out, say the words "With each breath out, I let my body breathe out all tension and all the things that may interfere with my becoming totally relaxed and comfortable."

Now take a deep breath in, repeating to yourself, "With each breath in, I breathe in relaxation."

And as you let this breath out, repeat, internally to yourself, "With each breath out, I let my body breathe out all tension and all the things that may interfere with my becoming totally relaxed and comfortable."

[Take a few slow, deep breaths in and out, and get a sense of the speed with which you will need to read these words to yourself.]

Now take another deep breath in, feeling the coolness of the air as it enters through your nostrils, and repeat silently, "With each breath in, I breathe in relaxation."

And as you let this breath out, let it be a feeling of letting go, and repeat, "With each breath out, I let my body breathe out all tension and all the things that may interfere with my becoming totally relaxed and comfortable."

Now take a deep breath in, repeating to yourself, "With each breath in, I breathe in relaxation." As you let it out, imagine you are a balloon letting out all the air, becoming completely flat and relaxed, and say to yourself, "With each breath out, I let my body breathe out all tension and all the things that may interfere with my becoming totally relaxed and comfortable."

Now let the air do the breathing for you, just as it does when you're asleep at night, and feel how your chest and abdomen gently rise and fall with each breath, letting each breath continue to relax you from head to toe.

Now, as your body continues to relax, close your eyes really tight, as though you were trying to keep soap out of them. Hold them tense for just a few seconds, and feel the tension in your eyelids.

Now, slowly let the muscles of your eyelids relax . . . relax . . . more and more relaxed with each breath. [Five second pause]

Notice how much your eyelids have relaxed already. They will continue to relax. And perhaps you will notice your eyes gently rolling upward behind your eyelids, and your eyelids feeling so relaxed, they just don't want to open at all. Now, as your eyelids become more and more relaxed, imagine ripples of relaxation flowing outward from your eyelids, like ripples flowing outward from a stone thrown into the water . . . flowing into your forehead . . . through all the muscles of your face . . . relaxing your jaw muscles and your lips . . . and flowing down through your neck and into your shoulders. Feel your shoulders releasing any tension; you may even feel them lower just a tiny little bit as the muscles relax.

Now feel the relaxation flowing down through your shoulders and your arms . . . flowing through your chest and through all the rest of your body. With each rising and falling of your chest and abdomen, your chest becomes more relaxed and all your internal organs are becoming more relaxed. Feel that relaxation flowing through your pelvis, relaxing all your pelvic organs . . . and flowing down through your thighs and your knees . . . your legs and your ankles and your feet . . . all the way down to the tips of your toes. Imagine your body is

resting in a soft tub filled with soothing, warm water, that your muscles are melting . . . all the tension is being absorbed by the warmth of the water.

YOUR SPECIAL SAFE HAVEN

[Next, describe a special place . . . your special place . . . a special haven that you can go to in your imagination. Maybe a place you've been in the past or a place you've always wanted to go but only seen pictures of. There might have been a time in the past when you were on vacation. . . . It might even have been a time early in your childhood. It can be a real or an imaginary place: The idea is to create a place where you feel completely relaxed and comfortable. Describe this place clearly to yourself, and slowly, so that it will make it easy for you to visualize it.

[As you describe it, describe the sensations in all your senses—what you see; the sounds around you; the temperature of the air; the movement of your body if you're moving, or its peaceful stillness if you are not; the smell of the air; even the tastes, if there are any tastes there. Use as much detail as you can. You may take from four to eight minutes for this description. Sometimes people have a long description at first when they are learning to relax, then later make another tape with a description of only one or two minutes in length. As you listen to the tape more often, your ability to relax quickly will increase. For children, ask them ahead of time what scene they would like to go to. They often like the beach, the mountains, or a beautiful park. Just as an example, we will give you a description of walking along the sand at the edge of the ocean. Here's an example. . . .]

Imagine you are on a magic carpet or in a time machine traveling through space and time—relaxing as you travel. Imagine you are traveling to a beautiful beach, perhaps on a peaceful tropical island. Even before you see the gentle waves out on the ocean, you can begin to feel the warm sand beneath your feet. Feel the pleasant dryness of the warm sand beneath

your feet. And as you move first one foot and then the other from side to side, you can feel the warm sand on the sides and the tops of your feet. As you push your toes gently into it, you can feel the dry granules of sand between your warm toes. Gradually you can begin to see this beautiful beach . . . dimly at first, then more and more clearly. Now, let yourself look down the beach . . . and see the warm, glowing, golden-white sand. Let your eyes follow the beautiful expanse of sand . . . and as you lift your eyes and look down this beautiful sandy beach . . . off to one side you can see the deep blue-green of the ocean. Listen . . . you can hear the sounds of the ocean waves rolling slowly to shore and see them breaking into watery white fingers of foam that glide smoothly over the wet sand. Walk over to the edge of the damp sand, and see the bright reflection of the sky in the thin film of water left behind as each wave strokes the wet surfaces and then rushes back down the slope. Feel the damp sand beneath your feet. White crests of waves slowly follow each other in toward the shore. And as you enjoy the deep, rich color of the ocean . . . perhaps you can feel the salty breeze blowing in, gently cool on the surface of your body. Take a deep breath in, savoring the pleasant fragrance, the smell of the sea. Perhaps even taste the slightly salty taste on your lips and tongue. And floating directly above you, you can see the cottony fluffs of pure white clouds . . . and a bird gliding through vast expanses of blue. Behind you is the bright sun, shining and pleasantly warming the skin of your back. Feel the warmth on the surface of your back, sinking deep into all the muscles of your back, relaxing you even more. And now, if you wish, you can go for a walk or a run down the beach. Perhaps you'd like to run on the firm, damp sand or on the soft, warm sand. Or if you like, you may like to wade into the water and feel its pleasant temperature. Immerse you body in it. Maybe you'd like to swim. Whatever you'd like to do, let yourself do it now. . . .

[Pause for fifteen to thirty seconds. . . .]

[After you have completed your description of your haven, your special place, say:]

As you listen to the rest of this tape, imagine yourself spending time in your haven, perhaps walking about, exploring it, enjoying it in any way that you wish.

[These first few steps should take about five to ten minutes. After you have finished with these initial steps, read the following affirmation phrases into your tape recorder, modifying them to better suit your situation or that of your child. Read them slowly and clearly, with a firm feeling of certainty: Read it with a voice that sounds as though you truly believe it, whether you do or not at this moment in time. Soon you will begin to believe it, and as you believe it, it will happen!]

STEP TWO: GIVING YOURSELF POSITIVE AFFIRMATIONS

With each breath in, breathe in warmth and relaxation . . . and with each breath out, release all the tensions and worries that disrupt life. Say to yourself:

"Day by day, I'm feeling better and better in every way. I'm feeling more control in my life.

- I have clear goals for my relationships: to develop and nurture kind, caring, loving relationships.
- I have clear goals for my work (or school): to do the best I can every day.
- I have clear goals for my physical health and mental health: always to do things to keep my body and my mind healthy.
- I focus energy every day on accomplishing my goals.

I expect to succeed in whatever I do. I am able to see myself succeeding at tasks before I start them. In this way, I program myself for success . . . and I see success. I understand that successful people sometimes make mistakes and have failures along the way. I do not expect perfection, but I learn from each mistake.

Every day, in every way, I am becoming the best person I can be. I learn from others. By learning from others, I expand my horizons on a daily basis.

I prepare carefully for each of my tasks and projects. I set myself up to win and I have let go of the old pattern of putting off tasks and thereby setting up failure. Every day I'm becoming more and more organized. . . . Organization is becoming a vital part of my nature. I realize that when I put something in its right place in the beginning, I am more likely to find it when I need it.

Every day I am becoming more focused, more alert, more wide awake and more filled with energy. Every day I'm becoming more interested in what I am doing, in whatever is going on around me, and the people around me. I work smart as well as hard, focusing my energy on the goals I have set for myself.

I am more flexible . . . more adaptable . . . more willing and able to change as needed. At the same time, I am more disciplined . . . more thoughtful.

My environment matters. . . . I will seek to be a positive force in my environment everyday. I surround myself with positive people, and people who believe in me. Similarly, I am more positive with those around me. I can step outside myself and understand the feelings of others, and I see things from their perspective as well as my own. I am free of fear of competition with others. I feel wonderful when I win; when I do not win, I learn. Competition spurs me on to be as good as I can be.

More and more, I accept myself as I am and I accept others as they are. . . . I accept things as they are, not as I think they should be. I compromise when it is necessary. I eliminate the ANTs and bad thoughts whenever they enter my mind. I own me, and I am in control of me . . . and I live with the inner voices that help and uplift me. I erase any voice that would try to tear me down. When I find anxiety, I am able to turn it into positive energy for creativity and positive change.

I have let go of the habit of giving up on myself. Instead, I give my best effort toward reaching the goals I have set for myself . . . and no matter what . . . I keep pursuing my fondest dream in my life.

[If you've decided to put a little more active music on at this time, you may do so.]

STEP THREE: VISUALIZING SUCCESS

Now visualize yourself in some future situation, perhaps a test or challenge or meeting that is coming up in the near future. Choose the kind of situation you might have had trouble with in the past, but this time, as you go through it, visualize yourself applying all the positive beliefs you've just repeated to yourself in your mind, and watch yourself being personally successful, no matter what the outcome of the situation is. Visualize yourself there, clearly and vividly; see and hear everything that is going on around you, and feel your body and your voice responding in the way you really want to . . . and the way that is healthy and wise . . . and see yourself being successful.

[Pause for about a minute or two, and then begin to read again.]

STEP 4: DEHYPNOTIZING YOURSELF

Now, as I count from ten down to zero, gradually feel yourself becoming more and more awake. Again, leave about three or four seconds between each two numbers. Ten, nine, eight . . .

Feeling yourself coming up, growing more and more awake.

Seven, six, five . . .

Feeling alert and full of energy.

Four, three . . .

Bringing the feelings of energy and relaxation with you as you come up . . . filled with energy and ready to do whatever you want to do next.

Two, one, zero.

Take a deep breath in. As you let it out, let your eyelids open and think to yourself, wide awake . . .

Feel your body beginning to stretch and move.

Now get up and walk around the room, and make sure you're fully wide awake before you do anything else.

The total time of the tape will be from fifteen to thirty minutes, depending on the pace of your voice, images, etc.

Now that you have made the tape for yourself or your child, listen to it once every day. This is important: The first few times you will find out how your body will react to the relaxation. Some people become so relaxed that they doze off to sleep for a bit. If that happens to you, great! Listen to the tape before you go to bed, or when you can catch a nap. Some people find that it takes them a while to be fully with it; they remain very relaxed for several minutes afterward, as if they were waking up from sleep. If the tape affects you that way, you want to make sure that you're clearly awake before you do anything that requires full concentration, like driving a car. Others can listen to the tape anytime, anywhere, and feel a relaxed energy flow through their bodies.

The most important thing is that you listen to your tape every day. You can change the content of the tape in any way that you think will be beneficial to you. This is your tape. Use it to strengthen your life.

Information on other self-hypnosis cassettes can be found at our Web site at *www.amenclinic.com* or on Dr. Miller's Web site at *www.DrMiller.com.*

CHAPTER 28

What to Do When ADD Treatment Doesn't Work

We have been able to help thousands of patients who were previously resistant to treatment through the new brain-based model given in this book. If you asked my assistant to repeat the most common phrase she hears me say, she would answer, "Dr. Amen says he loves his job."

But there are times that I struggle. And that's when treatment doesn't work—when, even through our best efforts, we cannot make a person better. Happily, treatment failures are uncommon in ADD patients when we use brain-based medicine, but there are cases.

Over the years, we have learned that patients for whom help is elusive usually fall into one of a number of recurring patterns:

- the wrong diagnosis
- the wrong medication or dose of medication
- interfering factors
- poor follow-through
- cutting corners
- the unknown

Here are some thoughts on each category and suggestions on what to do about them.

THE WRONG DIAGNOSIS

When another condition is misdiagnosed as ADD, inappropriate treatment is often prescribed. Not only will that be ineffective, but it can often make things worse. A classic example is bipolar disorder. Bipolar disorder is a cyclic mood disorder, with alternating ups and downs. If patients with bipolar disorder are given stimulant medication, it may trigger a manic or "up" episode, putting them at increased risk for psychosis.

Other ailments that have been mistaken for ADD include:

Asperger's syndrome—an autistic spectrum disorder characterized by repetitive thoughts, rigid cognitive function, and very poor social skills. Typically, people with Asperger's syndrome are academically behind and internally distracted, which makes them look as though they have ADD symptoms.

Substance abuse—especially marijuana, excessive alcohol use, use of inhalants, pain killers, etc. Drugs of abuse affect brain function and may cause a person to look hyperactive, restless, impulsive, and distracted. This is especially true for teenagers who start either marijuana or alcohol use. Either the intoxication or withdrawal state of marijuana or alcohol can cause a teenager to look as though he was inattentive ADD. Making things more confusing, many people with ADD abuse substances, and both problems are frequently present. This underscores the importance of a detailed history. If the ADD symptoms preceded the substance abuse then both are likely present. If there were no ADD symptoms prior to the substance abuse then substance abuse is likely the primary problem.

Depression—The numerous cognitive problems caused by depression can be misinterpreted as ADD. SPECT studies of people with depression show decreased activity in the prefrontal cortex, making their brains look as though they have ADD. This can be born out by the symptoms the depressed person exhibits. However, in the *non-depressed* state there are few or no ADD symptoms. Stimulants frequently increase moodiness in people who are depressed.

Learning disabilities, personality disorders, post-traumatic stress disorder, chronic stress, primary sleep disturbances such as sleep apnea, or other medical problems such as thyroid disease, may also be misdiagnosed as ADD, preventing effective treatment and healing.

THE WRONG MEDICATION OR DOSE OF MEDICATION

Another reason that treatment may not work is the use of the wrong medication or the wrong dose of medication. As we have seen in this book there are at least six distinct types of ADD and one treatment does not fit all. In fact, the most common ADD treatment (Ritalin) makes four of the ADD types *worse* when used alone. Proper, targeted medications and/or supplements are essential to effective treatments.

Even when the proper class of medication is used, i.e., a stimulant or an anticonvulsant, one person may respond to one medication while a different person needs another. For example, I have seen many patients respond to the stimulant Adderall even though they received no help whatsoever from the stimulant Ritalin. I have seen yet other patients get better from Dexedrine who had no luck with either Ritalin or Adderall. We have no way of knowing in advance which medication in a particular class is going to work best for a person. I suggest trying all the different medications in the appropriate class until you get the best response.

Another important variable is the particular dose of medication. Many people respond poorly to treatment because their doctors used the wrong dose of medication. Typically, doctors prescribe too small a dose. I've had many cases of folks who had no success on 10 mg of Adderall a dose, and were deemed treatment failures without ever trying 15 or 20 mg. Just as the wrong prescription for eyeglasses can make someone's vision worse, the wrong dose of medication can make things worse for an ADD patient. Too much medication is as serious a problem in that it can increase the possibility of side effects and noncompliance.

I have also seen generic medications cause treatment problems and confusion. In my experience, generic medication often works differently than the brand-name version. Sometimes it works better, often worse. For example, a close friend of mine with ADD responds very nicely to a specific generic form of Ritalin. She does not respond at all to other generics or brand-name Ritalin. We have done four trials with different forms of Ritalin with the same results.

One factor that few physicians consider is the difference between how women and men process medication. Due to hormonal factors, women have a higher percentage of body fat than men, which causes certain medications to be more or less available to the brain, necessitating the need for different dosages.

INTERFERING FACTORS

There are many independent factors that interfere with effective treatment and increase the likelihood of failure. Common ones include poor diet, lack of exercise, taking medication with orange juice or products containing citric acid, excessive stress, ineffective environments (home, work, school), poor relationships with treatment providers, excessive use of caffeine or nicotine, and taking other medications, especially those not reported to the doctor.

The wrong diet frequently interferes with treatment. As we've already seen, for Type 1 or Type 2 ADD too many carbohydrates causes wide blood sugar fluctuations and increased symptomotology. Type 3 ADD is usually helped with simple carbohydrates. Food can be used like medication—it can make things better or worse. It is hard to judge the effectiveness of medication when a child or teen eats nothing but simple carbohydrates, punctuated by high sugar and caffeine loads.

A lack of exercise or change in exercise can also make things worse. Intense aerobic exercise improves blood supply to the brain. Without exercise the dose of medication may need to be higher than it would with a good exercise regimen. Frequently, I have seen ADD children or teens do better when they are playing a high-aerobic sport such as basketball. But then they struggle after the season is over, and no one knows why the medication does not seem to work as well.

Citric acid (found in orange juice, other citrus juices such as grapefruit juice, lemonade, tomato juice, and in many preservatives) has been found to cause deactivation of some medications and should be avoided near the time of medication. Few doctors advise their patients to avoid these substances around the time of taking medication, and thus increase the likelihood of treatment failure. You do not have to completely avoid citric acid—just avoid in an hour before and after taking medication or supplements.

We have also seen that high levels of stress interfere with treatment. Stress causes an excessive release of corticosteroids from the adrenal glands. These stress hormones circulate to the brain and damage brain cells, especially in the temporal lobes. Chronic stress has a negative effect on cognition and diminishes the effectiveness of treatment. For example, if an ADD adult is being successfully treated, but then experiences a significant stress such as a job loss or divorce, the medication often needs to be adjusted.

A problematic or difficult environment (such as at home, work, or school) also contributes to treatment failure. You can have the right diagnosis and right treatment protocol, but if you are in a difficult marriage, have difficult parents or teachers, or have siblings who are abusing you, treatment will appear flawed and frequently fail. The environment needs to support the treatment.

A bad or poor relationship with the treatment provider is another common reason for failure. Whenever conflicts and miscommunication exists in the doctor-patient relationship, patients suffer. In the current medical climate, doctors are being pressured to see more patients in less time. As a result, they can miss important information or ignore the most healing part of medicine—the doctor-patient relationship. Work hard to find a doctor who is not only knowledgeable, but who is also kind and a good communicator.

Many will find it surprising that excessive caffeine or nicotine use can induce treatment failure. Both caffeine and nicotine cause blood flow constriction in the brain. In the short run, people who have a cup of coffee or a cigarette feel stimulated. In the long run, however, these substances, through the mechanism of decreased blood flow, intensify your ADD symptoms. These substances also diminish the availability of medication to the brain, requiring patients to take more than most people. Avoid all nicotine and much caffeine. Caffeine is found in coffee, tea, dark sodas, chocolate, and a number of medications. Nicotine is found not only in cigarettes, but also in cigars and chewing tobacco.

Over-the-counter medications, supplements, and herbs can also have a negative effect on treatment. These substances frequently interfere with treatment, especially when the doctor is unaware that patients are taking them. These substances may contain caffeine or ephedrine, causing cerebral vasoconstriction. Or, as in the case of St. John's wort, they may increase serotonin levels in the brain and effectively decrease dopamine levels, which may help Type 3 ADD, while making other types worse.

POOR FOLLOW-THROUGH

One of the most common reasons for ADD treatment failure is poor follow-through. Obtaining effective treatment requires patience and cooperation between doctor and patient. Many people with ADD are driven by the moment. They need things to work right away or they become frustrated, distracted, and do not follow through with treatment recommendations. Many medications take time to work, and people need to get adjusted to their positive or negative effects. Stopping or changing treatment too soon frequently causes failure. Many ADD patients also prematurely increase their medication. They reason that if a particular dose of medication doesn't work, they'll increase it the next time, despite directions from the doctor to go slowly. Or, they may give up or "say uncle" too early. They may try a treatment for a week or two, when some meds take three to eight weeks to be fully effective. Persistence is needed for effective treatment.

Along the same lines, many patients, despite effective treatment, get tired or irritated by needing treatment and prematurely stop taking medication or working their treatment plan. I warn my patients about this temptation, telling them to expect that they will want to stop treatment about a year into it. In my experience, even when patients are dramatically better, they forget what life was like before treatment and want to stop.

In addition, many people stop effective treatment because of erroneous information gotten from well-meaning but misinformed friends, relatives, popular news media, or Internet chat rooms. The amount of misinformation is larger for ADD than any other medical problem. One of the major problems with prematurely stopping effective treatment is that when it is restarted it may not work as well. I have a patient with ADD who responded very nicely to a combination of medication and dietary changes. After two years of benefit someone at her church told her that she heard negative information about her medication in an Internet chat room. She stopped her medication and became symptomatic as before. When she reinstituted treatment it did not work as before and it took us nearly another year to help her feel more balanced.

CUTTING CORNERS

Being too cost-conscious in getting the right help costs people more money in the long run than getting the best help up front. Many patients do not think about getting the best help they can. They try to save money in the wrong places. They just see the doctors on their insurance plan, even when those doctors are not properly trained or do not specialize in treating their particular problem. Being penny wise and dollar foolish can cause real trouble in ADD treatment. I have seen many, many patients who were told erroneous information by the pediatrician or family practice doctor, promulgating ADD myths, such as not taking medication in the afternoons or on weekends. Think of finding the best help available as an investment in your child or yourself. Here are a number of other areas where people try to cut costs that sabotage treatment:

- using generic medication to avoid the cost or insurance copay of the brand-name medication. Sometimes brand-name medication works much better than generic medication. It is usually worth trying both
- trying to stretch medication by taking less than the prescribed amount to make it last longer
- not keeping regular appointments with the doctor thinking that will save money, not realizing ineffective monitoring will decrease a treatment's effectiveness
- not following through with adjunct therapies, such as family or marital counseling, to save money, not realizing that attorneys for divorce litigation or getting a child out of legal trouble costs much more than effective treatment

THE UNKNOWN

There is still a lot that we do not know. As different as psychiatry looks now from the seventeenth century days of asylums and suspected demonic possession, will be how different psychiatry will look in a hundred years. In the past we blamed autism, schizophrenia, depression, bipolar disorder, and ADD on poor mothering, bad character structure, or having sin in your life. Thankfully, those days are mostly gone. In the next 100 years there will be many new discoveries that will enable us to help many more people. Clearly, we do not have all the answers, and as we learn more we will be able to help more and more people.

CHAPTER 29

How to Find the Best Help

A Resource Guide

Four questions that I am frequently asked are: When is it time to see a professional about ADD? What to do when a loved one with ADD is in denial about needing help? How do I go about finding a competent professional? When do you order a SPECT study? This chapter will attempt to answer these questions.

WHEN IS IT TIME TO SEE A PROFESSIONAL ABOUT ADD?

This question is relatively easy to answer. I recommend people seek professional help for ADD for themselves or their child when their behaviors, feelings, or thoughts interfere with their ability to reach their potential in the world, whether in their relationships, in their work, or within themselves. If you see persistent relationship struggles (parent-child, sibling, friends, romantic), it's time to get help. If you see persistent school or work problems, it is time to get professional help. If you see continued monetary problems, it's time to get help. Many people have told me they cannot afford to get professional help. I respond that it is much more costly to live with untreated ADD than it is to get appropriate help. If you see persistent self-esteem problems, or mood or anxiety problems, it's time to seek help. In my experience, if ADD remains untreated past the age of 9 years old, there is a very high chance of self-esteem and mood problems.

GAINING ACCESS TO YOUR OWN GOOD BRAIN

The internal problems associated with ADD can ruin lives, relationships, and careers. It is essential to seek help when necessary. It is also critical for people not to be too proud to get help. Pride often devastates relationships, careers, and even life itself. Too many people feel they are somehow "less than others" if they seek help. I often tell my patients that, in my experience, it is the successful people who seek help when they need it. Successful businesspeople hire the best possible outside consultants when they are faced with a problem that they cannot solve or when they need extra help. Unsuccessful people tend to deny they have problems, bury their heads in the sand, and blame others for their problems. If the ADD symptoms are sabotaging your chances for success in relationships, work, or within yourself, get help. Don't feel ashamed: Feel as though you're being good to yourself.

In thinking about getting help, it is important to put ADD in perspective. First, I have patients get rid of the concept of "normal versus not normal." "What is normal anyway," I ask. I tell my patients who worry that they are not normal: "Normal" is the setting on a dryer. Or that Normal is a city in Illinois. Actually, I spoke in Normal, Illinois, at a major university several years ago. I got to meet Normal people, shop at the Normal grocery store, see the Normal police department and fire department, and even be interviewed on the Normal radio station. I met Normal women. They were a very nice group, but really not much different from those folks in California. The Normal people seemed to have their share of ADD—which is why I was asked to speak.

I tell my patients about a study published in 1994, sponsored by the National Institutes of Health, in which researchers reported that 49 percent of the U.S. population suffer from a psychiatric illness at some point in their lives. Anxiety, substance abuse, and depression were the three most common illnesses. At first I thought this statistic was too high. Then I made a list of twenty people I knew (not from my practice). Eleven were taking medication or in therapy. Half of us at some point in our lives will have problems. It's just as normal to have problems as to not have problems. Again, it is the more successful people that will get help first. The same study reported that 29 percent of the population will have two separate, distinct psychiatric diagnoses and 17 percent of us will have three different psychiatric diagnoses. In my experience, very few people are completely without these problems. In fact, in doing research, one of the most difficult challenges is finding a "normal" control group.

One of the most persuasive statements I give patients about seeking help is that *I am often able to help them have more access to their own good brains.* When their brains do not work efficiently, they are not efficient. When their brains work right, they can work right. I often will show them a number of brain SPECT studies to show them the difference on and off medication or targeted psychotherapy, as a way to help them understand the concept. As you can imagine after looking at the images in this book, when you see an underactive brain versus one that is healthy, you want the one that is healthy.

WHAT TO DO WHEN A LOVED ONE IS IN DENIAL ABOUT NEEDING HELP

Unfortunately, the stigma associated with ADD or "psychiatric illness" prevents many people from getting help. People do not want to be seen as crazy, stupid, or defective. They often do not seek help until they (or their loved one) can no longer tolerate the pain (at work, in their relationships, or within themselves). Men are especially affected by denial.

Many men, when faced with obvious problems in their marriages, their children, or even themselves, refuse to see the reality of what's going on. Their lack of awareness and strong tendency toward denial prevent them from seeking help until more damage has been done than necessary. Many men are threatened with divorce before they seek help. Often, with ADD, many men had been diagnosed as children with hyperactivity and had been on medication. They hated feeling different from the other kids and resented taking medication, even if it was helpful for them.

Some people may say it is unfair for me to pick on men. And indeed, some men see problems long before some women. Overall, however, mothers see problems in children before fathers and are more willing to seek help, and many more wives call for marital counseling than husbands. What is it in our society that causes men to overlook obvious problems, to deny problems until it is too late to deal with them effectively or until significant damage occurs? Some of the answers may be found in how boys are raised in our society, the societal expectations we place on men, and the overwhelming pace of many men's daily lives.

Boys most often engage in active play (sports, war games, video games, etc.) that involves little dialogue or communication. The games often involve dominance and submissiveness, winning and losing, and little interpersonal communication. Force, strength, or skill handles problems. Girls, on the other hand, often engage in more interpersonal or communicative types of play, such as dolls and storytelling. Fathers often take their sons out to throw the ball around or shoot hoops, rather than to go for a walk and talk.

Many men retain the childhood notions of competition and that one must be better than others to be any good at all. To admit to a problem is to be less than other men. As a result, many men wait to seek help until their problems are obvious to the whole world. Other men feel totally responsible for all that happens in their families and admitting to problems is to admit that they have in some way failed.

Clearly, the pace of life prevents some men from being able to take the time to look clearly at the important people in their lives and their relationships with them. When I spend time with fathers and husbands and help them slow down enough to see what is really important to them, more often than not they begin to see the problems and work toward more helpful solutions. The issue is not one of being uncaring or uninterested: It is not seeing what is there.

Many teenagers also resist getting help, even when faced with obvious problems. They worry about labels and do not want yet another adult judging their behavior.

Here are several suggestions to help people who are unaware or unwilling to get the help they need:

1. Try the straightforward approach first (but with a new brain twist). Clearly tell the person what behaviors concern you. Tell them the problems may be due to underlying brain patterns that can be tuned up. Tell them help may be available—help not to cure a defect but rather help to optimize how their brain functions. Tell them you know they are trying to do their best, but their behavior, thoughts, or feelings may be getting in the way of their success (at work, in relationships, or within themselves). Emphasize access, not defect.
2. Give them information. Books, videos, and articles on the subjects you are concerned about can be of tremendous help. Many people come to see me because they read a book of mine, saw a video I produced, or read an article I wrote. Good information can be very persuasive, especially if it presented in a positive, life-enhancing way.
3. When a person remains resistant to help, even after you have been straightforward and given them good information, plant seeds. Plant ideas about getting help and then water them regularly. Drop an idea, article, or other information about the topic from time to time. If you talk too much about getting help, people become resentful and won't get help to spite you. Be careful not to go overboard.
4. Protect your relationship with the other person. People are more receptive to people they trust rather than to people who nag and belittle them. I do not let anyone tell me something bad about

myself unless I trust the other person. Work on gaining the person's trust over the long run. It will make them more receptive to your suggestions. Do not make getting help the only thing that you talk about. Make sure you are interested in their whole lives, not just their potential medical appointments.

5. Give them new hope. Many people with these problems have tried to get help, and it did not work or it even made them worse. Educate them on new brain technology that helps professionals be more focused and more effective in treatment efforts.
6. There comes a time when you have to say enough is enough. If, over time, the other person refuses to get help, and his or her behavior has a negative impact on your life, you may have to separate yourself. Staying in a toxic relationship is harmful to your health. Staying in a toxic relationship often enables the other person to remain sick. Actually, I have seen the threat or act of leaving motivate people to change, whether it is about drinking, drug use, or treating ADD. Threatening to leave is not the first approach I would take, but after time it may be the best approach.
7. Realize you cannot force a person into treatment unless they are dangerous to themselves, dangerous to others, or unable to care for themselves. You can only do what you can do. Fortunately, today there is a lot more we can do than we could have done only ten years ago.

FINDING A COMPETENT PROFESSIONAL WHO USES THIS NEW BRAIN SCIENCE THINKING

At this point, I must get forty to fifty calls, faxes, or e-mails a week from people all over the world looking for competent professionals in their areas who think in ways similar to myself and the principles outlined in this book. Because the principles in this book are still on the edge of what is new in brain science, these professionals may be hard to find. Still, finding the right professional for evaluation and treatment is critical to the healing process. The right professional can have a very positive impact on your life. The wrong professional can make things worse. There are number of steps to take in finding the best person to assist you:

- **Get the best person you can find.** Saving money up front may cost you in the long run. The right help is not only cost-effective but saves unnecessary pain and suffering. Don't just rely on a person who is on your managed-care plan. That person may or may not be a good fit for you. Search for the best. If he or she is on your insurance plan, great. But don't let that be the primary criterion.
- **Use a specialist.** ADD diagnosis and treatment is expanding at a rapid pace. Specialists keep up with the details in their fields, while generalists (family physicians) have to try to keep up with everything. If I had a heart arrhythmia, I would see a cardiologist rather than a general internist. I want someone to treat me who has seen hundreds or even thousands of cases like mine.
- **Get information about referral sources from people who know about your problem.** Sometimes well-meaning people give very bad information. I have known many physicians and teachers who make light of ADD and discourage people from getting help. The following is a quote from a family physician to one of my patients: "Oh, ADD is a fad. You don't need help. Just try harder." In searching for help, contact people who are likely to give you good information about subjects such as child psychiatrists, CHADD coordinators, and Internet ADD medical support groups, such as the one on Prodigy. Often support groups have members who have visited the professionals in the area, and they can give you important information about subjects such as bedside manner, competence, responsiveness, and organization.
- **Once you get the names of competent professionals, check their credentials.** Very few patients ever check a professional's background. Board certification is a key credential. To become board certified, physicians have to pass additional written and verbal tests. They have to discipline themselves to gain the skill

and knowledge that is acceptable to their colleagues. Don't give too much weight to the medical school or graduate school the professional attended. I have worked with some doctors who went to Yale and Harvard who did not have a clue about how to treat patients appropriately, while other doctors from less prestigious schools were outstanding, forward-thinking, and caring.

- **Set up an interview with the professional to see whether or not you want to work with him or her.** Generally you have to pay for their time, but it is worth spending time getting to know the people you will rely on for help.
- **Read the professional's work or hear the professional if possible.** Many professionals write articles or books or speak at meetings or local groups. If possible, read their writings or hear them speak to get a feel for the kind of person they are and their ability to help you.
- **Look for a person who is open-minded, up-to-date, and willing to try new things.**
- **Look for a person who treats you with respect, who listens to your questions and responds to your needs.** Look for a relationship that is collaborative and respectful.

I know it is hard to find a professional who meets all of these criteria who also has the right training in brain physiology, but these people can be found. Be persistent. The caregiver is essential to healing.

WHEN TO ORDER A SPECT STUDY; QUESTIONS ABOUT SPECT

I order SPECT studies for very specific reasons. Because of our very large database, I actually order fewer studies now than I did several years ago. Our extensive SPECT work has allowed me to be better at picking out brain patterns, clinically, that are responsive to certain treatments. Here are several common questions and answers about SPECT:

Will the SPECT study give me an accurate diagnosis? No. A SPECT study by itself will not give a diagnosis. SPECT studies help the clinician understand more about the specific function of your brain. Each person's brain is unique, which may lead to unique responses to medicine or therapy. Diagnoses about specific conditions are made through a combination of clinical history, personal interview, information from families, diagnostic checklists, SPECT studies and other neuropsychological tests. No study is "a doctor in a box" that can give accurate diagnoses on individual patients.

Why are SPECT studies ordered? Some of the common reasons include:

- evaluation of seizure activity
- evaluation of blood-vessel diseases, such as stroke
- evaluation of dementia and distinction between dementia and pseudodementia (depression that looks like dementia)
- evaluation of the effects of mild, moderate, and severe head trauma
- suspicion of underlying organic brain condition, such as seizure activity contributing to behavioral disturbance; prenatal trauma; or exposure to toxins
- evaluation of atypical or unresponsive aggressive behavior
- determination of the extent of brain impairment caused by the drug or alcohol abuse
- typing of ADD when clinical presentation is not clear.

Do I need to be off medication before the study? This question must be answered individually between you and your doctor. In general, it is better to be off medications until they are out of your system, but this is not always practical or advisable. If the study is done while on medication, let the technician know so that when the physician reads the study, he or she will include that information in the interpretation of the scan. In general, we recommend that patients try to be off stimulants at least four days before the first scan and remain off of them until after the second scan, if one is ordered. Medications such as Prozac (which stays in the body for four to six weeks) are generally not stopped because of practicality. Check with your doctor for recommendations.

What should I do the day of the scan? On the day of the scan, decrease or eliminate your caffeine intake and try to not take cold medication or aspirin. (If you do please write it down on the intake form.) Eat as you normally would.

Are there any side effects or risks to the study? The study does not involve a dye and people do not have allergic reactions to the study. The possibility exists, although in a very small percentage of patients, that a mild rash, facial redness and edema, fever, and/or a transient increase in blood pressure may result. The amount of radiation exposure from one brain SPECT study is approximately the same as one abdominal X ray.

How is the SPECT procedure done? The patient is placed in a quiet room and a small intravenous (IV) line is started. The patient remains quiet for approximately ten minutes with his or her eyes open to allow his or her mental state to equilibrate to the environment. The imaging agent is then injected through the IV. After another short period of time, the patient lies on a table and the SPECT camera rotates around his or her head. (The patient does not go into a tube.) The time on the table is approximately fifteen minutes. If a concentration study is ordered, the patient returns on another day.

Are there alternatives to having a SPECT study? In my opinion, SPECT is the most clinically useful study of brain function. There are other studies, such as quantitative electroencephalograms (QEEGs), Positron Emission Tomography (PET) studies, and functional MRIs (fMRI). PET studies and fMRI are considerably more costly and they are performed mostly in research settings.

QEEGs, in our opinion, do not provide enough information about the deep structures of the brain to be as helpful as SPECT studies.

Does insurance cover the cost of SPECT studies? Reimbursement by insurance companies varies according to the kind of plan. It is often a good idea to check with the insurance company ahead of time to see if it is a covered benefit in your case.

Is the use of brain SPECT imaging accepted in the medical community? Brain SPECT studies are widely recognized as an effective tool for evaluating brain function in seizures, strokes, dementia, and head trauma. There are literally hundreds of research articles on these topics. In The Amen Clinic, based on our experience over ten years, we have developed this technology further to evaluate aggression and nonresponsive psychiatric conditions. Unfortunately, many physicians do not fully understand the application of SPECT imaging and may tell you that the technology is experimental, but over 350 physicians in the United States have referred patients to us for scans.

SPECT RESOURCES

There are no centers like ours around the country. But there are many forward-thinking physicians and psychotherapists that understand the connection between the brain and behavior. Here is a list of physicians and psychotherapists across the country I refer to who are expert in diagnosing and treating Attention Deficit Disorder and understand the model I use based on brain SPECT imaging.

Physicians

ALASKA

William Larson, M.D.
7227 Bern St., Anchorage, AK 99507
(907) 344-2700
Practice limited to ADD in children and adults

ARKANSAS

William Collie, M.D.
2311 Biscayne Dr. #201, Little Rock, AR 72227
(501) 219-2300
Behavioral medicine and researcher

ARIZONA

Eric Greenman, M.D.
932 West Chandler Blvd., Chandler, AZ 85225
(480) 786-9000, Fax (480) 786-5190
Child, adolescent, and adult psychiatry—AACAP

CALIFORNIA

Dennis Alters, M.D.
2125 El Camino Real, Suite 104, Oceanside, CA 92054
(760) 967-5898
Child, adolescent, and adult psychiatrist
Author of *Wizard's Way*

Frank Annis, M.D.
288 Quinn Hill Ave., Los Altos, CA 94024
(650) 949-4244
Psychiatrist/specialty in adult ADD

Thomas Brod, M.D.
12304 Santa Monica Blvd. #210 Los Angeles, CA 90025
(310) 207-3337
Psychiatrist; sees older teens and Adults; board certified, assistant clinical professor at UCLA

Timmen Cermak, M.D.
45 Miller Ave., Suite 1, Mill Valley, CA 94941
(415) 346-4460
Psychiatrist

Nancy Cheney, M.D.
1014 San Juan Ave., Exeter, CA 93221
(559) 592-7300
Pediatrician

Steven Clark, M.D.
150 Tejas Place, Nipomo, CA 93444
(805) 474-8450
Family physician with a specialty in ADD and related disorders

Kirk Clopton, Ph.D., M.D.
Golden Hills Psychiatry, 1037 Sunset #100, El Dorado Hills, CA 95762
(916) 939-2343
Child, adolescent, and adult psychiatry

George Delgado, M.D., SAAFP
2012 Columbus Pkwy, Benicia, CA 94510
(707) 745-2705
Board certified family practice, special interest in child and adult psychiatry, depression, ADHD, and Bipolar disorder

Claire Friend, M.D.
1672 West Ave. J. Suite 110, Lancaster, CA 93534
(661) 940-4057
4560 California Ave. #410, Bakersfield, CA 93309
(661) 406-6964
Adult, child, and adolescent psychiatry

Dean Freedlander, M.D.
17705 Hale Ave. #H3, Morgan Hill, CA 95037
(408) 779-1221
Psychiatrist

R. S. Isaac Gardner, M.D.
525 College Ave. #211, Santa Rosa, CA 95404
(707) 575-7647
Psychoneuroendocrinology

Rick Gilbert, M.D.
9051 Soquel Dr., Suite F, Aptos, CA 95003
(408) 688-6712
Psychiatrist

Brian Goldman, M.D.
The Amen Clinic for Behavioral Medicine
350 Chadbourne Road, Fairfield, CA 94585
(707) 429-7181
Neuropsychiatry—children, adolescents, and adults; specializes in Asperger's Syndrome

Julie Griffith, M.D.
1875 South Eliseo Drive, Suite G, Greenbrae, CA 94904
(415) 925-1616
Pediatric neurology

Willard E. Hawkins, M.D.
745 South Brea Blvd., Suite 23, Brea, CA 92821
(714) 256-4673
Family physician with a specialty in ADD, and other mood and behavior disorders.

Martin Jensen, M.D.
30110 Crown Valley Pkwy. #108, Laguna Niguel, CA 92677
(949) 363-2600
Adult and child psychiatrist; specialty in anxiety, depression, ADD, addiction, fatigue, and insomnia; author of medical text on brain chemical imbalance

Janice Jones, M.D.
2220 Mountain Blvd., Oakland, CA 94611
(510) 482-8021
Psychiatrist

Lloyd J. King, M.D.
251 Hyde St., San Francisco, CA 94102
(415) 673-5700
Adult psychiatrist

William Klindt, M.D.
3880 S. Bascom Ave., Suite 217, San Jose, CA 95124
(408) 792-3210
Child and adolescent psychiatrist

Richard Lavine, M.D.
271 Miller Ave., Mill Valley, CA 94941
(415) 383-2882
Psychiatrist; specialist in addiction medicine

Jim McQuoid M.D.
825 DeLong Ave., Novato, CA 94947
(415) 209-9904
Psychiatrist

Emmett Miller, M.D.
P.O. Box 803, Nevada City, CA 95959
(530) 478-1807
The Amen Clinic for Behavioral Medicine
350 Chadbourne Road, Fairfield, CA 94585
(707) 429-7181
Psychotherapist specializing in ADD, deep relaxation, mind-body medicine, and hypnotherapy. Information on Dr. Miller's deep relaxation and imagery tapes can be found at www.DrMiller.com.

Fernando Miranda, M.D.
11260 Wilbur Avenue, Suite 303, Northridge, CA 91326
(818) 360-3078
or
3580 California Street, Suite 302, San Francisco, CA 94118
(415) 929-9405
Cognitive neurologist

Edward Oklan, M.D., M.P.H.
811 San Anselmo Ave., San Anselmo, CA 94960-2003
(415) 453-1797
The Amen Clinic for Behavioral Medicine, 350 Chadbourne Rd., Fairfield, CA 94585
(707) 429-7181
Adult, adolescent, and child psychiatry; expert in the use and interpretations of SPECT; diplomat, American Board of Psychiatry and Neurology

Jeri Owens, M.D.
The Amen Clinic for Behavioral Medicine, 350 Chadbourne Rd., Fairfield, CA 94585
(707) 429-7181
Psychiatrist

Robert Picker, M.D.
1224 Contra Costa Blvd., Concord, CA 94523
(925) 945-1447
General psychiatrist; specialty in ADD for adolescents and adults

Sharada Raghaven, M.D.
841 Blossom Hill Rd. #209, San Jose, CA 95123
(408) 629-3997
Board certified, American Board of Psychiatry and Neurology

Lucretia Reed, M.D.
1010 Slater Avenue, Suite 237, Fountain Valley, CA 92708
(714) 968-4202
Child, adolescent, and adult psychiatrist

Hugh Ridlehuber, M.D.
1301 Ralston Ave., Suite C, Belmont, CA 94402
(650) 591-2345
Child, adolescent, and adult psychiatrist

C. Herbert Schiro, M.D.
856 Richland Rd., Suite C, Yuba City, CA 95991
(530) 673-5331
Child and adult psychiatry

Herb Schreier, M.D.
Children's Hospital Oakland
747 Fifty Second St., Oakland, CA 94609-1809
(510) 428-3571
Chief of child psychiatry; researcher

Saad Shakir, M.D.
851 Fremont Ave., Suite 105, Los Altos, CA 94024
(650) 917-7510
14651 South Bascom Ave., Suite 250, Los Gatos, CA 95032
(408) 358-8090
Psychiatrist; clinical associate; professor of psychiatry at Stanford

Edward Spencer, M.D.
51 Marina Dr., Suite 821 B, Petaluma, CA 94954
(707) 763-6854
The Amen Clinic for Behavioral Medicine, 350 Chadbourne Rd., Fairfield CA 94585
(707) 429-7181

General neurology, SPECT brain imaging; epilepsy, dementia, migraine, and ADHD

Thomas Stiles, M.D.
660 Sanitarium Road Suite 102, Deer Park, CA 94576
(707) 963-8842
Endocrinology/Diabetes; Behavioral Internal Medicine

Matthew Stubblefield, M.D.
3303 Alma St., Palo Alto, CA 94306
(650) 856-0406
The Amen Clinic for Behavioral Medicine
(707) 429-7181
General child, adolescent, and adult psychiatrist; expert in ADHD and SPECT brain imaging

Lewis A. Van Osdel, III, M.D.I.
The Amen Clinic for Behavioral Medicine, 350 Chadbourne Rd., Fairfield CA 94585
(707) 429-7181
Child and adult psychiatrist; addiction psychiatry and expert in the use and interpretation of SPECT

Lawrence C. Wang, M.D.
1541 Florida Ave. #101, Modesto, CA 95350
(209) 577-3388
Pediatric neurologist

George L. Wilkinson, M.D.
702 Marshall St., Suite 410, Redwood City, CA 94063
(650) 367-0472
Adult psychiatry

Joseph Wu, M.D.
UC Irvine
163 Irvine Hall, Room 109 UC-BIC, Irvine, CA 92697-3960
(949) 824-7867
Associate professor of psychiatry; clinical director of UC Irvine Brain Imaging Center at the college of medicine

Ken Wulff, M.D.
1333 Lawrence Expwy., Bldg. 300, Santa Clara, CA 95051
(408) 236-6960
Adult and child psychiatrist

Stanley M. Yantis, M.D.
45 Castro Street, San Francisco, CA 94114
(415) 241-5601
The Amen Clinic for Behavioral Medicine, 350 Chadbourne Rd., Fairfield CA 94585
(707) 429-7181
Psychiatrist; clinical assistant professor at UC San Francisco; board certified in adult psychiatry

COLORADO

Daniel Hoffman, M.D.
8200 Bellevue Ave., #600E, Greenwood Village, CO 80111
(303) 741-4800
Neuropsychiatrist, neurofeedback, brain injuries (sees children and adults)

CONNECTICUT

James Merikangas, M.D.
One Bradley Rd., Suite 102, Woodbridge, CT 06525
(203) 389-7007
Neuropsychiatrist, Yale University School of Medicine

ILLINOIS

Rick Anderson, M.D.
815 Main St., Peoria, IL 61603
(309) 672-4648
Family practice

Georgia Davis, M.D.
1112 Rickard Rd., Suite B, Springfield, IL 62704
(217) 787-9540 Fax # (217) 787-9540/E-mail
gdavismd@springnet1.com
Child, adolescent, and adult psychiatry

Robert Kohn, D.O.
5404 W. Elm St. Place #Q, McHenry, IL 60050
(815) 344-7951
Brain SPECT; practice limited to neurology and psychiatry; assistant clinical professor of radiology at the University of Chicago

Dan Pavel, M.D.
University of Illinois, Chicago
1740 W. Taylor St. (m/c 931) Rm 2483, Chicago, IL 60612
(312) 996-3961
Chief, Nuclear Medicine

MICHIGAN

Jack Juni, M.D.
3601 West 13 Mile Rd., Royal Oak, MI 48073
(248) 545-8047
Brain SPECT expert; Academic Imaging Institute

NEBRASKA

Tom Jaeger, M.D.
2430 S. 73rd St. #201, Omaha, NE 68124
(402) 392-2205

Researcher; clinician; child psychiatrist; professor, Creighton University

NEVADA

Corydon G. Clark, M.D.
2235-A Renaissance Dr., Las Vegas, NV 89119
(702) 736-1919
Board certified in child, adolescent and general psychiatry; specializing in diagnosis and treatment of children, adolescents, and adults with attention deficit disorder, attention deficit hyperactivity disorder, Tourette's Syndrome, obsessive compulsive disorder, general anxiety disorders, and bipolar disorder

OKLAHOMA

Nancy Grayson, M.D.
6853 So. Canton Ave., Tulsa, OK 74136-3405
(918) 496-8050
Adult outpatient psychiatrist in private practice

OREGON

Keith Lowenstein, M.D.
9450 SW Barnes Rd., Suite 270, Portland, OR 97225
(503) 288-8617
Child, adolescent, and adult psychiatry

Rod Michaels, M.D., F.A.C.P.
1585 Liberty St. SE, Salem OR 97302
(503) 589-0714
Endocrinologist

Jeffrey Stevens, M.D.
Oregon Health Sciences, Department of Nuclear Medicine, 3181 SW Sam Jackson Park Rd., Portland, OR 97201
(503) 494-8468
Nuclear medicine physician

Laurance Taylor, D.O.
c/o North Bend Medical Center, 94180 2nd St., Goldbeach, OR 97444
(541) 247-7047
Osteopathic physician and surgeon; board certified; family practice in adult psychiatry

TENNESSEE

Michael A. Harris, M.D.
Executive Park S., 2700 S. Roan St., Johnson City, TN 37601
(423) 975-6922
Board certified adult psychiatrist

Robert Hunt, M.D.
2129 Belcourt Ave., Nashville TN 37212
(615) 383-1222
Medical director, Center for Attention and Hyperactivity; associate clinical professor of psychiatry, Vanderbilt Medical School

TEXAS

Paul Warren, M.D.
17103 Preston Rd., Suite 288, North Dallas, TX 75248
(972) 250-0498

VIRGINIA

Martin Stein, M.D.
1911 N. Fort Meyer Dr., Suite 907, Arlington, VA 22209
(703) 807-2471
Fax # (703) 807-2296, E-mail docstein@docstein.com
Private practice; affiliated with George Washington University; neuropsychiatrist

Lawrence Leightman, Ph.D., M.D.
933 1st Colonial Rd. #109, Virginia Beach, VA 23454

(757) 425-1969
Diagnosis in treatment of genetic disorder

WASHINGTON

Gregory Hipskind, M.D., Ph.D.
3015 Squalicum Pkwy., Suite 210, Bellingham, WA 98225
(360) 733-4140
Family physician with a specialty in ADD and related disorders

Theodore Mandlekorn, M.D.
7711 South East 27th St., Mercer Island, WA 98040
(206) 232-3456
Director of ADHD Clinic, Virginia Mason Medical Center

Terrance McGuire, M.D.
1715 114th Ave. SE #208, Bellevue, WA 98004
(425) 452-0700
Psychiatrist

Robert Sands, M.D.
3609 South 19th St., Tacoma, WA 98405
(253) 752-6056
Specialty in ADD, comorbid conditions; coaching and family therapy; familiar with SPECT scans

Psychotherapists

ALASKA

Kristie Fuller, Ph.D.
Langdon Clinic, 4001 Dale St. #101, Anchorage, AK 99508
(907) 550-2300
Clinical neuropsychologist

Linda Webber, Ph.D., and Leon Webber, D.Mn., L.M.F.T.
135 Christensen Dr., Suite 100, Anchorage, AK 99501
(907) 276-4910

Individual and family therapists with a specialty in couples, ADD, and related disorders

CALIFORNIA

Stuart Altschuler, M.F.T.
2127 North Bronson Ave., Los Angeles, CA 90068
(323) 993-1940
Psychotherapist, private practice

Joan Andrews, L.E.P., M.F.C.C.
1200 Quail Rd. #105, Newport Beach, CA 92660
(949) 476-0991

Cheryl Carmichael, Ph.D.
706 13th Street, Modesto, CA 95354
(209) 577-1667
Psychologist

Richard Baker, L.C.S.W.
655 University Ave., Suite 244, Sacramento, CA 95825
(916) 925-2442

Bobbi Carlson, Ph.D.
Las Encinas Hospital
2810 E. Del Mar Blvd., #12, Pasadena, CA 91107
(626) 585-0041
Psychologist; private practice; director of internship training

Dennis E. Gowans, Ph.D.
14603 East Whittier Blvd., Whittier, CA 90605
(562) 945-6471

Earl Henslin, Psy. D., B.C.E.T.S.
745 S. Brea Blvd., Suite 23, Brea, CA 92821
(714) 491-7831

Board certified expert in traumatic stress; diplomat in the American Academy of Experts in Traumatic Stress

Susan Jerome, M.A., M.F.T.
1200 Quail St., #105, Newport Beach, CA 92660
(949) 756-1642
Specializes in post trauma stress and adult ADD and related anxiety, depression, and couples issues

Linda Kozitza-Pepper, Ph.D.
825 DeLong Ave., Novato, CA 94945
(415) 899-1379
The Amen Clinic for Behavioral Medicine, 350 Chadbourne Rd., Fairfield CA 94585
(707) 429-7181
Licensed psychologist

Sheila Krystal, Ph.D.
1509 Euclid Ave., Berkeley, CA 94708
(510) 540-0855
Psychologist

Karen Lansing, M.F.C.C.
3060 Valencia Ave., Suite 6, Aptos, CA 95003
(831) 460-2550
Marriage, family, and child counselor

Jennifer Lendl, Ph.D.
1142 McKendrie St., San Jose, CA 95126
(408) 244-6186
Clinician and Research Psychologist; board certified expert in traumatic stress; certified sport psychologist
The Amen Clinic for Behavioral Medicine, 350 Chadbourne Rd., Fairfield CA 94585
(707) 429-7181
Psychologist

David Jarvis, Ph.D., Psychologist and Merlyn Jarvis, Ph.D., L.C.S.W.
3225 Verdugo Rd., Glendale, CA 91208
(818) 957-2060

Linda Lose, M.F.C.C.
4999 East Townsend, Fresno, CA 93727
(559) 252-0134

Michael McGrath, M.F.C.C.
825 DeLong Ave., Novato, CA 94945
(415) 899-1378
The Amen Clinic for Behavioral Medicine, 350 Chadbourne Rd., Fairfield CA 94585
(707) 429-7181
Psychologist

Daniel McQuoid, Ph.D.
745 South Brea Blvd., Suite 23, Brea, CA 92821-5310
(714) 491-7836
Licensed psychologist specialty in adult and adolescent in the area of ADD assessment compulsive addictive disorder and childhood trauma
3545 Long Beach Blvd., Long Beach, CA 90807
(562) 492-9162
Psychologist

Saeed Soltani, Ph.D.
1551 North Tustin Ave., Suite 540, Santa Ana, CA 92705
(714) 835-1700
Licensed clinical psychologist, specialty in the areas of compulsive disorder, ADHD, chemical dependency; forensic expert witness
Fountain Cedu School, Running Springs, CA
(909) 867-2722
Psychologist

Jocelyn Stoller, M.A.
1903 Broderick, Suite 4, San Francisco, CA 94115
(415) 346-4188
Educational consultant

Deborah Swain Ed. D.CCC-SLP
795 Farmers Ln., #23, Santa Rosa, CA 95405
(707) 575-1468
Speech language pathologist

Jennifer Tansey, Ph.D.
25401 Cabot Rd., Suite 213, Languna Hills, CA 92653
(949) 581-6623
Psychotherapist

Lawrence M. Wilcox
572 Rio Linda Ave., #104, Chico, CA 95926
(530) 521-4097
Clinical neuropsychologist

Andrew Yellen, M.D.
Heidi Yellen, M.A., Certified educational therapist
11260 Wilbur Avenue, Suite 303, Northridge, CA 91326
(818) 360-3078
Psychological and educational services for children and adults

FLORIDA

Ray Bowman, Ph.D.
6740 Crosswood Dr. N., Saint Petersburg, FL 33713
(727) 345-1234

NEVADA

Tom Blitsch, M.F.T.
1850 East Flamingo, Suite 137, Las Vegas, NV 89119
(702) 794-0317

OREGON

Alec Mendelson, Ph.D.
1550 N.W. Eastman Parkway, #208, Gresham, OR 97030
(503) 665-4357 Ext. 2
Child and adolescent psychologist; school-based psychological consultant

Ross Quackenbush, Ph.D.
189 Liberty St. N.E., #202, Salem, OR 97301
(503) 588-1010

WASHINGTON

William F. Bentley, Ph.D.
Eastside Creative Learning and Counseling
801 166th Ave., #102, Redmond, WA 98052
(425) 869-5885
Behavioral and learning management

Diane E. Hough, M.S., C.M.H.C., N.C.C.
9725 S.E. 36th St., #212, Mercer Island, WA 98040
(425) 869-3992
Specializing in individual, marriage, and family counseling

Neurofeedback Therapists

Susan Othmer
EEG Spectrum
16500 Ventura Blvd., Suite 414, Encino, CA 91436-2011
(818) 789-3456
www.eegspectrum.com for other training sites across the United States and internationally

Michael Linden, Ph.D.
30270 Rancho Viejo Road, Suite C, San Juan Capistrano, CA 92675
(949) 248-4399

Joel Lubar, Ph.D.
Department of Psychology, University of Tennessee
Austin-Pey #310, Knoxville, TN 37996-0900
(423) 637-9096

YOU KNOW YOU HAVE ADD WHEN:

it takes four alarm clocks going off for an hour to get you up in the morning
you are ready to go somewhere thirty minutes ahead of time and you still leave late
even you can't read your own handwriting
you read the paper, put on your makeup, and talk on the phone, all at the same time—while driving
your desk, room, and bookbag look like the leftovers from a nuclear bomb test
you take a stimulant and your mind calms down
you take a stimulant at bedtime and you feel relaxed enough to go to sleep
you try to listen to your partner at the same time you are reading a book and watching TV
you are making love and all you can think about is mowing the lawn
you incessantly tease the pets
your piles have children
you are addicted to the struggle but worn out by the struggle
you start your day with a worry
the first day of school your were out of step with others
learning to read
learning times tables
algebra
foreign language
going away to school
writing papers
getting projects in on time.

THE AMEN CLINICS

The Amen Clinics were established in 1989 by Daniel G. Amen, M.D. They specialize in innovative diagnosis and treatment planning for a wide variety of behavioral, learning, and emotional problems for children, teenagers, and adults. The clinic has an international reputation for evaluating brain-behavior problems and in the diagnosis and treatment of attention deficit disorder (ADD) and related problems. The Amen Clinics have the world's largest database of brain scans for behavioral problems in the world. Over the last ten years, they have performed over 10,000 brain SPECT studies.

The Amen Clinics also specialize in difficult diagnoses from a variety of symptoms and problems, including brain trauma, underachievement, school failure, depression, obsessive-compulsive disorders, anxiety, aggressiveness, cognitive decline, and brain toxicity from drugs or alcohol. Brain SPECT imaging is performed in the clinics.

By popular demand, the clinic opened a Southern California office in Newport Beach that focuses on neuropsychiatric evaluations and brain SPECT imaging. The clinic in Newport Beach is not a treatment center like the Fairfield Clinic, but rather an evaluation center. We have an extensive list of physicians and therapists in Southern California who understand the work of the Clinic and who can follow through with our recommendations.

The clinics welcome referrals from physicians, psychologists, social workers, marriage and family therapists, drug and alcohol counselors, and individual clients.

The Amen Clinic Fairfield
350 Chadbourne Road
Fairfield, CA 94585
(707) 429-7181

The Amen Clinic Newport Beach
4019 Westerly Place, Suite 100
Newport Beach, CA 92660
(949) 266-3700

www.amenclinic.com

BRAINPLACE.COM

Brainplace.com is an educational interactive brain Web site geared toward mental health and medical professionals, educators, students, and the general public. It contains a wealth of information to help you learn about the brain. The site contains over 300 brain SPECT images, hundreds of scientific abstracts on brain SPECT imaging for psychiatry, a brain puzzle, and much, much more.

VIEW OVER 300 ASTONISHING COLOR 3-D BRAIN SPECT IMAGES ON:

- Aggression
- Attention deficit disorder, including the six subtypes
- Dementia and cognitive decline
- Drug abuse
- PMS
- Anxiety disorders
- Brain trauma
- Depression
- Obsessive compulsive disorder
- Stroke
- Seizures

ON BRAINPLACE.COM YOU WILL BE ABLE TO:

- Test your abilities! Put together an interactive brain puzzle.
- Learn about the functions and problems of the prefrontal cortex, cingulate gyrus, temporal lobes, limbic system, parietal lobes, occipital lobes, and basal ganglia.
- Take the Amen Brain System Checklist to see how your own brain is working (or not).
- Obtain specific ideas for optimizing and healing each part of the brain.
- See which supplements can enhance brain function.

Index

ABOUT THE AUTHOR

Daniel G. Amen, M.D., is a clinical neuroscientist, psychiatrist, and the medical director of the Amen Clinics, located in Fairfield and Newport Beach, California. He is a nationally recognized expert in the fields of "the brain and behavior" and "attention deficit disorders." Dr. Amen has the world's largest database of brain-imaging studies for attention deficit disorders.

Dr. Amen did his general psychiatric training at the Walter Reed Army Medical Center in Washington, D.C., and his child psychiatry training in Honolulu, Hawaii. He has won writing and research awards from the American Psychiatric Association, the United States Army, and the Baltimore-D.C. Institute for Psychoanalysis. Dr. Amen has been published around the world. He is the author of numerous professional and popular articles, sixteen books, including *The New York Times* bestselling book *Change Your Brain, Change Your Life* and a number of audio and video programs. Dr. Amen is the coauthor of the chapter on functional brain imaging in the new *Comprehensive Textbook of Psychiatry.*

Dr. Amen is an entertaining and gifted speaker.